NEW YORK CITY

The Spiritual Traveler

NEW YORK CITY

THE GUIDE TO SACRED SPACES AND PEACEFUL PLACES

EDWARD F. BERGMAN

In Association with the New York Landmarks Conservancy

HiddenSpring

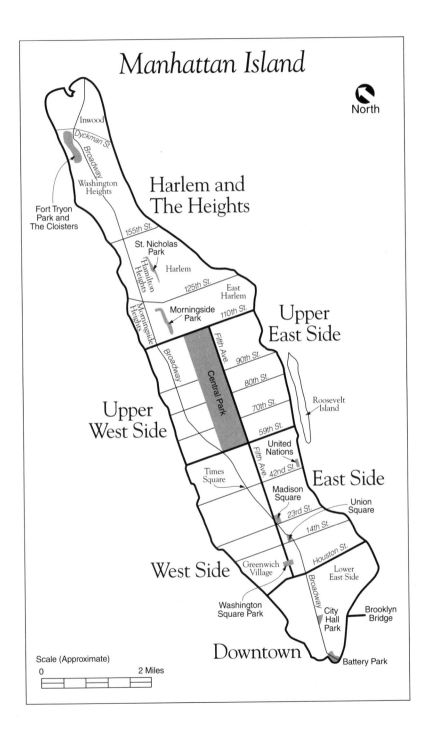

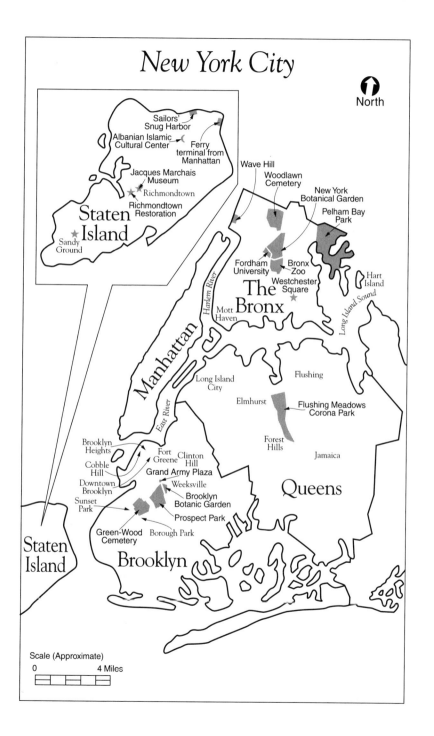

New York City

North

Sailors'
Snug Harbor
Albanian Islamic
Cultural Center
Ferry
terminal from
Manhattan
Jacques Marchais
Museum
Richmondtown
Richmondtown
Restoration
Staten
Island
Sandy
Ground

Wave Hill
Woodlawn
Cemetery
New York
Botanical Garden
Pelham Bay
Park

Harlem River

Fordham
University
Bronx
Zoo
Westchester
Square
Hart
Island

The
Bronx

Long Island Sound

Mott
Haven

Manhattan

Long Island
City

Flushing

East River

Elmhurst

Flushing Meadows
Corona Park

Forest
Hills

Brooklyn
Heights
Fort
Greene
Clinton
Hill
Grand Army Plaza
Cobble
Hill
Weeksville
Downtown
Brooklyn
Brooklyn
Botanic Garden
Sunset
Park
Prospect Park
Green-Wood
Cemetery
Borough Park

Jamaica

Queens

Staten
Island

Brooklyn

Scale (Approximate)

0   4 Miles

The cover image is a photomontage showing Bethesda Fountain in Central Park and an apartment building on Central Park West.

Cover design by Alexandra Lord Gatje
Book design by Saija Autrand, Faces Type & Design
Maps by Joseph Eric Busa

Library of Congress Cataloging-in-Publication Data

Bergman, Edward F.
    The spiritual traveler : New York City : the guide to sacred spaces and peaceful places / by Edward F. Bergman.
      p.   cm.
    Includes bibliographical references and indices.
    ISBN 1-58768-003-3 (alk. paper)
    1. New York (N.Y.)—Religion. 2. Sacred space—New York (N.Y.) I. Title.

  BL2527.N7 B47 2001
  291.3'5'097471—dc21

                                                     00-054051

Published by
HiddenSpring
An imprint of Paulist Press
997 Macarthur Boulevard
Mahwah, New Jersey 07430

www.hiddenspringbooks.com

Printed and bound in the
United States of America

Contents

ABOUT THE AUTHOR

Edward F. Bergman is chairman of geographic studies at Lehman College of the City University of New York. He has also taught at other universities around the world, and has lectured at many museums, including New York's Metropolitan Museum of Art, on such topics as New York City, world history, world geography and art. His previous writings about New York include *A Geography of the New York Metropolitan Region*, *Woodlawn Remembers: Cemetery of American History*, and a number of articles in *The Encyclopedia of New York City*.

The *S*piritual Traveler

Sacred journeys and sacred sites have been at the center of humankind's spiritual life from the very beginning. The Spiritual Traveler invites seekers of every faith and none to discover and connect with these ancient traditions and to find—either for the first time or anew—unique ways of pilgrimage in today's world.

PLEASE BE IN TOUCH

We have worked very hard to make this edition of The Spiritual Traveler as accurate and up to date as possible. However, any travel information could change at any time. If you think you have come across errors or omissions, please let us know. In addition, we would love to hear about your spiritual discoveries—any sacred spaces or peaceful places that you have found along the way, but not in this book. We will try to include them in upcoming editions. You can reach us at:

thespiritualtraveler@hiddenspringbooks.com.

LAST, BUT NOT LEAST

Please understand that the author, editors, and publisher cannot accept responsibility for any errors in this book or adverse experiences you might encounter while traveling. We encourage you to stay alert and be aware of your environment while on your spiritual journey.

"I have seen many things in my travels, and I understand more than I can express."—Sirach (Ecclesiasticus) 34:11, 12

A NOTE TO THE READER

Each entry for a house of worship in this book records: (1) the denomination or religion (unless it's clearly stated in its name); (2) its address, with cross-streets or avenues; (3) the date of the building. Some congregations commemorate the groundbreaking for their building, others the laying of the cornerstone, others the building's completion, first service, year of dedication, or year of consecration (usually when it's paid for). This book provides each building's date of dedication. Church cornerstones usually record two dates: that of the founding of the congregation and that of the laying of the cornerstone of the present building. Synagogue cornerstones usually give the date of the laying of the cornerstone according to both the Hebrew and the common calendar. (4) The architect of each building is listed next, if known. Research in archives has uncovered some names not given in most architectural guidebooks, or names that differ from those given in architectural guidebooks. (5) The last item listed for each entry is its telephone number. Most Manhattan buildings are in area code 212; the outer boroughs make up area code 718. If no area code is included, the reader can assume that it is 212. You need never be disappointed if you call ahead to be absolutely sure when a house of worship is open to visitors or when it will hold services.

Throughout the book "LM" indicates that a building is a New York City individually designated landmark, and "LMD" indicates that a building is within a New York City Landmark District. A building might be within a Landmark District but might not be an individually designated Landmark. Other buildings are both "LM" and "LMD." The New York City Landmarks Preservation Commission came into existence in 1965. It designates as landmarks structures that are at least thirty years old and are of noteworthy aesthetic, architectural, cultural, or historic significance. In 1973 the Commission's jurisdiction was extended even to interiors customarily open to the public, although interiors of houses of worship were explicitly excluded. The Commission can also designate historic districts that represent one or more styles of architecture or period of city history. Once individual or historic district designation has been made, alterations to a protected feature are prohibited without prior approval of the Commission. The Commission often allows new uses for buildings, with necessary adaptations, and the law even contains provisions for "hardship" cases.

In addition to the main entries, other spiritual sites in the immediate vicinity also reward a visit. The symbol ➨ introduces these spots right "around the corner."

Outdoor green spaces and peaceful places are noted by this icon.

All biblical quotations throughout the text are from the King James version. Quotations from the Qur'an are from the N. J. Dawood translation, fifth revised edition (New York: Penguin, 1993).

CHAPTER ONE

*I*ntroduction:
The Story of Spiritual Life
in New York City

SOME FORM OF SPIRITUALITY is essential to human life, and city dwellers follow many paths to find spiritual peace and strength. New York, one of the world's great cities, contains people following a great variety of paths. This book is a guide to specific places in the city associated with that search in the past and in the present.

There are the city's many houses of worship. Some faith groups refer to their facilities as "churches"; others call them "synagogues," "mosques," "temples," or "meetinghouses." These count among the city's most splendid monuments, and they contain rare treasures of sacred art and history. Each house of worship, however, is more than just a building. Each is a hub of activity for a community that comes together to pray, to celebrate, and to serve. Activities range from reading clubs to athletics, musical performances, educational programs, support groups, thrift shops, youth groups, and even cooking for soup kitchens or for shut-ins. This book introduces a selection of the major religious sites, according to considerations of spiritual and architectural beauty; active congregations representing each of the major faiths; and congregations of notable history in the life of the city. Our story is not just of the sacred spaces, but of the spirituality that created them.

Additionally, this book introduces some of the city's vibrant new spiritual centers. National polls reveal that nineteen in twenty Americans believe in God, and four in ten claim to attend religious services regularly. Not all of these believers belong to America's traditional mainstream denominations or religions. The full story of American spiritual life today includes not only the traditional religions of the world, but also more recent faiths. Mormonism, for example, was born in an upstate New York village in 1830, and it counts more than eleven million members worldwide today.

Many natural sites invoke spiritual repose or reflection. Our city parks are not, technically, consecrated, but Americans have long found a special spiritual consolation in nature, and New York's oldest trees or most restful oases of calm take their places in this book. Some Asian spiritual traditions emphasize God in nature, or God *as* nature, and botanical gardens in the outer boroughs feature traditional Asian landscape designs and plantings in which the contemplation of nature is interpreted as a form of worshipful meditation.

This book also draws your attention to some sites of historic events that evoke spiritual reflection, great sacrifices, or movements for human welfare: memorials to firefighters and police officers who gave their lives, war memorials, homes of writers of spiritual masterpieces, and locations where new initiatives in social service were launched.

The History of Spiritual Life in New York City

THE INDIGENOUS POPULATION

When Europeans first sailed into New York harbor, an estimated fifteen thousand Native Americans lived within today's New York City—perhaps thirty to fifty thousand in the metropolitan area. All spoke dialects of the Upper Delawaran family of languages, and they called themselves *Lenape*, or "real men." The Lenape were not politically or socially unified, but divided into a great number of loose-knit bands. Nor did they live in settled villages, but in seasonal campsites. Archaeologists have identified about eighty Lenape habitation sites within today's New York City, some two dozen fields, and a network of paths among them.

The Lenape diet included deer, game birds, fish, and shellfish. Piles of discarded shells from oysters gave today's Pearl Street (Manhattan) its name. They grew corn, beans, squash, pumpkins, and tobacco in the

WHAT IS NEW YORK?

An old joke insists that "They liked it so much, they named it twice: New York, New York." Historically, however, the city's boundaries have changed. Under Dutch rule (1625–64), the colony of the "Niew Netherlands," which included parts of New York and New Jersey, was governed from the city of "Niew Amsterdam." Under British rule (1664–1783), New Jersey was split off, and the name *New York* was given to both our city and Province in honor of the Duke of York. "New York City" included only the island of Manhattan until 1898; Brooklyn was a separate city. In 1898 a Greater New York City was consolidated, so all references to New York City, or to "the city," since 1898 mean to include all five of today's boroughs, which correspond with counties: Manhattan (New York County; 2000 population 1.5 million), Brooklyn (Kings County; 2.4 million), Queens (2.2 million), Staten Island (Richmond County; 0.4 million), and the Bronx (1.3 million).

woodland clearings, and introduced maple sugar, hominy, succotash, and tobacco to the Dutch. Their homes were longhouses built of bent saplings covered with sheets of bark, each of which housed as many as a dozen families. Because the Lenape moved frequently, they carried only lightweight possessions; they refused heavy Dutch iron cooking pots in trade. Their clothes were tanned animal skins. Hunting was a necessity, not a sport, and excessive killing was avoided.

We are certain of only a few specific sites that were sacred to Native Americans (see pp. 298, 333); several burying grounds have been moved or neglected.

The caves in Inwood Hill Park

NATIVE AMERICAN
SACRED SPACES

In contrast to European-American cultures, Native Americans developed beliefs, rituals, and ways of life that share the common theme of the sacredness of all aspects of everyday life and the natural world: There is no distinction between the sacred and the secular. By maintaining this holistic relationship with both the natural and the supernatural, plants, animals, objects, and other natural phenomena are endowed with souls and human traits.

Native American cultures believe that space has a sacred center and the "above" Earth and "below" are united. The monumental sacred spaces built by Native Americans provided a transition from the Earth-mound in Monroe, Louisiana (ca. 3750 B.C.E.), the vast circles, octagons, and bird-shaped mounds of the Southeast (ca. 1200 B.C.E.), and the Great Pyramid at Cahokia, Illinois (ca.1000–1300 C.E.). Other sites that hold a profound spiritual significance to Native Americans are natural settings, including creation-myth sites, sites of contact with spirits, places where valuable materials or medicines are obtained, and locations associated with legendary events.

Native Americans continue to experience the commonality of the sacred and the secular. In New York City, the Delaware are said to consider the swirling water of the Hell Gate area of the East River as a legendary portal to the underworld. For the Seneca Iroquois in Upstate New York, creation-myth sites are located at South Hill in the town of Naples and on the east side of Canandaigua Lake. A pilgrimage site for Catholic Native Americans is the National Shrine of Blessed Kateri Tekakwitha in Fonda, New York, commemorating a Mohawk woman (d. 1680) who became an ardent Catholic and to whom miraculous cures have been attributed (see p. 152).

Beginning in the early seventeenth century, Native American populations were decimated or displaced from their traditional lands by European settlers. Surviving tribes have adopted a wide variety of religious practices, often seeking to maintain or revive traditional spirituality, by embracing or rejecting modern life to varying degrees. Others practice Christianity as a result of conversions by missionaries over the past 400 years.

In New York City, the Native American population today is estimated at 35,000 (among 64,000 statewide), representing over 100 different cultures from across the country. This population includes traditionalists as well as followers of virtually every form of religion. The largest indigenous cultural group in New York State is the Northern Iroquois, comprised of several nations that share a similar language and culture. They originally lived along the St. Lawrence River in upper New York State and along the lower Great Lakes.

At the time of contact with Europeans, the Northern Iroquois village was a universe in microcosm. The forest edge surrounding the village represented the World's Rim. Anthropologist George R. Hamell has written about the significance of the forest edge, the deep woods, hollow tree trunks, rock faces, and berry islands as settings for rites-of-passage and interactions between humans and spirits. Deep springs, rivers, lakes, caves, rocky places, and the World's Rim are believed to be the dwelling places of ancestors and keepers of precious substances or medicines of well-being and the rituals associated with them.

Between 1000 and 1350 C.E., the Mohawk, Oneida, Onondaga, Cayuga, and Seneca Iroquois nations planted a Great Tree of Peace and formed a confederation called the Five Nations of the Haudenosaunee (People of the Longhouse). This gave them diplomatic, military, and economic power that lasted until the American Revolution. As the confederation dissolved and the Iroquois were confined to reservations in upper New York State and southern Canada, traditional social structures and customs were uprooted.

From 1799 to 1815, Handsome Lake, a charismatic mystic Seneca prophet, urged revitalization of the Iroquois society. He advocated maintaining traditional seasonal rituals, reinforcing family life and kinship ties, turning away from the scourge of alcohol, and adopting Quaker morality, while accepting the presence of the Europeans. Followers formed a church in the 1830s, known as the Handsome Lake or Longhouse Religion, which is still practiced among approximately half of the Iroquois.

In the nineteenth century, the Delaware Nation (also known as the Lenape) was completely displaced from New Jersey and Long Island and relocated to Oklahoma and Canada, eradicating the traditional culture.

Ceremonies took place in a "Big House," which was an adaptation of the longhouse dwellings. The Big House embodied spirit and nature: the tamped floor was the earth, the roof was the sky, two face masks carved on the center post represented the Creator, and the four walls were the four sides of the horizon. The building was aligned on an east-west (birth-death) axis similar to the Iroquois longhouse, with two fires ringed by a spiral "White Path" dancing circuit and seating sections for men and women of different groups. Their twelve-day New Year ceremony, staged in the fall after the harvest, included ritual enactment of the passage of life and the journey of the soul after death.

The American Indian Religious Freedom Act of 1978 requires federal agencies to evaluate their policies and procedures with the aim of protecting the religious freedoms of Native Americans. Many Native American practices and ceremonies that had been outlawed as being pagan and barbaric have been legalized. The return of exhumed human bones and other sacred objects in institutional collections to descendants is underway at the New York State Museum and nationwide as a result of the Native American Grave Protection and Repatriation Act of 1990. Cultural resources, including genesis-myth sites, locations of rituals, areas of spiritual encounter, and burial sites can be eligible for the National Register of Historic Places, receiving a degree of protection in the planning process for government-assisted projects.

—Kim E. Lovejoy

One Native American graveyard, for example, on Northern Boulevard near Little Neck Parkway in Queens, belonged to Long Island's Matinecock band. When Northern Boulevard was widened in 1931, the remains were removed and reinterred in the graveyard of Zion Protestant Episcopal Church (at Northern Blvd. and Douglaston Pkwy.). A monument in the cemetery shows a tree growing from a split rock, the symbol of the Matinecocks. Another ancient Native American burial ground at the western end of Alaska Street on Staten Island became a cemetery of a church, but today the church no longer exists, and the cemetery is abandoned.

The local indigenous groups did not build elaborate stone temples or complicated fortifications, as did the peoples of Mexico and Central and South America, so there is today very little evidence of the thousands of years of their presence. The only obvious link with them is evident in many place names still in use. Some describe the landscape (*Mosholu* in the Bronx, for example, means "clear water"; *Manhattan* means "hilly island"), some local products (*Jamaica* in Queens means "beaver"), others name the now vanished bands themselves (*Canarsie, Massapequa, Rock-away, Raritan, Hackensack, Tappan, Merrick,* and still others).

THE IROQUOIS LONGHOUSE

Function: Contemporary longhouses are the focus of Iroquois social, political, and religious life on the reservations in New York State and southern Ontario, Canada.

Origin: Archaeologists believe that by the mid–fourteenth century, longhouses built of sapling poles were flourishing in Iroquois villages. These multifamily dwellings housed clans related through the female line of descent. Longhouses of the eighteenth century were forty to four hundred feet long and from twenty to thirty feet wide, with shared cooking fires between compartments of individual families.

Architecture: At the close of the eighteenth century, followers of Handsome Lake revived the longhouse as a collective symbol. They met in a grange-type, rectangular hall built of logs with a shingled-gable roof. Although many longhouses in the nineteenth and twentieth centuries were built with stud frames and clapboard siding, the log structure has endured as an archetypal image and is being revived in contemporary longhouse construction. They are always long and rectangular, on an east-west axis, and have a fireplace or stove at or near each end. Inhabitants sit on rows of benches that line both long walls or on additional benches along the short walls. The open, central area is for the drummer's bench, dances, and other ritual activities.

Ceremonies: Iroquois ceremonies express gratitude to the Creator for sustaining gifts of life. There are seventeen ancient calendrical observances that predate the Handsome Lake Religion. Winter ceremonies are sponsored by the men and summer ceremonies by the women. Ceremonies involve public announcements, the Thanksgiving address, speeches and prayer, feasts, song and dance, reciprocity among the sexes and clans, tobacco burning, dream interpretations, confession of sins, and special paraphernalia.

Location: The Longhouse on the Tonawanda Seneca Reservation in Tonawanda, New York, is considered the "head fire." Other long-houses in New York are at the Allegheny Seneca Reservation in Cold Springs, at the Cattaraugus Seneca Reservation in Newtown, at the Onondaga Reservation in Onondaga, and the Mohawk Reservation at St. Regis.

—Kim E. Lovejoy

Leaders apportioned and adjudicated land use, but nobody owned land or had the right to transfer it out of tribal control, and the Native Americans frequently did not actually understand what Europeans meant when they wanted to buy land. Native Americans often returned to hunt or harvest unoccupied land that the Europeans insisted had been sold, and this caused unending friction. Peter Minuit, Director of the Dutch West India Company, "bought" Manhattan Island for sixty guilders' worth of trinkets in 1626, but we don't know who "sold" Minuit the island, what the "sellers" thought was happening, whether they had the right to sell it, or where this transaction took place. The Dutch bought Staten Island, or thought they bought it, on five separate occasions, and the English bought it again.

American Indian Community House (404 Lafayette St. ☎ 598-0100) in Manhattan administers cultural programs and service projects, and the Museum of the American Indian (see p. 83) supports Native traditions.

RELIGIOUS LIFE IN COLONIAL NEW YORK

Colonial New York had "established" churches, that is, official churches favored by the government. The Dutch established their Reformed Church, and when the English seized the colony in 1664, they established the Anglican Church. The degree of religious liberty allowed to other denominations varied, partly according to the mood or whim of the colonial governor and the wealth or power of the dissenters. For example, the Netherlands itself in the seventeenth century was a relatively liberal and tolerant state, but in New Amsterdam Governor Peter Stuyvesant sporadically persecuted Quakers, Lutherans, Jews, and other groups. The English colonial regime was more liberal, but English governors persecuted Presbyterians, Baptists, and other independently minded denominations.

The first cemetery of Congregation Shearith Israel, the Spanish and Portuguese Synagogue

Roman Catholics were banned under the Dutch and enjoyed only sporadic freedom of worship under the English.

Diversity nevertheless characterized the city's spiritual life. New York was, after all, a trading outpost, not a religious colony, like several New England settlements. Therefore, dissenters were generally tolerated if they profited the city, worshiped in private, and didn't make too much of a nuisance of themselves. Refugees from religious persecution elsewhere even found safety here. Jews, for example, came to New Amsterdam from Brazil. Many had settled in Brazil after the Dutch had taken that colony from Portugal in 1623, but they were forced to flee when Portugal retook Brazil in 1653. Protestants fled France when Louis XIV revoked their civil rights in 1685, and many of these people, called Huguenots, came to New York, joining earlier Huguenot settlers from what is today Belgium. The instructions sent to early British Governor Edmund Andros included an admonition "to permit all persons of what Religion soever, quietly to inhabit within the precincts of your jurisdiction, without giving them any disturbance or disquiet whatsoever for or by reason of their differing opinions in matter of Religion; Provided they give no disturbance to the public peace, nor do molest or disquiet others in the exercise of their religion."

THE REFORMED CHURCH

The Reformed Church, the established church of New Nether-lands, was the earliest European religious foundation of what is now New York City. In 1628, Jonas Michaelius (Latinized, as was common among European scholars at that time, from Michaelsen) arrived in Manhattan to minister to the Dutch and Huguenot settlers. He preached in Dutch in the mornings and French in the afternoons. Everardus Bogardus (Bogaert) replaced Michaelius in 1633, the year that the first church building was erected on what is now Pearl Street—the Church of St. Nicholas. Nicholas was chosen as patron saint of the settlement because the saint was the figurehead of the *New Netherlands*, the ship that brought the first colonists (see p. 208). Adam Roelantsen, the first schoolmaster, arrived on the same ship as Bogardus, and the school he started, now known as the Collegiate School (see p. 248), is arguably the oldest in the United States.

In 1642, during a period of tension between the Dutch and the Native Americans, the original church was replaced by a small stone church within the walls of Fort Amsterdam, where the Museum of the American Indian stands today (see p. 83). The church moved several times through later years, and its last home, at 48th Street and Fifth Avenue, made way for an office building that became a part of Rocke-feller Center in the 1940s. Today four "daughter churches" carry on the oldest continuous Protestant ministry in America: the Marble Collegiate (see p. 184), Middle Collegiate (see p. 125), West End Collegiate (see p. 248), and Fort Washington Collegiate. These successors are known as "Collegiate" because their ministers, serving their congregations as equals, are considered colleagues.

The early history of New Netherlands was unfortunately characterized by persecution of denominations other than Reformed. The Revised Freedoms and Exemptions of 1640 and 1650 stipulated that "no other religion shall be publicly admitted in New Netherlands except the Reformed." That was the rule in the Netherlands as well, but it had come to be interpreted that other groups would not be molested as long as they worshiped in private. Governor Peter Stuyvesant, however, wanted to impose religious conformity on the colony, and he often persecuted other denominations.

Britain's King William III (a Dutchman) granted the Collegiate Church a Royal Charter in 1696, making it the oldest corporation in the United States today. The churches prospered and multiplied, as German Reformed congregations formed, too. Additional churches were organized as new settlements were established in outlying areas. A few of these, standing among ancient gravestones, are some of the oldest churches in New York City. In 1789, when New York was chosen as the capital of the new United States, Pastor William Linn of the Dutch Reformed Church served as chaplain of the House of Representatives. Several of the older churches still refer to themselves as Dutch Reformed, but since 1867 the official name of the denomination has been the Reformed Church in America.

The Huguenots organized their own Église du St. Esprit in 1704, but they assimilated into New York society, their numbers dwindled, and in 1803 the parish joined the Episcopal Church. Today they worship (in French) at 109 East 60th Street, between Park and Lexington Avenues (☎ 838-5680).

The preponderance of Dutch people among the seventeenth-century population determined the preponderance of Dutch churches for some time, even under English rule. Governor Thomas Dongan, Andros's successor, reported in 1682: "New York has first a chaplain . . . of the Church of England; secondly a Dutch Calvinist, thirdly a French Calvinist, fourthly a Dutch Lutheran. Here bee not many of the Church of England; few Roman Catholicks; abundance of Quakers; Sabbatarians; Antisabbatarians; some Anabaptists, some Independents; some Jews; in short of all sorts of opinions there are some, and the most part of none at all. . . . The most prevailing opinion is that of the Dutch Calvinists." The Dutch had forbidden Roman Catholic worship, because until 1648 they were still fighting Catholic Spain. Governor Dongan, however, was himself Roman Catholic, and he attended the first celebration of mass in New York, in 1683.

We cannot be certain how many buildings were dedicated to religious worship during the colonial period, because only officially recognized denominations could build churches. Unrecognized denominations built churches anyway, but these buildings included a fireplace and a chimney in order to protect their ostensible status as a private dwelling. Furthermore, dedicated church buildings were expensive to build and maintain, and private homes could accommodate services of the small denominations. Therefore, despite the great variety of religious opinions, the number of

Trinity Church at the head of
Wall Street in 1866

church buildings increased slowly. Even the Anglicans did not get around to opening their first house of worship, Trinity Church, until 1698. Trinity rose on Broadway at the head of Wall Street, where the third structure of that name stands today (see p. 84). A visitor noted nine buildings fifty years later: Trinity Church (Anglican), the Old and the New Dutch churches, a Presbyterian church, a German Lutheran church, a German Reformed church, the French Protestant church, a Quaker meetinghouse, and a Jewish synagogue. In 1770 only fifteen religious buildings representing ten different faith groups served the city's 25,000 people.

No new churches were built during the War of Independence, and the British commandeered many existing buildings for stables and prisons deliberately to insult certain denominations. Religious freedom came with political freedom, and the number of sacred spaces in the city swelled as New York thrived economically and its population multiplied through the nineteenth century. By 1890 there were over 600 houses of worship in Manhattan. The combined membership of Christian and Jewish congregations was estimated to be over 700,000, approximately one-half of the total population.

Independent small communities dotted today's outer boroughs, and many of these areas underwent fewer drastic land use changes than Manhattan Island did. Therefore, some of the outer boroughs have a few very old churches. The Friends Meeting House in Flushing, Queens (1694, see p. 321), is actually the city's oldest structure in continuous use for religious purposes. As the outer boroughs grew and prospered, congregations in many neighborhoods built houses of worship of outstanding interest.

CHURCHES AND SYNAGOGUES MOVE UPTOWN

The earliest churches were built near the southern tip of Manhattan, where settlement first took hold. The John Street Methodist Church and Saint Peter's Roman Catholic Church, for example, the first of each of those two denominations, still stand on the sites where those congregations were founded in 1768 and 1785, respectively, although the buildings standing today are replacements of the originals (see pp. 87, 89). Saint Paul's Episcopal Chapel, built in 1766 on Broadway just a few blocks north of Wall Street, is Manhattan's oldest surviving church structure (see p. 92).

As settlement expanded northward on Manhattan, many congregations abandoned their historic sites downtown and built new religious properties uptown. (Congregations of African Americans were often forced to relocate uptown.) Many houses of worship were demolished, but others were purchased by new immigrant groups and, often, reconsecrated for new faiths or denominations. Thus, through successive waves of population replacement, some buildings still standing downtown have housed two or three congregations of as many different backgrounds. Some

The first Methodist preaching house on John Street, designed and built by Philip Embury. The 1768 painting by Joseph Beekman Smith shows Peter Williams, Captain Webb, and Philip Embury standing in front of the building.

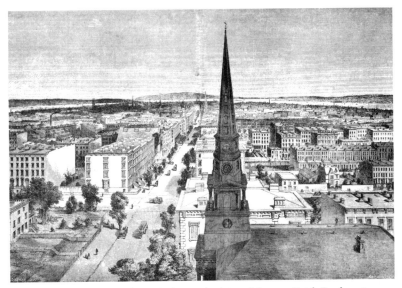

Fifth Avenue in 1859, looking south past the spire of the new Brick Presbyterian Church at 37th Street.

uptown congregations are in their fourth or fifth homes. For example, an early Baptist congregation organized on Norfolk Street in 1841 moved north to a new church on Fifth Avenue at 46th Street in 1861, moved again over to Park Avenue at 64th Street in 1922, and moved up to Riverside Drive in 1930 (see p. 286). Meanwhile, that Baptist congregation's original home on Norfolk Street came to serve a Russian Jewish congregation, Beth Hamedrash Hagodol, which still worships there today (see p. 113). When the Baptists left their Park Avenue building in 1930, they sold it to a historic Presbyterian congregation that had been founded on Mulberry Street in 1820, migrated to Broome Street in 1821, and to West 57th Street in 1878. Some Jewish congregations moved from the Lower East Side to Harlem as Harlem became fashionable at the turn of the twentieth century, but they later relocated south again—to the Upper East or West Side—as Harlem was settled by African Americans, who adapted some synagogues for Christian churches. The splendid Temple Israel, built in 1907 at 120th Street and Lenox Avenue, became the Mount Olivet Baptist Church when that congregation moved up from its original home on East 2nd Street—a building that is today the Russian Orthodox Church of the Protection of the Holy Virgin (see p. 270). Temple Israel migrated down to West 91st Street and still later over to East 75th Street.

In some cases congregations abandoned neighborhoods that were changing from residential districts to commercial or industrial quarters. The handsome profits these congregations enjoyed from the sale of their property often financed the construction of ever grander buildings farther north, more generously endowed. The story of the migration of historic black congregations to Harlem will be told on p. 261.

COMPETITION AMONG FAITH GROUPS

New York illustrates the argument that freedom of worship triggers competition among faith groups and that this competition actually increases overall support for religion. Religious participation has always been higher in American cities than in American rural areas and small towns, and the larger the city, the higher the participation rate. Houses of worship are convenient and accessible in cities, and the plurality of faith groups offers something for almost everyone.

Throughout America, leaders of all faiths were well aware of their competition, and many published handbooks providing tips on recruiting converts. In the 1830s a fiery young priest named John Hughes, who would later become New York's first Roman Catholic Archbishop, won national celebrity in a series of debates with Dr. John Breckinridge, a Presbyterian minister with little sympathy for the Roman Catholic Church. In 1843, Alexander Campbell, a founder of the Disciples of Christ, debated the nature of baptism with Dr. Nathan L. Rice, later to be pastor of Fifth Avenue Presbyterian Church. United States Senator Henry Clay of Kentucky presided. This debate was reported nationwide and later became a best-selling book. Public debates like these were the city's leading popular entertainment, but their appeal reflects genuine interest in religious matters.

Rivalry often expressed itself in architecture as well as in theology. Splendid houses of worship intended to proclaim both the rightness of that faith group and the righteousness of that congregation. Few faiths have remained outside this competition for splendor, as well as for favored sites and social prestige.

In addition, the number of activities thought appropriate to a congregation or even appropriate in a house of worship multiplied. Religious facilities did not always offer the broad range of activities for parishioners or of outreach to those in need that they do today. Well into the nineteenth century, church buildings were dedicated exclusively to worship

SANCTUARY AND
HOURS OF OPENING

Anyone seeking a quiet place to sit for meditation, prayer, or just a rest will be disappointed to learn that not all of the houses of worship listed in this book can remain open throughout the day every day. Staying open requires (unfortunately) personnel, and even volunteers cannot always fill the gap. We need a foundation like Britain's Open Churches Trust, founded by composer Andrew Lloyd Webber in 1994 to keep Britain's religious buildings open throughout the day.

Until we get one, however, visitors will sometimes encounter locked doors. The following is a list of houses of worship that are usually open during the day. Almost all Roman Catholic Churches remain open throughout most of the day, and the most generously endowed among other congregations are also able to stay open. Other buildings are open before and after services and at other special times, but these vary from year to year or even season to season.

This list is short, but a great many other sites not listed have offices within the building or next door, and someone there will usually be glad to let you in. In addition, virtually all schools, seminaries, and museums mentioned in the text are open most days of the week.

Downtown: Trinity, St. Paul's, and John Street Methodist.
East Side: Soka Gakkai International, the Church of the Incarnation, the Church of the Transfiguration, St. Bartholomew's, St. Peter's Lutheran, and St. Patrick's Cathedral.
West Side: Saint Mary the Virgin, Saint Thomas.
Upper East Side: Temple Emanu-El, the Upper East Side Islamic Cultural Center and Mosque, Holy Trinity.
Upper West Side: Church of Jesus Christ of Latter-Day Saints, Congregation Habonim.
Harlem and the Heights: Cathedral of St. John the Divine, St. Paul's nondenominational chapel on the Columbia University campus, Riverside Church.
Outer Boroughs: In Brooklyn, the Cathedral-Basilica of St. James, the Fatih Mosque; in Queens, St. George's Church, the Sikh Center of Flushing, the Hindu Temple of North America, the Thai Buddhist Temple, the Allen African Methodist Episcopal Cathedral; in the Bronx, Fordham University Chapel.

services. New York City's first parish house—a separate building for Sunday school classes and other church activities—was that of Holy Communion Church, opened in 1846 (see p. 177). When later waves of immigrants created vast neighborhoods of the poor, a new "institutional church" movement greatly expanded concern for the physical as well as the spiritual welfare of the less well-to-do. The typical institutional church offered a medical clinic, gymnasium, library, day nursery, cooking and sewing classes, and other training courses. Church properties expanded beyond the basic sanctuary as socializing and social service activities multiplied. A parallel movement among Jewish congregations in the early twentieth century added community centers onto synagogues. One prominent rabbi derided this development as "a *shul* (Yiddish for "synagogue") with a pool," but that descriptive phrase was proudly adopted by the proponents of these facilities.

By 1910 *Architecture* magazine would note: "Our metropolitan churches have become less and less houses of worship exclusively and more and more centers of social life. . . . They now include gymnasiums, athletic teams, clubs of various sorts whose obvious purpose is only slightly religious, but which have a real deep meaning in that they furnish a place of recreation in pure surroundings. . . . The buildings in which these great, modern, and heterogeneous activities are centered only partially resemble the parish churches of the past." Today it is unthinkable for a house of worship not to include at least a parish house, social hall, or similar facility.

A FEW OF NEW YORK'S "FIRST OR OLDEST IN AMERICA (OR EVEN THE WORLD)"

1. Oldest continuous Protestant ministry in America: New York's Reformed Church, which is also the oldest corporation in the United States.
2. The first Lutheran Church in America: St. Matthew's Lutheran Church in Inwood.
3. America's first Wesleyan Methodist Society: John Street Methodist Church.
4. Location where it is believed an African American first preached to a predominantly white congregation in America: John Street Methodist Church.

5. Location of the Thanksgiving service after George Washington was inaugurated the first U.S. president in New York, the nation's first capital: St. Paul's Chapel.
6. Shrine at the site of the home of the first American-born Roman Catholic saint: Elizabeth Bayley Seton Shrine.
7. Church whose pastors later served as the first bishop of Chicago and the first Roman Catholic chaplain to the U.S. Navy: St. Mary's.
8. Church to which a principal contributor was the first person to obtain citizenship through the process of naturalization prescribed in the U.S. Constitution: Old St. Patrick's.
9. Location of the investiture of the first American cardinal: Old St. Patrick's.
10. First American Baptist Church to be led by a black woman: Mariners' Temple.
11. World's first female ordained rabbi: Rabbi Sally Priesand, at Stephen Wise Free Synagogue.
12. Site of America's first "bread line": the close to the south of Grace Church.
13. The first bells in the world ever to be rung by means of electric switches: Most Holy Redeemer.
14. First Jewish temple to broadcast a webcast of a service: Temple Emanu-El.
15. First crucifixion scene ever placed on the exterior of a Christian church in the United States: St. Vincent Ferrer.
16. The first organ school in America: First Presbyterian.
17. Site of the first Lutheran theological seminary classes in the United States: St. John's Lutheran Church in Greenwich Village.
18. America's first asymmetrical Gothic church, the prototype for similarly picturesque churches all across the country: Holy Communion (deconsecrated).
19. America's first Gothic Revival-style church: St. Peter's Episcopal.
20. America's first Serbian Orthodox Cathedral: St. Sava.
21. Oldest school in the United States: The Collegiate School.
22. America's first "hanging balconies," that is, not supported by pillars: Marble Collegiate.
23. The world's first church constructed on a steel frame: St. Mary the Virgin.

24. The first church-owned-and-operated radio station in the country: Calvary Baptist.
25. The nation's first "Dial-a-Prayer" ministry: Fifth Avenue Presbyterian.
26. North America's oldest Jewish congregation, housed today in the first classical-style synagogue in America, but still owning another synagogue building that is the oldest in America: Shearith Israel.
27. Home of America's first indigenous society of priests: St. Paul the Apostle.
28. The first large-scale landscaped public park in the United States: Central Park.
29. Home of the first rabbi ever invited to open Congress with a prayer of invocation: B'nai Jeshurun.
30. The oldest Jewish university in America: Yeshiva University.
31. Shrine of the first American citizen to be proclaimed a saint of the Roman Catholic Church: Saint Frances (Mother) Cabrini.
32. The founding "mother" church of the A.M.E. Zion denomination: Mother Zion.
33. The first completely electrically lighted church in the United States, or probably the world: St. Francis Xavier.
34. The first figural stained-glass windows made in America: St. Ann and the Holy Trinity in Brooklyn Heights.
35. The first Romanesque Revival-style church in the United States: Our Lady of Lebanon in Brooklyn Heights.
36. The first auditorium-type seating plan for a church: Plymouth Church of the Pilgrims in Brooklyn Heights.
37. The first garden in the world to be designed for the blind, and also the first planned Japanese Garden in America: Fragrance Hill and the Japanese Garden at the Brooklyn Botanic Garden.
38. The first Hindu temple in the United States built according to ancient Hindu texts: the Hindu Temple of North America in Queens.
39. The world's first zoo founded as a scientific zoological research center: The Bronx Zoo.
40. The only Chinese Scholar's Garden in the United States: at the Staten Island Botanical Garden.
41. The oldest continuously inhabited free black settlement in the nation: Sandy Ground on Staten Island.

Brief Histories of a Few Faith Groups in New York

The following pages recount briefly the histories of several major faith groups in New York City, roughly in order of their historical appearance. These discussions do not attempt to record the development of doctrines or doctrinal disputes, but only an account of the organizational history of each group. The first church founded by European settlers, the Reformed Church, has been discussed on pages 10 and 11.

JUDAISM

New York's first two Jewish residents were Jacob Bar Simon and Solomon Pietersen, traders who arrived from Amsterdam in August 1654. The following month a ship brought twenty-three more Dutch Jews who had been driven from Brazil due to its recapture by Portugal after thirty years of Dutch rule there. Their ship, bound for Holland, had been seized by pirates. A few days later the pirate ship had been overtaken by a French frigate, the *Saint Charles*, which had brought them to New Amsterdam and thus forever earned its sobriquet, "The Jewish Mayflower." These twenty-five Jews together founded Congregation Shearith Israel ("remnant of Israel") and celebrated New York's first Rosh Hashanah in 1654. All of them were Sephardic Jews, or Sephardim.

Governor Peter Stuyvesant was furiously anti-Semitic, and he imposed special taxes on the Jews in lieu of military service, from which they were excluded. When a young butcher named Asser Levy petitioned the Dutch West India Company in Amsterdam directly to be allowed to help defend the city, Company directors admonished Stuyvesant to stop his persecutions, reminding him that Jews were significant Company stockholders. Levy's petition was granted, and today a lower Manhattan Street bears his name.

No structure for Jewish worship was constructed until 1730, and some of the furniture and fittings from this first synagogue are preserved at today's Shearith Israel on Central Park West (see p. 246). In 1789 Shearith Israel's Rabbi Gershom Mendes Seixas assisted at George Washington's inauguration—a scene recorded on the bronze doors of Trinity Episcopal Church (see p. 84).

Early in the nineteenth century, the Napoleonic Wars uprooted Jewish

FOUR HUNDRED YEARS
OF JEWISH SETTLEMENT

Five distinct groups of Jews settled in New York City. Each had its own language, customs and traditions, but all identified themselves as Jewish. It was this identity that contributed to their intense efforts to settle in the New World, for each group was fleeing from religious persecution in the lands they occupied. But their differences resulted in New York City becoming home to a vast variety of synagogues, each catering to its own specific group.

The first to arrive were twenty-three Sephardic Jews fleeing the Inquisition in Recife, Brazil, following the Dutch colony's capture by the Portuguese. The term *Sephardic* identifies them as Jews whose ancestors settled on the Iberian Peninsula in about the third century C.E. and where their descendants flourished until their expulsion in 1492. Their language was Ladino, or Judeo-Spanish, and many of their traditions, both cultural and religious, reflected their Hispanic heritage.

Ashkenazi Jews from parts of western and central Europe constitute the second group to arrive in New York City. *Ashkenazi* is the name medieval rabbinical authorities gave to lands along the Rhine River and is used to identify German Jewry and their descendants throughout Europe. Arriving in the years following the Revolutionary War and fleeing increasing unrest and persecution in Europe, German-speaking Jews brought with them a more liberal interpretation of their faith, which contributed to a three-part division among New York Jewry: Sephardim, and Ashkenazi Orthodox and Reform.

The third wave of Jewry began arriving in the 1880s; it was the largest group numbering over one million by the close of immigration in 1924. They were impoverished Yiddish-speaking Orthodox Ashkenazi Jews fleeing pogroms in eastern Europe following the assassination of Czar Alexander II in 1881. Their arrival caused alarm among established, acculturated New York Jewry, resulting in a division between the two groups that lasted well into the twentieth century.

By the time the fourth group of Jews began to arrive the Jewish population had begun to disperse throughout the city and boroughs, and social, economic and to a degree, religious interaction began to occur among the different groups. Conservative Judaism, an American Jewish compromise between the strict Orthodox and liberal

Reform movements, began to serve as a Jewish melting pot, where children from both groups could find common ground. It was these Jews who welcomed the survivors of the Holocaust. Few in number, traumatized by unspeakable events, penniless, it was the Holocaust survivors who galvanized the Jewish community and enabled them to welcome the city's last wave of Jewish immigrants: Jews fleeing the breakup of the Soviet Union. Like all the groups that preceded them, these Jews brought their own language, culture, and traditions.

—Marilyn J. Chiat

communities in Germany and Poland, and substantial numbers of Ashkenazim migrated to New York. In 1800 there were still fewer than 100 Jews in New York City, but in 1812 there were about 400, by 1846 some 10,000, and by 1880 about 60,000. At first the Sephardim and Ashkenazim worshiped together at Shearith Israel, but New York's first Ashkenazic congregation, B'nai Jeshurun, broke off from Shearith Israel in 1825 (see p. 253). As more Jews came to New York, still other synagogues were formed to represent different national origins or sects. In 1850 there were already fifteen synagogues of different groups in the city, and by 1859 there were twenty-seven.

Many of the Ashkenazim began to press for changes in the liturgy and practice of worship. These demands grew partly out of the German *Haskalah*, or Enlightenment, in the 1840s, but partly, too, out of local efforts to assimilate to their new home in America. They wanted prayers in a language they understood, and more sermonlike preaching. A progressive society called *Cultus Verein* sought advice from new "Reform" congregations that had been established in Charleston and in Baltimore, and the group soon established its own congregation in 1845. Its services offered a choir and sermons to educate the laity about Jewish issues (at first in German). Other changes came slowly through decades: the singing of hymns, instrumental music, the seating of men and women together, the abandonment of hats and prayer shawls for men, and the modification or abandonment of traditional dietary laws. When this group opened a new house of worship in 1847, they called it Temple Emanu-El ("God is with us"). This shocked the Orthodox, because they believed that as long as the Jews were scattered from the Holy Land, their houses of worship were only synagogues. The word *temple* was reserved for the temple in Jerusalem. The designation Temple Emanu-El by the new Reform congregation, however, expressed a desire to be at home in America.

Between 1880 and 1910 a third wave of about 1.4 million Jews came to New York, mostly from eastern Europe, and about 1.1 million stayed in the city. By 1910 these Jews made up a quarter of the city's population. These new immigrants organized hundreds of synagogues where they settled, on Manhattan's Lower East Side. Most of them were Orthodox, but they retained a wide array of distinctions based on sect, national origin, or even origin by individual village.

Many of these new immigrants prospered in New York and, as they did, they migrated out of the Lower East Side, first uptown, and then, with the con-

Temple Emanu-El's fourth home, which stood at the corner of Fifth Avenue and 43rd Street, in 1868.

struction of the subways, into the outer boroughs. Orthodox Jews believe that one must walk to Sabbath services (anything else is work). Therefore, some synagogues on the Lower East Side suffered years during which they lacked sufficient members to maintain their buildings or even to gather the ten men necessary to hold a service. (A renaissance of the Lower East Side is discussed on p. 109.)

Most of the estimated 1.2 million Jews in New York City today are of central or eastern European ancestry, although Sephardic immigration has increased in recent years from Turkey, the Middle East, and North Africa. Sephardic practice is also followed by a congregation of Falashas, from Ethiopia, and a congregation of African Americans. New York counts several congregations of Arabic-speaking Jews from Syria, Iraq, and Yemen. Hasidim number about 100,000. Hasidim ("pious ones") are followers of an ultra-Orthodox movement founded in eighteenth-century Poland.

There are two major Hasidic groups: Lubavitchers, from Poland, and Satmars, most of whom are from Hungary.

There are today four basic divisions in American Judaism: (1) Orthodox Judaism; (2) Reform Judaism; (3) Conservative Judaism, which tries to define a middle ground between Orthodox and Reform Judaism (for example, Conservative Jews will usually observe dietary laws, use Hebrew in prayer, and worship with their heads covered, but they will also mix English with their Hebrew, seat families together during services, and they may or may not have instrumental music and mixed choirs); and (4) Reconstructionist Judaism, which holds Judaism to be a human-centered rather than a God-centered religious civilization.

FEMALE SPIRITUAL LEADERS IN NEW YORK

Rebecca, Ruth, and Rachel count among the great heroines in Jewish tradition, and the New Testament includes Lydia, Phoebe, and Junia among the very earliest leaders of the Christian Church. Women have played leading roles in the spiritual life of New York City since its founding. In 1637, Anne Hutchinson was banished from Puritan Massachusetts when she preached that faith and grace alone could win salvation. She moved to Rhode Island and then to Long Island before settling in what is today the Bronx. Anne was eventually slain by Native American raiders in 1643. The Hutchinson River and Parkway in the Bronx commemorate her. The Hutchinson homestead is thought to have been near today's Seton Falls Park, which was named for the family of Elizabeth Seton, the first American-born Catholic saint (see p. 81), whose family later owned that land. Ann Lee, the English-born religious visionary, spent some time in New York City in 1774 before she established the Shaker movement upstate two years later.

To this day, women have held the pulpits of many New York houses of worship. Rabbi Sally Priesand, ordained at Hebrew Union College-Jewish Institute of Religion and installed at Stephen Wise Free Synagogue in 1972, was the world's first female rabbi. Today she serves in New Jersey. Dr. Suzan Johnson Cook served Mariners' Temple through the 1990s as the first black woman to lead an American Baptist Church; she serves today at the Bronx Christian Fellowship.

Shaykha Fariha presides at New York's Sufi Muslim mosque, and countless other women lead meditation and spiritual centers throughout the city. Elizabeth Seton and Mother Cabrini (see pp. 295) won recognition as Roman Catholic saints, but many people believe Dorothy Day (see p. 122), Alphonsa Hawthorne Lathrop (see p. 112), and Lillian Wald (see p. 109) also deserve sainthood.

Many women have lead righteous causes in New York. Brooklyn's Harriet Beecher Stowe spurred abolitionists with her antislavery novel *Uncle Tom's Cabin* (1852). When she first met Abraham Lincoln during the Civil War, the president allegedly asked, "Did this little lady really start this big war?" Harriet's brother was preacher Henry Ward Beecher (see p. 304). Mary White Ovington was a founder of the NAACP in 1909 and served as its unpaid executive secretary for many years (see p. 146). Many people would also nominate Margaret Sanger (1879–1966), who opened America's first clinic for birth control (a phrase she coined) in Brooklyn in 1916, went to jail for distributing contraceptives and information about them (in jail she lectured fellow inmates on family planning), but today appears on a U.S. postage stamp.

Sculptor Anna Hyatt Huntington's statue of St. Joan of Arc on Riverside Drive (see p. 257) was the first statue of a woman to be erected in New York City (not counting *Liberty* in the harbor). At the western end of Bryant Park, on Sixth Avenue at 42nd Street, stands the first major monument dedicated to a female New Yorker: the Josephine Shaw Lowell Fountain (Charles Platt, 1912). Lowell (1843–1905) worked tirelessly to improve conditions in New York's poorhouses and jails and the circumstances of working women. A statue of Eleanor Roosevelt (1884–1962) stands at Riverside Drive and West 72nd Street (Penelope Jencks, 1996). As first lady (1933–45) during the presidency of her husband, Franklin Roosevelt, and all through her life, Eleanor campaigned for the rights of labor, minorities, the poor, women, and young people.

BAPTIST

Jesus accepted baptism, but he never baptized anyone himself, so different Christian groups have felt differently about its necessity and the circumstances under which it should be performed. In 1657 the pastors of the

Reformed Church reported indignantly that "a fomenter of error, a troublesome fellow, a cobbler" from Rhode Island named William Wickenden "began to preach at Flushing, and then went with the people into the river and dipped them." Wickenden was promptly banished from New Netherlands. The Baptist movement slowly won new converts in the early eighteenth century, however, and Reverend Valentine Wightman regularly came down from Groton, Connecticut, to perform the rite—at first clandestinely, at night, but increasingly by day. Nicholas Ayres hosted meetings in his home after 1715, and he eventually formed a congregation that built a meetinghouse in 1728. When Ayres retired in 1736, however, the property was claimed by one of the trustees, and the congregation dissolved.

Today's First Baptist Church (see p. 251) was organized in 1745 by a group that named Reverend John Gano as pastor and built a meetinghouse on Gold Street. During the War of Independence, British troops commandeered the church as a stable, and the Baptist communicants were scattered, but the Baptist congregation survived. A new, larger church was built in 1802, after which this denomination became firmly established in the city. Baptists have formed associations for fellowship, but they have always insisted on the absolute autonomy of each local congregation. The first national denominational consciousness was achieved in 1814, with the organization of the General Missionary Convention of the Baptist Denomination.

Abyssinian Baptist Church (see p. 278) was organized in 1808 by "free colored" members of First Baptist, and through following years new immigrants formed their own Baptist churches as each group arrived: First German, 1846; First Swedish, 1853; First Italian, 1897; Norwegian-Danish, 1903; Bohemian, 1905; and so on, continuing to Haitian, 1965; Korean, 1976; Rumanian, 1979; Portuguese-speaking, 1982; Filipino, 1986, and Indonesian, 1993. New York's Baptists are split among several Conventions, but they make up one of the largest denominations in the city.

EPISCOPALIAN

British military chaplains inaugurated Anglican services soon after the Dutch surrender in 1664, and the Anglican Church remained the established church through the rest of the colonial period. In 1693 the colonial legislature called for the establishment of regular parishes throughout metropolitan New York, but Trinity Church was not granted a royal charter until 1697, and its first building was opened on Broadway at the head of Wall Street in 1698.

Soon after the War of Independence began, in 1777, New York's Provincial Congress adopted a constitution disestablishing the Anglican Church, prohibiting any form of religious establishment, and guaranteeing freedom of religion. At the end of the war, New York's Anglican clergy interpreted King George's recognition of American independence as

St. Peter's Episcopal Church, circa 1900

releasing them from their loyalty oaths, and in 1785 a General Convention organized a new "Protestant Episcopal Church"—"Protestant" to
distinguish it from Roman Catholic, and "Episcopal" to distinguish it from
Presbyterian and Congregational. (The word *Protestant* was dropped in
1967.) *The Book of Common Prayer* was rewritten to substitute prayers for
the U.S. president for the traditional prayers for the king of England. Episcopal Bishop Samuel Provoost served as chaplain of the U.S. Senate while
New York was the national capital from 1789 to 1791. These actions established precedents for today's worldwide Anglican Communion: independent national churches united by common bonds of history, theology, and a
relationship to the archbishop of Canterbury.

As settlement expanded, new parishes were defined, or new chapels
were opened in outlying residential areas, and these chapels eventually
became independent parishes. The Episcopal Church has remained one of
the most active and influential denominations in the city.

LUTHERAN

Lutherans counted among the first settlers in New Netherlands, and
they represented many nationalities: Dutch, German, Norwegian, Polish,
Swedish, and more. Jonas Bronck, for whom the Bronx is named, was an
early Danish Lutheran settler. All Lutherans, however, were united in
their loyalty to the Augsburg Confession (1530), written principally by
Philip Melanchthon and endorsed by Martin Luther.

In 1649 a New Amsterdam group organized and wrote to the Consistory (church council) of the Amsterdam Lutheran Church asking for
advice on forming a church and requesting that a pastor be sent. That
group of laypeople is considered the first Lutheran Church in America,
and the descendant of that organization is today's St. Matthew's Lutheran
Church in Inwood. In Amsterdam itself, however, the Lutheran Church
faced discrimination, so the Consistory did nothing for four years. New
Amsterdamers tried repeatedly to hold services and to recruit a pastor, but
they were blocked. A German pastor, Johannes Gutwasser, arrived in 1657
but he was deported. Lutherans did not enjoy freedom of religion until
after the English conquest in 1664, and even then they were unable to
attract a pastor until Jacobus Fabritius arrived from Amsterdam in 1669.
Within weeks he performed his first baptism, that of a fifty-year-old black
man who took the name Emmanuel. In 1670 the Lutheran congregation
bought land for a church building on Broadway, and the new Dutch pastor
who arrived in 1671 and served for twenty years, Bernhard Arnzius, firmly

established the denomination. German and English Lutheran churches multiplied, and a New York Synod was formed in 1786.

Through the nineteenth and even the twentieth centuries, New York Lutherans continued to be divided by synod and by nationality. In 2000, many of the Lutheran churches in New York still identified themselves as German, Swedish, Danish, Norwegian, or other nationality. They worshiped in seventeen languages.

METHODIST

In 1766, young Irish immigrant Barbara Heck was so shocked at the immorality of her friends' playing cards that she prevailed upon her cousin, Philip Embury, formerly a lay preacher in Ireland, to begin preaching in New York. Embury organized America's first Methodist Episcopal Society, introducing the movement that John Wesley (1703–91) had originated within the Church of England. Starting with only five people, Embury and the small society were soon joined by another lay preacher, Captain Thomas Webb, a British army officer who wore a patch over one eye and preached wearing his red uniform, his drawn sword laid across the pulpit. The congregation quickly outgrew a number of small rented meeting places and built its first chapel in 1768 on the site of the present John Street Methodist Church (see p. 87).

During the War for Independence, British officials assumed (incorrectly) that all Methodists were Loyalists, so Methodist services were not disturbed. After the War, however, the Methodist societies in America declared their independence from the Church of England. John Wesley sent Francis Asbury and Thomas Coke as superintendents (later called bishops) of American Methodism. A 1784 conference duly elected Coke and Asbury, and American Methodists formed the Methodist Episcopal Church in America, the first distinctively national denominational body. Asbury continued to preach on Staten Island for forty-five years. By 1850, Methodist churches counted almost three million members, one-third of all American church members. After a series of mergers, the United Methodist Church was created in 1968.

Many members of the John Street Church were black, and in fact a black man (whose name is not recorded) gave several sermons in this church in 1786—the first African American known to preach in any New York church. But a number of black members of the church grew disaffected by discrimination and left to hold their own services in 1796. In 1800 they incorporated their own Zion Church, which formed a separate denomination, the African Methodist Episcopal Zion Church (A.M.E. Zion), in 1820. Other congregations organized, and in 1848 that denomination recognized the New York congregation as the "Mother" church. That congregation is now located on 137th Street (see p. 277), and today the denomination counts about 1.5 million members in thirteen episcopal districts across the United States.

The New York dissidents had been encouraged by the example of Richard Allen, a Philadelphian who in 1787 had founded the Bethel African Methodist Episcopal Church. In 1816 that church joined with several other black Methodist churches to found the African Methodist Episcopal (A.M.E.) denomination, which eventually established parishes in New York City. Today it has about two million members nationwide. Its Allen Church in Jamaica, Queens, has one of the largest congregations in New York City (see p. 326).

THE RELIGIOUS SOCIETY OF FRIENDS (QUAKER)

Friends, though small in number, have played a significant role in New York's religious history. The Society was founded in England by George Fox (1624–91), and it took its name from John 15:15: "Henceforth I call you not servants . . . but I have called you friends. . . ." Friends traditionally gather in silence with the freedom for any member to speak if he or she chooses, or the assembly might spend an hour in meditation. They have no creed or statement of doctrine, and there is no minister or provision for a sermon. Fox wrote that individuals' experience of personal and direct relationship with God would "bid them Tremble," so they came to be called Quakers.

Their individualism was revolutionary, and it was treated as such wherever there was an established church. The New Netherlands Dutch shunned the first English Quakers when they arrived in 1657, but the Quakers were accepted by English dissenters who had settled some Long Island towns under Dutch patents. Governor Stuyvesant refused to extend freedom of worship to the Quakers, and one Quaker named Peter Hodgson was captured on Long Island, beaten, and then banished. The people of Flushing drew up a sharp reminder to Governor Stuyvesant that Flushing's patent guaranteed "liberty of conscience." This document, called the Flushing Remonstrance of December 27, 1657, was a forerunner to the First Amendment of the U.S. Constitution.

Friends continued to hold meetings, but Stuyvesant would not relent in his persecution. In 1662 a Quaker named John Bowne was arrested, imprisoned, and fined for holding meetings in his home. When he appealed to the directors of the Dutch West India Company, however, they ordered Stuyvesant to see to it that "the people's conscience should not be forced by anyone, but remain free in itself." Today the Bowne house in Queens is a public museum (almost within sight of the carved elephant gods guarding a Hindu temple down the street; see pp. 323–24). Persecution of Quakers generally ended after 1664. They were not permitted to vote until 1734, because an oath had previously been required of them in order to do so. Quakers refuse to take oaths. Even after 1734 they could not hold office. Manhattan's first meetinghouse was constructed downtown on today's Liberty Place in 1696.

CONGREGATIONAL AND PRESBYTERIAN

For much of local history, the Congregational and Presbyterian Churches have been virtually indistinguishable. Both groups accepted the Westminster Confession as their creed (written 1645–47, during the civil struggles in Britain) and shared the austere order of service originating in Calvinist Geneva. Pastors of each group were often called to churches of the other, and their forms of church government were similar. Strictly speaking, *congregational* describes a form of church government in which each individual church is autonomous. When we use the word *Congregational* to refer to a group of churches, however, or to an organized denomination, we are referring to one of the groups dissenting from the Church of England in the seventeenth century. Congregationalism came to America with the Pilgrims in 1620, and it dates back to 1643 in New York. Here, however, the strength of Presbyterianism acted unfavorably upon the growth of New England-style Congregationalism.

During the Dutch period, the area that is now the borough of Queens was settled by New Englanders under Dutch land grants. Once here, they tended to adopt the presbyterian form of church organization, that is, sole authority is vested in a body of presbyters or elders. Presbyterian church organizations were established on Long Island by the 1640s. New Amsterdam's Reformed Church found no theological objections to either Congregationalism or Presbyterianism.

Later Anglican colonial governors, however, occasionally tried to suppress both. English governors confiscated Congregational churches in Elmhurst and Jamaica (Queens) and gave them to the Church of England.

When Francis Makemie, the moderator of America's first Presbytery (church court, at Philadelphia in 1706), preached in a private house in Manhattan and baptized a child in 1707, Governor Lord Cornbury had him arrested and thrown into jail for "spreading pernicious doctrines." Makemie defended himself under the 1689 English Toleration Act. He was acquitted of disturbing the peace but required to pay court costs.

The First Presbyterian Church in Manhattan was organized in 1716 and began holding services on Wall Street in 1719. Presbyterian laymen were so active in the city's political, intellectual, and social life that First Presbyterian was called "the church of the patriots." John Witherspoon, a Presbyterian from Princeton, New Jersey, was the sole clergyman to sign the Declaration of Independence. During the earlier British civil wars of the 1640s, the Presbyterians had adopted the revolutionary slogan: "No bishop and no king." The government of the new United States finally achieved these goals—separation of church and state in a republic—prompting the indignant British aristocrat Horace Walpole to curse the American Revolution as "a Presbyterian rebellion." During the entire colonial period, the Anglican Church blocked the granting of a charter to the Presbyterians, so New York Presbyterians had had to register their property as owned by the Church of Scotland. They finally got a charter, and control of their own property, in 1784. When two additional Presby-terian congregations were established in New York—the Brick Church (1767, see p. 224) and the Rutgers Street Church (1796, see p. 247)—they remained collegiate with First Church until 1809. The Presbytery of New York City was formed in 1738, but it has had many geographical configura-tions before fixing today's boundaries of New York City.

The denomination grew rapidly, and by 1828 it was estimated that one-quarter of all churchgoers in New York attended one of the twenty-one Presbyterian churches. In 1851, 35 of the 110 churches in the city were Presbyterian. Today Presbyterian congregations nationwide are over-whelmingly white non-Hispanic, but more than half of the Presbyterians in New York City are nonwhite or Hispanic. In 2000 Presbyterian churches in the city included Chinese, Korean, Latin American, and African American congregations.

The Congregational General Association of New York was formed in 1824, but individual congregations still periodically switched their own designations between Presbyterian and Congregational. Many Congrega-tional churches merged with the Christian Church in 1931, and that denomination merged with the Evangelical and the Reformed Churches to form the United Church of Christ (UCC) in 1957.

ROMAN CATHOLIC

Roman Catholics were the last major religious group to gain the right to public worship in New York. The Dutch founders harbored bitter memories of their rule by Catholic Spain, and many of the colony's original settlers were refugee Protestants from Spanish-ruled Belgium or from France. The English, too, discriminated against Roman Catholics. There were no more than 200 Roman Catholics in New York City at the end of the War of Independence. By the middle of the nineteenth century, however, waves of Roman Catholic immigrants had made Roman Catholicism the largest denomination in the city. It still is, and it continues to be an immigrant church. Today, however, the immigrants are not from Europe, but from Latin America, Asia, and Africa.

The first Catholic priest in the New Netherlands was, however, treated cordially. The Jesuit (now Saint) Isaac Jogues arrived in 1643 on his way to carry the Gospel to the Mohawks. Returning from the wilderness, he heard the confessions of two Catholic colonists—a Portuguese woman and an Irishman—while waiting at Fort Amsterdam for passage back to Europe. Father Jogues was killed on a later mission among the Native Americans, in 1646, and he was canonized in 1930. A figure of him can be seen on the door to St. Patrick's Cathedral (see p. 151).

England's King James II, himself a Catholic, appointed Thomas Dongan as New York's first Roman Catholic governor in 1683, and the first mass in New York City was celebrated on October 30 in the fort chapel. This event is commemorated by a plaque on the Museum of the American Indian (see p. 83), which today stands on the site. Catholics enjoyed freedom of worship for only a few years, however, because James II was followed by Protestant kings who soon began to distrust all Catholics as potential traitors in Britain's struggles with Catholic France. These struggles culminated in the French and Indian War. A law of 1700 barred priests from entering the city under penalty of life imprisonment, and Catholics lost the vote and were barred from public office in 1711. At the time of the violent "Negro Riot" of 1741, John Ury was hanged as a conspirator after the jury had been turned against him by suggestions that he was a Catholic priest. He was in fact a Protestant schoolmaster, but his knowledge of Latin had made him suspect as a priest and agent of Spain. Until the British evacuated New York in 1783, Catholics had to meet in secret. For several years Father Ferdinand Steinmeyer, a German Jesuit living in Pennsylvania, visited New York periodically to conduct clandestine masses.

An Irish member of the Capuchin Order (Italian for "hooded ones"), Father Charles Whelan, was the first priest to arrive in New York after the War of Independence. He had served as chaplain to the French fleet during the war, been captured by the British, and spent a year as a prisoner on Jamaica before arriving in New York in 1784. He began holding services in the home of José Roiz Silva, a Portuguese merchant, and he slowly organized the tiny Roman Catholic congregation (about 200 people) before he left in 1786. Today the Church and Friary of Saint John the Baptist (211 West 30th St. between 7th and 8th Aves. 1872, Napoleon LeBrun. ☎ 564-9070) is the headquarters of the Capuchin Province of St. Mary–New York–New England.

Catholics at first imitated the Protestant form of church government. Prominent local citizens served as trustees and assumed responsibility for church finance and management. Accordingly, in 1785, several leading New Yorkers incorporated New York's first Roman Catholic Church. King Charles III of Spain, America's recent ally in the War for Independence, contributed toward the construction of the first church building. St. Peter's, located at the corner of today's Barclay and Church Streets—coincidentally, the site of the hanging of John Ury forty-five years earlier—was dedicated in 1786 (see p. 89). The trusteeship form of church government plagued the Roman Catholic hierarchy through the nineteenth century, but the hierarchy slowly established its authority.

In 1808 Pope Pius VII made New York the seat of a new diocese and appointed Richard Luke Concanen, an Irish Dominican living in Rome, as its first bishop. Concanen, however, died before ever reaching his post. The second bishop of New York, John Connolly, arrived from Dublin in 1815 a few months after a second church, St. Patrick's on Mott Street, had been dedicated by the visiting bishop of Boston, and Bishop Connolly chose this as his cathedral (see p. 116).

As Roman Catholics from Germany, Poland, and Ireland poured into the city, many native Protestants resented them as outsiders. Protestant mobs threatened the cathedral with torches on several occasions in the 1830s and 1840s, and Roman Catholic cathedrals in other U.S. cities were burned. In New York, however, Bishop John Hughes wrote, "There is not a [Catholic] church in the city which is not protected with an average force of one to two thousand men—cool, collected, armed to the teeth, and with a firm conviction, after taking as many lives as they could in defense of their property, to give up, if necessary, their own lives." This may have been a bluff, but it saved New York from mob rule and bloodshed.

Bishop Hughes, the fourth bishop and first archbishop of New York, announced his intention to build a new cathedral uptown on Fifth Avenue in 1850, the year that the see (ecclesial administrative region) was raised to an archdiocese. Hughes commissioned one of the largest churches in the world as a symbol that Catholics were claiming their rightful place in the community. He laid the cornerstone of the new St. Patrick's in 1858. In 1879 the new cathedral was dedicated, and Old St. Patrick's was demoted to the status of a parish church.

An 1869 engraving made from the plans for St. Patrick's cathedral. When this engraving was published, the walls of the building, then under construction, actually stood only fifty feet high.

Immigrants to New York usually settled into neighborhoods of identifiable ethnic or national character, so nineteenth-century New York parishes formed a mosaic of ethnicities. The churches themselves helped anchor the local character. Most second-generation Americans may have moved out of the old neighborhood, but they often wished to retain national differences in ceremony and service. The church hierarchy adapted to those wishes by allowing the formation of "national parishes" that could be attended by members of a specific nationality from all across the city. Between 1900 and 1920, half of all new parishes in Manhattan were such national parishes. Italians, for example, worshiped at St. Anthony of Padua on Sullivan Street and Our Lady of Mount Carmel in East Harlem (see pp. 164, 266), Poles at St. Stanislaus on East 7th Street (see p. 125), and the French at St. Vincent de Paul on West 23rd Street (see p. 176). Thus, some neighborhoods have two Catholic churches, one based on geography and the other representing ethnicity.

Today the Archdiocese of New York includes the boroughs of Manhattan, the Bronx, and Staten Island, as well as the upstate counties of Dutchess, Orange, Putnam, Rockland, Sullivan, Ulster, and Westchester. The boroughs of Brooklyn and Queens are included in the Diocese of Brooklyn, whose cathedral is the Cathedral of St. James (see p. 306). In 1997 the Archdiocese of New York estimated Catholics throughout the archdiocese to be 36 percent of Hispanic origin, 27 percent of Italian, and 19 percent of Irish origin. The percentage for Hispanics in New York City, however, was much higher than the 36 percent for the entire archdiocese.

Nearly all of the Roman Catholic churches in the city follow the Latin rite, but about a dozen conduct services in various Eastern rites. Four are Ukrainian, three are Carpatho-Russian, and others include the Armenian, Hungarian, Russian, Melkite, and Maronite rites.

Most Catholic parishes are conducted by diocesan clergy who are appointed by and answer directly to the bishops. Some of the parishes, however, are conducted by religious orders, such as the Jesuits, Augustinians, Dominicans, Paulists, or Franciscans. These priests are appointed by and answer directly to their religious superiors, who, in turn, work cooperatively with the bishops.

ORTHODOX CHRISTIAN

The term *Orthodox* covers about twenty denominations of eastern European or Near Eastern origin, all of which recognize the spiritual leadership of the patriarch of Constantinople (the former eastern capital of the Roman Empire, today's Istanbul). Nearly all of them are organized along national lines, and they follow the rituals of the traditional churches in their home countries. Each group claims to represent its nationality, so political turmoil in home countries has, in several cases, triggered the creation of more than one church in New York City claiming to represent that nation. This happened already at the time of the 1917 Russian Revolution; it occurred again when several eastern European countries came under communist domination after World War II, and it has happened again with the fall of communism after 1989. In still other instances, doctrinal disputes have caused the creation of rival national Orthodox churches.

The first Orthodox parish in New York City was organized in 1870 among Russian immigrants and converts, and Greeks formed their own

Holy Trinity Church in 1892. As each following national immigrant group reached a number sufficient to form its own Orthodox congregation, it did so. Today about one-third of the sixty-odd Orthodox houses of worship in New York City are Russian, and another third represent Greek organizations. Other Orthodox churches include the Albanian, Armenian, Bulgarian, Belorussian, Carpatho-Ruthenian, Ethiopian, Romanian, Serbian, Syrian Antiochian, and Ukrainian Orthodox churches.

UNITARIAN UNIVERSALIST

At the end of the eighteenth century, a wave of rationalistic philosophy affected intellectual circles in America. The Unitarian and Universalist churches, which merged in 1961 into a single denomination, both arose out of doctrinal conflicts within the Protestant churches of New England.

Unitarians do not accept the Christian doctrine of the Trinity. They hold different views about the person of Jesus, but most believe him to have been a spiritually enlightened human being who, through reason or intuition, came very close to God. American Unitarianism was officially born with the removal of trinitarian references from the liturgy at King's Chapel, Boston, in 1785. In 1794 John Butler preached Unitarianism in New York, and the city was also visited by the English scientist and Unitarian minister Joseph Priestley (the discoverer of oxygen). Philosopher and essayist Ralph Waldo Emerson offered the opening prayer at the ordination of a minister for the First Unitarian Church of Brooklyn in 1838. All Souls Unitarian Church in New York City (see p. 215) was formed in 1819, and it has always been Unitarian in theology and Congregational in church polity.

Universalism is the belief that all souls will eventually achieve salvation. In 1796 several prominent members of the John Street Methodist Church broke away to form a Universalist congregation, the Society of United Christian Friends of New York. A second Universalist Society organized in 1824, and today's Church of the Divine Paternity (founded 1838) on Central Park West at 75th Street, was the Fourth Universalist Society.

ADVENTIST

Adventist churches focus on the theme of the return, or second advent, of Jesus Christ to Earth. After that cataclysmic event, they believe, Jesus will reign in triumph. Therefore, Adventists are full of confidence and hope for the future, even if they may be pessimistic about the present. Adventism swept America in the 1830s and 1840s as a movement within existing churches, and only later did Adventists separate into individual denominations.

The largest group, the Seventh-Day Adventists, began to practice the observation of the Sabbath on the Seventh Day (that is, on Saturday) as early as 1844, but they did not adopt the name officially until 1860. Today the Church has eleven world divisions with a total of eight million members, only 10 percent of whom are in North America. Seventh-Day Adventists are evangelical conservatives, believing in the Bible as the literal revelation of God. Traditionally, they have allowed seminary-trained women to perform many rites, including marriage and baptism, but not to be ordained. Local churches in the United States, however, are challenging this tradition.

PENTECOSTAL

The term *pentecost* refers to an event that took place fifty days after Christ's resurrection, when the Holy Spirit enabled the first Christians "to speak with other tongues," that is, to speak unfamiliar languages (Acts 2:1–4.). Pentecostals believe that seeking and receiving this gift of tongues is a sign of baptism by the Holy Spirit. Other gifts of the Spirit may include healing, love, joy, prophecy, exorcism, and answers to prayers.

Pentecostalism began in the United States around 1900. There are a great many pentecostal churches in the United States today, and they differ widely in doctrine and in practice. They are united, however, in their belief in ecstatic experience. Most also believe in the Trinity, original sin, salvation through Christ's sacrifice, the virgin birth and divinity of Jesus, the divine inspiration of the scriptures, manifestations of the Holy Spirit, and future rewards and punishments. Services are generally demonstrative and energetic, and they usually observe the sacraments of baptism and the Lord's Supper. Most of their houses of worship in New York are modest buildings, although some congregations have purchased grander structures formerly occupied by other faith groups. The largest Pentecostal groups in the United States today are the Church of God in Christ, with almost six million members; the Assemblies of God (about 2.5 million); and the United Pentecostal Church (one million). All of these are represented in New York City.

ISLAM

Monotheism, the worship of one God, is believed to have been founded by Abraham (Hebrew for "exalted father"), and both Jews and Arabs claim literal descent from him—Jews through his son Isaac, and Arabs through another son, Ishmael. Muslims believe that the Arabs fell away from monotheism

A calligraphic rendering of "There is no God but God, and Muhammad is the prophet of God."

through the centuries after Abraham and Ishmael, but they were brought back by Muhammad (c. 570–632 C.E.). He founded Islam, which means "surrender [to God's will]." "One who surrenders" is a Muslim. The Arabic word for the one God is *al-ilah*, or Allah, a cognate of the Hebrew *eloh*, "god." The five essential duties of a Muslim, called the "Five Pillars," are belief in the one God, five daily prayers, generous giving of alms, fasting during one month (Ramadan), and, if possible, a pilgrimage (*hajj*) to Mecca at least once in one's lifetime. The Qur'an, the sacred scriptures of Islam, is a collection of writings revealed to Muhammad. Just as Christians see their religion as building on Judaism, adding the New Testament to the Old, so Muhammad envisioned his teachings as a continued evolution of monotheism. Muslims believe that Muhammad was the last of God's prophets, who also include Adam, Noah, Abraham, Moses, and Jesus.

The two main streams of Islam are Sunni and Shia, a division that arose out of a dispute among early Muslim leaders. About 85 percent of Muslims worldwide today are Sunni, but Shia Islam is the official religion of Iran. Through the centuries, differences in ceremony and in law have differentiated Sunnis from Shiites.

New York City's early black African residents probably counted a number of Muslims among them, but the first Islamic institution founded here was established in 1887 by Alexander Russell (Muhammad) Webb, an American who converted while serving as a U.S. diplomat in the Middle East. He taught and preached from a location in midtown Manhattan. In 1939 a Moroccan immigrant opened an Islamic Mission of America in Brooklyn Heights, and through the 1940s an increasing number of Arab Muslims settled in Brooklyn. The city's first purpose-built mosque was

Masjid al-Falah in Queens, which was opened by a group of Muslims from Pakistan and Bangladesh in 1982.

Today the number of Muslims in New York City is growing rapidly, through conversion, immigration, and family-size. There were probably 600,000 Muslims in the city by 2000, worshiping in about 100 mosques (*masjids*) ranging from humble storefronts to grand buildings. Muslims in New York come from many different countries, and they are very diverse. Nevertheless, many have found their faith to be a force bonding them here with Muslims from other countries and cultures. Most mosques may have been started by people from one or another nationality, but all welcome Muslims (and visitors) of any background.

America's Black Muslim movement was founded early in the twentieth century, but it won national recognition as the Nation of Islam under the leadership of Elijah Muhammad, who preached black separatism. The Nation opened its first mosque in Harlem in 1946. Malcolm X joined the Nation of Islam during a prison term (between 1946 and 1952), but he moved on to embrace Orthodox Islam before his assassination in 1965. The Nation's mosque in Harlem later followed his example, and took the name Masjid Malcolm Shabazz (see p. 268). Since Elijah Muhammad's own death in 1975, his son W. Deen Muhammad has led the main national group into Islam's mainstream. Louis Farrakhan broke with him and led a faction that still argued for separatism, but in February 2000 W. Deen Muhammad and Farrakhan announced that they had reconciled.

HINDUISM AND SIKHISM

Hinduism is the most ancient religious tradition in Asia. The oldest Hindu sacred texts (the *Vedas*) date to at least 1800 B.C.E., but the religion originated somewhere in central Asia long before that. It entered the Indian subcontinent with the arrival of central Asian peoples about the time of the writing of the *Vedas*. Hindus believe in one Supreme Consciousness, Brahman, whose aspects are realized in three deities: Brahma, the creator; Vishnu, the preserver; and Siva, the destroyer. These are coequal, and their functions are interchangeable. All other Hindu "gods," saints, or spirits are emanations of Brahman.

Sikhism is an offshoot of Hinduism based on the teachings of Guru (teacher) Nanak (c. 1469–1539 C.E.). Nanak tried to reconcile Hinduism and Islam, teaching monotheism and the realization of God through religious exercises and meditation. The Sikh's holy temple is in the city of Amritsar in northern India, where, under a series of gurus, the Sikhs long had an independent state before the British conquest. Sikhs believe that before Guru Gobind Singh, the tenth and last human guru, died in 1708, he "gave" the guruship to the Sikh scriptures, called the *Siri Guru Granth Sahib* (or *Adigranth*). These scriptures were compiled by earlier gurus, and they contain sacred writings by Hindu and Muslim teachers as well. The printed book itself is treated with special reverence.

Since the 1950s, and particularly after changes in the immigration law in 1965, what had been a trickle of Indian diplomats, students, and business executives to New York has become one of the major immigrant streams. As the number of Indians increased, many turned to religion to form an "Indian" cultural identity—especially since caste, regional, and sectarian differences often prevent an all-Indian identity in India itself. Indians at first rented space for worship, but in 1977 the Hindu Temple of North America opened in Flushing (see p. 324), and the Geeta Temple opened soon after in Elmhurst. In 1972 the Sikh Cultural Society dedicated a large temple in Richmond Hill (Queens). By 2000, New York City was home to approximately 100,000 Hindus and Sikhs, and they had built many houses of worship.

BUDDHISM

Siddhartha Gautama (c. 563–483 B.C.E.) was a northern Indian Hindu prince who, through meditation, achieved the status and title of *Buddha*, or "Enlightened One." He taught Four Noble Truths: (1) life involves suffering; (2) the cause of suffering is craving; (3) elimination of craving ends suffering; (4) craving can be eliminated by right thinking and behavior. This cessation of suffering is called *nirvana*, which means the "blowing out" of greed, hatred, and delusion.

The oldest surviving printed books are copies of the Buddhist texts, the *Pali Canon*, but as Buddha's teachings spread, sects and schools arose. The Theravada school of Buddhism ("doctrine of the elders") diffused across Southeast Asia, and today it is the state religion in Thailand and Sri Lanka. This school centers around the ideal of a monk striving for his own deliverance. Mahayana Buddhism (the "great vehicle," because it carries more people to nirvana), in contrast, which diffused throughout East Asia, idealizes the concept of the *bodhisattva*, someone who helps others achieve enlightenment. Mahayana thus recognizes numerous minor divinities. Mahayana monasteries arose in what is now Afghanistan, and the religion extended out from that focus of central Asian trade routes. In Bhutan, Tibet, and Mongolia, Buddhism evolved a special form called *Vajrayana*, which is known for its elaborate rituals and complex priestly hierarchy. Chinese Buddhists produced a new theory of spontaneous enlightenment, or *Ch'an*, which the Japanese called *Zen*.

Today Buddhism has several hundred million followers, but its adherents are hard to count because it is not an exclusive system of belief. Buddhist philosophy has won considerable influence in the modern Western world.

New York City is an important center of American Buddhism, partly because of its large population from countries that are predominantly Buddhist. The first Buddhists in New York City were undoubtedly Chinese immigrants in the mid–nineteenth century who worshiped in homes and secular societies. Japanese artist and writer Sokei-an Sasaki in 1930 formed the Buddhist Society of America, which was renamed the Zen Institute in 1945. The New York Buddhist Church (founded in 1938) created the American Buddhist Academy, which ordains priests, in 1948 (see p. 258). The Zen Studies Society was established in 1956 and today operates a Zen practice and training center on Manhattan's Upper East Side (223 East 67th St. ☎ 861-3333). The Zen Culture Society was founded in 1968, and the Chinese Institute of Chung-Hwa, the Buddhist Culture Meditation Center, opened in Elmhurst in 1979.

Many of today's Buddhist meditation centers are Zen, and these are usually led by Asian priests or Westerners who have long studied with Asian spiritual leaders. There is also a rising number of Buddhist temples built by new New Yorkers from China, Vietnam, Laos, Cambodia, and other countries. Lower Manhattan's expanding Chinese community, for example, supports at least thirty Buddhist temples, and other groups of Asian heritage have converted buildings in the outer boroughs into Buddhist temples or have constructed splendid new structures (see p. 325). One observer counted 112 Buddhist temples in New York City in 2000.

OTHER FAITH GROUPS

For reasons of space alone, the list above does not include all of the religious groups in the city. The great diversity of religions in New York ranges from the few hundred Baha'i followers of Baha'u'llah (1817–92), a Persian mystic who taught that "the fundamental purpose animating the Faith of God and His Religion is to safeguard the interests and promote the unity of the human race," to tens of thousands of followers of Santería, a religion developed in Cuba among slaves under Spanish rule. Santería incorporates elements of Roman Catholicism and the religion of the

African Yoruba people (see the box on p. 267). The Holy Spirit Association for the Unification of World Christianity was formed in 1954 in Korea by the evangelist Sun Myung Moon. The group registered in New York City in 1972 and bought a former hotel as its national headquarters. Reverend Moon was sent to prison for tax evasion in the 1980s, but the organization still has several churches in New York City. The International Society for Krishna Consciousness was formed in New York City by Swami Prabhupada in 1966. Krishna is a popular god considered an incarnation of Vishnu, a member of the Hindu Trinity. The society has its world headquarters in West Virginia and chapters worldwide.

New groups may well be forming every day, as New York continues to attract immigrants from around the world and to inspire spiritual movements.

GOING ON RETREAT

A number of New York City religious organizations operate retreat houses in the suburbs or upstate New York. These are most emphatically not "hotels," but are open to visitors for a few days of quiet rest and contemplation. Most offer discussion groups and opportunities for guided reading; some offer counseling. The Community of St. John the Baptist, for example, an Episcopal religious order for women, operates St. Marguerite's Retreat House in Mendham, New Jersey (☎ 973-543-4641); the New York Yearly Meeting of Friends (Quakers) operates Powell House Retreat Center in Old Chatham, New York (☎ 518-794-8811); the priests and brothers of the Franciscan Order offer facilities at Mount Alvernia in Wappinger Falls, New York (☎ 914-297-5706); and the American Burma Buddhist Association, with a temple at 619 Bergen Street in Brooklyn (☎ 718-622-8019), welcomes visitors to its Mahasi Retreat Center in Manalapan, New Jersey (☎ 723-792-1484). The Roman Catholic Carmelite Order operates Carmel Retreat in Mahwah, New Jersey (☎ 201-327-7090). This retreat, established in 1954, has its own gardens, but it also adjoins a state park. Nestled in the Catskill Mountains, the Zen Mountain Monastery in Mount Tremper, New York (☎ 914-688-2228) offers rigorous and authentic Zen training programs of lengths ranging from a weekend to several weeks. The Zen Studies Society (see p. 205) opened a meditation retreat, Dai Bosatsu Zendo, upstate in Livingston Manor in 1976 (☎ 914-439-4566).

Some retreat centers can even be found within the city limits. The Community of the Holy Spirit, an Episcopal community for women, welcomes visitors for short stays at its St. Hilda's House (621 West 113th St. ☎ 666-8249, ex. 304). The House of the Redeemer (Episcopal, 7 East 95th St. ☎ 289-0399) offers another opportunity. The Roman Catholic Jesuit Order offers retreat facilities at Mount Manresa on Staten Island (239 Fingerboard Rd. ☎ 718-727-3844), and the Roman Catholic Passionist Order operates Bishop Molloy Retreat House in Jamaica, Queens (86-45 Edgerton Blvd. ☎ 718-739-1229) as well as Cardinal Spellman Retreat House (5801 Palisade Ave., the Bronx [Riverdale] ☎ 718-549-6500).

The Census of the Faiths Changes with the City's Population

No official census has ever been taken either of houses of worship or of numbers of members of different faiths. A series of such censuses through the years, however, would reflect the changes in the city's ethnic and immigrant mix. In 1828 the twenty-one Presbyterian churches in the city attracted an estimated one-quarter of all churchgoers. The Episcopalians were next in number of houses of worship, with eighteen, followed by the Methodists (fourteen), the Baptists (thirteen), the Dutch Reformed (thirteen), and the Roman Catholics (four). There were two synagogues.

Since then, some denominations have all but disappeared, while others still serve numerous members. The Episcopal Church has remained strong for three hundred years despite the shrinking of the population of English background. Maybe this is because Episcopal programs have welcomed newcomers, who often accept a new religious affiliation in a new home. Today the Episcopal Diocese of New York holds weekly services in fourteen languages. Also, immigrants from the West Indies have always been important in New York history, and many of those who come from former British colonies are already Anglican. New York's Episcopal Church has also long been a wealthy church; it received at first generous land grants, and it has continued to receive gifts and endowments from wealthy members. Combine these facts with Episcopal movements in the nineteenth century to build glorious houses for the Lord, and you understand why many of New York's sacred designated City Landmarks are Episcopal churches.

Among Jews, Sephardim arrived first. Ashkenazim came and founded their own synagogues later. The Roman Catholic Church was established by French and Irish settlers. They were joined by Germans, then Italians and Slavs at the end of the nineteenth century. Today Hispanics make up the largest share of Roman Catholics, but Asians and Africans are also strongly represented in Roman Catholic congregations. Koreans and Chinese fill New York's Methodist and Presbyterian churches. New immigrants bring faiths to the city that were historically not strongly represented—such as Islam and Hinduism. Virtually every major faith on Earth is today represented in New York.

In 1990 Professors Barry Kosmin and Seymour Lachman of the City University of New York surveyed New Yorkers' religious affiliations. Here is what they found:

Affiliation Claimed

Roman Catholic	43.4% of all respondents
Jewish	10.9
Baptist	10.7
Protestant (other than denominations listed individually)	6.8
Methodist	2.9
Pentecostal	2.3
Episcopalian	2.2
Muslim	1.5
Various Eastern religions	1.4
Lutheran	1.3
Presbyterian	1.2
Jehovah's Witness	1.1
Eastern Orthodox Churches	0.8
Unitarian	0.4
Mormon	0.2
Alternative religions (Scientology, Eckankar, etc.)	0.1
Agnostic	7.4
Other or unclassified	3.6
Refused to answer	1.9

These numbers were compiled by a telephone survey, so they do not necessarily reflect the percentages of New Yorkers who belong to specific houses of worship, nor do they measure the importance people actually accord religion in their lives. The dominance of Roman Catholics, Baptists, and Jews reflects the city's population base, but the tremendous number and variety of creeds also reflects the city's continuing experience of new immigration.

THE NEWEST NEW YORKERS

More than one million immigrants came to New York City between 1990 and 2000, raising the foreign-born share of the city's population from 28 to 40 percent, the highest percentage since 1910. These newcomers augmented the city's ethnic diversity. The number of New Yorkers born in the former Soviet Union, for example, tripled, from about 81,000 to 229,000. South Asians from India, Pakistan, and Bangladesh more than doubled, from 67,000 to 146,000. Dominicans remained the leading Latino group, with their numbers rising more than two-thirds, from 230,000 to 387,000, and Mexicans nearly quadrupled from 35,000 to 133,000.

Kennedy International Airport in Queens claims to be the "Gateway to America." So many newcomers have in fact made that borough their home that its 167 nationalities and 116 languages make it the most diverse county in the United States today.

A 1990 estimate of the houses of worship in the city numbered 3,571, led by Baptist with 471, followed by Jewish (437); Roman Catholic (403); Pentecostal (391); Episcopal (163); Lutheran (161); Presbyterian (159); Methodist (123); Seventh-Day Adventist (116); Apostolic (72); Russian Orthodox (69); Christian Church of North America (63); Muslim (60); Jehovah's Witnesses (54); Church of Christ (50); and on down to just one Baha'i Temple. Through the 1990s and into the twenty-first century, the number of mosques and of Hindu, Buddhist, and Sikh temples has been growing rapidly.

CHAPTER TWO

What to Look For in New York's Houses of Worship

Houses of worship have historically been among New York's largest and tallest buildings, and their steeples long dominated its skyline. That of Trinity Church was the highest point in colonial New York, and for sixpence visitors could climb to the top for a breathtaking panorama of the city, the fort, and the boats in the harbor (see p. 84). When St. Patrick's Cathedral's twin 330-foot spires were topped off in 1888, they could be seen from twenty miles away (see p. 151). Many sacred spaces in New York City are large enough to seat 2,000 or more worshipers. The Cathedral of St. John the Divine—601 feet long and, at the west front, 207 feet wide—could contain twenty-seven basketball courts (see p. 281).

Today, however, all of these houses of worship are dwarfed by massive office buildings, apartments, and stores. When commercial buildings first overtopped the spires of houses of worship, many observers found it symbolic of an unfortunate reversal in society's values. In 1913 the Woolworth Corporation's new headquarters rose in the Gothic architectural style that was associated with churches; the world's tallest building at the time was ironically dubbed "the cathedral of commerce." This was said approvingly by some, but derisively by others.

Some sacred spaces are surprisingly large because their neighborhoods were more residential in the past. In 1900, Lower Manhattan was the most densely populated place the Earth has ever seen, with 640,000 people per square mile. The island's population peaked at 2.3 million in 1910, and most people lived in the southern half. Houses of worship were built to serve large local populations, larger percentages of which probably also attended services regularly. For example, at the end of the nineteenth century, 10,000 people attended services at St. Stephen's on East 28th Street each Sunday, whereas today that is an area of offices, with fewer neighborhood residents (see p. 141).

Some buildings, such as the Church of St. Thomas More, were isolated country facilities when they were built, so today a visitor stumbling upon them seems carried back to a time long before skyscrapers rose around them (see p. 222). Many were originally surrounded by burying grounds, but New York eventually forbade new burials in the city center, and most burial grounds have been built over. Their occupants were disinterred and laid to rest in new cemeteries farther out from the city center. Only a few quiet churchyards still exist in the heart of the city, and they are important for their rarity, calm and historical significance. A surprising number of houses of worship, however, have managed to reserve a tiny garden or planted seating area next to the building. These are usually open to the public.

This chapter suggests principal features to look for in houses of worship of different denominations and faiths. The entries for the individual buildings throughout the rest of the book, however, will not conform to a "checklist" of criteria, but treat each place according to its unique points of interest, whether they be its members' beliefs, the congregation itself, the building, or its history, or the artworks it contains. A few of New York's houses of worship have their own guidebooks (including St. Patrick's, St. John the Divine, and Trinity), and many others have free or inexpensive pamphlets guiding you through the building.

Architectural Elements

THE PLACEMENT AND SHAPES OF BUILDINGS

Churches traditionally face east. Worshipers in synagogues face toward Jerusalem; in New York City that is east. Mosques are designed so that the congregation faces Mecca. Given the constraints of crowded New York real estate, however, not all New York churches, synagogues, and mosques have been able to observe an eastward orientation on the exterior plan, even if they can design the interior to achieve it.

"FENG-SHUI" IN MANHATTAN

The placement and design of temples, gravesites, homes, and even whole cities is called *feng-shui* in Chinese. Feng-shui originated in early philosophical questioning of humankind's place in nature. It was practiced in China by the third century C.E., and from China made its way into Vietnam, Korea, and Japan. Migrants from East Asia have more recently spread interest in feng-shui around the world, and today it exercises increasing influence on the real estate market, architecture, and interior design. Buildings in New York have hired feng-shui consultants to guarantee propitious alignment of design features, including doors and windows, mirrors, fountains, and plantings.

The street grid of Manhattan, planned in 1811, happens to be oriented so that on four days of the year you can stand in the middle of any cross-street and see the sunrise or sunset: Sunrise on January 2 at 7:20 A.M. E.S.T. and December 10 at 7:10 A.M. E.S.T.; sunset on May 28 at 6:20 P.M. E.D.T., and July 12 at 8:30 P.M. E.D.T. There is no record that this was intentional.

The shape of a house of worship can itself reveal something about the congregation's beliefs. The most embracing plan is probably a square or circle, especially if the altar, pulpit or *bimah* is placed in the center of the congregation.

A rectangle is a more common plan for a building, but the placement of the entrance and of the focal point of the interior conveys symbolic meaning. Seventeenth-century Protestants, for example, placed the entrance in the middle of one of the long walls, and the pulpit in the middle of the other long side. This was generally considered to be a "democratic" design, and it is called the **meetinghouse style**.

The alternative design for a rectangular building is to place the entrance on one of the short sides (at one end), and to place the altar and pulpit at the other end. This design imitates the law courts in ancient Rome, and it is called the **basilica** design, from the Greek word for "royal." It requires the congregation to come forward to approach the altar or pulpit. This design has always been considered hierarchical, so it was explicitly rejected by many early Protestants. New York's earliest Presbyterian churches, for example, were built square or as meetinghouses specifically to avoid the connotations of the basilica form. This architectural term, by

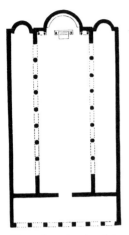

Floor plan of a church in the basilica style with a narthex and three aisles

the way, should not be confused with the special designation "basilica," which the Pope awards to Roman Catholic churches of special historical or religious merit. Many places of worship, churches in particular, are divided into three parts: the **narthex**, an enclosed porch or vestibule at the entrance; the **nave**, at times divided by columns, piers and side aisles; and the **chancel**, which may have an **apse**.

A church in the form of a **Latin cross**, called **cruciform**, is considered even more hierarchical than a basilica design. The arms of the cross are called **transepts**, and the area where the transepts intersect the nave is called the **crossing**. The altar may be placed in the center of the crossing, or it may be pushed back away from the congregation into the chancel. The further the altar is removed from the congregation, the more ceremonial the plan is considered. A place to walk around behind the altar is called an **ambulatory**, and chapels may radiate from that.

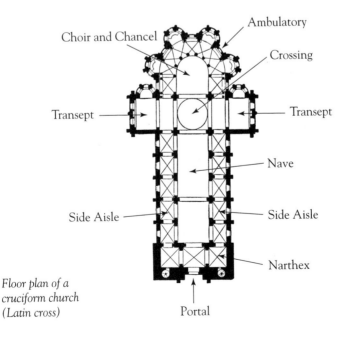

Floor plan of a cruciform church (Latin cross)

On a **Greek cross** plan, all arms radiating from the crossing are of equal length.

Any church may have a tower with a belfry and steeple over the entrance, over the crossing, or placed asymmetrically, picturesquely, somewhere along the side of the sanctuary. A **flèche** is a small spire, usually over the crossing, and usually containing a small bell. Domes may be found in buildings of classically inspired styles: Romanesque, Renaissance, Baroque, or Classical Revival.

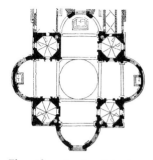

Floor plan of a church in the form of a Greek cross

A well-designed narthex in an urban house of worship serves as a "decompression chamber" from the hustle and bustle of street activity into the sanctuary of quiet contemplation. It may also accommodate fellowship and social assembly after a service.

Due to high real estate costs, few houses of worship have free space around them. Midblock sites are usually more affordable than corner lots, so architects are challenged to ensure adequate natural lighting. Many sacred buildings have clerestories. A **clerestory** (clear story) is often found in a basilica plan building where the side aisles are lower than the central

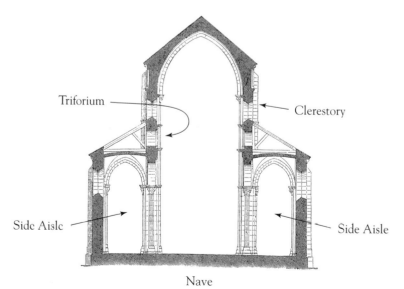

Triforium

Clerestory

Side Aisle

Side Aisle

Nave

A cut-away view of a Gothic church

nave, and it has windows allowing light into the interior. Simply put, it is that part of the nave which rises above the side aisles and contains windows. Clerestories are important sources of light (gas lighting was introduced in the 1820s, but electric lighting not until the 1880s), and they also inspire people to look up and, perhaps, elevate their thoughts. Clerestory windows may not be conspicuous, so if they are stained glass, they may be in abstract patterns, which are less expensive than figural windows. In some sacred spaces, abutting buildings may dictate that the number of windows on one side may not match the number on the other, and in still others, beautiful windows may today be blocked by new neighbors.

Architectural Styles

Congregations and their architects have always been concerned with the philosophical or historical associations of architectural styles. Well-known architectural images have great power. The common association of the Gothic style with Christian churches, for example, is a powerful metaphor.

Many of New York's houses of worship were built in the nineteenth century, when new building materials were introduced, such as iron and steel, but many of them echoed historic styles and even revived them. Their architects, however, were not simply archaeological reconstructors. They treated styles of the past as architectural vocabularies with which they could "say things" that were altogether their own. The use of historical styles was defended by the great Prague-born architect Leopold Eidlitz. "What forms," he asked, "are we to take: Egyptian or Greek, or Roman, or medieval?" He answered, "Take them all, familiarize yourself with them all; but when you reproduce them, be careful to keep them separate, and to use only such as were originally used together, lest by mixing forms of different periods you produce discord."

No attempt to classify New York buildings in historical styles can be completely successful. Many builders were ignorant of stylistic purity, and frequently they inadvertently mixed styles in one or another of their buildings. Architect Samuel A. Warner proclaimed his 1854 Marble Collegiate Church to be in the Romanesque Revival style, which was just then coming into fashion, but observers today label it Gothic Revival with minor Romanesque details (see p. 184). Furthermore, many New York houses of worship have been built through the course of years, and during those years the congregations' preferences changed. Different parts of these buildings may be in different styles. This is common among the old churches of Europe, and some American architects deliberately mixed styles in order to imitate and suggest such age—despite Eidlitz's admonition against the practice. For these reasons the architectural guidebooks of even the American Institute of Architects and of the New York City Landmarks Preservation Commission assign individual buildings to different stylistic categories.

As mentioned, even the dating of houses of worship may be difficult. Some congregations commemorate the groundbreaking for their building, others the laying of the cornerstone, others the building's completion, first service, year of dedication, or year of consecration (usually when it's paid for). This book provides each building's date of dedication.

For general reference, the characteristics and connotations of the most popular sacred styles will be discussed in the following pages, in which we trace a history of architectural fashion from the late eighteenth into the early twentieth century. Some outstanding houses of worship have been built in modern and postmodern styles, too, and several of these are featured in the text.

The Wren-Gibbs, Georgian, and Colonial Revival Styles

Manhattan's oldest surviving church building, St. Paul's (1766; see p. 92), exemplifies a style developed by Sir Christopher Wren, who designed fifty-one new churches after London's Great Fire in 1666. Wren's classical style was successfully copied by James Gibbs, whose most famous church was London's St.-Martin-in-the-Fields (1726). Gibbs published the plan of St. Martin's in *A Book of Architecture* (1728), and the architect of our St. Paul's, possibly a Thomas McBean, probably studied Gibbs's book.

The distinguishing exterior features of this **Wren-Gibbs style** include the combination of a classical **portico** (porch) with a tower and steeple. Wren transformed the Gothic spire into a classical square tower surmounted by a pyramidal or telescoping spire. He often centered the tower on the façade with the principal entrance at its base. At St. Martin's, Gibbs perched the tower and steeple further back onto the roof ridge, concealing its structural support, and put a monumental portico with freestanding columns across the entire façade. At St. Paul's in New York, the west façade is the original façade. Try to imagine it as it was when it was built, with a lawn sloping down to the Hudson River. This façade is typical of Wren. The tower projects through the façade, and a small portico protects the door into the tower. The grand façade on the eastern end of St. Paul's, facing Broadway, was added three years later. This portico looks more like that of St. Martin's in London, and when architect J. C. Lawrence added a steeple onto St. Paul's tower in 1794, he followed the lines of Gibbs's steeple at St. Martin's. Today most visitors enter St. Paul's through the grand Broadway portico, but in fact they are "sneaking in" behind the altar, rather than approaching the altar through the church from the west, as is proper in a basilica plan. Other common attributes of Wren-Gibbs churches include giant **pilasters** (flat columns against walls), a stone **belt course** (or string course—a horizontal line of stones marking a division) separating two stories of windows, and a continuous **balustrade** on top.

Wren-Gibbs church interiors were among the first specifically designed to meet the requirements of Protestant worship, which focuses on preaching. Clear sightlines and audibility were essential; Wren actually called his churches "auditories." At St. Paul's, fluted columns (that is, with grooves) that are mounted on bases and attached to the balconies seem to support a complete vaulting system. This **vaulting** does not carry any weight; it is only decorative, but it does amplify the minister's voice. Balconies allow more of the congregation to be close to the minister by doubling up. Sounding boards often hover over wineglass-shaped pulpits. The windows in such churches were originally clear, and the interiors were bright, allowing the congregation to see the minister and to read in their own prayer and hymn books. The walls usually have a lower row of short windows and an upper row of higher rounded windows. At St. Paul's, a **Palladian window** (a large arched central window flanked by lower rectangular windows) fits behind the altar. This late-Renaissance Italian feature enjoyed considerable popularity in England in the seventeenth and eighteenth centuries.

Many American builders owned copies of Gibbs's *Book of Architecture*, and the Wren-Gibbs type of church was further popularized by America's first how-to handbook, Asher Benjamin's *The Country Builder's Assistant* (1797). This book inspired many of the Congregational churches in New England, although economical New Englanders frequently omitted the enormously expensive porticos.

The term **Georgian** often refers to the architecture of the reigns of England's first three Georges (1714–1820). The Georgian style was classical, imitating northern Italian late-Renaissance architecture, particularly that of Andrea Palladio. Characteristics include a formal dignity and symmetry, solid proportions, ornate frames for doorways, stone **quoins** (blocks used to reinforce or decorate the corners), and Palladian windows.

Wren-Gibbs and Georgian classical architecture enjoyed new popularity in the United States in the 1920s and 1930s, when it was called **Colonial Revival**. The Brick Presbyterian Church (see p. 224) and the Third

Church of Christ, Scientist (1924, Delano & Aldrich) at 585 Park Avenue (at 63rd St.) are good examples.

Greek Revival

Late-eighteenth century archaeology spurred an interest in antique architecture and decoration, and both Greek and pre-Imperial Roman styles found favor in the United States. Greek architecture was thought to represent democratic government, and Roman to represent republican government. Thomas Jefferson's Virginia state capitol (1785–92), modeled after the Roman Maison Carrée in Nîmes, was the modern world's first example of a public building in the temple form.

The most easily identifiable features of **Greek Revival** buildings are a portico across the front and a roof with a ridge running from front to back. All doors and windows are **trabeated** (rectangular, because built with posts and beams), because ancient Greeks did not use arches. Glass windows are clear.

By the 1820s, the Greek Revival style flourished for churches. In New York City, temple fronts were often combined with steeples, but a few purer Greek temple-front churches still stand from the 1830s and 1840s. All have at least an impressive Greek temple façade. Four notable surviving examples are St. Joseph's on Sixth Avenue (1834), St. James on James Street (1837), St. Peter's on Barclay Street (1838), and the Mariners' Temple on Oliver Street (1842) (see the box on p. 89).

Gothic Revival

The romantic movement idealized the Christian medieval past and spurred a **Gothic Revival style** of architecture. **Pointed arches** are the most typical feature, but other characteristics include **buttresses** (structures built against walls for support), stained-glass windows, **tracery** (curvilinear openwork shapes creating a pattern within openings), large **rose windows** (circular windows with tracery), and sculpture with medieval inspiration.

The Gothic Revival style gained

A Gothic pointed arch

A rose window

popularity rapidly after Episcopal Bishop John H. Hopkins of Vermont, who was well-known in New York City, published *An Essay on Gothic Architecture* (1836). The appropriate architectural features were detailed in *The True Principle of Pointed or Christian Architecture* (1841), by the Englishman A. W. N. Pugin. Pugin argued that Gothic is the only style appropriate for Christian churches.

Early Gothic Revival buildings are usually monochromatic, but later buildings, called **High Victorian Gothic**, often used stone in contrasting colors. The light and dark horizontal banding on New York's first example, Jacob Wrey Mould's Church of All Souls (1854, since demolished), won its nickname "The Church of the Holy Zebra." Architect P. C. Keely's Roman Catholic Church of St. Bernard on West 14th Street (between Eighth and Ninth Aves., 1875) is a very good example.

Gothic Decoration Is Not Gothic Construction

Some nineteenth- and twentieth-century churches were built according to medieval Gothic methods of construction, but others only display Gothic decoration. True Gothic construction, the Gothic of the Middle Ages, is the grandparent of the modern skyscraper. In those buildings a skeleton of strong piers—stone in the Middle Ages, steel in the present— supports the building. The walls are not holding up the building but are themselves being held up by the skeleton. They are mere curtains to keep out the rain. The Gothic churches of Europe and modern skyscrapers everywhere demonstrate that curtain walls can even be made of glass. The construction of Europe's great Gothic cathedrals, however, absorbed the efforts and finances of whole communities for decades, or even centuries, and nineteenth-century American congregations demanded fine new houses of worship in a hurry. Therefore, most nineteenth-century Gothic Revival churches in America are Gothic in their design and decoration, but they were not built according to medieval Gothic construction methods.

America's first Gothic Revival buildings were made of wood, and Gothic-style details and decoration were added. Even structural elements that have no function in wooden buildings were copied from the medieval stone buildings. For example, Gothic cathedrals need buttresses along the outside to support the high walls against the outward thrust of the heavy stone roof vaults. Sometimes even freestanding piers, called **flying buttresses**, extend supporting arms against the wall. In wooden churches, however, the vaults are made of plaster. From inside, these are indistinguishable from stone vaults, but they are hung from wooden roof supports, more or less as in any plaster ceiling. With plaster vaults, weight-supporting buttresses are unnecessary, but many wooden Gothic Revival churches have them anyway. These buildings are often called **Carpenter's Gothic**, to differentiate them from true **Stonemason's Gothic**.

A *Gothic finial*

Architects later chose to cover even iron and steel skeletons with Gothic-style decorations. The Church of St. Mary the Virgin, for example, is actually the world's first steel and concrete church (see p. 188). Iron supports the Gothic Revival St. Patrick's Cathedral (see p. 151). Both St. Mary's and St. Patrick's have buttresses, but the buttresses serve no structural function. Self-consciously modern architects disdain such buildings, calling them "dishonest." Architect Ralph Adams Cram (1863–1942) demanded "rigid honesty in church building, where any willful falsity approaches the point of sacrilege. . . . If a church is not honest—honest in its design, its construction, its decoration—it is nothing." Nevertheless, such churches remain among the most beloved across America. In fact, our need to have buildings *appear* certain ways, however they happen to be constructed, demonstrates the power that tradition and symbolism have in our lives. The architect of St. Mary's, Napoleon Le Brun, built many New York churches in a variety of styles.

Cram himself attempted true Gothic-style construction. He insisted on building St. Thomas's out of masonry in the traditional manner, using structural steel only for the roof **truss** (see p. 190). Construction of the Cathedral of St. John the Divine, also true Gothic, has absorbed the energies of the New York community for over one hundred years (see p. 281).

New York's Gothic-Style Churches

New York's first Gothic-style church was Old St. Patrick's Cathedral on Mott Street, designed by Joseph Mangin in 1809 (see p. 116). The fire that swept that building in 1868, however, destroyed the façade, and little of what we see of Old St. Patrick's today conveys its original Gothic-style details. Old prints reveal that Mangin's grasp of the style was insecure. A more genuine Gothic Revival style came with the design of St. Peter's Episcopal Church (1838; see p. 179), the details of which came from Bishop Hopkins's book.

Richard Upjohn cinched the popularity of the Gothic with his design for Trinity Church (1846; see p. 84), which was immediately hailed as a masterpiece. Upjohn wrote a handbook for the construction of wooden churches for poor rural parishes, *Rural Architecture* (1852). It provided patterns for churches that still stand from the Midwest across to the Pacific Northwest. Richard Upjohn's son, Richard M. Upjohn, joined him to design the wonderful Gothic-style entrance gates to Green-Wood Cemetery in Brooklyn (1861, see p. 317), and younger Upjohn designed the beautiful Gothic Revival Christ Church in the Bronx (5030 Riverdale Ave. at West 252nd St., 1866).

James Renwick, Jr., followed Richard Upjohn, Sr., as the leading designer of Gothic-style churches in New York. Renwick was only twenty-five years old when he received the commission to build Grace Church, and he was twenty-eight in 1846 when Grace opened its doors (see p. 130). The Gothic Revival style came to be associated with the Episcopal denomination, as exemplified by Trinity, Grace, and numerous more modest parish churches, a surprising number of which still survive scattered around the city, often surrounded by skyscrapers. Many New Yorkers were surprised when Roman Catholic Bishop John Hughes chose Renwick to design the immense cathedral Hughes wanted in the Gothic Revival style, but Hughes intended to proclaim by his choice of size, architect, and style that Roman Catholics had "arrived." Other denominations, including Congregationalists, Methodists, and Baptists, were attracted to the beauty of the Gothic Revival style, and they incorporated Gothic features into their buildings, but they retained the liturgical arrangement of their interior spaces (for example, they were seldom cruciform). Greater Metropolitan Baptist Church and the Abyssinian Baptist Church in Harlem, for example (see pp. 273, 278), are Gothic-style on the outside, but simple open preaching spaces—auditorium-style—on the inside.

Romanesque Revival

Richard Upjohn designed Brooklyn's Church of the Pilgrims (today's Our Lady of Lebanon, 1846, see p. 302) in the **Romanesque Revival style** before he designed Manhattan's Trinity in the Gothic style. Soon thereafter architect Robert Dale Owen argued in *Hints on Public Architecture* (1849) that Romanesque-style architecture represented American democratic Christian values better than the Gothic style could. Romanesque was the architectural style that had *preceded* the Gothic in European history, but in New York it enjoyed a revival of interest *after* the revival of interest in the Gothic style. Reverend Leighton Parks, rector of St. Bartholomew's Church, later identified five characteristics of Romanesque architecture that he believed carry spiritual significance: The **round**

A Romanesque round arch

arch to him signified thankful acceptance of life on Earth, rather than the striving toward heaven represented by the Gothic pointed arch. Parks argued that the chancel should be in the form of an apse. The chancel is the area in which the clergy performing a service move or sit; an apse is a semicircular area terminating a space. An apsidal chancel, in Parks's view, recalled the early democratic church organization, when there were no bishops' thrones, but the whole clergy sat on benches around the wall of the apse. Third, a dome would symbolize the tents first used for worship among the Jews. Fourth, the purity of clear glass, rather than stained glass, would represent redemption, and, fifth, a bell tower (or campanile), which was a Romanesque architectural innovation, would reflect the idea that the church was open to new ideas. St. Bartholomew's Church, which was designed for Parks's congregation, exemplifies the Romanesque Revival style (see p. 153). Romanesque Revival churches also often have **wheel windows**—large round windows having distinctly radiating spokes. If the churches' façades have two towers, one is usually taller than the other. A particularly ornate form of medieval Romanesque architecture, called

Byzantine, is characterized by complex vaulting, large open spaces, and lavish decoration with precious marbles, mosaics, and gilding. St. Anselm's Church in the Bronx (see p. 331) is modeled on the prototype for Byzantine churches—Hagia Sofia in Istanbul. Similarly, J. H. McGuire's Holy Trinity Roman Catholic Church on Manhattan's West 82nd Street (1912) is a Byzantine Revival gem. (Art collector William Randolph Hearst once attended a funeral there and made an offer to buy the altar.)

A wheel window

Ralph Adams Cram, the proponent of the Gothic Revival style, adopted Romanesque Revival for Christ Church, Methodist, on Park Avenue (see p. 198). Cram explained, "... the Protestant congregation was averse to Medieval Catholicism both by inheritance and doctrine . . . [so] let us go back to the first style that was evolved to express the Christian religion, long antedating the Gothic of the Catholic West. A Byzantine basis is what we should use." Byzantine or Romanesque was seen by a number of Protestants at the time as postclassical, specifically Christian, and yet pre-Catholic.

America's master of the Romanesque Revival style was undoubtedly Henry Hobson Richardson (1838–86), although his individual stamp differentiates his work from European precedents. **Richardsonian Romanesque** is characterized by stone construction, round arches framing deeply recessed windows and doors, rough textures, and a horizontal heaviness to the buildings. New York has no churches by Richardson himself, but fine Richardsonian churches include St. Martin's and St. Luke's (both Episcopal; see pp. 271–72) and the West-Park Presbyterian Church (165 West 86th St., 1890, Henry F. Kilburn).

Classicism: Renaissance Revival and Beaux-Arts Styles

The École des Beaux-Arts in Paris was founded in 1796 in order to monitor French artistic training. It taught all period styles, but it emphasized **classical** forms, that is, ancient Greek, Roman, and the ways that the

Renaissance revived those. The first American to study at the École was Richard Morris Hunt, who would later design the bronze doors at Trinity Church.

The firm most often associated with the **Renaissance Revival style** in New York was McKim, Mead and White. Charles Follen McKim and Stanford White had both worked with H. H. Richardson, and in 1879 they set up their own office with William Rutherford Mead as a third partner. The three began their careers by building informal summer homes, but they ended as the champions of classical formal traditions. Judson Memorial Church is an example of their classical work (see p. 168). St. Francis De Sales Roman Catholic Church (135 East 96th St., 1903) is a Renaissance Revival church designed by the architectural firm of O'Connor and Metcalfe.

During the Italian Renaissance, sculptors, architects, painters, and other artists often collaborated on great churches and other buildings. When several American artists collaborated at the 1893 Chicago World's Fair, one of them, Augustus Saint-Gaudens, stated boldly, "This is the greatest gathering of artists since the fifteenth century," thus dubbing their work the **American Renaissance**. We will note examples of American Renaissance collaboration at New York churches, including Trinity, St. Bartholomew's, Ascension (see p. 171), and St. Paul the Apostle (see p. 236).

Another offshoot of Beaux-Arts training was a slightly later, more refined, classical style typified by the work of Carrère and Hastings. Thomas Hastings's grandfather was a composer of sacred music (he wrote the music for "Rock of Ages"), and his father was a Presbyterian pastor. Hastings and his partner John Merven Carrère, the son of a Baltimore coffee dealer of French descent, designed a number of New York's outstanding buildings, including the Humanities and Social Science Division of the New York Public Library (see p. 186) and several fine churches in a variety of styles. These include Fort Washington Presbyterian, the First Church of Christ, Scientist (see p. 243), and St. Mary's of Manhattanville.

As a descriptive term, **Beaux-Arts** is usually reserved for buildings of a particularly lush classicism, almost baroque in character, that was thought to be appropriate for late-nineteenth-century urban grandeur. These buildings, typically including museums and court houses, boast large stone bases, grand stairways, paired columns on bases, monumental attics, grand arched openings, medallions, and sculptural figures. The Museum of the American Indian (see p. 83) is a good example.

Synagogues

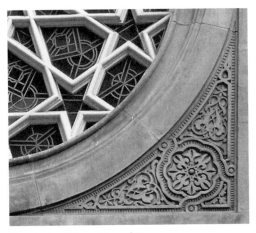

Façade detail from Central Synagogue

In order to be a synagogue, a structure only needs to be a place where at least ten adult male Jews (a **minyan**, the minimum necessary for a proper service) assemble regularly for prayer. *Synagogue* comes from the Greek *synagein*, "to bring together." Some traditions prescribe architectural details, but these have been open to interpretation or change through the years. For example, the synagogue should be the tallest building in the city, but this cannot always be achieved.

Any synagogue must have an **ark**, which is a receptacle containing the Torah scrolls, and the ark should be placed against the wall facing Jerusalem (in New York, the eastern wall). **Torahs** (scrolls containing the first five books of the Hebrew scriptures: Genesis, Exodus, Leviticus, Numbers, and Deuteronomy) are handwritten in Hebrew on leaves of parchment sewn together to create scrolls. Portions of the Torah are read on the Sabbath and during festivals. The Torah scrolls may have small caps (*rimmonim*) of silver or brass. Shearith Israel's archives preserves a Torah desecrated by British soldiers in New York during the Revolutionary War, but an imperfect Torah cannot be used. Torahs are considered sacred second only to human life, and they are, in fact, buried when they are no longer usable. In front of every ark hangs a continuously burning lamp (today often electric), the *ner tamid*. This symbolizes the eternal light that burned in the Temple in Jerusalem. As a rule, the congregation sits at right angles to the ark in more traditional synagogues, but facing it in more liberal ones.

The wall facing Jerusalem may also display a painted curtain. It is said that when the Messiah comes to Jerusalem, the curtain will part to reveal a view of the city. Traditional Jewish congregations interpret the Second

Commandment's prohibition against "graven images" (Exodus 20:4) to prohibit the representations of humans or animals in decor, so there will be no figural art in those synagogues. (All Muslims and the most traditional Protestant denominations also observe that prohibition, but other Christians, including Roman Catholics, believe that God's appearance on Earth as Jesus Christ moderated that commandment. See John 1:14). Stenciling, usually of ornate geometric or foliate patterns, is popular on the walls of synagogues (although seldom of words, as can be found in some Christian churches and in mosques). Repositories to the right or left of the ark may contain the "little scrolls," the Books of Ruth, Esther, or others. Vases may hold almond branches, as in the Temple in Jerusalem (Numbers 17:8), and mounted tablets may display the Ten Commandments.

Each synagogue has a platform (**bimah** to the Ashkenazim; **tebah** to the Sephardim) with a lectern from which the Torah is read. One tradition holds that this must be located in the center of the synagogue so that everyone can hear, but many Reform synagogues place the *bimah* in front of the ark along the eastern wall. At Temple Emanu-El (Reform), for example, the *bimah* stands directly in front of the ark. The **cantor** may stand on the *bimah* or at a separate lectern.

Another common decorative object is a **menorah**, or candelabrum. Seven-branched menorahs were found in Solomon's temple in Jerusalem. We can see them on the Arch of Titus in Rome, which was erected in 81 C.E. to commemorate the capture of Jerusalem and the looting of the Temple eleven years before. Orthodox synagogues generally avoid having seven-branched menorahs because they want to avoid imitating the Temple, but Reform synagogues might have seven-branched menorahs. A special menorah is used during the festival of Hanukkah. The nine-branched menorah (eight plus the one to light the others) used in that ceremony symbolizes the holiday.

Orthodox synagogues have no instrumental music (an organ immediately reveals that the synagogue you are in is not Orthodox); the congregation worships with covered heads, and men and women sit separately. In Reform, Conservative, and Reconstructionist synagogues, there is no segregation by sex.

Synagogues have always reflected the community and time in which they were built. The first synagogue in New York City, built in 1730, was modeled after the Great Sephardic Synagogue of Amsterdam. When nineteenth-century migrations brought more Ashkenazim to New York, many new congregations at first simply purchased existing Protestant church buildings and adapted them for use as synagogues. These buildings were given rabbinical approval because they did not contain any statuary or other graven images, and the ark could often comfortably fit into what had been an apse. The oldest surviving built synagogues in New York City were patterned after Christian churches. The Gothic Revival structure built for Congregation Anshe Chesed (see p. 118) still stands on Norfolk Street, but this style was soon associated with Christianity so exclusively that few other Gothic-style synagogues are to be found.

Horseshoe arch

Newer synagogues reflected a mixture of contemporary tastes and the architectural styles of the peoples' countries of origin. For example, New York's Central Synagogue (see p. 158) is a superb example of the **Moorish Revival style** popular in nineteenth-century Berlin and Budapest. These buildings have horseshoe-or keyhole-shaped arches and other features meant to recall the period when Judaism flourished in Muslim Iberia. Later Jewish migration from eastern Europe inspired styles based on the traditional *shtetl* (village) architecture of that region. These wood-frame structures often incorporated twin towers and onion domes.

Arnold Brunner, the first American-born licensed Jewish architect (1857–1925), criticized the Moorish Revival style as strengthening "the impression that the Jew was necessarily an alien, and did not wish to be regarded as an American." Brunner designed his first synagogues in Romanesque forms, but incorporating Islamic and Byzantine elements. An example was the home of Shaaray Tefila, which Brunner built on West 82nd Street in 1894—today the Ukrainian Orthodox Cathedral of St. Volodimir. At the very end of the nineteenth century, archaeological discoveries in the Holy Land provided classical models for synagogues. Congregation Shearith Israel's current building on Central Park West (see p. 246) was the first synagogue to adopt the classical style.

Early in the twentieth century, interest in Moorish and Byzantine Revival styles reawakened, often including central domes and giant single-arch façade portals, as at B'nai Jeshurun (see p. 253) and Temple Emanu-El (see p. 200). Today synagogues are built in every conceivable style.

Mosques (Masjids)

Islam means "surrender [to God's will]," and "one who surrenders" is a *Muslim*. When Muslims gather for Friday midday prayers and a sermon (**khutba**), it must be in a space whose purity reflects that of the believers. A mosque is fundamentally an enclosure for community prayer, not ritual. Muslims traditionally show very little concern for the architectural "style" of the building in which they pray. The imam (prayer and community leader) at Manhattan's first purpose-built mosque, the Islamic Cultural Center (see p. 227), has emphasized, ". . . in America, people are interested in understanding people through their architecture. This is not really our way, but I think that this can be seen as a new era for the mosque. Since this is America, the mosque should be made in an architectural language that Americans understand. Still, that has nothing to do with Islam."

Mosques can properly be built in any architectural style, but they often reflect those of Islam's Middle Eastern cradle. Characteristic features suggest shelter—originally from the hostile desert environment—including courtyards with covered arcades, and pools and channels of water. Tall slender towers called **minarets** are used to call the people to prayer. Unlike Christian steeples, minarets often stand apart from the body of the mosque.

Masonry domes, vaults, and arches span the large interior spaces, and although mosques may have few windows, intricate grills will allow light to filter in. Muslim architects created the horseshoe arches that were later copied on synagogues. All mosques will have facilities for ritual purification, usually at or near the entrance. Muslims believe one must wash one's arms, hands, face, and feet before praying. Interior walls are often elaborately carved plaster or stone, or surfaced with brilliantly colored, glazed tiles. Islam prohibits figural art, so it has developed a rich decorative art based upon abstract geometric patterns and natural flower and plant forms. Quotations from the Qur'an, the sacred text of

Geometric design

BELLS AND MINARETS

The purpose of bell towers and minarets is the same: to call the faithful to prayer or services. Christians use bells, and Muslims use criers called *muezzins*. Some New York churches have bells that date back to the eighteenth century: Trinity Church, Middle Collegiate, Brick Presbyterian, St. George's in Queens, and others. While American mosques rarely project the call to prayer outside the mosque, bells, too, in New York seldom ring, for three reasons: First, not all members of any particular congregation can be called by its bells because they do not live in the neighborhood. Only the Catholic Church and, to a degree, the Episcopal Church define parishes and encourage their members to attend their local parish church. Members of other faith groups choose a house of worship that may or may not even be the nearest of their denomination. Many church members travel long distances to attend services where they choose. Members of St. Luke's Lutheran Church on Manhattan's West Side, for example, drive in weekly from Long Island. Therefore, ringing bells would not reach the members of those congregations. Second, the people who *do* live near a particular church may not be members of it, and some of them do not want to be disturbed by ringing bells. And third, bells are expensive to maintain. Many historic bells in New York church steeples simply do not work any longer.

Islam, in the flowing forms of Arabic calligraphy, are also used to splendid effect.

The main feature of a mosque's interior is the **mihrab**, a shallow apse in the wall that identifies the direction of Mecca. That wall is called the **qibla**, and in New York it is the east wall. The *mihrab* is sometimes interpreted as a symbolic door or gateway to heaven, and it may boast decorative arches or pilasters. The members of the congregation, arranged in parallel rows, pray facing the *qibla*. Near to the *mihrab* are usually two pulpits. A small one, called a **kursi**, may be used by the imam to lecture or preach on ordinary occasions. The other is the **minbar**, a high pulpit, often canopied, reached by a straight staircase. The *minbar* is used only during Friday services and on holidays. There are no pews; the congregation stands and kneels, and women pray separately from the men. Music does not play a part in Muslim prayer, so mosques have no choir loft or organ.

Hindu Temples

Hindu temples in America are usually designed flexibly to accommodate a great variety of divine images or languages, or even to serve as cultural or community centers. New York's one genuine purpose-built temple does, however, reflect traditional considerations (see p. 324). The principal structural symbols in Hindu sacred architecture are mountains and cavelike spaces within them. Mountains are symbolic in many ways. They aspire to reach heaven, so they provide a base for our own upward thrust toward heaven. Furthermore, they are often interpreted as the abode of the gods, or at least potentially sites where gods may appear. A temple represents an earthly model of the entire cosmos, so it should resemble a mountain, which is the center of that cosmos. Few Hindu communities in America can afford the lavish sculptures and bas-reliefs of deities found on the exteriors of temples in India, but a spire (***rajagopuram***) may mark the main entrance. Otherwise, many Hindu temples may not be identifiable from the exterior.

Inside, cavelike spaces represent the womb's generative and regenerative powers. There are many variations in Hindu temple architecture, but most temples have a large room (***natmandir***) where worshipers sit or stand. This room will usually have an east-west alignment. The image of the principal deity resides in the womb-chamber (***garbhagriha***) of the temple at the western end, gazing toward the rising sun and the approaching devotee. Traditional details and figures are often imported from India. Temples traditionally have no pews or chairs; the only seat is reserved for the god.

Sikh Temples

A Sikh temple is called a *gurdwara*, which means "Gate to the Guru." It may be a home, rented space, or specially built temple, but the focus will always be on the scriptures, which are usually covered with a cloth at the front of the room, under a canopy. Sikhs avoid turning their backs to them. Worshipers and visitors must leave their shoes in an entry area, and everyone sits on the floor as an act of humiliation, equality, and respect. During services, hymns are sung and the scriptures are read. There are virtually no "decorative" requirements for a *gurdwara*, nor is there any additional architectural symbolism.

Buddhist Temples

The primary Buddhist monument is the dome-shaped *stupa* (the upper part of which evolved into the *pagoda* of East Asia). The form derives from ancient royal funeral mounds, but it was adopted by Buddhists as a reliquary. According to legend, Buddha's remains were divided into ten portions, and a consecrated mound was built over each relic. Later stupas were constructed for the remains of other holy figures such as saints and monks. As in Hinduism, the dome represents a symbolic mountain, and its interior represents the womb. Buddhist stupas have an inner chamber, called the "cosmic egg." These features of a mountainlike form protecting an inner chamber can best be seen at the Thai Buddhist Temple (see p. 325).

Inside, Buddhist temples vary widely. Most, but not all, feature at least one main altar. It may hold a statue of the main Buddha for that temple, and it is usually located at the front of the sanctuary. The altar itself is a symbolic mountain, and that symbol can be enhanced by the addition of a terrace or tiers of altars. Side altars often contain statues or pictures of the founder of the temple's lineage, which is a line of teachers and student followers through history. Some temples have pews, whereas others have just pillows or meditation cushions on the floor.

A pagoda

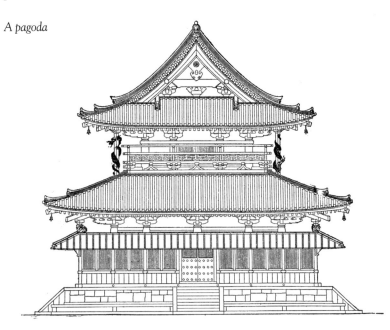

Church Interiors

The interior design of any Christian house of worship will reveal something about the beliefs of the people who worship there.

High or Low

A distinction commonly used to differentiate churches is between **High Churches** and **Low Churches** (usually capitalized in this special meaning). This expresses the degree to which any congregation believes that pomp and ceremony are appropriate for religious celebration. High Churches favor ceremony, formality, and elements of mystery, ornate vestments, candles and incense, and artistic and symbolic decorations, including crosses (especially **crucifixes**, which are crosses with an image of the crucified Christ on them). Low Churches, by contrast, forego decoration and ceremony. They express their piety in plain and simple furnishings and ceremonies.

The distinction between High and Low can sometimes be drawn not only between denominations, but even among individual churches within one denomination. For example, a movement in nineteenth-century England called the Oxford movement wanted to bring the Church of England back to its roots in medieval Catholicism. That meant going "Higher" by emphasizing the importance of the sacraments with exalted rituals and accompanying furnishings, and even making changes in church architecture. The movement wanted wider aisles for processions and apses to emphasize the altar (traditional Anglican churches were flat-ended). These new High forms and ceremonies came to be called **Anglo-Catholic**. The Oxford movement's American counterpart, the Ecclesiological Society, was founded in New York in 1848, and *The New York Ecclesiologist* was America's first periodical devoted to architecture and design. Virtually every Episcopal church discussed in this book (Ascension, Grace, Holy Apostles, Incarnation, St. James, and others) was rebuilt Higher in the late-nineteenth or early-twentieth century. Chancels were deepened or decorated more elaborately; transepts were added; altars replaced communion tables; reredoses were added, and crosses or even crucifixes were displayed. Architect Richard Upjohn, a High Church man, gave Trinity Church a deep chancel to emphasize the mystery of services, and he even insisted on raising a cross on top of the church's steeple. At the time, the display of crosses was considered terribly High Church. St. Peter's Episcopal Church (see p. 179) displayed no cross, and Trinity's vestry approved the display by only one vote. St. James displayed no cross until the 1880s. The "Reformed Episcopal Church" broke off from America's Episcopal Communion in protest in 1873 and stayed Lower, but there are few congregations of that denomination today.

Ritual or Nonritual

A second differentiation can be drawn between ritual and nonritual churches. **Ritual (or liturgical)** faiths, which include the Catholic and the High Episcopal churches, focus their worship on the altar. The altar is given great visual prominence as the site of the ritual sacrifice of the Eucharist, and the entire congregation must have an unobstructed view. The altar may be covered or protected by a **baldachin**, which is an ornamental canopy usually supported by columns. Houses of ritual worship also usually need space for processions and for the numerous clergy. These requirements will usually result in a large narthex, at least one wide aisle, and a broad and deep chancel. Ritual churches may also need a **sacristy**, which is a room near the chancel where the robes and altar vessels are stored and where the clergy vest themselves for services.

Changes in Roman Catholic liturgy defined at the Second Vatican Council in 1965 necessitated architectural changes in Roman Catholic churches. Before Vatican II, the priest celebrated the mass in Latin with his back to the congregation. He faced an altar attached to the back wall of the sanctuary, and this area was set off by a communion rail. Today, however, the mass is celebrated in the language of the people, and the priest faces the congregation across a free-standing altar. This liturgical change raised the problem of what to do with the existing, frequently ornate altars and the communion (or altar) rails that created a barrier between the priest and the congregation. Generally, rails have been removed, and new low altars have been built forward from the back wall, often at the crossing.

Several other details to look for in Roman Catholic and other ritual churches derive from their belief in the doctrine of transubstantiation. This is the belief that the ceremony of mass reenacts Christ's last supper. Christ's words to his disciples, "This is my body, which is given for you," are interpreted literally. **Transubstantiation** means that in the act of consecration of the host, an ordained priest is the instrument for transforming bread and wine into the actual human flesh and human blood of Christ. Any leftover portions of this transubstantiated bread are, therefore, still the body of Christ. These portions will be kept in a small repository, called a **tabernacle**, on or near the altar. Most Roman Catholic churches have some consecrated hosts in the tabernacle all the time, and its presence is noted by the burning of the **vigil light**, or **sanctuary lamp**, which usually hangs beside the tabernacle and is usually red in color. This host may be brought to the sick or dying, or it may be exposed for worship in a candle-stick-sized object called a **monstrance**.

Most Protestant faiths do not believe in transubstantiation, but believe that the communion is a symbolic sharing of bread and wine. Episcopalians leave undefined the nature of the communion bread and wine. Some Episcopalian and Lutheran churches speak of the "Real Presence" in the Eucharist when received but not necessarily when reserved.

Roman Catholic churches may display relics of saints in **reliquaries** on altars or in dedicated chapels. In Catholic teaching, relics are devotional objects, like holy water and the rosary. It is not necessary to believe in them; that is, they are not *de fide* (essentials of the faith). A **shrine** is a special chapel dedicated to the worship of a particular saint, and shrines often contain relics of that saint. The Church of St. Jean Baptiste, for example, displays on a side altar a relic of St. Peter Julian Eymard (1811–68; canonized 1962), founder of the Order of the Most Blessed Sacrament (see p. 210). New York has the complete remains of two Roman Catholic saints: St. Datian at Most Holy Redeemer (see p. 123) and St. Frances Cabrini at her own shrine building (see p. 295).

Orthodox churches are also ritual churches. In them, the sacrament of the Eucharist is performed by the priest out of sight, and the bread and wine are brought forth from that holy place. An **iconostasis**, or screen covered with icons (sacred images), conceals that space, and the priests' doorway through the iconostasis is called a Royal Door (because Christ, the King of Heaven, passes through it in the form of the Eucharist).

Nonritual (or nonliturgical) denominations include most Protestant groups—Methodist, Baptist, and so forth, as well as some Low Church Episcopalians. For these groups the most important part of the service does not consist of performing rituals at an altar, but of listening to the Word, so their liturgy and church design focus on the pulpit. The entire congregation must be able to see the pulpit and to hear the sermon. The ideal form for nonritual churches is the auditorium, a preaching space in which the largest possible congregation can be brought within the range of the human voice, as in Wren's "auditories."

Nonritual churches do not require either a large chancel or pathways for processions, but a wide center aisle may facilitate communion. A table may be set up all the way from the head to the foot of the aisle, and members sit at the table in relays to be served the bread and wine by elders.

Altars in these churches are not elaborate. Often they are not even called altars, but communion tables. For the Presbyterians and other Calvinist faiths in early New York, as for the Puritans in New England and some groups still today, a simple wooden table, the Lord's Board, sufficed. Even at New York's Trinity Episcopal Church (then High Church) as late as 1877, several parishioners objected to the installation of an ornamental **reredos** (also called a **retable** or **altar screen**) behind the altar that draws attention to it. Through the years, altars in almost all churches have grown increasingly conspicuous. Sometimes a rich fabric or tapestry, called a **dossal**, hangs behind and over the altar. Well into the twentieth century, however, when altars replaced communion tables in some older New York City churches (St. Peter's Episcopal, for example), many parishioners chose to leave, hot with indignation.

Many old New York City churches have been redesigned through the years, and what we see today is very different from what was first built. Almost all have evolved in two seemingly contradictory ways. On the one hand, almost all denominations have accepted items of decor once thought exclusively ritualistic: the display of crosses, deep chancels, frescoed or painted walls, stained glass, reredoses, and altars. In contrast to this decorative trend, almost all houses of worship have come to accommodate the elements of worship that are emphasized among the nonritual denominations; that is, their design has shown greater concern that all parishioners be able to see and hear all elements of the service. This may reflect the democratization of religious worship in a democratic country.

Holy water stoup at the entrance to Our Lady of Good Counsel

Furnishings

Most Christian churches have three basic items: a **pulpit**, from which the minister delivers the sermon; an **altar** or **communion table**, from which the sacrament of the Eucharist, or the Lord's Supper, is shared; and a **font**, for the sacrament of baptism. Some churches

PIPE ORGANS

Anyone interested in New York pipe organs might begin with a four-CD boxed set of *The Great Organs of New York*, issued by Bischof and Vitacco of New York in 1996. The recordings are accompanied by a booklet that gives details on each of the twenty-seven organs played in the recordings plus "A Brief History of Organs in New York City" written by Arthur Lawrence. In addition, a number of individual congregations have issued recordings of their organ or of their choir. You will usually find notice of these posted in each church or synagogue.

Each organ is a completely unique mix of sets of pipes in an acoustically unique environment. Each is suitable for and usually heard playing a different type of music, depending upon the specific liturgy, the traditions of that denomination or individual congregation, and the tastes of the music director or organist of any day. This is still to say nothing of the tastes and prejudices of the listeners. Still further, each organ is in a different state or condition. Some of what, by general agreement, *would* be the finest organs in the city are wheezing along at only a fraction of their capacity, because the cost of maintaining and restoring these mighty instruments is prohibitive.

also have a **lectern,** or Bible stand. Lecterns often display an eagle, the symbol of St. John's Gospel, which begins "In the beginning was the Word." Christian Science churches have two lecterns for the two readers.

Many Roman Catholic and some Episcopalian churches have confessionals, although these booths are being replaced in most churches by reconciliation rooms. Roman Catholic and Orthodox churches also have containers for holy water at church entrances, so that entrants can cross themselves, in remembrance of their baptism.

Pews

Today, most churches allow people to sit wherever they choose, but this was not true in the past. Pews were pieces of real estate held by regular members of the congregation, and few were available for visitors. "Free" churches did exist, but these were usually chapels in poor neighborhoods supported by wealthy churches elsewhere.

As the city grew, however, anonymity grew, the city's floating population increased, and some people began to feel that churches should

welcome all visitors. Therefore, St. Mary's (Episcopal) Church, in Manhattanville, abolished pew rental in 1831; it was possibly the first church
in America to do so. As annual pledges and weekly collections came to
replace pew rent as the main source of income for most churches, slip pews
replaced box pews. The box pews that still exist in a few New York City
churches are generally open to all on a first-come-first-served basis.

Orthodox congregations traditionally stood during services, but today
many Orthodox churches offer seating.

Other Interior Furnishings

Most decorations in ecclesiastical buildings carry symbolic meaning,
and the study of these is called **iconography**. One of the most common
symbols is paired first and last letters of the Greek alphabet, alpha and
omega, (A and Ω). This signifies that all things begin and end in the Lord
(Revelation 22:13).

Churches dedicated to specific saints feature their portraits. The
patron of a church is often represented on the **trumeau** (the column in the
center of the main door holding up the **tympanum** above), and saints can
be identified by distinctive objects they carry or have around them, called
attributes or **emblems**. These usually symbolize the personality of the
saint, the saint's occupation or acts, or how the saint suffered martyrdom.
The four evangelists, Matthew, Mark, Luke, and John, for example, are traditionally accompanied by an angel, a lion, an ox, and an eagle, respectively. All four symbols are often winged. Sometimes only the four
emblems are shown, in which case they are called the **tetramorph** (Revelation 4:7). The tetramorph can be found somewhere, if you search, in
most Christian churches. The chancel window at Trinity Church displays
the four evangelists plus St. Peter (holding the keys to heaven) and St.
Paul (with the sword with which he was beheaded—also, symbolically, the
sharp sword of the Word of God and of the Spirit). Most churches will
celebrate the annual feast days of their patron saints. The special veneration of the Virgin Mary, called Marian devotion, is almost exclusively
Roman Catholic, Anglo-Catholic, and, to a lesser degree, Orthodox. The
decor of many New York churches includes portraits of renowned theolo-
gians, scientists, or other secular workers, in addition to those of saints.
Roman Catholic churches may display the **stations of the cross**, which are
fourteen specific scenes from Jesus' trial and crucifixion.

Decor may reveal the congregation's nationality or ethnicity. You
might look for national patron saints (Stephen of Hungary, for example)
or foreign-language inscriptions. African Methodist Episcopal Churches

Christ and the tetramorph at Riverside Church

frequently display anvils, because an old Philadelphia blacksmith shop served that denomination in 1793 as America's first black-owned house of worship. Some churches display the American flag or New York State flag and a denominational flag. Roman Catholic churches often fly the Vatican flag; its left half is yellow, and the right half depicts the papal crown above St. Peter's keys.

If the denomination or nationality of a church has changed, symbols of the previous group may remain. Mount Olivet Church in Harlem, for example, built as a synagogue, still displays the six-pointed star, the **Magen David**. The woodwork in St. Teresa's Roman Catholic Church downtown on Rutgers Street, built as Rutgers Street Presbyterian Church, still displays the thistle, the emblem of Scotland. Encyclopedias of symbols have been compiled, but in any church you can ask the priest or minister to help you interpret or identify those you see.

Stained Glass

Stained-glass windows can provide great artistic and spiritual delight in any house of worship, and New York City displays some of the finest stained glass in America. As with other aspects of architecture and decoration, stained glass has gone through cycles in and out of favor. The large-scale use of stained-glass windows was introduced in Europe's Gothic cathedrals. As discussed above, Gothic construction allowed glass curtain walls, and worshipers enjoyed the radiant effects of shimmering color and their symbolic meaning.

Early Protestant leaders, and later the "Age of Reason" turned against stained glass. Its designers thought that whereas clear glass represented the clarity of reason, stained glass represented mystical, vague, and romantic sentiments and emotions. Also, clear glass does illuminate the interior better. Many old churches in Europe replaced their stained glass with clear glass.

In New York, the window glass in the Wren-Gibbs style and in the Greek Revival style churches was originally clear. The Gothic Revival in the 1900s, however, brought stained glass into the newly built churches, and it was even put into older churches. St. James Roman Catholic Church, for example, built in a pure Greek Revival style, has stained-glass windows today.

The stained-glass windows for the Gothic Revival churches of Saint Ann and the Holy Trinity in Brooklyn Heights (see p. 301) and Holy Apostles in Manhattan were made by William Jay Bolton (1816–84), America's first artist in stained glass. William Morris, the leader of England's nineteenth-century Arts and Crafts movement, set up a workshop, trained craftsmen, and hired the best contemporary painters—his friends, the Pre-Raphaelites Dante Gabriel Rossetti, Ford Maddox Brown, and Edward Burne-Jones—to design windows. Manhattan's Church of the Incarnation (see p. 147) displays fine examples of this school of stained glass.

As a general rule through the nineteenth century, Episcopal churches imported their windows from England, whereas Roman Catholic churches imported theirs from Catholic France or Bavaria, notably the work of Mayer of Munich. Mayer, still in business, was founded in 1847, and its artists provided ecclesiastical decorations, including windows, statues (as at Most Holy Redeemer, see p. 123), crucifixes, mosaics, and sacred vessels for many New York churches. Franz Zettler, Franz Mayer's son-in-law, specialized in stained glass.

Early Gothic Revivalists saw stained-glass windows as pictures painted *on* glass. They were bright, but basically imitation three-dimensional representations of saints or of sacred scenes. Toward the end of the nineteenth century, however, architects and artists came to appreciate the beauty of true medieval stained glass—mosaics of bits of colored glass held together by veins of lead to form pictures. Some American architects and glass-workers achieved new masterpieces in the medieval fashion. Ralph Adams Cram was responsible for the publication of Henry Adams's *Mont Saint Michel and Chartres* (1913), the first literary appreciation of Gothic art. In the book, Adams cited the French architect Viollet-le-Duc's conclusion that blue was the dynamic agent in medieval windows. The windows at the French cathedral of Chartres, for example, are rich in true blue glass (not painted), so Charles Connick (1875–1945) used lots of blue in New York. The windows at St. Vincent Ferrer are beautiful examples (see p. 202). The syntheses of stained glass and architecture achieved at St. Vincent's, at St. Thomas's, and at the Cathedral of St. John the Divine follow European precedents (see pp. 190, 281). Individual medieval European and American stained-glass windows can be seen in the Metropolitan Museum of Art (see p. 206) and, especially, at the Cloisters (see p. 296).

Louis Comfort Tiffany (1848–1933) and John LaFarge (1835–1910) developed a new form of glass that is called *opalescent* here, but still identified as "American glass" in Europe. They created glass with exaggerated textures and color variations and then used those variations, often in layers, as part of their compositions. Many Protestant and Jewish congregations whose religious beliefs forbade figural decorations approved stained-glass abstractions. Even landscapes were theologically innocent: nature seen as the manifestation of the benevolent Deity. (Many nineteenth-century churches have colored glass that features simple geometric or floral patterns; that is not true stained glass, but *stock glass*. Patterns were not designed for individual windows, but mass-manufactured and cut into the required shapes.)

Other outstanding stained-glass artists in New York included William Willet (1867–1921), Louise Howland King (1865–1945), D. Maitland Armstrong (1836–1918), and Wright Goodhue (1905–31). Artists in the studios of J. & R. Lamb and of Frode Rambusch (founded in 1857 and 1898, respectively, and both still in operation) designed ecclesiastical decorations and sacred items, as well as windows. Unfortunately, many churches have lost their archives, many firms and artists have lost their records, and many windows are not signed. Therefore, many of New York's most beautiful windows cannot be attributed for certain—even as to country of origin.

Stained glass is expensive and nonessential, so it was often the last thing installed—long after the house of worship was completed. Therefore, a building's windows may conflict with its overall architectural style.

In other cases, the donor of the windows insisted on an inconsistent style. Many New York Gothic Revival churches, for example, have opalescent windows, which are an art nouveau style.

Regrettably, we rarely see the stained glass in New York's sacred spaces to best effect. The interiors are usually well lit, so the windows reflect the interior light and appear as brilliant opaque surfaces. By contrast, when sunshine passes through stained glass into houses of worship that are dark inside, the walls disappear, and the glass is resplendent. One expert reports that a light meter at the crossing at New York's St. Patrick's Cathedral reads about fifteen foot-candles of light at midday; the meter records one foot-candle at the crossing at Chartres Cathedral in France.

Visiting a House of Worship

Houses of worship generally welcome visitors of all faiths.

Different congregations do hold services on different days at different hours. For example, the principal services of the week in mosques are on Friday at noon, and in Christian churches on Sunday morning. Synagogues hold services Friday evening and Saturday morning. Call each individual congregation for times and further details.

Houses of worship do not vary much in the behavior expected. In all, respectful quiet is always appreciated. Eating or drinking is prohibited. Some houses of worship will have dress codes posted, and these usually require at least long trousers for men; women's clothing should cover the arms, and hems should reach below the knee (to the ankles in mosques). Women's heads should be covered in mosques. In conservative and orthodox synagogues, women traditionally cover their heads, and men are requested to wear a small skull cap (*yarmulke*). In many houses of worship, men are asked to remove headgear. All visitors to mosques, Sikh temples, and to some Hindu temples—including worshipers—remove their shoes. If you have any questions, simply telephone ahead of your visit.

Don't be confused by moments of sitting, standing, or kneeling during services. You may wish to follow the lead of those around you, but if that makes you uncomfortable, few regular worshipers will take offense if a visitor remains quietly seated.

It is rude to photograph individuals at their private devotions, but most sacred places will allow you to photograph portions of the interior. If you are in doubt, ask an official present for permission.

CHAPTER THREE

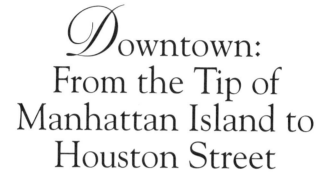

*D*owntown:
From the Tip of
Manhattan Island to
Houston Street

I T WAS AT THE SOUTHERN END of Manhattan that the Dutch established their colony of
Nieuw Amsterdam in 1625. The settlement's wall
(today's Wall Street) crossed the island only about 500
yards from the island's tip, and "the Broadway," following an Indian trail, led up the center of the island,
eventually becoming a road to the north. Today the
small-scale crooked streets among the skyscrapers and
canyons of the financial district reveal the pattern of
the old colony, but not a single building from the Dutch period still stands.
British rule replaced Dutch in 1664, but when New York became the first
capital of the new United States in 1789, the city still covered only about
ten blocks north from the Battery at the island's southern tip.

As New York developed into the leading commercial center and port
of the United States, development pushed northward swiftly and relent-
lessly. City Hall stood on the northernmost fringe of town when it was
built in 1811, so builders covered its north side in common brownstone
instead of marble, because no one ever expected the building to be seen
from that side. By 1820, however, New York had expanded another ten to

fifteen blocks, and by 1850 the city limits had pushed north two miles to 14th Street. South Street along the East River was a "street o' ships," a thick forest of masts marking the congested port. As commerce crowded out families, residential areas receded northward.

Waves of nineteenth-century immigrants packed into crowded tenements northeast of City Hall: Chinatown and, north of that, Little Italy. Further to the east, beyond the Bowery (once a path to Governor Stuyvesant's "Bowery," or farm) is the Lower East Side. That area's original Irish and German settlers moved north and were replaced by Russians, Poles, and especially eastern European Jews. Most of the upwardly mobile Jewish immigrants left as quickly as possible. The Lower East Side is still a first stop for immigrants, but today they are often Hispanic or Chinese, as Chinese immigration has multiplied and Chinatown expanded. Traditional denominations have struggled to answer the spiritual needs of the new settlers. A walk through the neighborhood will reveal synagogues as well as storefronts transformed into Buddhist temples.

The northwestern part of Lower Manhattan is today's fashionable *TriBeCa*, the TRIangle BElow CAnal Street. To the north of that lies Greenwich Village.

From the Battery
Up along the West Side

Where It All Began
BATTERY PARK

Battery Park, at the southern tip of Manhattan, is named for a row of guns that long stood along the old shoreline, approximately the line of today's State Street. The park is all landfill. A tablet in the northern part of the park, by Battery Place, memorializes the Walloons, French-speaking Protestants from today's Belgium, who came fleeing religious persecution and made up a significant segment of the city's seventeenth-century population. The memorial was given by the government of the Belgian province of Hainaut in 1924. Nearby stands a memorial to those who served in the Korean Conflict (1991, G. MacAdams). Still other memorials in the park remember the Coast Guard, those who gave their lives in World War II, and Wireless Operators. The American Merchant Marine Memorial (1991, Marisol), just offshore, portrays three merchant mariners standing on a sinking ship. A fourth man in the water, who is almost completely submerged at high tide, reaches up for their assistance. The harrowing sculpture is based on a photograph taken by a U-boat captain who had torpedoed the ship and who watched it go down with all hands.

The most important building in the park is **Castle Clinton National Monument** (LM, 1807, John McComb, Jr. ☎ 344-7220), originally constructed to protect the harbor from naval invasion. It was built about 300 feet off the shore, to which it was connected by a wooden causeway. Congress declared it a National Monument in 1946, and today it is administered as a museum by the Department of the Interior.

Battery Park affords a fine view of two historic islands, Liberty Island and Ellis Island, both of which are operated by the National Park Service and can be reached by tourist boats. The **Statue of Liberty on Liberty Island** (LM, dedicated 1886; sculptor F. A. Bartholdi; pedestal by Richard Morris Hunt. ☎ 363-3200) was donated by a group of French citizens whose purpose was to encourage the French people to defend their own republican government. The American public soon reinterpreted the statue to symbolize America's welcome to immigrants. Gustave Eiffel designed her structural support system three years before he built the tower in Paris.

Neighboring **Ellis Island** houses the U.S. Immigration Station (LM, 1898, Boring & Tilton; restored 1991, Beyer Blinder Belle and Notter Finegold & Alexander. ☎ 363-3200). Here immigrants were subjected to a brisk and fateful examination. Most were "processed" in a couple of hours, and sixteen million passed through Ellis Island to become American citizens between 1897 and 1954. A minority, however, was rejected, or lingered on appeal. Today the main halls feature exhibitions about the island's history.

The First American-Born Saint
CHURCH OF OUR LADY OF THE ROSARY AND SHRINE OF SAINT ELIZABETH BAYLEY SETON
Roman Catholic. 8 State St., between Pearl and Whitehall Sts. 1965, Shanley & Sturges. ☎ 269-6865

Elizabeth Bayley Seton (1774–1821), who was canonized as the first American-born saint in 1975, was born into an Anglican home of wealth and privilege. Her father was the health officer of the Port of New York and professor of anatomy at King's College, today's Columbia University. She married William Seton, a prominent shipping merchant, in 1794, and the young couple moved into a house at 8 State Street. Unfortunately, William soon fell ill and lost his fortune. The Setons went to Italy in the hope of his recovery, but William died there in 1803, leaving Elizabeth a penniless young widow with five children. She was so moved by the tender care that she and her husband had received from Roman Catholics in Italy that she started studying Catholicism when she returned to New York, and in 1805 she shocked her family and friends by converting to it. Shortly thereafter, she moved to Baltimore, and there she opened a school that is considered the beginning of America's parochial school system. She also founded America's first religious order, the Sisters of Charity. In 1817 Mother Seton, as she was then known, sent three Sisters of Charity to New York to open an orphanage, and Sisters still serve in New York schools and orphanages. The Church of Our Lady of the Rosary stands today on the site of the early Seton family home.

The building next door at 7 State Street (LM, 1793, attributed to John McComb, Jr.) serves as the rectory of the shrine, and it has its own fascinating history. It is one of the oldest buildings in Manhattan and the only survivor of New York's first era of great mansions. Its façade boasts delicate late-Georgian detailing, including oval windows in the west wall and a graceful wooden portico that follows the curved line of the street. The tapered Ionic columns are said to have been made from ships' masts. In 1883, the Mission of Our Lady of the Rosary for the Protection of Irish Immigrant Girls was founded in this building in order to look after the thousands of young Irish girls arriving in America. Many were without hope or promise, and they often found themselves in indentured servitude or worse. The Mission befriended more than 170,000 of them.

AROUND THE CORNER

➡ Author **Herman Melville** (1819–91) was born in a house right through the block, at 6 Pearl Street (no longer standing).

➡ Across State Street, tiny **Peter Minuit Plaza**, named for the director of the Dutch West India Company, contains a small memorial to the city's first Jewish settlers, who arrived here fleeing persecution in Brazil.

➡ One block north of Broad Street (between Water St. and South St.) stands the **Vietnam War Memorial** (1985, Wormser and Fellows). Letters home from U.S. servicemen and women who died in the conflict are engraved on a wall of translucent green glass. The letters' honest simplicity has deeply moved visitors to this site, but the plaza was rebuilt in 2000 (E. Timothy Marshall & Associates). The redesign includes engraved names of all New Yorkers who died in the Vietnam War, new plantings, and a map set into the pavement.

Native American Treasures

THE NATIONAL MUSEUM OF THE AMERICAN INDIAN (LM)

1 Bowling Green at the foot of Broadway. 1907, Cass Gilbert. ☎ 514-3700

This branch of the Smithsonian Institution occupies a Beaux-Arts building that served as the city's Custom House from 1907 to 1973. Remarkable features include the monumental *Four Continents* by Daniel Chester French in front of the building, individual sculptures representing our trading partners high on the façade by other leading sculptors, plus the rotunda ceiling painting by Reginald Marsh. The interior gleams with rich marbles.

The collection was formed by George Gustav Heye, who, upon his death in 1957, left over 800,000 objects plus 86,000 images of Indian life. The Smithsonian absorbed the collection in 1989, under a mandate from Congress to preserve, study, and exhibit the life, languages, literature, history, and arts of Native Americans. The collection had never been entirely catalogued, and Native American political and spiritual leaders have come from all over the Americas to help identify objects. The New York museum holds only part of the collection; the rest will be housed at the Museum of the American Indian on the Mall in Washington, D.C. The changing exhibitions here are enriched by regular demonstrations of Native American artistic techniques and performing arts.

The building stands on the site of the original Fort Amsterdam. Author, abolitionist, and social reformer **Julia Ward Howe** (1819–1910), author of "The Battle Hymn of the Republic," was born in a house on this site. One of America's first great songwriters, **Stephen Foster** (1826–64; "Oh Susannah," "Camptown Races," "My Old Kentucky Home," "Old Black Joe," etc.) lived around the corner at 6 Greenwich Street. Up at 124 Greenwich Street, a Presbyterian minister named **Dr. Sylvester Graham** (1794–1851) served a cracker he had invented to residents of his boarding house. None of these buildings still stands.

AROUND THE CORNER

➡ The **U.S. Post Office** on Bowling Green, originally the Cunard Building (LM, 25 Broadway. 1921, B. W. Morris) contains iron work by Samuel Yellin, frescoes, murals, and rich marbles in one of New York's most spectacular interiors.

Mother of Churches
TRINITY CHURCH AND GRAVEYARD (LM)

Episcopal. Broadway at the head of Wall St. 1846, Richard Upjohn. ☎
269–6640. Pamphlets available in the narthex, and guidebooks and a map
of the graveyard in the small shop.

Edgar Allan Poe grumbled, "Any structure of the so-called Gothic
order must of necessity be an incongruous work, unless it be an exact copy,
and then it must be unfit." Nevertheless, Gothic Revival architecture
became the fashion in the 1840s. The new homes of Trinity Church, First
Presbyterian Church (see p. 173), and Grace Episcopal Church (see p.
130) were all dedicated in the same year.

The current building was actually the third Trinity Church built on
this site. The first had opened in 1698 (thanks to the pirate Captain Kidd,
who lent a runner and tackle to hoist the stones), but it burned down in
1776. President Washington attended the consecration of the second, in
1790, but that one had to be demolished in 1839 after a heavy snowfall
endangered its roof. This replacement copies the English perpendicular
Gothic style, characterized by a high clerestory over side aisles, and crenellated and pinnacled parapets along the walls. Worshipers enter through
the immense square tower at the front. The tower (281 feet high) may
actually be a bit too big for the medium-sized church behind it, but today
the tower itself is dwarfed by surrounding skyscrapers. When Trinity was
cleaned in 1990, surprisingly, a pink building emerged from one that had
for years been very dark.

Trinity parish is famously wealthy, thanks to Queen Anne, who, in
1705, gave it the Queen's Farm of 215 acres stretching north from the
church. Trinity has given away 97 percent of this land through the years,
much of it in support of other churches in New York City and State, across
the United States, and even abroad, earning the name "Mother of
Churches." Trinity has retained thirty-one buildings, making it still one
of New York's largest commercial landlords. Trinity's royal patrons also
granted it the rights to all drift whales or anything else that washes up on
Manhattan's shores, but today Trinity surrenders those rights to the City
Sanitation Department.

Before you enter the church, note the three bronze doors added in
1896. The sculpted portals were designed by architect Richard Morris
Hunt, and different artists executed each set of doors and tympanum
above. Karl Bitter designed the main portal, Charles Henry Niehaus the
south doors, and J. Massey Rhind the north doors.

Inside, rows of columns support the nave vaulting, but the ceiling is really plaster suspended from wooden trusses, not stone. The design of Trinity's chancel triggered a battle over liturgical practice and church design. Architect Upjohn, a High Church man, made it as large as the church's governing body would let him, and he clearly separated it from the nave by elevating it up steps and by throwing a heavy arch across the ceiling at the line of demarcation; the arch is supported by huge columns. He differentiated the nave from the chancel even on the exterior. The exterior buttresses (which are structurally unnecessary) are exaggerated at the divide, and the roof line of the nave continues out over the chancel beyond the end of the side aisles.

Still other aspects of the interior mark this as a High Church. For example, the focus of visual interest is the altar, not the pulpit. An enormous reredos—one of the first large reredoses in the United States, installed in 1877—occupies the whole thirty-five-foot width of the chancel and rises to the sill of the chancel window. Its carvings include twelve apostles plus a crucifixion scene, seven other scenes from the life of Christ, and, on top, angels holding musical instruments. The large chancel window, designed by Upjohn himself and among the earliest pieces of stained glass designed in this country, presents Christ flanked by the four evangelists and Saints Peter and Paul. Worshipers at Trinity have included two reigning queens (Liliuokalani of Hawaii in 1887 and Elizabeth II of England in 1976) and two Princes of Wales, the young men who went on to become Kings Edward VII (in 1860) and his grandson Edward VIII of England (in 1919).

All Saints' Chapel, added at the west end of the north aisle in 1913, with its own entrance from Broadway, reserves the Blessed Sacrament for emergency ministrations to the sick. Its architect, Thomas Nash, also designed the baptistery near the northeast corner of the chancel. Rooms in the Bishop Manning Memorial Wing on the southwest corner (1966, Adams & Woodbridge,) exhibit church treasures, such as the silver communion vessels given by Queen Anne, and also materials about the history of Trinity and New York City.

The graveyard around the church serves as a small park for local office workers. The oldest marker is that of Richard Churcher, who died at the age of five in 1681, suggesting that this land was a cemetery even before Trinity parish was established in 1697. The winged hourglass and skull and crossbones on Richard's stone remind us that time flies, and of what lies beyond. Famous Americans interred in this yard include first

Trinity Graveyard

secretary of the treasury Alexander Hamilton, steamboat inventor Robert Fulton, Captain James Lawrence (Commander of the USS *Chesapeake* during the War of 1812, who immortalized himself with his dying command, "Don't give up the ship"), Albert Gallatin (Jefferson's secretary of the treasury), and Francis Lewis, the only signer of the Declaration of Independence buried in Manhattan. The Martyrs' Monument (1852), a tall Gothic-style memorial to American patriots who died in British prisons in New York during the Revolutionary War, stands at the northeast corner of the yard. The last interment in Trinity graveyard was in 1832.

One weathered brown slab bears the inscription "Charlotte Temple," whose unhappy love affair was supposedly the basis for *Charlotte Temple, a Tale of Truth,* by Susannah Rowson. The 1791 book tells how Charlotte, an impressionable young girl, falls in love with a British officer and elopes with him to New York. He abandons her, and she dies after giving birth to his daughter. The book was one of America's first best-sellers, going through over 200 editions by 1903. The author insisted that it was based on a true story, but historians have disproved that. In the 1850s, for an unknown reason, Trinity stonecutters chiseled Charlotte's name into this slab, and it soon became a popular destination for melancholy romantics— "a shrine of unhappy love," said *Leslie's Weekly* in 1897. The whole thing was probably just a publicity stunt for the book.

The small head of a cherub over the gate at the back of the churchyard, opening onto Trinity Place, was a gift from London's church of St. Mary-le-Bow, built by Christopher Wren in 1680 but destroyed in a 1941 bombing raid. Columbia University began as King's College in a small frame schoolhouse in this yard in 1754, and today 1754 are the last four digits of the school's telephone number.

America's First Methodist Congregation
JOHN STREET UNITED METHODIST CHURCH (LM)
44 John St., between Nassau and William Sts. 1841, William Hurry. ☎ 269-0014

This, the first Wesleyan Society in America, was founded in 1766. The present building, the third on the site, reminds us of *The Methodist Discipline* (1784): "Let all churches be built plain and decent and with free seats as far as possible; but not more expensive than is absolutely unavoidable; otherwise the necessity of raising money will make rich men necessary to us, and if dependent upon them and governed by them, farewell Methodist discipline, if not doctrine too." The brownstone façade is classical, with two-story round-arched windows flanking a Palladian window over a broad entrance door. The intimate interior preserves architectural fragments of the two earlier buildings, including the wide board flooring, entrance stairway, pews, foot warmers, the light brackets along the balcony, and the pulpit (carved by Philip Embury himself—see p. 29) high on a single pillar, reached by a winding stair. Some of the timbers shaped by Philip Embury for the first church on this site are today beneath the pulpit at **Park Avenue United Methodist Church** at 106 East 86th Street (1927, Henry Pelton).

A small museum downstairs displays a clock sent as a gift by John Wesley, the English founder of Methodism; the Bible and hand-carved lectern used by Philip Embury; as well as portraits and other relics relating to the history of Methodism in the United States.

AROUND THE CORNER
➡ **The Titanic Memorial Lighthouse** (Fulton St. between Pearl and Water Sts. Installed here 1976, Charles E. Hughes III.) was originally erected atop a downtown building (since demolished) by public subscription in 1913, one year after the *Titanic*, bound for New York, sank with a loss of over 1,500 lives. It now marks the entrance to the **South Street Seaport** complex (LMD) of restored historic shops and ships, plus a museum.

REMEMBERING THE TITANIC

The Titanic departed from Southampton, England, for her maiden voyage to New York on April 10, 1912, representing the highest attainment of engineering technology. Despite the publicity given to the ship's first-class quarters, her expected profits were to come from the many immigrants in steerage. The great ship sideswiped an iceberg just before midnight on April 14, 1912, and sank at 2:20 A.M. on the 15th, taking over fifteen hundred passengers and crew members with her.

Several New York sites commemorate the *Titanic*. She was to have docked at Pier 59 at West 20th Street. Today that is the Chelsea Piers Sports complex, where large photos on its promenade show the crowd waiting for news outside the pier and the arrival of the rescue ship *Carpathia* at Pier 54 at West 14th Street on April 18, 1912. Straus Park on West 106th Street between Broadway and West End Avenue commemorates Ida and Isador Straus, owners of Macy's Department Store. Isador would not get into a lifeboat until all of the women and children had been saved, and Ida refused to leave without him, so they perished together. Straus Park includes a granite fountain and bench (designed by Evarts Tracy) and a reclining figure of Memory, by Augustus Lukeman. The bench quotes the Song of Solomon 8:7, "Many waters cannot quench out love—neither can the floods drown it." A plaque on Macy's 34th Street entrance also remembers the couple.

Incorporated into Central Park's eastern wall at Fifth Avenue at 91st Street is a memorial to William J. Stead (sculptor G. J. Frampton, architects Carrère and Hastings), who also went down with the *Titanic*. Stead was a British journalist and one-time resident of New York. The plaque is a copy of one on the Embankment along the Thames in London.

Several churches, including Grace Church and the Cathedral of St. John the Divine, contain memorials to others who perished in the disaster.

New York's First Roman Catholic Parish
SAINT PETER'S (LM)
22 Barclay St. at Church St. 1837, John R. Haggerty and Thomas Thomas.
☎ 233-8355

Peter (d. ca. 64 C.E.) was, along with his brother Andrew, one of Christ's first disciples. Originally named Simon, he received from Jesus the name Peter (Aramaic *Cepha* or Latin *Petrus*, "rock") as a sign of the role he would play in the founding of the church. Tradition has it that he was the first bishop of Rome, where he suffered martyrdom, and that, thinking himself unworthy to suffer the same fate as Jesus, he asked to be nailed to the cross upside down, as he is often shown in art.

"GREEK TEMPLES" IN NEW YORK

St. Peter's, St. James (p. 99), the Mariners' Temple (p. 101), and St. Joseph's (p. 167) are all Greek temple-style churches. St. Peter's is probably the grandest. New York's only church of comparable grandeur was the Thirteenth Street Presbyterian Church (between 6th and 7th Aves., 1846), but that building has been deconsecrated and

St. James Roman Catholic Church

converted into apartments, and the only remaining Greek Revival temple as fine as St. Peter's Church is the **Federal Hall National Memorial**, a few blocks away on Wall Street (LM, 1833–42).

St. James, the Mariners' Temple, and St. Joseph's exemplify variations on a design called *distyle in antis*, which means "two columns between end walls." The main entrance is in an alcove cut into the façade behind the columns, and the side blocks are terminated by paired *antae* (pilasters). At St. James and at St. Joseph's the columns are Doric, and at the Mariners' Temple they are Ionic. The architects of all three buildings added doors to the traditional classical formula. St. James has two side entrance doors right on the façade, and both the Mariners' Temple and St. Joseph's have two more doors tucked into the sides of the alcove. These doors originally gave access to stairways leading to balconies.

PIERRE TOUSSAINT

A bronze plaque on the façade of St. Peter's Church commemorates parishioner Pierre Toussaint (1766–1853). Toussaint was the slave of a family that fled a 1787 slave uprising in Haiti and settled in New York. Toussaint's owner died, but Toussaint continued to support the family by becoming a hairdresser to wealthy women. He was freed in 1807 and married (at St. Peter's) in 1811. He was a gentle, religious man who gave financial assistance to Catholic charities and orphanages, helped a number of slaves buy their freedom, and ministered to plague victims. The intersection of Barclay and Church Streets was named for him in 1989, the same year that the Archdiocese of New York initiated the process that could eventually earn him recognition as a saint. He reached the first step, being declared "Venerable," on December 18, 1996. He was originally buried in Old St. Patrick's Churchyard, but his remains have been moved to the crypt at St. Patrick's Cathedral (see page 151).

Prominent New Yorkers incorporated the Roman Catholic Church in 1785 and assumed responsibility for church finance and management. The Spanish ambassador lay the cornerstone for the first church because Spain's King Charles III had contributed for it, and, in gratitude, the church trustees reserved the front pew in perpetuity for any visiting Spanish delegation. That pledge was restated in 1976 as part of the church's commemoration of the U.S. bicentennial. The church was originally adorned by gifts from the people of Puebla, Mexico, whose bishop knew the pastor of St. Peter's since their student days at a seminary in Bologna, Italy, in the 1770s. Even after Old St. Patrick's (see p. 116) became New York's cathedral, St. Peter's retained its social preeminence, so its priests entertained European Catholic visitors. Reverend John Power, for example, St. Peter's pastor from 1822 to 1849, discussed religion in America with Alexis de Tocqueville and provided ideas that found their way into Tocqueville's masterpiece, *Democracy in America*. Elizabeth Seton converted to Catholicism in the earlier church here, and she regularly attended St. Peter's.

The Greek Revival temple that is today's St. Peter's, the second building on the site, raised the level of architectural ambition for New York churches. Most earlier churches had been constructed of rubble masonry with brownstone trim—such as nearby St. Paul's Episcopal (see p. 92). St. Peter's, by contrast, boasts finely dressed granite, which is much harder to carve than brownstone, laid in ashlar, that is, regular blocks. (Its east wall, obscured from public view, was left raw unfaced brick.) Furthermore, St. Peter's boasts a full-width projecting portico supported by six tall free-standing Ionic columns. The pediment contains a statue of Peter holding his attribute, the keys to heaven. It was probably carved by a carver of ships' figureheads; it looks like one. No cross was put on top of this pure Greek-style temple until sometime after the 1890s.

St. Peter's interior was originally as grand as its exterior. Its walls were plain white plaster articulated by pink stone, fluted pilasters, and a gilded ceiling, but now it is painted pale green picked out with occasional gilding. Natural light flooded the sanctuary through clear glass windows. Today's stained-glass windows by Charles Connick, while beautiful, have reduced the natural light. Interior details still include molding around the ceiling, plasterwork, and crystal chandeliers.

The elaborate pedimented former high altar echoes the Ionic colonnade of the portico, and today it forms an enormous reredos flanked by niches, fluted pilasters, and statuary. The crucifixion scene above the tabernacle is one of three paintings donated to the first St. Peter's by the Spanish diplomatic delegation.

AROUND THE CORNER

➼ **Battery Park City** was built on landfill on the lower west side of Manhattan. Just inside Battery Park City may be found the **Police Memorial**, dedicated in 1997 to officers killed in the line of duty. Stuart Crawford designed an outdoor room of granite walls enclosing a fountain and pool. A wall records the officers' names and the dates on which they died. Battery Park City includes considerable park space and a esplanade along the Hudson River.

➼ The **Museum of Jewish Heritage** (Kevin Roche, John Dinkleloo & Associates ☎ 509-6130), opened in Battery Park City in 1997, is dedicated to educating visitors about the Jewish experience before, during, and after the Holocaust. Its collections include over 2,000 photographs, almost 1,000 artifacts, and many original documentary films. A new wing will open in 2003, tripling the museum's size.

➼ The construction of a museum of women's history, to be known as the **Museum of Women: The Leadership Center**, is proposed for a nearby site.

➥ A five-mile ribbon of parkland is now under construction all the way from Battery Park to West 59th Street. The new strip park, to be called **Hudson River Park**, will involve repairing the Civil War–era seawall and the huge rotting piers along the shore. The target date for completion of the park is 2005, when it is intended to offer a continuous riverfront esplanade with lawns and flowers, bicycle and running trails, and playgrounds.

Manhattan's Oldest Church
SAINT PAUL'S CHAPEL AND YARD (LM)
Episcopal. West side of Broadway between Fulton and Vesey Sts. 1766, possibly a Thomas McBean. ☎ 732-5564

Paul (d. ca. 67 C.E.) is, after Jesus himself, probably the most important figure in the history of Christianity. Born as Saul into a Jewish family of Greek culture, he originally persecuted Christians, but one day he was blinded by a glorious light and heard Christ asking him, "Saul, Saul, why persecutest thou me?" (This event is represented on the façade of St. Paul the Apostle, p. 236.) Saul's vision triggered his conversion. His blindness was cured, he was baptized, and he changed his name to Paul out of humility (Latin *paulus* means "small"). He became an extraordinary missionary, as is known through the Acts of the Apostles and his own writings, which make up much of the New Testament.

The architecture of St. Paul's, Manhattan's oldest surviving church building, is described in the chapter "What to Look For" (see p. 53), but here we might note a few additional features. St. Paul's was built of rough-dressed local stone with brownstone trim at the windows and quoins. The tower was raised and the steeple added in 1794 by James C. Lawrence. The top of the tower is a replica of the Choragic Monument of Lysicrates, in Athens (ca. 334 B.C.E.). Thomas Jefferson had the Corinthian capitals of this classical monument copied for the Hall of Representatives (part of the U.S. Capitol) in Washington, D.C., where they can still be seen.

St. Paul's interior is maintained in traditional colors, with cream and gilded woodwork. Thirteen of the fourteen cut-glass chandeliers are original, handmade in Waterford, Ireland, and date from 1802. The gray and white marble paving was very fashionable in England in the late eighteenth century. The pulpit and communion rail predate the Revolution, as the Prince of Wales' coronet and six feathers on the pulpit defiantly proclaim. Pierre L'Enfant, the French military engineer who laid out Washington, D.C., designed the golden sunburst over the high altar, with Mount Sinai in clouds and lightning, the Hebrew word for God in a gilded triangle, and two gilded tablets recording the Ten Commandments.

St. Paul's was the site of a Thanksgiving service after George Washington's inauguration as the first U.S. president on April 30, 1789. This service (depicted on the south door at Trinity Church—see p. 84) was repeated in 1889 with President Benjamin Harrison and again in 1989 with President George Bush. While New York served as the nation's capital from 1789 to 1791, George Washington worshiped at St. Paul's. His pew in the north aisle was rebuilt in 1960, although without its original canopy. Washington must have taken satisfaction from the fact that during the War of Independence, what became his pew had

St. Paul's Chapel

been occupied by Prince William (later King William IV), Lord Cornwallis, and other British officials. On the wall beside it hangs the first rendering of the great seal of the United States, adopted in 1782; it may have hung here in 1789. Other notables who worshiped in St. Paul's include the Marquis de Lafayette and President Grover Cleveland. In the south aisle, the arms of New York State hang above the pew of the governor of New York. Against the west wall is a bust by John Frazee of John Wells, a leading jurist and coeditor with Hamilton of the *Federalist Papers*. Note that Frazee crowned Wells with native American plants instead of the traditional acanthus.

New York's first public monument to a Revolutionary War hero is beneath St. Paul's Broadway portico outside. Major General Richard

Montgomery was killed during the United States' disastrous attack on Quebec on December 31, 1775, and Congress immediately ordered the U.S. representative in Paris, Benjamin Franklin, to commission a memorial. The monument, by Jean-Jacques Caffieri, was installed here in 1789. On it, an altar supports a broken column (symbol of a hero's life cut short) with a funerary urn on top. The shadow that this monument cast through the Palladian window above the altar prompted the congregation to commission L'Enfant's redesign of the interior. General Montgomery fell in Quebec, but his remains were brought here in 1818 and entombed in the wall. Montgomery Place, the home his widow, Janet Livingston Montgomery, built about ninety miles north on the Hudson River, in Annandale, is today a public museum.

St. Paul's churchyard offers another restful oasis in lower Manhattan. Notables interred here include Dr. Philip Turner, surgeon general during the War of Independence; John Bailey, who made George Washington's sword, now in the Smithsonian Institution; Étienne Bechet, Sieur de Rochefontaine, the most distinguished French officer buried in the United States who fought for our independence; Sir John Temple, Britain's first ambassador to the United States after independence; and Richard Colles, who built New York's first waterworks and prepared the plans for the Erie Canal. The remains of Richard Coote, earl of Bellemont and royal governor of New York, Massachusetts, and New Hampshire from 1697 to 1701, lie here. (He described New York as "the growingest town in America.") The yard is said to harbor a ghost. Actor George Frederick Cooke (d. 1812) has supposedly been seen looking for his head. It was allegedly sold after his death to pay doctors' bills, and the skull was used in productions of *Hamlet*. Edmund Kean, a leading English actor, paid for Cooke's monument.

AROUND THE CORNER

➡ **City Hall Park** (LMD), just across Broadway from St. Paul's, was set aside as common land by the Dutch colonial government and served first as a pasture, then as a public gathering place. The Common witnessed numerous public protests, speeches, celebrations, and executions. Later in the eighteenth century a section of it near Chambers Street served as a burial ground, but nobody knows how many bodies may still rest there today. More than 250 American soldiers were hanged by the British from a gallows constructed there during the War of Independence. In 1999 the Park was reconstructed with new plantings, benches, and a Victorian fountain. **City Hall** itself, still the official seat of the city govern-

GEORGE WHITEFIELD AND
THE GREAT AWAKENING

On November 15, 1739, several hundred people gathered in the Common, today's City Hall Park, to hear George Whitefield, a twenty-five-year-old preacher who had already won quite a reputation. His fiery denunciations of lazy clergy had gotten him banished from Church of England pulpits, so he had taken to preaching in the open air. Here in New York, Trinity Church, the colony's established church, and even the Dutch Reformed Church had refused him their pulpits, but it was rumored that the Presbyterians—always making trouble in the eyes of the establishment—would let him speak again in their church later in the evening. Whitefield's sermon in the Common that day stressed the need for individuals to experience a "New Birth," without which there could be no salvation. Whitefield, along with Jonathan Edwards in New England and a few other preachers throughout the colonies, triggered a wave of piety known as "the Great Awakening" that swept the colonies.

Newspapers reported that hecklers on the fringes of the crowd were "Giggling, Scoffing, Talking and Laughing," but most of the crowd was "hush'd and still," their faces glowing with "solemn Awe and Reverence." Whitefield even drew attention to the hecklers as examples of "the boldness and Zeal with which the Devil's vassals serve him." The sermon was such a success that over 2,000 people jammed the Presbyterian Church that evening, and for each of the next four days Whitefield preached in the Common in the morning and the Presbyterian Church in the evening.

Whitefield noted that "I find that little of the work of God has been seen in [New York] for many years," but "I have not felt greater freedom in preaching and more power in prayer since I came to America than I have had here in New York." He returned to New York in the spring of 1740, and again that autumn. During those visits, a stage erected in the Common allowed between five and seven thousand people to hear him at a time. He continued to attack complacent and corrupt leaders of both church and state, and he called for humane treatment of slaves and their instruction in Christianity.

The Great Awakening was the first of many waves of spirituality that have swept New York, often triggered by a single charismatic preacher. Through the twentieth century the pulpits of New York's houses of worship, its outdoor parks, Madison Square Garden, and even its concert halls were filled with eager hearers of Stephen Wise, Billy Graham, Bishop Fulton J. Sheen, Norman Vincent Peale, Malcolm X, Harry Emerson Fosdick, Adam Clayton Powell Sr. and Jr., and many others, and still today New York's finest spiritual speakers fill large halls.

Whitefield's last sermon was delivered in the open air in Exeter, Massachusetts, in 1770, the day before he died in Newburyport, where he is buried.

ment, is an example of neoclassical architecture (LM, 1802–11, Joseph Mangin and John McComb). The New York County Courthouse behind City Hall (52 Chambers St., J. Kellum and L. Eidlitz, 1881) will be the new home of the Museum of the City of New York (see p. 206).

A Sacred Site Recovered
AFRICAN BURIAL GROUND (LMD)
Corner of Duane and Elk Sts.

Black slaves arrived in New Amsterdam almost with the first Dutch settlers, and in 1644 a free black community began when eleven blacks were freed and given plots of land to farm. Throughout the entire colonial period, New York had one of the largest black populations in North America. In the 1740s, about 21 percent of the city's population was black, most of whom were slaves, and as late as the War of Independence, the city was second only to Charleston, South Carolina, as a center of urban slavery.

THE NEW YORK STATE
FREEDOM TRAIL COMMISSION

In 1997 the New York State Legislature created a commission charged with identifying and marking places across New York State that are significant in the history of black Americans. Some are well-known and documented, such as the African Burial Ground, but most are not preserved, and no signs previously marked these street corners or buildings. In March 2000, the Commission submitted a draft list of several hundred places across the state worthy of designation, some thirty of which are in New York City.

The earliest document mentioning this burial ground is dated 1713, but burials may have occurred here before then, and it is not certain that everyone buried here was either African or slave. The 5.5 acre cemetery was in use until 1794, and the total number of interments may have been 20,000 or more. Many restrictions were placed on the burials of enslaved Africans. For example, the number of people in attendance was limited to twelve, and the burials had to take place during daylight, which was contrary to some African customs. Nevertheless, the slaves retained some traditions. "The Heathenish rites," complained Reverend John Sharpe in 1713, "are performed at the grave by their countrymen." Archaeological evidence suggests that those buried were generally wrapped in shrouds fastened with brass pins, and some, but not all, were placed in coffins. They were buried with their heads toward the west, so that they would face the rising sun.

The African Burial Ground had been largely forgotten by the early nineteenth century and, as in many other places in Manhattan, advancing construction and development swept over this cemetery without bothering to disinter the dead. In 1991 the federal government began construction of an office building at Broadway and Duane Streets, just north of City Hall, and a portion of the burial ground was excavated. Some 390 human remains were disinterred, of which an estimated 92 percent were of African origin and 45 percent were of children under the age of thirteen. Burial artifacts included shroud pins, African trade beads, coins, mariners' medals, and copper jewelry. In response to widespread protests, the government altered its building plans and created a pavilion area, where burials are still undisturbed. The remains that were excavated

The Triumph of the Human Spirit *by Lorenzo Pace (dedicated in 2000), is a stylized form of the headdress of the Bamana people of Mali, representing the mythical antelopes who taught the people how to farm.*

have been studied to determine cause of death, place of birth (from chemical analyses of tooth enamel), and, if of African origin, original place of ancestry (through DNA). All remains are to be reinterred by 2002. A bronze medallion embedded in the sidewalk in nearby Foley Square in 2000 bears the words of Maya Angelou's poem "Still I Rise," and a new sculpture, *The Triumph of the Human Spirit*, by Lorenzo Pace, soars into the sky.

AROUND THE CORNER

➥ A plaque on the exterior of the office building at 5 Varick Street records that this site was where John B. Russworm and Samuel E. Cornish launched **Freedom's Journal** on March 16, 1827, the first black-owned-and-operated publication in the United States. Russworm, born in Jamaica, was the second black college graduate in the United States (from Maine's Bowdoin College). Cornish had been born in Delaware, studied for and received Presbyterian ordination in Philadelphia, and was recruited by prosperous evangelicals to found, in 1824, the First Colored Presbyterian Church, on Elm Street near Canal Street. *Freedom's Journal* called for abolition of slavery nationwide and denounced racism and discrimination in every aspect of American life. Reverend Cornish resigned as editor after only a few months, and Russworm carried on until 1829, when he himself migrated to Liberia, never to return. Despite *Freedom's Journal's* short life, it inspired other black men and women of letters. By the Civil War there were more than forty black-owned-and-operated newspapers in the United States.

➥ **Masjid al-Farah** (245 West Broadway, south of Canal St. ☎ 334-3582) was founded in 1980 by American followers of Shaykh Muzaffer Ashki Efendi, a twentieth-century Sufi master, and it has established other branches across the United States and Mexico. Services of worship, teaching, and music are held here weekly. The nearby bookstore, Sufi Books (227 West Broadway. ☎ 334-5212) is affiliated.

➥ The **Museum for African Art** (593 Broadway between Prince and Houston Sts. ☎ 966-1313), opened in 1993, is one of America's few museums devoted to the art of sub-Saharan Africa. Its permanent collection is small, but it hosts and generates rotating and traveling exhibitions. The museum interior, designed by Maya Lin (architect of the Vietnam Veterans' Memorial in Washington D.C.), lies behind an 1860s cast-iron storefront and contains a gift and book shop in addition to display spaces.

buildings for many years, but in the 1950s the financier Bernard Baruch, whose ancestor Rachel Rodriguez Marques was buried here in 1733, bought and donated the adjacent land for a city park. The Daughters of the American Revolution provided markers for the eighteen Jewish Revolutionary War veterans who rest here, and an annual Memorial Day service is still held. The cemetery may be viewed from the sidewalk.

➡ At the corner of the Bowery and Division Streets stands a **statue** of the Chinese philosopher **Confucius** (K'ung Fu-tzu, c. 551–479 B.C.E.) by Liu Shih, donated to the City of New York by the Chinese community in honor of the U.S. bicentennial. Confucianism is one of several Asian systems of belief, including also Taoism and Shintoism, that might be categorized as ethical systems or philosophies rather than religions. They focus on appropriate behavior (*orthopraxy*) rather than belief in a set of philosophical or theological arguments (*orthodoxy*). Several do not even address theological questions such as the nature of God or the gods, or life after death. Confucius taught a system of "right living" preserved in a collection of sayings, *The Analects*. People may attain heavenly harmony by cultivating knowledge, patience, sincerity, obedience, and the fulfillment of obligations between parents and children, subject and ruler.

A Mission to Sailors
MARINERS' TEMPLE (LM)
Baptist. 12 Oliver St., just off Chatham Square. 1845, attributed to Isaac Lucas. ☎ 233-0423

An enormous ship's bell to the right of the portico reminds us that this congregation was founded to serve the sailors on the busy East River, where New York City's shipping concentrated until the end of the nineteenth century. The New York Domestic Missionary Society established the Mariners' Temple in 1843 and housed it in this building, a former Baptist church, in 1863. This church welcomed immigrants of many origins and denominations, and it actually inspired other Baptist churches both in the United States and abroad. When the waterfront activity moved from the East River to the Hudson River, membership in this church declined. Today its congregation is a mix of neighborhood residents.

Isaac Lucas, recorded as the builder, adapted a design popularized by architect Minard Lafever. Mariners' was built of random stone, but where it is visible to the street it was plastered to a smooth finish and marked with false joints to look like the architecturally appropriate smooth cut stone. You can see the unplastered stonework on the exposed northwest wall.

Mariners' Temple

The interior of Mariners' has suffered fewer changes than St. James's interior (see p. 99). In the front of the nave, large Corinthian columns between Corinthian pilasters echo the façade and define an elevated platform with a lectern. Smaller Corinthian columns support the balcony around three sides. Crystal chandeliers hang from a ceiling that is a masterpiece of decorative plaster work. A central rosette medallion is set against a coffered wheel. Between the wheel spokes, the design is picked out with carefully framed simpler rosettes, and the design swirls outward to cover the entire ceiling. The tall windows (square-headed, as is appropriate to Greek architecture) that illuminate both the aisles and the galleries are of clear glass, as they would have been originally.

Oliver de Lancey, for whom this street is named, remained loyal to George III during the War of Independence, serving as a brigadier general in the British Army. His property was confiscated, and he died in exile in 1785.

A Congregation that Has Been Irish, Italian, and Chinese in a
Church that Has Been Lutheran, Episcopalian, and Catholic
CHURCH OF THE TRANSFIGURATION (LM)
Roman Catholic. 25 Mott St. 1801, original architect unknown; 1868 additions, Henry Engelbert. ☎ 962-5157

This parish was founded by a nineteenth-century Cuban refugee who spent half his life fighting for the rights of Irish immigrants in New York. Father Félix Varela fled a Spanish death sentence for agitating for Cuban independence and arrived in New York in 1823. By the time he left thirty years later, he had founded two parishes and two schools, opened orphanages, tended the sick and dying during recurrent cholera epidemics, and risen to become vicar-general of the New York Diocese. For decades he was one of the most literate defenders of Catholicism in America, contributing to all the leading journals and newspapers. He even published New York's first Spanish-language newspaper, which advocated independence for Cuba and the abolition of slavery in the United States. A 1997 U.S. postage stamp honors him as a "Social Reformer," and a plaque on St. James Church, another parish he founded, commemorates his work. In 1998, during Pope John Paul II's visit to Cuba, Father Varela was declared to be "Blessed," a significant step toward sainthood.

The building was built as Zion English Lutheran Church, and it also served an Episcopal congregation before being purchased by Transfiguration Catholic parish (founded by Father Varela in 1827 on Ann Street) in 1853. It is built of the same rubble masonry as St. Paul's (see p. 92), but its details are less sophisticated: brownstone entablature and quoins, a triangular pediment, and a simple tower penetrating the front gable. The façade has the typical three windows over three entrances, and all of the windows are pointed. (This is one of New York's three Georgian-Gothic churches on the Lower East Side; see p. 105.) In 1868 the copper-clad octagonal belfry and spire were added, and the interior was redecorated in the Gothic style.

Behind the altar is a large painting of the transfiguration of Christ, which is described in all four Gospels. Here is the story from Matthew 17: "And after six days Jesus taketh Peter, James, and John his brother, and bringeth them up into an high mountain apart, and was transfigured before them: and his face did shine as the sun, and his raiment was white as the light. . . . behold, a bright cloud overshadowed them: and behold a voice out of the cloud, which said, 'This is my beloved Son, in whom I am well pleased; hear ye him.'"

Elizabeth Seton's Sisters of Charity opened a girls' school here in 1856 (Mother Cabrini taught there), and the Christian Brothers opened a boys' school in 1857. The Irish of the parish originally relegated the Italians to worship in the basement, creating, needless to say, tensions between the two groups, but when priests of the Salesian Society (founded in Turin, Italy, in 1875) took over in 1902, they brought the Italians upstairs. The Salesians also established a mission to the local Chinese. Thus, this church was a key institution in both "Chinatown" and "Little Italy" from the 1920s to the 1950s. Comedian Jimmy Durante belonged as a boy, and singer Enrico Caruso attended services. Most of the time since 1949 the church has been a responsibility of the Maryknoll Fathers, who have a long history of missionary work and service in China.

AROUND THE CORNER

➥ **The Museum of the Chinese in the Americas** (formerly the Chinatown History Museum. 70 Mulberry St. at Bayard St., second floor. ☎ 619-4785) offers a variety of changing exhibitions, plus two permanent exhibitions: "Where Is Home? Chinese in the Americas," a collection of photographs and artifacts; plus "Family Portraits," photographs of area residents.

An Old Church with a New Congregation
FIRST CHINESE PRESBYTERIAN (LM)
61 Henry St. at Market St. 1819, original architect unknown. ☎ 964-5488

The First Chinese Presbyterian Church

Colonel Henry Rutgers donated this land for a Dutch Reformed church, but the building came to be known as the Sea and Land Church after Presbyterians bought it in 1866 and began offering services tailored for sailors from the nearby docks. Both shipbuilding and import-export trade concentrated along the lower East River through most of the nineteenth century, and it was from nearby docks that the *Empress of China* sailed in 1785, the first vessel ever to sail from America to China. Trade with China grew so rapidly that, by the late 1850s, a ship was arriving from China each week. Chinese sailors or merchants were probably the first Chinese New Yorkers, and a distinct enclave of Chinese soon developed in New York. Between 1882 and 1943 Chinese immigration was restricted, so the Chinese population here grew slowly. In the ports of China itself, however, Presbyterian missionaries were converting many Chinese, and Presbyterians began missionary work among Chinese in New York with services in a hotel on Worth Street in 1868. Reverend Huie Kin, who was called to the ministry in 1885, started a mission that became the First Chinese Presbyterian Church in 1910. That congregation shared this building with the Sea and Land Church for many years, but it assumed full responsibility after Sea and Land dissolved in 1972. Today the old building is the focus of a lively congregation and community.

This is one of three historic churches on the Lower East Side that have Georgian bodies but Gothic pointed-arched windows (the others are St. Augustine's and the Church of the Transfiguration). They were built twenty-five years or so before the architectural fashion known as the Gothic Revival started, so it is possible that their builders remembered the Gothic windows of churches back in England and put windows of the Gothic type into these more up-to-date Georgian volumes. Thus, these churches are referred to as Georgian Gothic.

New York's Largest Buddha Image
MAHAYANA TEMPLE BUDDHIST ASSOCIATION
133 Canal St. at the Bowery. 1997 conversion of a movie theater by Yung Foo Don. ☎ 925-8787

This temple has tried to create a street façade that resembles or reminds worshipers of a traditional Buddhist pagoda. Large red columns support a porch roof over the ground-floor doorway, and a false façade has been attached to the wall of the building above that. This façade shows a balustraded wall with steps at either end fronting an elaborate pagoda of three pavilions, each two tiers high, with red columns and green tile roofs. Above the façade, the building wall has been painted bright yellow.

On the sidewalk, two stone lions guard the door, which opens into a small lobby where a brazier full of sand holds incense sticks burning before a shrine to Kuan Yin, the Buddha of Mercy. Kuan Yin is sometimes spoken of as masculine, sometimes feminine. As you step down a ramp from the lobby into the main sanctuary, the yellow altar to your right holds small paper inscriptions wishing blessings on the spirits of the deceased, and the red altar on your left carries blessings for those still alive. New York City's largest Buddha image, a fifteen-foot-high gilded statue, is seated above the

The Mahayana Buddhist Temple

altar in the main sanctuary. Buddha smiles benevolently, his right hand raised in a three-fingered blessing. The altar before him, laden with offerings of the faithful, is framed by tall "light pagodas"—beautiful cones of lights. Two large drums are used by the priests during chanting for the purpose of "centering" the worshipers, or helping them find calm. The huge iron bell (six feet high), brought from China, that hangs in the back of the sanctuary is rung (by swinging a log) only on special holidays. Illustrations of the life of the Buddha line the walls, which is additionally decorated with bright red columns, a tapestry showing several dragons, and crystal chandeliers. The space itself is open and free of furniture.

Orthodox Grandeur
THE ELDRIDGE STREET SYNAGOGUE (LM)
Orthodox. 12–16 Eldridge St., just off Canal St. 1887, Peter and Francis Herter. ☎ 219-0888.

The main sanctuary of this extraordinary building was virtually abandoned for forty years, only to be rediscovered in the 1970s as a time capsule of the opulence of a bygone day. It was New York's first synagogue to be built by eastern European Jews, many of whom were prominent businessmen, solidly Orthodox in their faith and opposed to Reformed and Americanized Judaism. The congregation's name, Khal Adath Jeshurun Anshe Lubz, means "the Community of the people of Israel with the people of Lubz." In 1891 *The Century Magazine* reported that the congregation consisted of "lawyers, merchants, artisans, clerks, peddlers, and laborers."

The building's flamboyantly eclectic brick and terra-cotta façade combines Moorish horseshoe arches with both Romanesque- and Gothic-style details. Twin stair towers flank a recessed central bay that houses a large wheel window and is crowned by an arcaded gable. The Magen David appears in the roundels of the window.

The large sanctuary lies under a seventy-foot-high barrel-vaulted ceiling bordered with hemispherical domes supported by slender columns with Moorish-style capitals. The women's gallery rings the space above. The ark is a copy of the façade carved in Italian walnut, and curtains painted on

The Eldridge Street Synagogue

the wall seem to hide a view of Jerusalem. The *bimah* sits in the center of the room, illuminated by brass torchères at its corners. Brass chandeliers with glass shades hang from the ceiling, and gas jets ring the columns. The pews were bought used from a Christian church, so, incongruously, they show a trefoil Christian motif. The synagogue doesn't share any walls with neighbors, so light streams in from round-arched stained-glass windows (none are figural) on all four sides. Elaborate designs were originally stenciled on the upper walls, and gold stars on the deep blue ceiling.

The synagogue counted 4,000 members in 1900. Worshipers here included the artist Ben Shahn; performers Eddie Cantor, Paul Muni, and Edward G. Robinson; and scientist Jonas Salk. Membership fell, however, as Jews moved away from the Lower East Side. The main auditorium was sealed in the 1930s, but services were held in the basement whenever a minyan could be gathered. The "rediscovery" of the building by architectural historians in the 1970s triggered its designation as a City, State, and Federal Landmark. Since then the nonprofit Eldridge Street Project has been established to restore it to serve as a museum of Jewish and Lower East Side history, as well as a house of worship. Services downstairs have not been interrupted, so every Jewish holiday has been celebrated in this synagogue since 1887.

AROUND THE CORNER
➡ **The Sung Tak Buddhist Temple** (LM, 15 Pike St., between E. Broadway and Henry St. 1903, Alfred E. Badt) occupies a Romanesque Revival style building that was originally built as a synagogue for the Congregation B'nai Israel Kalwarie, the "Sons of Israel of Kalwarie" (on the Polish–Lithuanian border). Twin lateral staircases approach the worship space above a high basement that provides room for shops.

Sung Tak Temple

THE SYNAGOGUES
OF THE LOWER EAST SIDE

The eastern European Jews who settled in the Lower East Side organized an estimated 600 synagogues between 1880 and 1910. Most were Orthodox, but they retained distinctions based on sect, national origin, or even individual village. Abraham Cahan's novel *The Rise of David Levinsky* (1917) tells how David, an immigrant from Russian Poland, goes to the synagogue maintained by people from his hometown as soon as he arrives in New York. The first "Sons of Antomir" synagogue is "a ramshackle little frame building," but, as the men of Antomir succeed in America, they are able to buy and convert "an impressive granite structure, [formerly] a Presbyterian church." David himself eventually wins wealth as a garment manufacturer.

As many such immigrants prospered and migrated out of the Lower East Side, the membership of many synagogues fell below the number necessary to maintain their buildings or even to gather the ten men necessary to hold a service. Most recently, however, young Jewish couples are moving back into the neighborhood abandoned by their own grandparents. The center of the revival is the Cooperative Village, a complex of buildings stretching along Grand Street from Essex to the East River Park. They were built between the 1940s and the 1960s, after the old tenements were torn down. Today the neighborhood's Jewish population totals an estimated 50,000 people; they support thirty functioning synagogues, new schools, shops, kosher food stores (fliers found in the neighborhood advertise classes teaching "kosher sushi cooking"), and restaurants. America's oldest continuously operating *mikvah*, for ritual bathing (founded in 1904), still stands at 313 East Broadway (west of Grand St.), and it is serving new young visitors.

Innovative Social Services
HENRY STREET SETTLEMENT (LM)
263, 265, and 267 Henry St. at Montgomery St. (two houses dating from the 1820s, and a third with a newer façade from 1900). ☎ 766-9200

In 1893 Lillian Wald (1867–1940), a middle-class woman of German-Jewish descent, founded the Nurses' Settlement to provide medical care to poor immigrants in the Lower East Side. Philanthropists Jacob Schiff and

Morris Loeb purchased two old row houses for the organization's use, and soon visiting nurses from the Settlement attended thousands of patients throughout the city seven days per week, for free. This was the beginning of public nursing, including that of school nurses, in the United States. The Settlement's activities expanded to include recreational and educational programs—partly in an effort to "Americanize" the area's new eastern European Jewish population—and it eventually opened several houses throughout Manhattan and the Bronx. In 1944 the nursing service became the independent Visiting Nurse Service, but the Settlement still provides a broad selection of programs for young people, families, and the elderly in a neighborhood that is today largely Chinese and Hispanic.

The Henry Street Settlement Playhouse, one block north at 466 Grand Street, started as a location for amateur theatricals, and graduates of its acting courses include Gregory Peck, Tammy Grimes, Diane Keaton, Eli Wallach, and Lorne Greene.

New York's Only Slave Balcony
SAINT AUGUSTINE'S (LM)
Episcopal. 290 Henry St., between Montgomery and Jackson Sts. 1828, attributed to John Heath. Enlarged 1849. ☎ 673-5300

Augustine (354–430 C.E.) was born in what is today Algeria. After early years spent in dissipation (he was the sorrow of his mother, Monica, who is today the patron saint of mothers with unruly children), he converted and reformed, becoming eventually a bishop and writer. His *Confessions* (an autobiography up to his conversion) and *The City of God* have found countless readers.

St. Augustine's is the only church left in New York that has a gallery originally built for slaves. We cannot, however, be certain that slaves ever sat in this gallery, because the church was under construction when slavery was abolished. New York's State Legislature declared the children of slaves free if the children were born after July 4, 1799, and granted freedom to slaves born before that date at the age of twenty-four for women and twenty-eight for men. Therefore the last slave in New York would have received his freedom on July 4, 1827.

In 1876 the corrupt political leader William M. "Boss" Tweed hid in this gallery during his mother's funeral down below. He was a fugitive from the law because he had siphoned millions of dollars out of the city treasury. (One has to doubt that the police were really doing their best to find him.)

St. Augustine's is one of the three landmark churches with Georgian bodies but Gothic-style windows (along with First Chinese Presbyterian and The Transfiguration—see p. 102 and 104). Tradition has it that the fieldstones for its walls were dug from Mount Pitt, near the present intersection of Grand and Pitt Streets, which was a fortified spot during the Revolution. A double pediment and a projecting tower give the church's façade a special elegance, in addition to the typical three windows over three doors. The two-story windows along the nave are set in brick-arched frames, but the doors have stone lintels. Cut stone was expensive, so wood was used for the main cornice, which extends completely around the building and tower, and for the eaves.

Inside, the altar stands in front of an arched recessed chancel wall. Both the wineglass pulpit, which still has a three-feather Prince of Wales crest on the sounding board suspended above, and the organ date from 1830. The galleries are simple paneled wood carried on fluted cast-iron columns.

This building was built as All Saints' Free Church ("free" because no pew rent was charged), but when the congregation from St. Augustine's Church merged with that of All Saints' in 1949, the congregation took St. Augustine's name.

Financed by a Roll
BIALYSTOKER SYNAGOGUE (LM)

Orthodox. 7–13 Bialystoker Pl. (formerly Willett St., between Grand and Broome Sts.) 1826, original architect unknown. ☎ 475-0165

A bialy is a kind of an onion roll that originated in Bialystok, a city in northeastern Poland, and in 1905 a congregation of Jews from Bialystok bought this building (a former Methodist church) partly with the proceeds from a bakery over on Grand Street. It is today the oldest structure in the city to house a synagogue.

The façade is severely plain, with a simple pediment, no belt course or quoins, and three round-arched windows over its three doors. A low flight of steps sets the building off from the street. The Polish congregation designed an interior decor that is quite lavish. Three sculpted crowns and two rampant lions top the gilded ark, designed in Italy. The ceiling and wall murals depicting the signs of the Zodiac and scenes of Jerusalem have recently been restored. The oak wash basin in the lobby—a feature unique to this synagogue—was originally a wine barrel, donated by Schapiro's Winery, which still exists on Rivington Street. The synagogue operates a nursing home at 228 East Broadway.

New York's First Roman Catholic Bell
SAINT MARY'S
438 Grand St. West of Pitt St. 1833, original architect unknown. ☎ 674-3266

The first St. Mary's Church to rise on this site was pillaged and burned to the ground by an anti-Roman Catholic mob in 1831, just four years after it had been dedicated and five years after the parish had been established. Perhaps the arsonists had been particularly enraged by its bell; St. Mary's had been the first Roman Catholic church in the city to have one. St. Peter's and St. Patrick's churches were organized before St. Mary's, but the priests at those churches were largely Irish, and Ireland had no tradition of church bells because Ireland's English rulers had prohibited them. The Augustinian Fathers at St. Mary's treasured their bell, which had, in fact, been purchased from an old Presbyterian congregation. The fire destroyed the bell, but the congregation struggled to rebuild after the fire, and today the body of this church, dedicated in 1833, is New York's second oldest Roman Catholic church structure. It was built as a Greek Revival temple with a grand Doric portico, but in 1864 that façade was removed and replaced by the present twin-spired red-brick façade.

The first priest at this new St. Mary's, Father William Quarter, later served as the first bishop of Chicago, and in the 1880s St. Mary's Reverend Charles Parks became the first Roman Catholic chaplain to the U.S. Navy. Parishioner Alphonsa Hawthorne Lathrop, the youngest daughter of novelist Nathaniel Hawthorne, founded the Dominican Sisters of Hawthorne, who still operate **St. Rose's Home** for people suffering from incurable cancer (at 71 Jackson St. in New York City and six others in other states).

In 1871, St. Mary's was extended to the rear by architect L. J. O'Connor. Today religious paintings enrich the apsidal chancel, and a stained-glass skylight illumines what was the high altar, which was designated a "Privileged Altar" by Pope Pius IX in 1878. Another skylight dome is found over the crossing, and stained-glass windows from Mayer of Munich, dated 1888, line the nave. After the Brooklyn Bridge opened in 1883, the Irish Catholic population of this area began to move over to Brooklyn, and St. Mary's fell into a slow decline for some time. The parish population is diverse today; masses are held in English, Spanish, and Chinese.

New York's Chief Rabbi
CONGREGATION BETH HAMEDRASH HAGODOL (LM)

Orthodox. 60–64 Norfolk St., between Broome and Grand Sts. 1850, original architect unknown. ☎ 674-3330

This Gothic Revival building was built as the Norfolk Street Baptist Church, but it also served, in turn, an African American Zion Baptist congregation and then a Methodist congregation before it was purchased in 1885 by the Jewish congregation occupying it today. Beth Hamedrash Hagodol, the "Great House of Study," is the oldest Russian Orthodox synagogue in America, having been founded on Allen Street in 1852. When Rabbi Jacob Joseph from Vilna was appointed rabbi of this congregation in 1899, he was given the short-lived unofficial title "Chief Rabbi of New York City."

A few Gothic-style exterior details can be seen, despite smooth stuccoing and a cream paint job with brown trim: the band of quatrefoils on the two towers, an iron fence, and the pointed window arches. Inside, the ornate ark and pulpit, center *bimah* with etched glass lamps, and colorful wall paintings all testify to its role as a synagogue.

Congregation Beth Hamedrash Hagodol

A Unique Community
CONGREGATION KEHILA KEDOSHA JANINA
Orthodox. 280 Broome St., between Eldridge and Allen Sts. 1927, Sidney Daub. ☎ 431-1619

The individuals who founded this synagogue in 1906 were neither Sephardim nor Ashkenazim (see p. 21), but Romaniotes, from the Greek city of Janina. The first documentation of a Jewish colony in Janina dates from the seventh century C.E., but oral tradition has it that the Romaniotes were remnants of a group who, after the destruction of the Temple in Jerusalem in 70 C.E., were sent back to Rome in slave ships. A storm forced the ships to land on the coast of today's Albania, whence the Jews made

Congregation Kehila Kedosha Janina

their way to the city of Janina in northwest Greece, and there they developed their unique customs and rites over the next 1,900 years. When Sephardic Jews were expelled from Iberia in 1492, some of them went to settle among the Romaniotes. Between 1890 and 1935, a large number of Romaniotes migrated to New York and opened four synagogues, but this is the only one left today. It is in fact the only Romaniote synagogue in the Western Hemisphere. The members of the congregation use Sephardic prayer books but have their own prayers and rituals. The interior was originally lit by a large skylight, today covered. The *tebah* is in the center of the room and the ark on the north wall. In 1997 the congregation celebrated its seventieth anniversary by opening a small museum of their community history on the second floor.

AROUND THE CORNER
➥ *Tenement* became synonymous with the many five-or six-story apartment buildings constructed to house immigrants. A residential floor typically had four small apartments (each about 325 square feet) and an

unlighted staircase rising through the center of the building. **The Lower East Side Tenement Museum** (97 Orchard Street, between Delancey and Broome Sts. ☎ 431-0233), opened in 1988, recreates such an early housing unit and presents scenes and exhibitions about immigrant life and housing. When 97 Orchard Street was completed in 1864, the privies were in the backyard, but legislation slowly improved housing conditions, as displays in this museum explain.

The Cantors' Carnegie Hall
FIRST ROMANIAN AMERICAN CONGREGATION
Orthodox. 89 Rivington St., between Orchard and Ludlow Sts. 1888, original architect unknown. ☎ 673-2835

This building, a rare example of Romanesque Revival architecture on the Lower East Side, originally served as a Methodist church. That congregation, however, moved out four years later and sold the building to Shaaray Shomoyim ("Gates of Heaven"), which had been organized as the First Romanian Congregation about 1860, but reorganized and added the word "American" to its name in 1885. The elaborate interior seats almost 1,600 people, which makes it one of the largest houses of worship in the city. Entertainers George Burns, Red Buttons, and Eddie Cantor were all members. The synagogue earned the name "the cantors' Carnegie Hall" because of the outstanding cantors who sang here. They included Jacob Pincus Perelmuth (otherwise known as opera star Jan Peerce) and his brother-in-law Reuben Ticker (Richard Tucker), whose funeral was held at the Metropolitan Opera House when he died in 1975. (The tiny park across from the Metropolitan Opera House today—between Broadway and Columbus Avenues and West 66th Street—is **Tucker Park**, with a 1979 bust of the tenor by Hebald.)

The First Romanian American Congregation

The World's Spiritual Traditions
THE OPEN CENTER (LMD)
83 Spring St. east of Broadway. ☎ 219-2527. A small bookshop offers a variety of spiritual texts.

The Open Center is a nonprofit, holistic learning institution founded in 1983 and dedicated to individual and cultural renewal. The Center's five main areas of inquiry are (1) spiritual practices; (2) cultural studies and the arts; (3) psychology and inner development; (4) holistic health; and (5) social and ecological issues.

The Center offers more than 600 programs every year dealing with the world's spiritual traditions, including training, conferences, lectures, and performances ranging from mind-body medicine to stress-reduction techniques to social and environmental issues. Attendance numbers over 15,000 people per year. The Center does not endorse any one religious philosophy, but encourages study of all the world's spiritual traditions, including meditation and Eastern spirituality. Its second-floor meditation room, open to all, offers a peaceful retreat.

AROUND THE CORNER
➡ **Lorenzo Da Ponte** (1739–1848), librarian, friend of Casanova, and librettist for Mozart (*The Marriage of Figaro, Don Giovanni,* and *Cosi Fan Tutte*), died in a house that stood at 91 Spring Street. He had come to America in 1805, but failed as a grocer in Sunbury, Pennsylvania. Clement Clarke Moore (see p. 179) had found him there and persuaded him to come to New York, where he taught Italian privately to, among others, the poet Fitz-Greene Halleck and Julia Ward Howe. He eventually became professor of Italian language and literature at Columbia University, and his library formed the nucleus of the university library's holdings in Italian literature.
➡ **The Poet's House** (72 Spring St. ☎ 431-7920) offers one of America's largest collections of poetry books open to the public.

New York's First Roman Catholic Cathedral
OLD SAINT PATRICK'S (LM)
Mott St. at Prince St. 1815, Joseph Mangin. ☎ 226-8075

Patrick (385?–461? C.E.) was born in today's Wales, but he was captured and enslaved by raiders at age sixteen and taken to Ireland. After six years he escaped and spent some years, perhaps, in France, when a dream inspired him to return to Ireland to preach Christianity. Christianity existed there, but it had made small headway. Legends recount how he used the three-leaved shamrock to explain the mystery of the Trinity, and how he drove all snakes off the island. He is Ireland's patron saint.

This building, the original Roman Catholic cathedral of New York, was begun in 1809, the year after New York became a diocese, but it was not completed until 1815, and it was demoted to the status of a parish church after the new cathedral uptown was consecrated in 1879 (see p. 151). Nevertheless, this building holds a lot of history. One generous contributor toward its construction was Anthony Trapani, a rich merchant born in Meta, Italy, who was the first person to obtain citizenship through the process of naturalization prescribed in the U.S. Constitution. In 1835 nativist mobs, aroused by the influx of Irish immigrants, threatened to destroy this building; the wall around it may well have been built as a defensive measure. John Neumann (1811–60) was ordained here in 1836, the year he arrived from his native Bohemia. He served as a missionary in western New York State and eventually rose to become bishop of Philadelphia. He was canonized as a saint in 1978, and the next year a shrine was dedicated to him in the new St. Patrick's uptown. John Hughes, the first bishop to be consecrated in New York, was consecrated here in 1838. President Lincoln wrote Pope Pius VIII to recommend that Hughes be made the first U.S. cardinal, but Hughes died before he was elevated. Hughes' successor as archbishop, John McCloskey, was invested in Old St. Patrick's as the first American cardinal in 1875.

The church's appearance has been greatly altered by a fire in 1866 and several subsequent restorations and redesigns. It was originally in a version of the Gothic style, but it is hard to tell from what we see today. The original shell was, however, decorated with Gothic touches, such as a Gothic-style tripartite façade with a large window with elaborate tracery in the center. Each of the rough gray fieldstone side walls has eight tall pointed windows.

Inside, cast iron columns support the vaulted roof. The wide wood reredos depicts a rank of saints standing in niches. France's King Louis Philippe sent six stained-glass windows for St. Patrick's in 1846, but they didn't fit, so they went to a little Jesuit college that had just been founded up in the Bronx. They still adorn Fordham Chapel today (see p. 329).

North and south of the church a brick wall encloses Old Calvary Cemetery, which was originally the cemetery for St. Peter's Church. Pierre Toussaint (see p. 90) was originally buried here, but disinterred and reinterred under the altar of the new St. Patrick's in 1983.

AROUND THE CORNER

➡ A few nearby buildings are related to Old St. Patrick's. **St. Michael's Russian Catholic Church** (LM), at 266 Mulberry Street, was designed in 1859 by James Renwick, Jr., and William Rodrigue, the same team that worked on the new St. Patrick's. This little brownstone and brick Gothic Revival building was built as the chancery office. For some years it served as the office for the cemetery, but after World War II it was given to Catholics of the Russian Rite.

➡ The **Convent and Girls' School** (LM) around the corner at 32 Prince Street was originally an Orphan Asylum. The institution was founded in 1817 by Mother Seton's Sisters of Charity (see p. 81), but this elegant building, for which no architect is known, dates from 1826. The entranceway, with slender Corinthian columns and a fanlight, is one of the few complete late-federal style doorways in the city.

New York's Oldest Purpose-Built Synagogue
ANSHE CHESED/ ANGEL ORENSANZ FOUNDATION (LM)
176 Norfolk St., between Houston and Stanton Sts. 1850, Alexander Saeltzer. Not generally open to the public.

This Gothic Revival building is the city's oldest structure specifically built as a synagogue, and for a time it was the city's largest. Anshe Chesed ("People of Kindness"), New York's third Jewish congregation, organized in 1828, built it. After that congregation moved away, the building served two other congregations in turn. By 1975, however, with the continuing migration of Jews from the

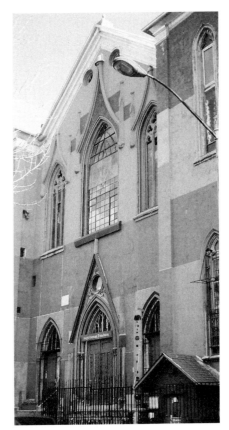

Anshe Chesed/Angel Orensanz Foundation

Lower East Side, the building was abandoned and padlocked. In 1986, Spanish sculptor Angel Orensanz and his brother Al bought it for a studio and gallery. Regular Sabbath services resumed in 1997 under the auspices of an organization called the Shul of New York. In 2000 the new congregation found in Texas an historic Torah made in Slonim, Belarus. Since a congregation from Slonim worshiped here early in the twentieth century, the Torah may actually have been used in this building and now has returned newly restored to it. The building is no longer used exclusively as a synagogue, but is now being used for weddings, fashion shows, and the filming of music videos.

CHAPTER FOUR

$\mathcal{T}$he East Side: From Houston Street to East 59th Street

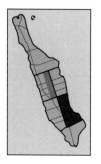

THE AREA EAST OF BROADWAY from Houston Street to 14th Street was once grand. In the 1830s, the homes of New York's leading families lined Lafayette Street. Eventually these rich migrated northward, and first Germans and then a variety of other European immigrant groups moved into this part of the East Side. In the 1960s the area came to life as a "hippie" neighborhood, and now it's had a resurgence, with new restaurants and boutiques lining its streets.

South of 4th Street, Broadway divides East from West Manhattan, but north of Washington Square, Fifth Avenue is the demarcation. Continuing northward on the East Side, one passes through Union Square, Gramercy Park, and Murray Hill. Both Union Square and Murray Hill were named for farms, while Gramercy took its name from an early nineteenth-century real-estate development centered on a still-surviving private park. At the end of the nineteenth century, Murray Hill became an enclave of elegant mansions, many of which survive. The East 40s and 50s developed as the heart of commercial Midtown East after the construction of Grand Central Terminal (the first one, built in 1871, was replaced by the present one in 1913), but numerous late-nineteenth-century mansions and churches still stand.

Houston Street to East 23rd Street

The Catholic Worker

ST. JOSEPH HOUSE AND ST. MARY HOUSE

Respectively, 36 East 1st St. (☎ 254-1640); and 55 East 3rd St. (☎ 777-9617). Original construction dates and architects unknown.

Many people called Dorothy May Day (1897–1980) a saint in her own lifetime, but she scoffed, "I don't want to be dismissed so easily." A native of Brooklyn, she became interested in socialism while an undergraduate at the University of Illinois, returned to New York, converted to Catholicism, and in 1933 founded, with French-born Peter Maurin, the weekly *The Catholic Worker*. The paper explored pacifism, utopianism, and Catholic social thought, and it sold for only a penny. Circulation reached 185,000 by 1940. Meanwhile, Ms. Day opened soup kitchens here that fed over 1,000 people per day, and she encouraged the opening of similar "houses of responsibility" across America. Her autobiography, *The Long Loneliness*, appeared in 1952. In March, 2000, the Vatican approved starting the process by which Ms. Day might eventually be canonized; this approval grants the title "Servant of God."

The Catholic Worker's opposition to World War II lost it many readers and supporters, but today it's still published at St. Mary House for 90,000 subscribers (at 25 cents per year), some 10,000 of whom live outside the United States. The privilege of reserving the Blessed Sacrament at St. Mary's private chapel was granted to Ms. Day, and it has been renewed by each of New York's archbishops. St. Mary's and St. Joseph's houses (named for Jesus' mother and foster father) still provide food and a variety of social services today.

AROUND THE CORNER

➥ Several private cemeteries were built in this area in the 1840s and 1850s, but only two survive (both LM). **The New York Marble Cemetery**, the city's first nonsectarian cemetery, was built on a half-acre bounded by 3rd Street, Second Avenue, 2nd Street, and the Bowery in 1831, but today it is largely hidden inside the block. Investors built 156 underground vaults and sold them to upper-class residents of nearby neighborhoods. There are no monuments, but owners' names are recorded on plaques around the walls. In 1832 the same group built the **New York City Marble Cemetery** at 52–74 East 2nd Street, between First and Second Avenues. U.S. President James Monroe was interred there briefly, and members of the prestigious Lenox and Roosevelt families rest there still. Both cemeteries can be viewed from the street, but neither is today open to the public.

➥ The **Liz Christy Garden** at the corner of Houston and Bowery Streets, founded in 1973, is one of the first of now over 1,000 community gardens throughout New York City. Volunteers tend raised beds of flowering plants, vegetables, and berry bushes. Trees provide shade and a touch of countryside.

The German Catholic Cathedral
MOST HOLY REDEEMER
Roman Catholic. 173 East 3rd St., between Aves. A and B. 1852, original architect unknown. ☎ 673-4224

This church is both big (80 feet by 127 feet) and astonishingly high, to inspire you to look up and think of heaven. Great height is typical of churches administered by Fathers of the Redemptorist Order, which was the first male Roman Catholic religious community to establish a permanent foundation in New York. Bishop Hughes invited them from Germany in 1842, when Germans were second only to the Irish in the city's Catholic community. This parish was established in 1844, and its church soon won the nickname, "the German Catholic Cathedral."

The first small church was dedicated here in 1844, but this new and grander replacement was consecrated in 1852 by an "all-star cast." New York's first archbishop, John Hughes, presided; the celebrant of the mass was Bishop (now Saint) John Neumann, and Bishop John McCloskey (later America's first cardinal) preached the sermon. During the consecration, a relic of Henry II, emperor of Germany from 1014 to 1024, was sealed into a niche in the altar. (Henry was canonized as a saint in 1146, and he is portrayed in the window in the St. Elizabeth Seton chapel in the south aisle at St. Patrick's Cathedral.)

Most Holy Redeemer has been altered several times, but certain original features remain. It was built in the Byzantine Revival style, and its original red brick exterior was covered with polished granite and limestone in 1912. The façade's three richly decorated gables are divided into three entrances by four massive pillars. The tower and spire originally rose to 250 feet, but in 1912 the tower was redesigned to look Romanesque and lowered to 232 feet. The bells in this tower were the first in the world ever to be rung by means of electric switches, a system devised by a parishioner named Rebeschung, on January 11, 1914.

The interior is divided into three naves by tall pillars standing on high bases. Christ reigns in majesty from the apse over the main altar, and that painting is illumined from above through a stained-glass skylight in the form of a dove. The ceiling vaulting is painted azure. The side aisles lead to side altars in enormous niches with curving open framework baldachins.

The side aisles are lined with shallow chapels. A reliquary chapel (last on the right) contains the bones of St. Datian (under a wax effigy), plus relics of Jesus' manger, the pillar at which he was scourged, the true cross, the girdle of the Virgin Mary, the mantle of St. Joseph, and other relics of St. Ann, St. Lazarus, St. John the Baptist, and St. Anthony of Padua. (A list is posted on the wall.)

Today this church where 10,000 German New Yorkers used to hear mass at several liturgies every Sunday no longer serves a specifically German parish, but it remains the parish church for about 250 Catholic families, half English and half Spanish-speaking, from a great many nations.

AROUND THE CORNER

➤ **Asian Classics Institute** (321 East 6th St., between First and Second Aves. ☎ 475-7752) offers programs and instruction in Buddhism and meditation. The institute also operates a bookstore at 211 East 5th Street.

Anchor of a Community

SAINT GEORGE'S UKRAINIAN CATHOLIC CHURCH

30 East 7th St., between Second and Third Aves. 1977, Apollinaire Osadca. ☎ 674-1615

The Ukrainian Catholic Church recognizes the authority of the pope in Rome, but it retains some national traditions in its liturgy. The Ukrainian rite was first celebrated in New York at **St. Brigid's** (119 Ave. B, founded in 1848) in 1890, but the Ukrainians got their own church in 1905. After several moves, they occupied this new house of worship in 1977. It is of pale yellow brick with limestone trim in a characteristic Ukrainian style. A high dome representing heaven caps a Greek cross. Inside, a mosaic of Christ Pantocrator proclaims, "I am the Resurrection and the Life." The façade features a central mosaic of Christ and smaller mosaics showing Ukrainians in native costumes before two famous Ukrainian cathedrals, that of St. George in L'viv and of St. Sofia in Kiev. Still another mosaic shows St. George slaying the dragon above the inner doorway.

This church is the focal point for the local Ukrainian community. The block-long street beside the church is Taras Shevchenko Place, named for a nineteenth-century Ukrainian poet. Behind the church is a school, where Ukrainian students learn the language, and next door to the church to the east is a twelve-story rectory and cooperative apartment complex, completed just after the Ukraine declared its independence in 1991. Surma, a shop featuring Ukrainian items, has been across the street (7 East 11th St.) since 1918 (right next to McSorley's, one of New York's oldest bars, dating to 1854). The Ukrainian community plans to build a museum of Ukrainian life and history at 222 East Sixth Street.

AROUND THE CORNER

➥ **St. Stanislaus Roman Catholic Church** just down the street (101 East 7th St., between First and Second Aves. 1901, unknown architect. ☎ 475-4576) was organized in 1872 as New York's first Polish parish. Stanislaus (1030–79) was a medieval bishop of Cracow. The church is lovingly maintained, and a portrait bust of the Polish Pope John Paul II (by Andrew Pitynsky, 1991) stands in front.

New York's Liberty Bell

MIDDLE REFORMED COLLEGIATE CHURCH

112 Second Ave., between 6th and 7th Sts. 1892, S. B. Reed. ☎ 477-0666

Middle Collegiate's bell was the first to tell New Yorkers of the signing of the Declaration of Independence in 1776, and it has celebrated many important events in our nation's history. The bell had been cast in Amsterdam in 1729, receiving its distinctive tone from having been made partly of silver coins contributed by Amsterdam congregations. It hung in several New York Collegiate churches before being installed here in 1950. It rings every Sunday morning from 10:45 until 11:00 and for every presidential inauguration; it also tolls every president's death.

This building is the third home of Middle Collegiate Church, one of the Reformed churches that trace their ancestry to the first church in New Amsterdam, founded in 1628. The church's large west window, which almost fills the gable of the façade, shows the arms of the Dutch church, the symbolic lily among thorns, the church amidst its enemies (Song of Solomon 2:2), and the seal of the Collegiate Church. The church structure is a rough limestone Gothic-style building with asymmetrical towers flanking the gable facing Second Avenue. The church's property has an L shape, so the parish house faces East 7th Street, and the interior passage linking the two buildings is brightened by a Tiffany skylight.

The recently restored interior has no columns; the wood-panel ceiling is supported by three longitudinal trusses and five pairs of Gothic-style spandrels. The marble pulpit and communion table were both brought from the Netherlands in the eighteenth century, and both served this congregation in earlier homes downtown. The walls are stenciled with decorative patterns and religious quotations in gold leaf. The interior is lit naturally by the window in the west wall, plus sixteen small windows set into the roof. The church is in the middle of a block, so it shouldn't be expected to have windows along the sides of the nave. Middle Reformed, however, boasts ten large Tiffany windows in the side walls depicting religious themes derived from drawings by Dresden artist Heinrich Hofmann. How was this accomplished? Louis Tiffany's friend Thomas Edison personally devised and installed a system of backlighting for them. Edison's work had to be torn out and replaced in the 1990s; it wasn't up to the standards of today's building code!

"Right Makes Might"
COOPER UNION (LM)
East 7th St. to Astor Pl., Fourth Ave. to the Bowery. 1859, F. A. Peterson.
☎ 353-4100

This free public college, open to both men and women and originally requiring no credentials other than "a good moral character," was founded by the generosity of inventor Peter Cooper (1791–1883), who thankfully recognized that his wealth had come from "the cooperation of multitudes." It was the first college to offer adult education courses, many given in the evenings for those who worked during the day. A statue of Cooper by Augustus Saint-Gaudens, who was an evening student at the school, with a marble base and canopy by Stanford White, sits in the tiny square on the south side of the building. The Italianate brownstone Union building is America's oldest extant building framed with iron beams, which Cooper developed from rails milled in his own factories. Cooper's beam system later evolved into the steel skeleton that supports modern skyscrapers.

In the Great Hall downstairs, on February 27, 1860, presidential candidate Abraham Lincoln denounced the Dred Scott Supreme Court decision that allowed an owner to take a slave from free territory back to the South. "Thinking it wrong as we do," he asked, "can we yield to them? If our sense of duty forbids this, then let us stand by our own duty fearlessly and effectively. . . . Let us have faith that right makes might, and in that faith let us, to the end, dare to do our duty as we understand it." The speech was widely publicized, and three months later Lincoln received the Republican nomination; in November he won the election. Earlier on the day of the Cooper Union speech, Lincoln had been captured in a flattering portrait by society photographer Mathew Brady, and Lincoln was later to say, "Brady and the Cooper Institute made me president."

Other speakers in this hall make up an honor roll of great Americans, including Mark Twain, Susan B. Anthony, Frederick Douglass, Ulysses S. Grant, Booker T. Washington, Elizabeth Cady Stanton, Woodrow Wilson, and many more. The American Red Cross, Volunteers of America, and the National Association for the Advancement of Colored People (NAACP) were all founded in this hall.

Manhattan's Oldest European Religious Site
SAINT MARK'S IN THE BOWERY (LM)
Episcopal. Second Ave. at 10th St. 1799, original architect unknown. Square belfry, clock tower, and steeple added 1828, Town & Thompson. Chancel, 1836. Cast-iron portico, 1858. Restored 1978, the Edelman Partnership. ☎ 674-6377

This land was consecrated over 350 years ago, and it has never since been used for any secular purpose. It is, therefore, the oldest European reli-

gious site in continuous use in Manhattan. Governor Peter Stuyvesant erected a chapel here when it was his country residence, "The Bouwerie." In 1672 he was buried in a vault under that chapel, and in his will he left the chapel to the Dutch Reformed Church. Eventually Dutch Reformed services were discontinued, and the Stuyvesant family offered to build a new Episcopal church here. This church was incorporated (by parish-ioner Alexander Hamilton) as a new parish in 1799. Stuyvesants continued to join their ancestors in the family crypt until 1954, when the vault was finally sealed after

St. Mark's in the Bowery

the burial of the governor's last descendant in the male line, Augustus Van Horne Stuyvesant, Jr.

St. Mark's is the second oldest church building in Manhattan, after St. Paul's (see p. 92), and renovations through years kept pace with architectural fashions. The rubblestone walls, trimmed round-arched windows, and simple triangular pediment reveal its late-Georgian beginnings. The front has the typical three round-arched windows above three doors, and the sides have two tiers of round-arched windows. St. Mark's is simpler than St Paul's: It lacks a belt course, balustrade, key stones, and quoins. The Greek Revival steeple was added later, and the Italianate cast-iron portico was added another generation later. These parts work well together because they are all forms of classicism.

Several pieces of sculpture decorate the grounds. Two Florentine marble lions (the symbol of Mark, the evangelist and author of one of the four Gospels) flank the main doorway, and outside the portico stand two granite statues of Native Americans (Aspiration and Inspiration) by Solon Borglum, whose brother Gutzon sculpted Mount Rushmore. A bust of Daniel Tompkins (1774–1825) stands at the west end of the porch. Tompkins, who is buried in the graveyard, was a four-term governor of New York and a two-term U.S. vice president. Nearby Tompkins Square is named for him. The graveyard also contains Thomas Emmet, an Irish patriot who fled to America when the British learned that he and his brother had advised Napoleon on an invasion of England (his brother was hanged); New York mayor and diarist Philip Hone; Revolutionary War hero Colonel Nicholas Fish; and members of several prominent New York families. In 1878 this cemetery was the scene of a sensational body snatching. The remains of department store magnate A. T. Stewart were stolen and held for ransom. When they were eventually returned, his widow had them reinterred under the new Episcopal cathedral she endowed in Garden City, Long Island. A handsome 1838 iron fence surrounds the yard, and a plaque memorializes poet W. H. Auden, who lived nearby and was a parishioner. Architect Frank Lloyd Wright designed a group of apartment towers to rise out of this churchyard, but the Depression stopped that project.

St. Mark's interior has suffered several terrible fires, so it retains very little original detail. Cast-iron columns support a gallery on three sides. The lower-level stained-glass windows (including one of Peter Stuyvesant on the east wall) date from the nineteenth century, but those in the upper tier were installed in 1982. Today the fixtures are all movable so the space can be used to continue St. Mark's traditional sponsorship of performing arts. In the 1920s, poets Edna St. Vincent Millay, Vachel Lindsay, and Kahlil Gibran (see p. 173) served on St. Mark's Arts Committee.

AROUND THE CORNER

➥ St. Mark's members sponsored a red brick and terra-cotta missionary chapel just down the street. Today that chapel is the **St. Nicholas Carpatho-Russian Orthodox Greek Catholic Church** at 288 East 10th Street (1884, James Renwick, Jr., and W. H. Russell. ☎ 254-6685). Its present congregation has taken loving care of it since obtaining the building in 1937.

➥ Some of the sycamore trees in **Tompkins Square Park** (between Aves. A and B, 7th St. and 10th St.) are thought to be among the oldest trees in New York City (200 years or more). The Square appeared already on the 1811 map of Manhattan, and it was designated to remain public grounds in perpetuity.

THE GREAT TREES
OF NEW YORK CITY

There are about 2.5 million trees in New York City. Some are native species: Dense forest of oaks and hickories covered much of the city for centuries before Europeans arrived. Other species were imported. A peach tree that Dutch Governor General Peter Stuyvesant himself planted on his farm in today's Lower East Side succumbed to a wagon accident only in 1847. As early as 1708, the Common Council granted residents of Broadway permission "to plant trees before their lots and houses," and by 1791 citizens were petitioning the Council itself to "afford them cool and shaded walks" along the city's avenues.

In 1985 the City Department of Parks and Recreation asked New Yorkers to nominate their favorite trees, for reasons of unusual size, species, form, or for historical associations. The Department then published in 1990 *Great Trees of New York City*, which listed 120 Great Trees. By the time the second edition of that booklet was printed in 2000, fifteen of the original choices had died, but a few new choices were added. Some of these Great Trees will be mentioned subsequently (the booklet itself can be obtained at the Parks Department Headquarters, Fifth Ave. at 63rd St. in Manhattan).

➥ A few blocks north, **Madina Mosque** (401 East 11th St. at First Ave. ☎ 533-5060), was founded by a group of Bangladeshis in 1976, but it has been enlarged and beautified through the years. Today the call to prayer is broadcast through a bright blue and green minaret, decorated with calligraphy, built on the back roof of the nineteenth-century storefront building.

Where the "Quality" Worshiped
GRACE CHURCH (LM)
Episcopal. 800 Broadway at 11th St. 1846, James Renwick, Jr. Landscaping, 1881, by Calvert Vaux & Co. ☎ 254-2000. A guidebook is available in the office.

When Grace Church opened, diarist Philip Hone noted: "This is to be the fashionable Church. . . . The pews . . . brought [such] extravagant prices . . . that the word of God, as it came down to us from fishermen and mechanics, will cost the quality who worship in this splendid temple about three dollars every Sunday. This may have a good effect; for . . . if they do not go regularly to Church, [they] will not get the worth of their money."

Grace was soon *the* place for services and ceremonies, always choreographed by sexton Isaac Brown, immortalized by Edith Wharton in *The Age of Innocence*. Brown ran a profitable undertaking and carriage-rental operation on the side, and although he admitted that Lent was "horridly dull," he insisted that "we manage to make our funerals as entertaining as possible." One of America's first publicized "celebrity weddings" occurred at Grace, when P. T. Barnum sponsored that of Colonel Tom Thumb (thirty-three inches tall) and the equally diminutive Lavinia Warren in 1863; from Grace the newlyweds departed for Washington to be received by President Lincoln in the White House. In the 1880s the editor of *Home Journal* defined "Society" as those "who keep carriages, live above Bleecker, are subscribers to the opera, go to Grace Church, have a town house and a country house, and give balls."

This church, the second home of a congregation organized in 1809, was completed in the same year as Trinity, two miles down Broadway, but whereas Trinity is brownstone, Grace is gleaming marble (quarried by convicts from upstate Sing Sing prison). Broadway abruptly veers to the west at 10th Street, so Grace's spire terminates the view up Broadway from the foot of Manhattan. Broadway veers just here because Henry Brevoort, James Renwick's uncle, refused to let the city drive either Broadway or 11th St. through his apple orchard. Little did Brevoort know that his nephew would eventually beautify that parcel of old family land. When

Renwick received the commission to build Grace, his only training had been in engineering, and he'd never seen a Gothic church. Nevertheless, Grace is one of New York's finest examples of the Gothic Revival style. Renwick was still a vestryman at the time of his death (1895), as his father had been before him. A bust of the architect glowers down from the west wall of the north transept, where he appears so dignified that prayers have mistakenly been addressed to him as to a saint.

A tympanum above Grace's main entrance at the base of the tower on Broadway illustrates Peter and John healing the lame man (Acts 3:2–10). A fine rose window pierces the gable above. Higher up, traceried belfry openings soar until the tower sprouts pinnacles and launches an octagonal spire topped with a cross. Along the exterior walls of the nave, buttresses alternate with pointed-arched windows, and a crenellated parapet—as on medieval castles—tops the walls.

The style is Gothic, even if the construction method is not. The elaborately ribbed vaulting inside is of lath and plaster, not stone. Bright limestone has gradually replaced the original plaster on the interior walls, and the floor is a mosaic. Grace Church is one of many Episcopal churches founded Low (Renwick never shared Upjohn's commitment to the Ecclesiological movement—see p. 69) but which have crept Higher. Its chancel has been deepened twice, and Renwick himself designed the richly carved reredos and the altar, on which stands an inlaid marble Tiffany cross.

Across the garden to the north, the rectory (where many New Yorkers dream of living) boasts as many Gothic-style pinnacles and details as the church does. Its two wings are identical, but decorated differently in an effort to make the building picturesque. The urn in the garden, a gift of an early rector, was found during excavations in Rome. When found, it allegedly contained coins from the years 54 to 68 C.E., just when Nero was persecuting the earliest Christians.

To the south is a chantry (small chapel) with a tympanum by sculptor Lee Lawrie. Until 1905 the Vienna Bakery stood on the corner lot to the south. Each evening it gave away products unsold during the day (by some accounts the first "bread line"), but its purchase by the church guaranteed protection of this green space and the vista up Broadway to the church spire.

Through the block, on Fourth Avenue, Grace School (opened 1894) has expanded and consolidated behind the historic façades of a number of the church's auxiliary buildings from the turn of the century. One of them housed New York's first day-care center.

An Old Church Finds New Life
SAINT ANN'S SHRINE AND ARMENIAN CATHOLIC CATHEDRAL

Roman Catholic and Armenian Catholic. 110 East 12th St., between Third and Fourth Aves. Façade 1847, original architect unknown; body 1871, Napoleon LeBrun. ☎ 477-2030

When St. Ann's parish was founded in 1852, its first pastor and his assistant, John Murray Forbes and Thomas Scott Preston, shocked Protestant New York by converting to Catholicism after having served at fashionable St. Luke's Episcopal Church. Five years later Reverend Forbes gave the city more to talk about by returning to the Episcopal Church and eventually becoming the first permanent dean of the General Theological Seminary (see p. 180). Father Preston remained at St. Ann's, helped found the woman's Order of the Divine Compassion, and is today remembered in the name of a Bronx High School.

In 1871 St. Ann's, dedicated to the mother of the Virgin Mary, moved up here from its first home on Astor Place. This building had been constructed in 1847 as a Baptist church, but it had served as home for Temple Emanu-El since 1856 (see p. 200). St. Ann's congregation kept the old building's façade and tower, but tore down the body of the church and hired parishioner Napoleon LeBrun to build a new one. His finished work, in French Gothic style, was hailed by *The New York Catholic* as "the most gorgeous of our Catholic temples." The earlier façade probably explains why St. Ann's is seldom noted among LeBrun's works today.

St. Ann's entered her glory days in LeBrun's "new" building. The church enjoyed the largest income of any Catholic parish in the city and hosted the American premiere of Verdi's *Requiem* in 1874. The marble baptistery to the left of the entrance, a memorial to a popular priest, dates from that era. In the 1920s the church was refurbished. Tearing down old balconies and putting new stained glass in the windows (abstract windows in the clerestory above two tiers of figural windows in the nave and eight more figurals in the apse!) brightened the interior. A papal rescript of August 29, 1929, declared St. Ann's "The American National Shrine of the Motherhood of St. Ann." The church was further adorned with a new marble shrine and reliquary, floor, altar and reredos, altar rail, and statues.

After World War II, the neighborhood changed and could no longer support its many Catholic churches, so St. Ann's suffered hard times. The church is no longer a parish church, but two groups have breathed new life into it. In 1983, at the request of Pope John Paul II, its use was granted to the Apostolic Exarchate for Armenian Catholics. Also, a community of

Ecuadorians was granted the right to bring a copy of the Madonna of Quinche from their homeland. The Lady, a small statue of the Madonna and Child, is installed in an exquisite gilded shrine, and Ecuadorian women regularly change the beautiful and elaborate dresses they have sewn for her. Each week planes from Ecuador bring fresh long-stemmed roses to adorn the sanctuary.

Today St. Ann's offers masses in English, Armenian, Spanish, and, by special dispensation, traditional Latin.

AROUND THE CORNER

➡ **Immaculate Conception Roman Catholic Church** (LM, 406–412 East 14th St., between First and Ave. A. 1896, Barney & Chapman. ☎ 254-0200) was built by Grace Church (see p. 130) as an Episcopalian chapel and social service center in what was then a poor immigrant neighborhood. Today we see only half of what this complex once was, but it still resembles a medieval urban church, looking after the spiritual, educational, and physical needs of its parish. The style of the buildings is late-Gothic or early-Renaissance French, featuring a bold tower on 14th Street, a church, and a small chapel. The buildings to the east of the tower were originally a hospital and community center, but are today clerical housing and offices. The central parking lot used to be a courtyard, and buildings on 13th Street included the rectory, a clubhouse, and the parish building with parlors and a reading room, Sunday school and cooking classes, and even a gym and swimming pool. The Roman Catholic Church bought this property in 1943. The belief in the Immaculate Conception—that Mary was born without sin—was proclaimed Roman Catholic dogma in 1854.

UNION SQUARE

14th to 17th Sts., between Fourth Ave. and Broadway.

Union Square took its name from the fact that it was the spot where the Bowery and Bloomingdale Road (today's Broadway) came together, that is, united. The park opened in 1831, and it was soon surrounded by elegant mansions, theaters, and concert halls. From the Civil War until well into the twentieth century, workers' rallies and political protests were often held here. The area went through a period of decline after World War II, but in the 1990s it sprang to life once again. The equestrian statue on the south side of the Square shows George Washington reclaiming New York from the British on November 25, 1783, and it stands just a few feet from where the event actually happened (Henry Kirke Brown, 1856). Other statues in the Square include one of Abraham Lincoln (Brown,

1868), and one of the Marquis de Lafayette, the French hero of the American War of Independence, and Washington's good friend (Frédéric-Auguste Bartholdi, 1873). This statue was a gift to the people of New York from the government of France in thanks for New Yorkers' help during the Franco-Prussian War (1870–71); this statue helped Bartholdi win the commission for the Statue of Liberty a few years later.

A **statue of Mohandas Gandhi** (1869–1948) by Kantilal Patel (1986) stands in the pedestrian triangle at the southwest corner of Union Square. In 1893 the Indian-born British-educated lawyer was thrown off a segregated train in South Africa. He had bought a first-class ticket by mail, not knowing that a "colored" man wouldn't be allowed to use it. He dedicated the rest of his life to fighting injustice—nonviolently. He fought for rights in South Africa before returning to India, where he was instrumental in the achievement of independence. The statue shows him wearing a simple dhoti, reminding us of his asceticism and the freedom that comes from renouncing material possessions.

Nearby, six bronze relief panels by sculptor Greg LeFevre depict a 1909 garment factory strike and other milestones in the history of the International Ladies Garment Workers' Union. A rally of 30,000 workers here in 1882 launched what eventually became the annual Labor Day holiday.

"All-Encompassing Compassion"
SOKA GAKKAI INTERNATIONAL
7 East 15th St., between Fifth Ave. and Union Square. 1887, R. H. Robertson. ☎ 727-7715

Soka Gakkai International (SGI) has grown out of an organization founded among Japanese school teachers in 1930. Its goal was to reform the educational system based on the theory of *soka*, or "value-creation," and on the Buddhist philosophical ideas of Nichiren (1222–82 C.E.), dedicated to empowering individuals to develop their unique creative potential. The organization eventually ran afoul of Japan's military government, which disbanded it in 1943 and imprisoned its leaders as "thought criminals." After World War II, the organization sprang to life again and expanded its mission to include not only education, but human rights and individual development. Buddhism is often thought of as a religion that leads to individual withdrawal and meditation, but the Nichiren tradition is more of a missionary or reaching-out kind. Soka Gakkai founded this international organization in 1975 to coordinate its worldwide membership and to promote "infinite respect for the sanctity of life and all-encompassing compassion." The New York SGI Center offers a library, a bookstore, meeting rooms, and lectures, in addition to facilities for Buddhist meditation and worship.

Its red brick and brownstone Romanesque Revival building has always housed groups dedicated to doing good. It opened as a branch of the Young Women's Christian Association, and in 1917 it became "People's House," occupied by labor unions and institutions. The International Association of Machinists occupied it from 1956 until 1988, and since the building reopened in 1995, SGI has won architectural awards for the care with which architect Anita B. Brandt restored it.

Economist and moral crusader **Henry George** (1839–97) died in an upper floor of a hotel that faced Union Square on the corner of East 15th Street. His writings on equitable systems of taxation influenced policies in North America, Australia, and Western Europe.

"In Christ There Is No East or West"
SAINT GEORGE'S (LM)
Episcopal. Rutherford Pl. at East 16th St. 1848, Blesch and Eidlitz. ☎ 475-0830

George (said to have lived in the fourth century C.E.) seems to have been an early soldier-martyr born in today's Turkey, but little is known of his life. The legend that he killed a dragon actually convinces some people that George himself is just a myth. He is, nevertheless, popular throughout parts of Europe, and the patron saint of England, of soldiers, and of boy scouts.

Trinity Church opened a small chapel dedicated to St. George downtown in 1749. George Washington attended a Christmas service at that first St. George's, and Washington Irving was baptized there. St. George's became an independent parish in 1811, and soon thereafter the congregation decided to relocate to the north. They accepted the offer of a plot on Stuyvesant Square from Peter Stuyvesant III, even though this area was then described as "a howling wilderness." (The offer was shrewd, because the church increased the value of all of Stuyvesant's neighborhood property.) This church was begun in 1846—the year both Grace Church and the present Trinity Church were dedicated—and it was dedicated two years later. Its Romanesque Revival style proves that the Ecclesiological movement's fascination with Gothic Revival architecture had not hypnotized everyone (see p. 69). Fire hollowed out the building in 1865 (a small cross made from remnants of the original communion table hangs in the sacristy), but it was rebuilt by Leopold Eidlitz. Two very tall spires, however, had been weakened by the fire, and they had to be removed in 1889.

St. George's rector through those years, Dr. Stephen Higginson Tyng (served 1845–78), was an evangelical, and one of the most famous orators of his day. He strongly opposed the High Church efforts of many of his Episcopal colleagues, insisting that a church is a gathering place to hear sermons. That purpose is well served by St. George's vast open interior: a long, wide, three-aisled basilica without a clerestory. It is inconsistent with the Romanesque style to have balconies (they're a Renaissance innovation, as in Wren's churches), but St. George's balconies bring the congregation closer to the preacher and increase capacity to 1,500, which made St. George's New York's largest Episcopal church for many years. The high ceiling (long the highest in the city), supported by carved beams ornamented in gold, improves the acoustics. Abstract stained-glass windows line the nave, but figural windows are found in the vaulted apse. Tyng instructed Eidlitz explicitly that the "communion table" should not resemble an "altar," and a reredos was forbidden. Another Low Church feature was the Lord's Prayer printed in large easy-to-read letters on the apse wall (encouraging the participation of the congregation), but that was painted over some years ago. The musician, theologian, and medical missionary Albert Schweitzer (1875–1965) suggested the placement of the new organ that was installed in 1958.

Banker J. P. Morgan, one of the richest and most powerful men in America at the turn of the nineteenth to the twentieth centuries, was senior warden here for many years, and he, along with Rector William S. Rainsford (whose bust by Daniel Chester French can be seen in the right aisle) made St. George's a leading "institutional church." It offered vocational schooling, fresh air camps, medical and dental clinics, and it opened its parish house game rooms, shower facilities, and gymnasium to poor community residents. St. George's won the grand prize at the 1907 Paris International Exposition for its "socialized work." One of Morgan's gifts was the carved rolling pulpit, which can be pushed right to the center of the church during sermons.

Harry T. Burleigh was the featured baritone soloist at St. George's from 1894 until 1947. Burleigh, the son of former slaves, popularized spirituals and adapted many of them to the concert stage. He composed over 300 songs, including "Deep River," and hymns, including "In Christ There Is No East or West." He also helped Antonin Dvořák adapt traditional black melodies for Dvořák's "Symphony of the New World." Morgan had enormous respect for Burleigh, and Morgan specified the songs he wanted Burleigh to sing at his funeral, held here April 14, 1913. Seven years later, an escaped mental patient tried to assassinate J. P. Morgan, Jr., as he was leaving St. George's. The bullet killed Dr. James Markoe, a Morgan family friend.

The Byzantine-Romanesque Revival chapel fronting the square directly north of St. George's, designed by M. C. and H. L. Emery, opened in 1911, St. George's Centennial year. The reading every Sunday at the chapel service is from an 1846 Bible formerly used at the Church of the Holy Communion, with which St. George's parish merged, together with Calvary Church, in the 1970s.

AROUND THE CORNER

➥ The Gothic Revival **Calvary Church** (LMD) stands at 273 Park Avenue South (at 21st St., 1847, James Renwick, Jr. ☎ 475-1216). Calvary is the hill outside Jerusalem where Christ was crucified. This church boasts 141 stained-glass windows, a Tiffany mosaic fountain, and a particularly fine organ. Jenny Lind sang here, President Teddy Roosevelt worshiped here, and he stood as godfather to his niece Eleanor (see p. 25) when she was baptized from here in 1884. Calvary's Reverend Edward Washburn supplied the model for Dr. Ashmore in Edith Wharton's novel *The Age of Innocence*.

CALVARY CHURCH AND ALCOHOLICS ANONYMOUS

The two stained-glass windows to the south of Calvary Church's central doors were given in memory of Rowland Hazard, known as "Rowland H." in the early days of Alcoholics Anonymous. In 1931 Hazard, realizing that he was an alcoholic, consulted the celebrated psychiatrist Dr. Carl Jung in Zurich. Jung treated him for a year, but then announced that he could be of no further use to Hazard: What Hazard needed was a religious experience. At that time, Dr. Samuel Shoemaker, the rector of Calvary Church, was the head of the Oxford Groups, an organization that emphasized spiritual values in daily living. The Oxford Groups had helped an alcoholic New York stockbroker named Bill W. get sober, and Bill and Dr. Bob S., a surgeon in Akron, Ohio, founded Alcoholics Anonymous in 1935. Hazard was one of their first members. Wilson later wrote Dr. Jung that his "candid and humble" advice to Rowland Hazard "was beyond doubt the first foundation stone upon which our Society has since been built." Alcoholics Anonymous counts almost two million members today.

Meetinghouses for Two Quaker Groups (Both LM)

The Society of Friends in America suffered a schism in 1828. One group adopted some tenets of evangelical Christianity, including more formal church services, and came to be called Orthodox. The other group, lead by Elias Hicks, held more traditional simple meetings. During the schism, the Hicksites built a meetinghouse on Stuyvesant Square (see below), and the Orthodox built a new meetinghouse a few blocks away on Gramercy Park South (see p. 139). When the groups reunited in 1955, they retained the meetinghouse on Stuyvesant Square (named, ironically, for the Dutch governor who had persecuted the Friends in the seventeenth century). The other meetinghouse is today a synagogue.

FRIENDS MEETING HOUSE

15 Rutherford Pl. at East 15th St. (on Stuyvesant Square). 1861, Charles T. Bunting. ☎ 673-5750

Architect (and Friend) Charles Bunting translated the simple dignity of Friends' worship and the quiet dignity of their apparel into a red brick building so austere that it could be "modern architecture." Many features are reminiscent of the Greek classicism popular twenty years earlier. A panel with the building's date can be seen on the front gable below a lunette window. The granite block for mounting a horse and the hitching post at the southeast corner of the building once stood before the home of Friend William Penn in Philadelphia. Penn had founded Philadelphia ("place of brotherly love") as a refuge for Quakers.

The yearly meeting of Friends from throughout the tristate region was held in this building from its construction until the 1940s, when the fire

The Friends Meeting House on Rutherford Place

department protested against so many people staying in the building during the session. Today's congregation includes members of a variety of ethnic and national backgrounds, and nearly all have joined as adults, rather
than having been brought up as Friends.

AROUND THE CORNER
➡ Some of the English elms across Rutherford Place on **Stuyvesant
Square** (between Rutherford Place and Perlman Place from 15th to
17th Sts.) are thought to be as much as 200 years old. Rutherford
Place is named for Colonel John Rutherford, who served on the committee
that laid out Manhattan's street grid beginning in 1807.
➡ The modern concrete, mosaic, and stained-glass church on the south
side of Stuyvesant Square is **St. Mary's Catholic Church of the Byzantine
Rite** (246 East 15th St. at Second Ave. 1963, Brother Cajetan J. B. Bau-
mann, O.F.M. ☎ 677-0516). The Byzantine-Jacobite, or Ruthenian, rite
uses the Old Slavonic liturgy.

THE BROTHERHOOD SYNAGOGUE
Conservative. 28 Gramercy Park South. 1859, Gamaliel King & John Kellum. Remodeled as a synagogue 1975, James Stewart Polshek & Partners.
☎ 674-5750
　The Orthodox Friends commissioned the prominent firm of King and
Kellum to build their austere but carefully-detailed Italianate meeting
house. The side walls are plain brick, but the handsome pedimented façade
features sandstone from Ohio. This building was a refuge for slaves fleeing
north along the Underground Railway, and later a service for distressed
travelers established by this congregation led to the formation of the Travelers' Aid Society in 1905. After the two groups of Friends reconciled, this
building eventually came to house a Conservative Jewish congregation.
　The Garden of Remembrance, dedicated in 1982, on its eastern
side, a serene courtyard planted with honey locust trees, commemorates the deceased members of the congregation and the Jews who perished
in the Holocaust.

AROUND THE CORNER
➡ **Gramercy Park** (LMD), at the foot of Lexington Avenue between 20th
and 21st Streets, was laid out by property developer Samuel Ruggles in
1831. It is to this day a private park. You may admire it, but you cannot
enter it unless you have a key, and keys are available only to residents of
buildings facing the park.

A Masterpiece Rises from Ashes
CHURCH OF THE EPIPHANY
Roman Catholic. 373 Second Ave. at 22nd St. 1967, Belfatto & Pavarini.
☎ 475-1966

Matthew 2:1–12 records that a star announced to certain Oriental Magi (Latin for "wise men") the birth of a king in Judea. Guided by the star, they discovered the infant in a house in Bethlehem, worshiped him, and presented him with gifts. Matthew does not say how many magi there were, nor give their names. The Roman theologian Tertullian (160–230 C.E.) first spoke of them as kings, referring to Old Testament prophecies such as Isaiah 60:3 ("And the Gentiles shall come to thy light, and kings to the brightness of thy rising"), and the Christian philosopher and scholar Origen (185–254 C.E.) set the number at three. In the eleventh century a tradition arose of naming them Caspar, Melchior, and Balthasar. The day of the Magi's visit has traditionally been celebrated as *Epiphany*, or "appearance," referring to the manifestation of God in Christ, and closing Christmas observances on January 6.

A stained-glass window over the entrance to the Church of the Epiphany shows the Adoration of the Magi, and, in it, a realistic portrayal of the Madonna and Child contrasts sharply to the modern style in which the Magi are portrayed. This disparity seems deliberate, as if to set off the Holy Family, but in fact the Madonna and Child are fragments of an Epiphany window by Mayer of Munich that stood behind the high altar at an earlier Church of the Epiphany on this site. That grand 1870 Romanesque Revival church, designed by Napoleon LeBrun, was destroyed by fire on the night of December 20, 1963. For awhile, services were held in the auditorium of the Metropolitan Life Insurance Company a few blocks away, but this new church was dedicated in 1967. The purplish-brown brick building has been called "The most positive modern religious statement on Manhattan Island." It is free and expressionistic, with a high open tower that seems to thrust a tall cross heavenward. The corner of the site offers a courtyard with plantings and seating.

East 24th Street to East 42nd Street

Restoring a Masterpiece
OUR LADY OF THE SCAPULAR
AND SAINT STEPHEN

Roman Catholic. 149 East 28th St., between Lexington and Third Aves. 1854, James Renwick, Jr. Extended to the north 1866. ☎ 683-1675

Stephen (d. 34 C.E.) was the first known martyr for Christ. Acts 6:8 tells that he was a man "full of faith and power, [who] did great wonders and miracles among the people." He was denounced as a blasphemer and stoned to death as Saul (not yet converted) stood by and approved.

In 1853, the same year that James Renwick, Jr., became involved in the planning of the new St. Patrick's Cathedral (see p. 151), he contracted to design this church, the second home of St. Stephen's parish. Whereas St. Patrick's is Gothic-style, St. Stephen's is brownstone and brick Romanesque Revival. St. Stephen's was enlarged in 1866, but that may have been part of the original plan—intended as soon as the church was able to buy the property behind it.

The decoration of the enlarged St. Stephen's was entrusted to Constantino Brumidi (1805–80), who has been called "the last great master of the Italian Baroque tradition." Brumidi had begun his career painting for

Our Lady of the Scapular and St. Stephen

rich patrons—including the Vatican—in his native Italy, but he became involved in obscure revolutionary activities and was given the choice of jail or exile. In 1852 he sailed for the United States.

In America he found work at St. Stephen's and, simultaneously, at the United States Capitol in Washington. In the Capitol, Brumidi painted parts of the House of Representatives chamber, many committee rooms, and scenes along several corridors. The Capitol dome holds his huge fresco, "The Apotheosis of George Washington," which shows Washington entering heaven in the company of other famous Americans (including Benjamin Franklin, Samuel F. B. Morse, and Robert Fulton) escorted by the gods of classical mythology. Brumidi designed the frieze in the Capitol rotunda and painted about one-third of it, but the work was not completed until 1954.

Brumidi's grand conception for the interior of St. Stephen's is a rare surviving example of his work in churches. Behind the altar, he mounted a twenty-two-by-forty-four-foot painting of the crucifixion. Scholars are uncertain why Brumidi placed Mary Magdalene at the foot of the cross right in the center of the composition. This is unusually prominent, considering that only the Book of John mentions her presence at the crucifixion. Brumidi placed Mary Magdalene equally prominently in his only other work in New York (a fresco crucifixion scene behind the altar at P. C. Keely's 1870 **Church of the Holy Innocents** at 128 West 37th St.).

Brumidi lined the walls of St. Stephen's with murals of the Sacred Heart, the Immaculate Conception, and saints, and he adorned the choir lofts with arcades of saints—a total of about forty-five separate scenes. Furthermore, he may have covered the interior with trompe l'oeil ("fool the eye" illusionistic painting) of pillars and other monumental architectural details, but these were all covered with paint and stucco long ago. Today St. Stephen's is beginning to restore these interior decorative finishes. It has been hypothesized that Brumidi even designed the 100 figural stained-glass windows by Mayer of Munich that line the nave, as well as the two rose windows in each arm of the transept. Brumidi's assistant Fillipo Costaggnini probably designed the stations of the cross.

The Church of Our Lady of the Scapular, which formerly stood a few blocks away, merged with St. Stephen's parish in 1990, and the former was demolished. A scapular is a short sleeveless garment worn by members of certain religious orders. The pastor at that church had triggered a scandal in 1911, when the parish sold chances on a Flanders automobile. Anthony Comstock, the president of the Society for the Suppression of Vice, raided the church and halted the raffle.

"The Little Church around the Corner"

THE CHURCH OF THE TRANSFIGURATION (LM)

Episcopal. 1 East 29th St., between Fifth and Madison Aves. 1849, but with additions through decades by leading architects, including F. C. Withers, Henry Vaughan, Ralph A. Cram, and Richard Upjohn. ☎ 684-6770. A guidebook is available in the office.

This famous church is actually a rambling collection of picturesque structures built around a quiet garden. It received its nickname in 1870, when the pastor of a fashionable church nearby declined to officiate at the funeral of actor George Holland because theater people were considered disreputable. The pas-tor suggested to Hol-land's friend Joseph Jefferson (the leading comic actor of the day) that "the little church around the corner" might hold the servic-es. Jefferson replied, "God bless that little church around the cor-ner." At Holland's funeral, newspapers re-ported, "many a well-known comedian . . . sat silent and dejected in the gloom." Rever-end George Houghton officiated.

The Church of the Transfiguration

Transfiguration has enjoyed a reputation as a church for those in the performing arts ever since. The funerals of playwright Dion Boucicault, author O. Henry (William S. Porter), and actor Edwin Booth (who retired after his brother assassinated President Lincoln) were all held at Transfigu-ration, and Sir Henry Irving, Dame Ellen Terry, Tallulah Bankhead, Sarah Bernhardt, and Sir Rex Harrison attended services when in New York.

Visitors enter the garden through a lich-gate, a small structure with a green copper roof. Unusual in an urban setting, lich-gates were used in suburban America as a resting place for coffins before burial. This one was donated by Mrs. Franklin Delano, FDR's great-aunt. A path leads to the church's main entrance in the central tower. The exterior reveals

Transfiguration's several snug spaces. The arched windows to the left open into two chapels and the baptistery. The long roofline to the right covers the nave. A transept ending in a small apse extends south from the nave (back toward the street). The angle where the nave and the transept meet incorporates an octagonal tower, the base of which is another chapel. This multiplicity of nooks and crannies, with generally low ceilings, produces a sense of intimacy.

The ornate brick and brownstone Gothic Revival rectory to the west harbored fugitive slaves in the 1850s. Several blacks took refuge here during New York's 1863 draft riots while a mob howled for their lives. Reverend Houghton advanced on the mob resolutely hefting the church's processional cross and demanding, "Stand back, you white devils; in the name of Christ, stand back." For forty years after that incident, a black couple, George and Elizabeth Wilson (he a former slave and she a freewoman) worked at Transfiguration, and they are memorialized by a window at the end of the south transept.

In 1880 Transfiguration built a small chapel in what was then countryside up at 120 West 69th Street, between Columbus Avenue and Broadway (architect William H. Day) but sold it in 1897. It is today's **Christ and Saint Stephen's Episcopal Church**, a charming little building set behind a broad green lawn and overshadowed by apartment buildings.

➦ AROUND THE CORNER

The tiny **Pinkerton Garden** at Second Avenue at 29th Street is a vest-pocket park designed to trigger interest in the environment.

➦ **The Interfaith Center of New York** (40 East 30th St., between Fifth and Madison Aves; ☎ 685-4242) works to apply the spirituality and wisdom of all of the world's religious traditions to our daily lives and to conflicts in local communities and among nations. Interfaith programs offer educational materials; international exchange; training in conflict resolution and mediation; spiritual and cultural events; information and networking services; liaison with the United Nations and New York agencies; and an art gallery, a gift shop, and tourist information.

The First Christian Nation
SAINT VARTAN CATHEDRAL OF THE ARMENIAN ORTHODOX CHURCH IN AMERICA
Second Ave. at East 34th St. 1968, Walker O. Cain. ☎ 686-0710

Each Easter Sunday, a dozen doves are released on the plaza in front of the Armenian Cathedral, symbolizing Christ's sending his apostles out into the world. It is believed that two of those "doves," the apostles Thad-deus (also called Jude) and Bartholomew, brought Christianity to Arme-nia. Christianity became the state religion in Armenia in 301 C.E., when St. Gregory the Enlightener saw Jesus in a vision descend to Earth. At that site was erected the Cathedral of Holy Etchmiadzin, which means "where the only-begotten descended." Thus, Armenia is recognized as the world's first Christian nation, and Etchmiadzin is today the seat of the present supreme patriarch, Karekin II, enthroned in November 1999, 132nd in the line from Gregory.

New York's first celebration of the Armenian Liturgy occurred at Grace Episcopal Church in 1889. The United States got its own Armenian diocese and bishop in 1898, first seated in Worcester, Massachusetts, but moved to New York in 1927. In 1933 the church suffered a schism, partly because Etchmiadzin was then under Soviet control, but partly due to internal Armenian struggles. On Christmas Eve, 1933, the primate was assassinated while in procession at **Holy Cross Church** (580 West 187th St.). (**St. Illuminator's Cathedral of the Armenian Orthodox Church** at 221 West 27th St. today represents one of the splinter groups.)

St. Vartan's Cathedral is set back from and elevated above the sur-rounding streets on a plaza that is embellished only by a monumental 1968 bronze sculpture, *The Descent from the Cross*, by Reuben Nakian. The cathedral is an imposing and dignified limestone-faced building with a conical top on a high dome, reflecting traditional Armenian church archi-tecture. Its corners are marked by curious dovetailing in the form of crosses. High above the door on the façade, Vartan the Brave, a fifth-century warrior prince, receives the blessing of the religious leader Catholicos Hovsep before battle with the Persians, who threatened Arme-nia's Christian culture and independence. Both men in fact lost their lives in an historic struggle.

Armenians have their own alphabet (created early in the fifth century C.E. by St. Mesrob, who is venerated at a side altar), and in the center of the dome one Armenian letter signifies "He Who is," which is what God answered when Moses asked his name (Exodus 3:14). Eight stained-glass windows around the dome depict the creation (the artist mercifully divid-ed the work of the first day into two). Small traditional crosses are embed-ded in the walls—never crucifixes, because Armenians lay emphasis on the cross as a symbol of the resurrection. The altar itself sits on a high platform called a *bema* (just as in a synagogue), and a chancel before the *bema* holds chairs for clergy. In an Orthodox church the iconostasis always conceals the altar, but in an Armenian church a curtain opens and closes across the *bema* to reveal or to conceal the altar at different times during services. A fragment of reserved Blessed Sacrament in a monstrance always sits on the altar.

Gandhi's and Nelson Mandela's Church in New York
THE COMMUNITY CHURCH

Unitarian. 40 East 35th St., between Park and Madison Aves. 1948, Maurice Salo. ☎ 683-4988

Mohandas Gandhi, whose statue stands in Union Square Park (see p. 134), had few personal possessions, but one he treasured was a small plaque from the Community Church of New York honoring him for his work. It was sent to him in 1932, and it is today displayed with Gandhi's spectacles and sandals in the Gandhi Museum in Delhi, India. The Community Church, founded in 1825 as the Second Congregational Unitarian Society, has always been dedicated to human freedom and civil rights. Its Pastor John H. Holmes (served 1907–49) was a founder of both the American Civil Liberties Union and the National Association for the Advancement of Colored People. Member Mary White Ovington was the unpaid executive secretary of the NAACP for its first fifteen years, and eventually her ashes were placed in the altar of the church's chapel. Community's first black member was designated head usher in 1915 and stood at the door to signal that this was an integrated church, and back then there weren't many in New York (or in all of America). Community members later led the fight for African UN delegates to enjoy access to Manhattan restaurants and hotels. Community Church continues to honor its historic commitments. It housed the American offices of South Africa's African National Congress, and when Nelson Mandela made his first visit to New York City in 1990, shortly after his release from prison but before being elected President of South Africa, he stopped for a private visit to Community Church.

Isaiah beats swords into plowshares on the façade of the red brick modernist building (Isaiah 2:4). The interior is a simply articulated preaching space.

AROUND THE CORNER

➡ Just down the street stands the **New Swedenborgian Church** (112 East 35th St. 1859, James Hoe. ☎ 685-8967). Swedenborgianism is based on the teachings of Emmanuel Swedenborg (1688–1772), a Swedish scientist, philosopher, and mystic. Swedenborgians believe that people are essentially spirits clothed with material bodies, and that religion touches all areas of our lives. New York's first society organized in 1816, and early members included Henry James, Sr., author Richard Dana, and painter George Inness. This whitewashed Italian Renaissance-style building, almost hidden on a leafy plot, is the only Swedenborgian church in New York City today.

Treasures Within
CHURCH OF THE INCARNATION (LM)
Episcopal. 205 Madison Ave. at 35th St. 1865, Emlen T. Littell. Rebuilt after an 1882 fire by D. & J. Jardine. ☎ 689-6350. Pamphlets are available in the narthex.

The Church of the Incarnation opened as a chapel of Grace Church in 1850, but it became an independent parish in 1852. Its Gothic Revival exterior guards an extraordinary collection of ecclesiastical art.

The chancel painting of the Adoration of the Magi is by John LaFarge, and sculptor Daniel Chester French designed the massive oak communion railing. Martin Luther, John Knox, John Bunyan, and Florence Nightingale (in her nurse's cap) can be identified in the north clerestory windows above the altar. Louis Saint-Gaudens (brother of Augustus) designed the baptismal font, a bronze figure of John the Baptist standing in a shallow bowl of Sienna marble. The Civil War hero Admiral David Farragut (who

The Chapel of the Resurrection in the Church of the Incarnation

commanded at the 1864 Battle of Mobile Bay, "Damn the torpedoes! Full speed ahead!") was a parishioner here, and he is memorialized by a marble-relief portrait in a medallion resting on the sculpted prow of a battleship. Also on the north wall is a memorial to Henry Eglington Montgomery, the second rector of this church. It was designed by Henry Hobson Richardson, the distinguished Boston architect (see page 60). This is the only monument in New York known to have been designed by Richardson. On the south wall, the memorial to onetime rector Arthur Brooks was designed by Henry Bacon and includes a bronze portrait bust by Daniel Chester French. These two artists later collaborated to create the Lincoln Memorial in Washington, D.C. Incarnation's south wall also carries a Tiffany marble, onyx, and glass memorial to Arthur Brooks's brother Phillips Brooks, an Episcopal bishop of Massachusetts who wrote the words to "O Little Town of Bethlehem."

The stained-glass windows constitute a catalogue of some of the best glassmaking in England and the United States in the 1880s. They include the work of Tiffany, LaFarge, Holiday, Clayton & Bell, William Morris, C. E. Kempe, and others. Windows by Edward Burne-Jones are especially rare in the United States, and his *Virgin Mary and Dorcas* (representing Faith and Charity) at Incarnation (the easternmost window on the north wall of the nave) illustrate why critic Quentin Bell said Burne-Jones portrayed "a world without tears or laughter, a world in which no violent emotions exist, in which every one is quietly and decently sad."

Look for the pew marked "Delano," where Franklin Delano Roosevelt sat at his mother's funeral.

Manuscripts and Precious Books
THE MORGAN LIBRARY (LM)
On the northeast corner of 36th St. and Madison Ave. ☎ 685-0008

The Morgan Library, begun as banker J. P. Morgan's personal collection, contains one of the world's largest stores of medieval illuminated manuscripts; two Gutenberg Bibles; tiny portraits of Martin Luther and his wife Katharina von Bora, painted from life by Lucas Cranach; and much else of spiritual interest (unfortunately not all of it regularly on display). A medieval gold triptych made in Stavelot, Belgium, is decorated with enamel scenes of the finding of the true cross and of the conversion of the Emperor Constantine to Christianity. The triptych contains what some people believe to be both a piece of the true cross and one of the nails used in Jesus' crucifixion. Morgan's original private library building faces East

36th Street (33 East 36th St., 1906, McKim, Mead & White); the later building on the corner of 36th and Madison was built as a public museum (1928, B. J. Morris), and the 1853 brownstone mansion on the southeast corner of 37th and Madison was from 1904 to 1943 the home of J. P. Morgan, Jr. All three buildings are today connected internally.

 The covered courtyard between the two buildings along Madison Avenue offers seating and sandwiches in a relaxing atmosphere.

East 43rd Street to East 59th Street

THE UNITED NATIONS AREA

The eighteen acres of the **United Nations** (First Ave. at 46th St., ☎ 963-7713) are not part of New York City, or even of the United States, but belong to the member nations as international territory. The UN attracts over a million visitors annually, who tour its buildings and learn about its workings. The complex includes the tall slab of the Secretariat building, with offices for the administration; a low horizontal building for conferences; and the domed General Assembly building.

The Dag Hammarskjöld Memorial Chapel, with stained-glass windows by artist Marc Chagall, can be found against the west wall of the Visitors' Lobby. Hammarskjöld, a Swedish statesman, greatly expanded the UN's role in world peacekeeping during his tenure as secretary-general from 1953 to 1961. He died in an airplane crash in today's Zambia while trying to negotiate peace in the Congo, and he was awarded the Nobel Peace Prize posthumously in 1961.

 The UN complex includes extensive public gardens set with works of sculpture given by member governments.

There are several sacred spaces and peaceful places in the immediate area. **The Church Center for the United Nations** (44th St. at First Ave. 1962, William Lascaze. ☎ 661-1762) is a modernist nondenominational church featuring a stained-glass sculptured wall, *Man's Struggle for Peace and Brotherhood*, by Henry Willet.

Holy Family Roman Catholic Church (315 East 47th St. 1965, George J. Sole. ☎ 753-3401) is dominated by a tall gray granite and aluminum bell tower. Pope Paul VI conducted an interreligious meeting at Holy Family on October 4, 1965, marking the first occasion that a reigning Roman pontiff visited a parish church in North America. The church

St. Mary's Garden

treasures a gold, ivory, and stone chalice that was used at the papal mass at Yankee Stadium later that day. The contemporary windows are by Rambusch Studio.

St. Mary's Garden, to the west of the church on East 47th Street, provides a tranquil retreat, with a small "waterfall," a bridge over a pond, and plantings.

To the east of the church, the Japan Society (333 East 47th St. 1971, Junzo Yoshimura and Gruzen & Partners. ☎ 832-1155) offers a tranquil landscaped interior garden and changing exhibitions about Japanese art and life.

On the south side of 47th Street, the entire length of the block is set aside as Dag Hammarskjöld Plaza. This is often the site of ethnic/political/or religious demonstrations directed to the attention of UN members.

The gardens in Tudor City (LMD), an apartment complex between 41st and 43rd Streets constructed along high abutments above First Avenue in the 1920s, offer a restful oasis. The buildings all face inward toward the gardens because when this gracious complex was built, it was surrounded by slaughterhouses and other industrial activities.

The United Presbyterian Church of the Covenant (LMD, 310 East 42nd St. 1871, J. C. Cady. ☎ 697-3185) ended up a full story above street level when 42nd Street was regraded for the construction of Tudor City. A staircase had to be built reaching up to the church entrance. The church has an intimate interior, with fine stained-glass windows and delicately carved wood.

The **Ford Foundation** (LM), which supports humanitarian efforts around the globe, allows public access to the "forested" atrium lobby of its New York headquarters. (321 East 42nd St., between First and Second Aves. 1967, Kevin Roche, John Dinkeloo & Associates.)

The Irish Are Here
SAINT PATRICK'S CATHEDRAL (LM)
Roman Catholic. East side of Fifth Ave., between 50th and 51st Sts. 1879, James Renwick, Jr., and William Rodrigue. Archbishop's residence (452 Madison) and rectory (460 Madison), 1880, both James Renwick, Jr.; Lady Chapel, 1906 by Charles T. Mathews. ☎ 753-2261. Guidebooks are available in the shop.

This site was miles out of town when St. Peter's Catholic Church bought it in 1828 for a burial ground, and even in 1853, when Archbishop John Hughes boldly envisioned it as suitable for a new cathedral, the city had hardly reached 42nd Street. By the time the cathedral was dedicated in 1879, however, New York's most exclusive residential district had grown up around it. Today St. Patrick's still defines, for many people, the center of New York City.

Archbishop Hughes chose the architect and style specifically to proclaim that the Roman Catholics—the Irish in particular—had "arrived." Hughes had himself arrived from Ireland at the age of twenty in 1817, and when ground was broken in 1853 for the new St. Patrick's, half of the 814,000 people of New York City (then only Manhattan) were foreign-born, and half of the foreign-born were Irish. James Renwick, Jr., developed the design together with the archbishop's own brother-in-law, William Rodrigue. During construction, Archbishop Hughes lived with his in-laws nearby on Lexington Avenue, and he frequently visited the construction site, reportedly incurring his loving sister's wrath by tromping through mud and clambering up on high scaffolding with no concern for his own health or safety. Hughes can be seen discussing the cathedral plans with Renwick in a small window designed and donated by Renwick on the west wall of the south transept. Archbishop Hughes died in 1864, so he did not live to see his cathedral dedicated. His successor, however, Archbishop McCloskey, had Hughes's coat of arms, rather than his own, set over the main door.

St. Patrick's design is based on that of the Cathedral of Cologne, Germany. That cathedral was begun in 1248, but its towers weren't actually completed until 1880. St. Patrick's towers were finished in 1888, rising 330 feet from square bases to octagonal lanterns to traceried spires. The twin-towered façade differentiated it from New York's single-towered Protestant Gothic Revival churches. A steep gable between the towers holds a rose window twenty-six feet in diameter. The building has exterior buttresses, but it doesn't really need them because an iron framework supports the walls. The eastern end of the roof sprouts a lacy flèche.

The three-foot-high figures on the bronze doors represent, from top to bottom, on the left, St. Joseph; St. Isaac Jogues, the first Catholic priest in New York; the Blessed Kateri Tekakwitha, called the "Lily of the Mohawks" ; at top right St. Patrick (see p. 116); St. Frances Cabrini (see p. 295); and St. Elizabeth Ann Seton (see p. 81).

The cathedral's plan is cruciform, with the altar toward the east. Clustered white marble piers divide the huge interior (306 feet long and 48 feet wide) into a central aisle and two high side aisles. The piers' ornamented capitals and the elaborate vaulting draw your eye to the ceiling 108 feet above, decorated with (plaster) ribs with foliated bosses (knobs carved like flowers) at the intersections. Both sides of the nave are lined with shallow aisle chapels dedicated to various saints. The second chapel in the north aisle, dedicated to Saints Bernard and Bridget, provides a hint of Ireland. Its doorway, flanked by clustered green columns, is a replica of one in a twelfth-century chapel in County Louth, Ireland.

The high altar and bronze baldachin (rising fifty-seven feet) provide a focal point for the sanctuary. The archbishop's throne (*cathedra*, in Latin) is on the north side of the altar; St. Patrick stands on the column in front of it, appropriately holding a shamrock. The pulpit is on the south side. The stations of the cross around the walls of the transept won first prize for religious art at the Chicago World's Fair of 1893. Many visitors recognize the marble *Pietà* in the south aisle of the ambulatory; William Ordway Partridge based it on Michelangelo's *Pietà* in the Vatican. From the crossing you can get a good view back to the rose window in the west façade and the organ in the loft beneath it. The Lady Chapel behind the altar was added in 1906; its Vermont marble gleams more brightly than does the granite of the rest of the cathedral. The chapel's windows tell of the fifteen mysteries of the rosary; in one of them, a Bolshevik revolutionary topples a cross from the roof of a church. Directly opposite the Lady Chapel is the entrance to the crypt, where lie Archbishop Hughes, the cardinals of New

FULTON J. SHEEN

Fulton J. Sheen (1895–1979) was born in Illinois, studied in the United States and abroad, and was ordained a priest in 1919. He quickly won fame as a charismatic speaker, and in 1930 he started broadcasting a Sunday evening *Radio Catholic Hour*, the success of which was followed by the even more successful television show, *Life Is Worth Living* from 1952 to 1957. The weekly program of spiritual advice won an Emmy, and its rating even topped that of comedian Milton Berle (who quipped, "At least I'm losing my ratings to God.") From Sheen's opening greeting to his parting words ("Bye now, and God love you!") viewers were treated as his intimate friends. He synthesized mainstream Protestantism with a reassuring vision of Catholicism as patriotic and traditional, presented a clear-cut moral vision, and thus reached a diverse audience and paved the way for religious ecumenism. He rose to a bishopric, and many of his books, and even a six-hour videotape of a retreat with him, remain available. The block of East 43rd Street between Lexington and Third Avenues, in front of **Saint Agnes Church**, his home parish, is today "Fulton J. Sheen Place."

York who succeeded him, several rectors of this church, and Archbishop Fulton J. Sheen. The remains of Pierre Toussaint (see p. 90) were moved to this crypt after he was declared "venerable" by John Paul II in 1983. The cardinals' *galeros* (flat ceremonial red hats with tassels all around—no longer awarded to new cardinals) are suspended from the ceiling of the sanctuary high above the altar.

"Strangers Welcome"
SAINT BARTHOLOMEW'S (LM)
Episcopal. Park Avenue between 50th and 51st Sts. 1923, Bertram Goodhue. ☎ 751-1616. Guidebooks are available in the narthex.

When the rector of St. Bartholomew's feared that his congregation was getting too elitist 100 years ago, he took out newspaper advertisements for its services—among the first placed by any church. He even put a sign out front: "Strangers Welcome." Strangers are still welcome to "St. Bart's," whether they seek a moment of prayer or meditation, or just a casual visit. And it repays a visit, for this splendid church was meant to be "a great gift of beauty to the city," according to its rector when it was built, Dr. Leighton Parks. The New York Central Railroad had just electrified and covered its tracks. With the trains underground, Park Avenue was developing into an elegant boulevard. The congregation had been founded downtown in 1835 and moved up to Madison Avenue at 44th Street in 1876, but as that neighborhood became commercial, the congregation decided to migrate north again. Dr. Parks specified a Romanesque-style building designed for preaching and for good music (see p. 59).

The low flat-roofed structure of white limestone facing Park Avenue is the narthex, and its portal is itself an extraordinary work of art. The portal had been commissioned for the church on Madison Avenue; architect Stanford White modeled it on that of the Romanesque Church of Saint Gilles in Gard, Provence, France. The congregation insisted that it be disassembled and reinstalled as part of the new church, but here architect Bertram Goodhue put it on a projecting narthex. A screen of marble columns and a sculptural frieze of biblical scenes (very Rodin-esque) unify its three doorways. Each doorway has a tympanum, a panel below that, and a pair of bronze doors with six panels. The center door was designed by Andrew O'Connor and Daniel Chester French; the north portal by Herbert Adams; and the south portal by Philip Martiny.

High on the façade, figures of four famous preachers—Martin Luther, Paul, Francis of Assisi, and Phillips Brooks (see p. 148)—stand to signal this church's dedication to preaching. The knives at the very top of the gable indicate the method by which, legend has it, Bartholomew suffered martyrdom; he was flayed. Bartholomew was one of the twelve apostles, but nothing else is known of him. His church here is cruciform, and the crossing is covered with an octagonal dome with mosaics on the exterior and topped with a golden cross. The architect's original scheme proposed a tower resembling a huge rocket ship that would have doubled the height of the church.

The narthex is rich and mysterious. Marble columns standing inside marble walls support a five-domed ceiling on which golden mosaics by Hildredth Meière illustrate the story of the creation, illuminated by standing torchères. Many of the features of St. Bartholomew's, including the interior of the narthex, are modeled after the eleventh-century Basilica of San Marco in Venice, a masterpiece of the Byzantine style. Stepping into St. Bartholomew's itself, one's immediate impression is of simple volumes and surfaces lustrous with marble, tile, or mosaic. The space is well designed for music. Conductor Leopold Stokowski first came from Europe to direct the choir here, and St. Bartholomew's pipe organ is the largest in

St. Bartholomew's Church

New York City, with eleven divisions distributed around the church, including one in the dome. Sculptor Lee Lawrie created the elaborately carved marble altar, lectern, pulpit, and communion rail. Neither Goodhue nor Reverend Parks wanted St. Bartholomew's to have stained-glass windows (they're not appropriate to this architectural style), but outstanding examples have been installed through the decades. The twenty-four-foot wheel window in the south transept, for example, should be of one uniform tint, as it is in San Marco, lending a soft golden glow to the interior of the church. St. Bartholomew's congregation, however, demanded more color, so the window was filled with multicolored stained glass.

🍃 The Memorial Garden at the southwest corner of the church's property, designed by William Hamby in 1968, offers a pleasant place to sit among two small fountains, a course of water running through geometric channels, modernist curved seats, and gingko trees. Lunch and dinner are served here in pleasant weather.

Behind St. Bartholomew's on Lexington Avenue, the 570-foot General Electric Tower was specifically intended by its architects to resemble a campanile (a freestanding bell tower) for the church (originally the RCA Building, 1931, Cross & Cross). It features matching salmon brick, chamfering, and an open tracery crown.

Greenacre Park

AROUND THE CORNER

➡ To the east of St. Bartholomew's, **Greenacre Park** on 51st Street between Second and Third Avenues (1971, Hideo Sasaki) is one of the city's finest "vest-pocket parks." Its rock walls, stream that feeds a waterfall, magnolia trees, and banked woodland plantings bring nature into the city.

Universal Brotherhood
THE NEW YORK THEOSOPHICAL SOCIETY
240–242 East 53rd St., between Second and Third Aves. ☎ 753-3835

The Theosophical Society was organized in 1875 by Helena Blavatsky, a Russian-born naturalized American citizen, and Colonel Henry Olcott, a prominent Civil War veteran, lawyer, and journalist. Madame Blavatsky, as she was known, had traveled widely in search of spiritual knowledge, and she introduced many spiritual traditions of the East to the West. In 1879 she and Colonel Olcott moved to India and established an international headquarters in Adyar, a suburb of Madras (today's Chennai), where it remains. Today the Society has branches in sixty countries. U.S. headquarters are in Wheaton, Illinois, and about 120 branches and study centers can be found around the country.

The Society's goals are "to form a nucleus of the universal brotherhood of humanity, . . . to encourage the comparative study of religion, philosophy and science," and ". . . to investigate unexplained laws of nature and the powers latent in humanity." The Society sponsors classes and lectures in New York, as well as a bookshop (The Quest Bookshop next door) that offers texts on topics ranging from astrology to Zoroastrianism.

Home of Sacred Jazz
SAINT PETER'S
Lutheran. Lexington Ave. at 54th St. 1977; Hugh Stubbins & Associates. ☎ 935-2200

Several New York congregations demolished their freestanding churches and built office or residential towers with new sanctuaries tucked inside, but St. Peter's congregation, founded in 1862 and on this site since 1904, sold Citicorp its property on the condition that Citicorp would build them a new freestanding church. Thus we have a modern church in the form of a rock ("Thou art Peter, and upon this rock I will build my church" [Matthew 16:18.]) sitting on a plaza at the base of a fifty-nine-story aluminum-encased building rising above the church on colossal ten-story-high supports. The church, faced with granite, is set at a forty-five-degree angle to the street to emphasize its independence, and doors open onto both Lexington Avenue and 54th Street, as well as into the bank center. The church's only exterior decoration is a cross on Lexington Avenue designed by Italian sculptor Arnaldo Pomodoro.

St. Peter's has a lobby, for in addition to its main sanctuary and chapel, St. Peter's has a 250-seat theater, a music room, and a studio. The main worship space is a spare ivory-painted terraced room, with boxy red oak furniture. The sanctuary is illumined by a skylight that stretches up and over the entire vaulted ceiling, eighty-five feet above the pews, and by vertical strip windows. A tall sixteenth-century Dutch wrought-iron cross stands behind the altar, and the freestanding pipe organ serves as another piece of sculpture. The baptismal font at the entrance provides a constant murmur of running water. The pews are removable, so the interior space flexibly allows for song, dance, sermons, or music performances.

The Erol Beker Chapel of the Good Shepherd, just off the lobby, is reserved exclusively for worship, prayer, and meditation. This all-white room, measuring only twenty-eight feet by twenty-one feet, was created by American sculptor Louise Nevelson. Ms. Nevelson designed the sanctuary lamp, altar fabrics, vestments, and the wall sculptures, which are assemblages of white-painted found wooden objects. "The Chapel," she wrote, "was designed to be universal; it's a symbol of freedom. . . . If people can have some peace while they are there, and carry it with them in their memory bank, that will be a great achievement for me."

St. Peter's is one of the most culturally active congregations in the city, renowned for its use of jazz in a sacred context. Reverend John Garcia Gensel, who served here from 1965 until 1993, was a friend of Duke Ellington, who dedicated to him his composition, "The Shepherd Who Watches Over the Night Flock." The church's grand piano once belonged to Billy Strayhorn, the Duke's collaborator, who composed "Take the A Train." Thelonius Monk's funeral was held here in 1982. Today, the church offers noon jazz concerts through the week, jazz masses, and jazz vespers on Sunday afternoons.

The Ark Stood High
CENTRAL SYNAGOGUE (LM)
Reform. 652 Lexington Ave. at 55th St. 1872, Henry Fernbach. ☎ 736-3100

On August 28, 1998, this historic building suffered a terrible fire. Firefighters had to shoot water through the stained-glass windows, heavily damaging the exquisite interior woodwork and stenciled walls. Eventually the roof collapsed, resulting in additional destruction. In the aftermath, the walls were found to be structurally sound and the wooden ark marred but towering over the ruins. The damaged prayer books were buried at Linden Hill Cemetery in Queens, and the congregation set to work rebuilding its masterpiece home.

This is the oldest building in continuous use as a synagogue by the same congregation in New York State. Congregation Ahawath Chesed ("Lovers of Mercy") was organized on the Lower East Side among Bohemian Jews in 1846 and worshiped in four other locations before moving into this building. That congregation was joined here by Congregation Shaarey Hasomayim ("Gates of Heaven") in 1898, and the combined congregation took the name Central Synagogue in 1920. The cornerstone for this building was laid by Rabbi Isaac Mayer Wise, one of the founders of Reform Judaism in the United States, and his son served here as rabbi.

This building was inspired by the Great Dohany Street Synagogue in Budapest, Hungary, and it is one of the best of New York's Moorish-style synagogues. A projecting central block of the façade boasts an elaborate geometric rose window above three portals. Flanking twin 122-foot towers start as squares but become octagons topped by globes. Light and dark

Central Synagogue

stones alternate in the window arches, and the dark stone surfaces are crisscrossed with light stone bands. When the building opened, the congregation paid for special streetlights on the sidewalk that were reproduced in 1989.

By January 1, 2001, a new roof was in place, framed entirely in beams of Douglas fir up to twenty feet long and twelve inches across (fir actually performs better than steel, which would have buckled under the heat of the fire). Black and red slate was being laid in geometric patterns on the roof, the decorative cresting was being restored to the parapets, and the copper globes on top of the twin towers were being regilded. Inside, they're replacing the elaborate stencilwork, adding new chandeliers in the cusps of the horseshoe arches along the balcony and sconces under the balcony.

Korean Schools of Buddhism
MANHATTAN WON BUDDHISM CENTER
431 East 57th St. at the East River. Building converted 1995, ☎ 750-2774.

This school of Buddhism, founded in Korea in 1916, focuses on meeting the spiritual needs of the laity. No Buddha images are found here, for it is believed that they distract from the living Buddhas you meet every day and the potential Buddha in yourself. The center offers a complete program, including regular meditation sessions and even Sunday services. Won Buddhism traditionally has a high percentage of women priests.

Those interested in learning about the other Korean schools of Buddhism may visit the **Korean Cultural Service** (460 Park Ave. at 57th St., 6th floor ☎ 759-9550), which offers a multimedia lending library and an art gallery and sponsors lectures, seminars, exhibitions, and performances. **The Korea Society** (950 Third Ave. at 57th St., 8th floor ☎ 759-7525) also offers a range of educational opportunities.

AROUND THE CORNER

➥ Tiny **Sutton Place Park**, overlooking the East River at the eastern end of East 57th Street, provides a quiet outdoor oasis in this neighborhood. Its life-sized wild boar sculpture, *Porcellino*, is a copy of a Florentine original.

CHAPTER FIVE

𝒯he West Side: From Houston Street to West 59th Street

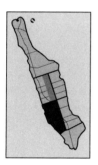

In THE 1790s, the country estates to the north and west of old New York were sold off, subdivided, and developed. Greenwich Village grew up along the Hudson River as weavers, sail makers, and craftspeople moved into modest new homes, and many New Yorkers fled there to escape the recurrent epidemics of smallpox, yellow fever, and cholera that ravaged the city in the 1790s and early 1800s. When a grid was established for Manhattan streets in 1811, Village residents successfully protested the redesign of their maze of existing streets, so it's still easy to get confused there today. In the 1830s, prominent families built town houses on Washington Square, but the fashionable elite soon migrated further north. By the 1850s the Village had become a quiet middle-class backwater. African Americans and Irish and Chinese immigrants moved in at the end of the nineteenth century, and Italians settled in the tenements south of Washington Square. Writers and artists discovered the affordable housing stock, and they firmly established the Village's reputation as America's "Bohemia" by World War I.

The area from 14th to 23rd Streets, known as Chelsea, was developed as a middle-class suburb, but the Hudson River Railroad opened along

Eleventh Avenue in 1851, and for the next hundred years the railroad tracks and the docks along the Hudson determined the character of Manhattan's far West Side: commerce, industry, and working-class housing. West 23rd Street enjoyed a heyday as a theatrical center in the 1880s, a period from which the Chelsea Hotel survives, and the blocks on Sixth Avenue to the south, lined with limestone and cast-iron dry-goods palaces, came to be known as "the Ladies' Mile." This area was in decline by the 1930s, but it has revived, and buildings have been restored to their original elegance.

To the north, the garment center developed early in the twentieth century from 34th to 59th Streets, and Times Square focused on the theatre. Tunnels under the Hudson River from New Jersey and under the East River from Long Island were completed in 1910, bringing trains to McKim, Mead, and White's masterpiece Pennsylvania Station on 33rd Street. This solidified West Midtown as a commercial and industrial hub. The destruction of Penn Station in 1963 triggered the historic preservation movement that eventually saved its East Side companion, Grand Central Terminal (plus sacred spaces and many other buildings throughout the city).

Greenwich Village

Rare Plants and Birds
SAINT LUKE IN THE FIELDS (LM in LMD)
Episcopal. 485 Hudson St., just south of Christopher St. 1822, Clement Clarke Moore and James N. Wells. Restored and expanded after a 1981 fire by Hardy Holzman Pfeiffer Associates. ☎ 924-0562

This church, named for Luke the Evangelist, is one of Manhattan's oldest church buildings and the centerpiece of an early example of site planning. Clement C. Moore helped design the church itself (and served as first pastor to the congregation), but James Wells is generally credited with having designed the entire block bounded by Christopher, Barrow, Greenwich, and Hudson Streets. A burial ground and garden in the middle of the block were shielded from public view by town houses, the vicarage, and a parish house.

The burial ground has vanished from the interior of the block, and the row of thirteen houses on Greenwich Street was demolished in the 1950s to make way for expansion of St. Luke's School (founded 1894),

The garden of St. Luke in the Fields

but much of Wells's plan still survives. Today a two-acre garden of walks and lawns in the interior of the block is open to the public, and, because of the garden's orientation and the heat-retaining qualities of the brick walls, the garden boasts species seldom seen so far north, including pomegranate, rosemary, and figs, plus rare bird and butterfly visitors.

Originally, seven houses stood on each side of the church, but only three remain on each side, dating from 1825–26. They are some of the best examples of federal architecture remaining in the city, and among the few whose builder we know. Number 487, Wells's own house, the widest and finest, was later the childhood home of novelist Bret Harte, author of *Tales of Roaring Camp* and *The Outcasts of Poker Flat*. Today it is the parish office.

St. Luke's congregation was formed in 1820 when the Greenwich Village settlement was isolated from the Manhattanites still clustered at the southern tip of the island. After a disastrous fire in 1886, the original congregation moved uptown and formed a new St. Luke's in Harlem (see p. 272). Trinity parish bought the ruin, reopened it as St. Luke's Chapel in 1892, and reestablished it as an independent parish in 1976.

The church is a simple country church, although it is among the first built of brick rather than rubblestone. Its square tower projects much further forward through the gable than usual, and it lacks a steeple. The finishing detail is severely plain. The new interior design, necessary after a

1981 fire, restored the lost simplicity of the original Federal style. Several scenes from the 1990 movie *Longtime Companion* were filmed in this church.

AROUND THE CORNER
➥ A few blocks to the north, the **New York Center of the Nimatullahi Sufi Order** holds meditation sessions on Thursday and Sunday evenings (306 West 11th St., between Hudson and Greenwich Sts. ☎ 924-7739).

Two Early Italian Catholic Parishes
SAINT ANTHONY OF PADUA
155 Sullivan St. at Houston St. 1888, Arthur Crooks. ☎ 777-2755

The Italian population of New York City increased sharply at the end of the nineteenth century. From 20,000 in 1880, their numbers rose to 220,000 by 1900 and about 550,000 by 1910. Most of these immigrants had been landless peasants fleeing the poverty of southern Italy. Archbishop Hughes created an Italian parish dedicated to St. Anthony of Padua, but he dissolved it when he found its pastor collecting money in the "Irish" parishes without his permission. Hughes's successor, Archbishop John McCloskey, invited Franciscan fathers to organize a new St. Anthony of Padua parish in 1866, so this is New York's oldest Italian national parish. Anthony of Padua (1195–1231) was born in Lisbon, Portugal, and served as a Franciscan missionary in North Africa before ending his life in Italy. His sermons, many of which have survived, remain popular.

Corner lots are the most valuable real estate, and in New York the Catholic Church could seldom afford them. On the day of the public sale of this lot, however, a terrible storm kept away all bidders but one Franciscan priest. He bought the land at a good price, happily insisting that "St. Anthony looks after his own." Aside from the new St. Patrick's, Gothic Revival was rarely used for New York's Roman Catholic churches in the nineteenth century (plus Gothic had never been a popular style in medieval Italy), so architect Crooks gave the Italians a more appropriate Romanesque-style church. Two rows of eight columns separate the long, high central nave, culminating in a marble apse, from the side naves, each of which ends in a semicircular chapel.

St. Anthony's sponsors a feast honoring its patron saint each year in early June, beginning with a procession of the saint's image through the streets, then an outdoor fair in the evenings with rides, carnival games, and street food. (The late-summer street festival of San Gennaro is run by a group affiliated with the **Church of the Most Precious Blood**, another Franciscan church at 113 Baxter St.).

Father Fagan Square around the corner at Sixth Avenue and Prince Street is named for a member of St. Anthony's clergy who died while leading others to safety during a fire at the church's monastery on Thompson Street in 1938.

OUR LADY OF POMPEII

25 Carmine St. at Bleecker St. 1928, Matthew Del Gaudio. ☎ 989-6805

Our Lady of Pompeii (named for a painting above the altar) is just a couple of blocks away from the church of St. Anthony. Many Italians suffered such hardship while migrating to America in the late nineteenth century that Bishop Giovanni Scalabrini founded in Italy in 1887 the St. Raphael Society for the Protection of Italian Immigrants, St. Raphael being the patron saint of travelers. Archbishop Corrigan of New York wrote to Italy asking for missionaries to found a St. Raphael Society here, and these men ("Scalabrinians") founded the parish of Our Lady of Pompeii in 1892. Frances Cabrini (see p. 295) worshiped in this parish's first church building.

The current church, the parish's second home, is a grand classical building, albeit finished with stone only on the façade and part of the Bleecker Street side, where the rest is yellow brick. Its single high tower (double arcades topped by a circle of columns topped by a dome surmounted by a cross) emphatically marks the corner. Charles Borromeo (1538–84), patron saint of the Scalabrinians, stands high on the façade. He was made a cardinal by his uncle, Pope Pius IV, at the age of twenty two. He eventually played an important role in the Council of Trent, which reformed the Catholic Church, and in 1563 he was named bishop of Milan. He established Sunday schools and seminaries, and he was said to have set a personal example of virtuous living.

A stained-glass window installed in the west wall of Our Lady of Pompeii in the 1930s illustrates the beatitude "Blessed be the Peacemakers" (Matthew 5:9). It praises the freedom the Catholic Church enjoys in the United States. When this window was installed, Catholicism felt threatened by fascism in Europe and South America. In the stained-glass window honoring the sacrament of marriage (east wall), the tall priest can be identified as Father Antonio Demo, pastor here from 1899 until 1933.

The square across from the church at the intersection of Carmine and Bleecker Streets and Sixth Avenue was named **Father Demo Square** in 1941 by Mayor Fiorello La Guardia.

AROUND THE CORNER

➥ **James J. Walker Park,** a couple of blocks south (between Hudson St. and Seventh Ave. South, St. Luke's Place and Clarkson St.), was the burying ground of St. John's Chapel (torn down in 1918) from 1801 until it was taken over as a public park in 1896. No documents record how many people were buried there, but few were disinterred and moved, and the space is paved today.

America's First Lutheran Seminary
SAINT JOHN'S EVANGELICAL LUTHERAN CHURCH (LM in LMD)
81 Christopher St., between Seventh Ave. and Bleecker St. 1821, original architect unknown. Altered 1886, Berg & Clark. ☎ 242-5737

This church was built on the site where the first Lutheran theological seminary classes in the United States began in 1797. Reverend John C. Kunze, pastor of a downtown Lutheran church, held the classes in his country home here. Later, a legacy from pioneer Lutheran pastor Reverend John C. Hartwick funded Hartwick Seminary in upstate New York. When Pastor Kunze died, his country home was sold to the Eighth Presbyterian Church, which replaced his home with this building. The Presbyterians sold the church building to St. Matthew's Episcopal congregation in 1842, and that congregation worshiped here until St. John's Lutheran congregation bought the building in 1858, thus neatly returning the land to the denomination that had owned the property first.

John was a Galilean fisherman when he and his brother James were called from mending their nets to follow Jesus (Mark 1:19). Tradition has always identified John as the unnamed "disciple whom Jesus loved," who leaned on Jesus' chest at the last supper, and to whom Jesus on the cross confided the care of his mother.

This building has been called modified Federal style. Three sets of doors are topped by three arched windows set among fluted pilasters, which extend to the bottom of the pediment. The pediment is surmounted by a small octagonal tower, topped by a dome, topped by a ball and cross. The Romanesque-style first story and the parish house next door to the west reveal changes made in 1886 to keep up with architectural fashion.

AROUND THE CORNER

➥ The bar-restaurant Marie's Crisis (59 Grove St.) is the site of the house where **Thomas Paine** (1737–1809) died. His 1776 pamphlet *Common Sense* convinced many Americans of the need for independence, and *The*

Crisis, written during the war when America's fortunes were at their lowest point ("These are the times that try men's souls . . ."), inspired many to carry on the struggle. He was a deeply spiritual man who believed in God and immortality, but his disagreements with most established religions caused him to be shunned by most church organizations. When a young member of a Presbyterian church choir shook Paine's hand at the end of his life, the boy was reprimanded for it.

➥ The **Northern Dispensary** (165 Waverly Pl., on triangle with Waverly Pl. and Christopher St. 1831, H. Bayard, carpenter. Restored 1997, John Ellis & Associates.) was founded as a public clinic in 1827 and operated until 1989. Edgar Allan Poe was treated here for a cold in 1837.

An Outspoken Priest
SAINT JOSEPH'S (LM in LMD)
Roman Catholic. 371 Sixth Ave. at Waverly Pl. 1834, John Doran. Repaired and altered by Arthur Crooks after fire damage in 1885. ☎ 741- 1274

St. Joseph's parish was founded in 1830, but anti-Catholic prejudice made it difficult to buy a site in the then small suburban village of Greenwich, so this building was not dedicated until 1834. The dedication service was attended by a number of men who would play important roles in American Catholicism. The sermon was preached by Father Constantine Pise, who had been the first Catholic priest to serve as chaplain to the U.S. Senate. The presiding deacon was Father William Quarter, later first bishop of Chicago, and the subdeacon was Father John McCloskey, later America's first cardinal. Father John Hughes (see p. 151), who would later become New York's first archbishop, was also present. The priest here from 1857 to 1880, Father Thomas Farrell, dedicated his efforts to African Americans' struggle for equality. He threatened to return to his native Ireland if the South won the Civil War, and in his will he left $5,000 to found New York's first Catholic church for blacks. To prod the diocese to action, the will stipulated that if the parish weren't founded within three years, the money would go for a Protestant orphan asylum! The stained-glass window of the Sacred Heart in the south wall at St. Joseph's was Father Farrell's gift to this parish.

When the **Church of Saint Benedict the Moor** was founded on Bleecker Street in 1883—barely meeting Father Farrell's deadline—it was the first church for black Catholics north of the Mason-Dixon Line. Benedict (1526–89) was the son of African slaves on an estate in Sicily. He was freed at an early age, and when he was later insulted because of his color, his dignified and patient bearing attracted the attention of a group of Franciscan hermits who asked him to join them as a lay brother. In 1898 Benedict's church moved into a previously Protestant Evangelical church building at 340 West 53rd Street (1869, R. C. McLane & Sons), where its parishioners today are largely Hispanic.

The façade and sides of St. Joseph's Church show two different architectural styles, revealing its construction in a period of transition between styles. The front is Greek Revival: Doric columns *distyle in antis* (see p. 89). The round-headed windows that Arthur Crooks added to the façade are not only stylistically incorrect (Greek-style architecture has rectangular openings) but reveal only the staircases to passersby. The building's side walls, by contrast, reflect the style of earlier Georgian churches. Random courses of rubblestone are pierced by tall round-headed windows. At the corner of the building, the two styles meet, and the Georgian style prevails. There are quoins (Georgian) rather than antae (Greek). Curiously, a classical Greek frieze encircles the building as if to pull it together.

The Missionary Spirit
JUDSON MEMORIAL BAPTIST CHURCH (LM)
51–55 Washington Square South. Church 1893. McKim, Mead & White; tower and hall 1895–96, all same architect, all LM. ☎ 477-0351

The impetus for this church was Reverend Edward Judson's wish to memorialize his father, Reverend Adoniram Judson (1788–1850), the first American Baptist missionary to Asia. Reverend Adoniram Judson had gone to Burma in 1813, compiled an English-Burmese dictionary, and set to work to translate the Bible. *Adoniram* means "my Lord is exalted"; (1 Kings 4:6), and Adoniram Judson's portrait in stained glass can be seen in today's **Central Presbyterian Church** (Park Ave. at 64th St.), which was originally Park Avenue Baptist Church.

Edward Judson's own mission was here—to provide health, nutrition, education, and recreation programs in what was then a poor immigrant neighborhood. The location was chosen between the gentry who still occupied Washington Square and the poor immigrant district to the immediate south. The church's dedication ceremonies reflected the earnestness of the sponsors: They included a seminar on "The Problems of a Great City." "Missionary work" was intended here, too, for Judson hoped to convert the neighborhood's Italian Roman Catholic population. John D. Rockefeller supported young Judson's goals, so he made a generous contribution for the building. Today the congregation maintains its reputation for social activism, and it is affiliated with both the Baptist Church and the United Church of Christ.

The complex included a church, adjacent bell tower, and an apartment house to generate revenue. All are in yellow brick with creamy terra-cotta trim, and the church additionally features inset marble panels framed in terra-cotta. The pale colors created a sensation when the church went up in a city of brownstone. The church has an elaborate entrance between the sanctuary and the 130-foot tower. Half-round steps lead up to a platform over which marble columns support a decorated arched hood.

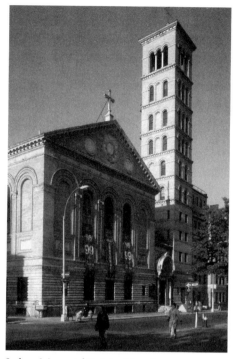

Judson Memorial Baptist Church

Inside, the marble relief of angels was designed by Augustus Saint-Gaudens and carved by Herbert Adams. Freestanding angels guard the pipes on the gilt and gesso organ screen. The windows by John LaFarge are one of this church's treasures. Twelve portray the apostles, each standing fifteen feet high in a round-topped niche framed by pilasters, as sculptures would be in a Renaissance church. LaFarge created five additional windows, including a rose window in the south wall and another for which, it is alleged, his mistress posed as an angel (the round one on the stairwell).

The congregation still occupies the church, but the tower and hall to the west were sold to support church programs, and today both are residences for New York University students. Frank Norris, author of *The Octopus* and *The Pit*, once lived in the tower, and poet Edwin Arlington Robinson lived in Judson Hall in 1906.

AROUND THE CORNER

➥ The park that is today **Washington Square** (LMD) was designated a potter's field in 1797, just in time to receive hundreds of victims of the next year's yellow fever epidemic that took over 2,000 lives— about one in twenty of the city's total population. The square was also the site of public hangings—many of them from the 300-year-old 70-foot-tall English elm in the northwest corner of the park. English elms were among the first nonnative trees planted in North America, and this venerable example, a "Great Tree" (see p. 129), is one of the oldest trees in the city. Washington Square was acquired for a public park in 1823, but hundreds, if not thousands, of people may still lie beneath it. The seventy-seven-foot-high marble Washington Arch, at the foot of Fifth Avenue, was erected in 1892 to the design of Stanford White. It replaced an earlier one up the block of wood and plaster that commemorated the centennial of George Washington's 1789 inauguration. On the north side, two statues show Washington as "First in War" (on the east, 1918 by Herman MacNeil) and "First in Peace" (west side, 1916 by Alexander Stirling Calder).

➥ A block away from Washington Square, at the northwest corner of Washington Place and Greene Street, stands today's **Brown Building**, site of an historic 1911 tragedy. The proprietors of the Triangle Shirtwaist Manufacturing Company on the upper floors habitually locked the exit doors to keep the 500 employees from leaving their sewing machines. At about 4:30 P.M. on March 25, a fire somehow started. One hundred forty-six girls died in less than fifteen minutes, most of them by jumping from the windows. The tragedy inspired the organization of labor unions in the garment industry and the passage of fire protection legislation by the state. A memorial service is held on this corner each anniversary of the fire.

➥ Just across Greene Street, at 21 Washington Place, lived philosopher and theologian **Henry James** (1811–82), and here both of his sons were born: **William James** (1842–1910), philosopher, psychologist, and author of *The Varieties of Religious Experience*, and the novelist **Henry James, Jr.** (1843–1916).

➥ In 1978 the City Parks Department tried to recreate on a small plot on the northeast corner of Houston Street and LaGuardia Place a mix of species typical of seventeenth-century Manhattan Island, the forest "inhabited by Native Americans and encountered by the Dutch settlers." Several of the species originally in this **Time Landscape**, however, have not survived on today's busy street corner.

➥ **Still Mind Zendo** (120 Washington Pl., ☎ 691-2972), located in a private brownstone with a garden in the back, teaches Zen without requiring belief in Buddhist metaphysics.

A Center of Jewish Education
HEBREW UNION COLLEGE/ JEWISH INSTITUTE OF RELIGION
1 West 4th St. 1979, Abramovitz, Harris & Kingsland. ☎ 674-5300

Hebrew Union College, founded in Cincinnati by Rabbi Isaac Mayer Wise in 1875, was the first institution of Jewish higher education in the United States. It was intended to train rabbis for the Reform movement. In 1922 Rabbi Stephen S. Wise founded the Jewish Institute of Religion in New York; in 1950 the two institutions merged on West 68th Street next door to the Stephen Wise Free Synagogue, and later they moved to this new location. This building houses the Petrie Synagogue, with windows, ark, and eternal light by Israeli artist Yaacov Agam, and the Joseph Exhibition Center, which offers changing exhibits focusing on Jewish life and culture.

A Presidential Wedding
CHURCH OF THE ASCENSION (LM in LMD)
Episcopal. 36 Fifth Ave. at 10th St. 1841, Richard Upjohn. ☎ 254-8620. A pamphlet available in the narthex catalogues the stained-glass windows.

The Church of the Ascension was the site of New York's only presidential wedding. The romance began one weekend in 1844, when prominent New Yorker David Gardiner and his daughter Julia were President John Tyler's guests on an excursion aboard the *USS Princeton*. An explosion aboard the ship killed Mr. Gardiner, and just three months later, on June 26, Julia married the President. Tyler, aged fifty-four, was a recent widower with children older than their new twenty-two-year-old stepmother. Julia was a debutante who already at the age of eighteen had appeared in an ad for a department store ("I'll purchase at Bogert & Mecamly's. . . . Their Goods are Beautiful & Astonishingly Cheap. . . ."), one of America's first celebrity product endorsements. Julia reigned for nine months as the White House hostess, launching a tradition by insisting that the band play "Hail to the Chief" whenever her husband entered a room.

Ascension congregation had been organized in 1827, but this church was only three years old in 1844. It had been the first church built on Fifth Avenue, then a dirt road terminating at 23rd Street, and it sat in the

The Church of the Ascension

middle of undeveloped land. Its Gothic Revival design predates Upjohn's Trinity Church. Worshipers enter through a central tower that rises above arched windows to a belfry. The nave itself is high, with a clerestory and side aisles. The rector at the time was a Low Church man, and, wanting no room "for High Church doings," he bought the land behind the church himself and built a house to prevent Upjohn from building a deep chancel (see p. 69). The parish only later bought the house as a rectory. Ascension became known as "the Low Church Cathedral," offering good sermons, good music, and plain decoration. Nothing savoring of ritualism was allowed; even flowers were forbidden until the twentieth century.

In the late 1880s the chancel was remodeled under the direction of Stanford White, and it is a splendid example of American Renaissance decor. The centerpiece is John LaFarge's enormous mural, *The Ascension of Christ into Heaven*. One of its sources is Raphael's *Transfiguration*, now in the Vatican Galleries, but the figures of the apostles are derived from Italian Renaissance painter Palma Vecchio; LaFarge painted the background landscape from sketches he had made while on a visit to Japan; and the overall style echoes the painters Titian and Delacroix. The mural is set in an architectural frame and decorations by Stanford White. Louis Saint-Gaudens created the marble relief just below the mural in which two symmetrically prone angels fly above the altar holding a chalice with the inscription: "This do in remembrance of me." D. Maitland Armstrong created mosaics of kneeling angels and designed the altar, and White's partner Charles McKim designed the pulpit. This decor obviously raised the appearance of the church Higher, but the redesigners still couldn't do anything about the flat shallow chancel.

Some of the stained-glass windows are among the best in New York. John LaFarge's *Nicodemus Coming to Jesus by Night*, the westernmost window on the south side of the nave, is among his finest anywhere.

Ascension was New York's first church to be faced with brownstone, a sandstone that takes its distinctive chocolate color from iron deposits. It soon became so popular for houses (the rectory at 7 West 10th St. was one of the first) that today "brownstone" is synonymous with row house.

From November 9, 1929, until the late 1960s, Ascension stood open for prayer or meditation twenty-four hours a day seven days of the week. The front doors didn't even have a lock, and Ascension was known as "The Church of the Open Door."

AROUND THE CORNER
➡ Eighteen West 10th Street was long the home of **Emma Lazarus** (1849–87). In her sonnet "The New Colossus," the Statue of Liberty lifts her lamp "beside the golden door." The sonnet is today engraved on the Statue's pedestal. Later, the Lebanese-born mystic and poet **Kahlil Gibran** (1883–1931) lived at 51 West 10th Street (now replaced by an apartment building 45–57). His book *The Prophet* has brought inspiration to countless readers.

Intolerance Solves No Problems
FIRST PRESBYTERIAN CHURCH (LM in LMD)
48 Fifth Ave. at 12th St. 1846, Joseph C. Wells. South transept 1893 McKim, Mead & White. Chancel added 1919. Church house: 1960, Edgar Tafel. ☎ 675-6150

First Presbyterian is one of New York's richest churches in both historic associations and artistic treasures. The congregation dates back to 1716, and after U.S. independence it received the first religious charter granted by the first New York State Legislature, which its pastor served as chaplain. George Washington was sworn in as president on this church's Bible in 1789.

Harry Emerson Fosdick preached here in 1922 his famous plea for Christian toleration, "Shall the Fundamentalists Win?" (see p. 286). His sermons attracted so many people that the church installed loudspeakers for people gathered outside to hear. A new plaque installed in 1998 features a portrait of Fosdick with a quotation: "When will the world learn that intolerance solves no problems?"

This building is only the second home of this historic congregation. The building's architect, an English immigrant who was later a founder of the American Institute of Architects, designed a crenellated central entrance tower embellished with quatrefoil tracery. The Gothic Revival body of First Presbyterian seems to have been modeled on St. Saviour at Bath, England.

The nave windows are by D. M. Armstrong, Tiffany Studios, Francis Lathrop, and the Lamb Studios. The church has been modified considerably since its construction. McKim, Mead & White added a south transept chapel for additional seating, and a chancel was added in 1919. The blue rose window above the reredos was a gift of Robert de Forest, the founder of the American Wing of the Metropolitan Museum. The Alexander

Memorial Chapel (1937), named for a longtime pastor, features a Scottish motif— thistle, heather, and ivy, and its three stained-glass windows show the cathedral of Iona, a Scottish crusader, and the Ionic cross of St. Martin.

The church house on the north side of the church was designed by Edgar Tafel,

First Presbyterian Church

who had apprenticed to Frank Lloyd Wright in the 1930s and worked on the house "Falling Water" in Pennsylvania. The parish house echoes the church in many ways, but it maintains its individuality. Its horizontal lines, respect for materials, and stylized lettering typify the "prairie style" of Tafel's teacher, Wright, but make a dignified individual statement.

AROUND THE CORNER

➤ The tiny cemetery at 72–76 West 11th Street, just east of Sixth Avenue, called **Shearith Israel's Second Cemetery** (LMD), is in fact the third, but it is the second of which we know the location. Interments took place here from 1805 to 1829. Most of the bodies were removed when

The second cemetery of Congregation Shearith Israel, the Spanish and Portuguese Synagogue

11th Street was widened, but Ephraim Hart, a founder of the New York Stock Exchange, still rests here.

➡ The Portico Place Apartments was originally the **13th Street Presbyterian Church** (LMD, 143 West 13th St. 1846, attributed to Samuel Thomson; deconsecrated and converted 1982, Stephen B. Jacobs & Associates). This was one of the best Greek Revival churches in the city, modeled on the Theseum in ancient Athens.

➡ **East West Books** (78 Fifth Ave. between 13th and 14th Sts. ☎ 243-5994) carries titles on psychology, Western religious traditions, and interfaith spirituality, but specializes in Eastern religions and boasts New York's largest and widest stock of books on Buddhism. Here you can also find meditation aids, including cushions, incense, statues, posters, magazines, videos, and music.

West 14th Street to West 42nd Street

New York's First Spanish and French Roman Catholic Churches
OUR LADY OF GUADALUPE
229 West 14th St., between Seventh and Eighth Aves. 1902, Gustave Steinback. ☎ 243-5317

At the turn of the twentieth century, New York's Spanish-speaking community was almost entirely Spanish or Mexican, and its greatest concentration was in this West Side neighborhood. Father Venance Besset, a French member of the Assumptionist order serving in New York, recognized the need for Spanish-speaking churches. Father Besset called on fellow Assumptionists to come from Chile to help, and in 1902 they established this, the mother church of Spanish-speaking New Yorkers, dedicated to the patroness of the Americas. The Virgin of Guadalupe appeared in 1531 near Mexico City, where a basilica today houses an image of the Virgin on cloth that many believe was created miraculously. For this New York church, an 1845 brownstone row house owned by the Delmonico family (owners of the popular restaurant) received an astonishing new white Spanish baroque façade, a church was created in the interior, and Spanish-language masses and social services began. Social activist Dorothy Day (see p. 122) worked here, and Trappist monk Thomas Merton (see p. 291) spoke warmly of this church in his book *The Seven Storey Mountain*. Our Lady of Guadalupe even houses Manhattan's oldest ongoing Boy Scout troop—Troop 304.

Father Bessett later also founded Our Lady of Esperanza (see p. 295).

SAINT VINCENT DE PAUL

127 West 23rd St., between Sixth and Seventh Aves. 1857, original architect unrecorded. ☎ 243-4727

This was New York's first French-language Catholic congregation, founded in 1842 on Canal Street and relocated here in 1857. Vincent de Paul (1580–1660) dedicated his life to the service of the poor, and a charitable society of laymen was founded in Paris in his name in 1833. This church's limestone classical façade with Corinthian pilasters was added onto an older building in 1939, the centennial of the foundation of the Fathers of Mercy, the order of priests who founded the parish and staffed it until 1960. They displayed the first Christmas crèche in New York. The opalescent

St. Vincent de Paul

stained-glass windows and a series of brilliant murals trace the history of Christian France: the baptism of King Clovis, St. Denis in Paris, St. King Louis, Joan of Arc, and other episodes. Edith Piaf, the French singer beloved as "the little sparrow," married singer-composer Jacques Pills here on September 20, 1952. Marlene Dietrich, who served as witness, gave the bride a cross set with diamonds.

AROUND THE CORNER

➡ Richard Upjohn's 1846 former Episcopal **Church of the Holy Communion** (Sixth Ave. at West 20th St., LM), today deconsecrated and a nightclub, was the first asymmetrical Gothic Revival church in America and the prototype for similarly picturesque churches all across the country. Worshipers here included prominent financiers John Jacob Astor, Cornelius Vanderbilt, and Jay Gould, but its congregation dwindled and eventually merged with St. George (see p. 135) and Calvary (see p. 137).

➡ **The Center for Jewish History** (15 West 16th St. between Fifth and Sixth Aves. Remodeled in 2000 by Beyer Blinder Belle. ☎ 294-8301) is a partnership of the American Jewish Historical Society, the YIVO Institute for Jewish Research, the Leo Baeck Institute, and the Yeshiva University Museum. Changing exhibitions of historical artifacts, books, manuscripts, and ceremonial objects tell the history of Jewish life and traditions.

➡ **Tibet House** (22 West 15th St. between Fifth and Sixth Aves. Second floor of an apartment building. ☎ 807-0563) is one of New York's most prominent resource centers for Tibetan religion and culture. Founded in 1987 by Columbia University professor (and friend of the Dalai Lama) Robert Thurman, Tibet House presents all aspects of Tibetan civilization and spirituality in its library, gallery, newsletter, exhibitions, lectures, concerts, and conferences. **The Tibet Center** (107 East 31st St., 5th floor. ☎ 779-1841), founded in 1975, also offers a variety of evening activities and programs, plus a reference library open to the public.

Roman Grandeur on 16th Street
SAINT FRANCIS XAVIER
Roman Catholic. 30 West 16th St., between Fifth and Sixth Aves. 1882; P. C. Keely. ☎ 627-2100

The souvenir book of the dedication of St. Francis Xavier in 1882 exulted: "The emotion first excited is that of admiring surprise. . . ." The building is a Roman basilica, and whereas "Gothic . . . impresses with the solemnity and deep mysteriousness of religion. . . . The Basilica, on the other hand, exhilarates the mind with the joyousness, the boldness, and the grandeur of faith. . . ."

St. Francis's exterior hints at the grandeur within. Its monumental porch and vestibule with vaulted stone ceilings spill out over the sidewalk. Its granite façade is bold and exuberant. A broken arched pediment above the central niche holds a statue of the patron saint, topped by an arcade, embellished volutes, and a large pediment surmounted by a cross.

Inside, massive stone columns support a lofty vaulted and richly decorated ceiling. The dedicatory book continues: "The lavish profuseness of foliations, moldings, cornices, etc., surpasses even the Renaissance in luxuriance. . . . Yet it is all blended [with] good proportion, harmony of tone, lightness of handling and lofty grandeur. . . ." High-relief ornamentation includes soaring angels and life-sized gesturing saints. A triforium surrounds the nave. This is a church of the Jesuit order, of which Francis Xavier (1506–52) was one of the earliest members. He brought Christianity to Japan, China, and to India, where he is buried, and he is the patron saint of missionaries. Here in his church he soars to heaven in a ceiling medallion high above the crossing. The church boasts many stained-glass windows by Tiffany and Mayer, but few of them are figural, so as not to distract our eye from the walls, which are covered with frescoes. Bavarian artist William Lamprecht lived in America between 1868 and 1901 and painted religious scenes at many churches. At St. Francis he covered the walls with scenes from the life of Christ and the lives and works of the saints. (He was paid almost five times as much as the building's architect.) It is said that Stanford White frequently visited St. Francis to admire the statue of the Madonna on the east side-altar, his favorite in New York. The rich marble transept altars are dedicated to the Sacred Heart and to Aloysius Gonzaga, the patron saint of young students, who died at age twenty three in 1591 while caring for plague victims.

The parish was founded in 1851, and this is its second home. Part of the money to pay for the first St. Francis Church, as well as for decorations, vestments, and sacred vessels still used was the gift of Catholics in Mexico, just as the diocese of Puebla had adorned St. Peter's 100 years earlier (see p. 89). In 1893 the church was illuminated with over 2,000 electric lights and claimed to be "the most complete electrically lighted church in the United States."

The first member of Spanish royalty ever to visit the New World, the Infanta Eulalia, worshiped at St. Francis Xavier in 1893. Her trip commemorated the anniversary of Columbus's voyage, financed by her ances-

Left: The Bialystoker
Synagogue

Above: Jacques Marchais
Museum of Tibetan Art

Below: The Hindu Temple
of North America

Above: The Friends Meeting
House on Rutherford Place

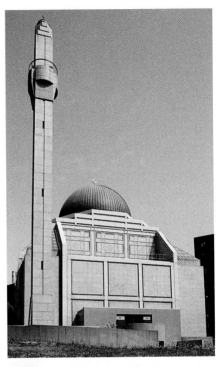

Above: Brooklyn Botanic Garden

Right: The Upper East Side Islamic Cultural Center and Mosque

Below: St. Jean Baptiste

Right: Central Synagogue

A cloth labyrinth at the Cathedral of St. John the Divine

The West Side Community Garden

Left: St. Peter's Episcopal Church, the Bronx

Below: St. Francis Xavier

The General Theological Seminary

tor Queen Isabella 400 years earlier. Thomas Merton (see p. 291) heard the call to be a priest during a benediction in the lower church at St. Francis's.

Jesuits have been in New York since 1846, when Bishop Hughes invited a group of exiled French Jesuits then living in Kentucky to take charge of both his new college and seminary at Fordham (see p. 329) and also this parish. They established a college and church here on 16th Street, first called Holy Name of Jesus, but changed to St. Francis Xavier in 1851.

America's First Gothic Revival Church
SAINT PETER'S (LMD)
Episcopal. 344 West 20th St., between Eighth and Ninth Aves. 1838, James W. Smith, after designs by Clement Clarke Moore. ☎ 929-2390.

St. Peter's three buildings tell a story of changing tastes in architectural styles and of one man, Clement Clarke Moore (1779–1863), developer, organist, scholar, preacher, architect, builder, and the author of "A Visit from Saint Nicholas." He wrote it in 1822 but refused credit until he included it in a book of his poems dedicated to his children in 1844.

Moore inherited a large estate called Chelsea, stretching from today's 21st to 24th Streets, from Eighth Avenue to the Hudson River, and he set out to develop the property. His father had been the rector of Trinity Church and Episcopal bishop of New York, so first he generously donated land for the General Theological Seminary (see p. 180) and another lot for St. Peter's Church. Moore himself drew up designs for a church flanked by a chapel and a rectory, all three in the Greek Revival style just coming into fashion. The chapel (346 West 20th St., today the rectory) opened in 1832. It was a simple Greek-style temple, one of the first in the city, albeit with engaged brick pilasters instead of freestanding columns. Moore donated an organ and served as organist.

The congregation proceeded to put in the foundations for a larger church in the same style, but then a parishioner returned from England praising the Gothic Revival style newly popular there. The congregation adopted that new idea, and Moore, with the assistance of architect-builder James W. Smith, relying on drawings of Oxford's Magdalene College and on Bishop Hopkins's *Essay on Gothic Architecture* (see p. 56), created America's first Gothic-style church. It is constructed of rough Manhattan schist trimmed with granite. Worshipers enter at the side of the fine high tower that projects from the front, so the tower base, housing a winding double staircase, serves as a narthex.

Wood rot required the removal of original wooden porches on the sides of the tower, but their shadows can still be traced on the façade. Wooden finials were taken off the top of the tower in the 1920s, but the tower was restored in the 1990s, and its clock repaired.

The interior of the church has been rebuilt repeatedly. The original communion table and the communion rail at which Moore knelt have been preserved in a small chapel against the east wall. Stained glass replaced clear glass windows.

The parish hall to the east (finished in 1871), a red brick Victorian Gothic building with lancet windows and a crenellated tower, is today the home of the Atlantic Theatre Company. This company was founded in Chicago in 1985 by playwright David Mamet and actor William H. Macy.

The wrought-iron fence along the street is older than any of the buildings. It was a hand-me-down from Trinity Church in 1837, when Trinity was putting up its third building (see p. 84). Washington, Hamilton, and Robert Fulton may have known this railing.

AROUND THE CORNER
➡ **Shearith Israel's Third Cemetery** (LMD), at 98–110 West 21st Street, just west of Sixth Avenue, accepted interments from 1829 until 1851. Since then Shearith Israel has held cemetery property on Long Island (see p. 246).

An Oasis
GENERAL THEOLOGICAL SEMINARY (LMD)
Episcopal. Entire block from Ninth Ave. to Tenth Ave., between West 20th and West 21st Sts. Built between 1836 and 1960. ☎ 243-5150

The grounds of General Theological Seminary are private, but they are open to visitors, and they offer one of Manhattan's most tranquil oases. The Episcopal Seminary was founded in 1817, and classes were held in St. Paul's Church (see p. 92) until Clement Moore (see p. 179) began to develop his Chelsea estate property and donated this block for a new campus.

West Hall (1836) was the second building constructed, but it is the oldest still standing. Eventually Charles C. Haight developed a plan for a double quadrangle of Gothic-style dark brick buildings with brownstone and pressed-brick trim. These were constructed between 1883 and 1902. Hoffman Hall (1899), at the west end of the campus, features a grand entrance and stairway to an elegant oak-paneled dining hall with a fireplace at one end and a gallery high above the other. The ceiling is barrel-vaulted, coffered, and elaborately carved. The Chapel of the Good Shepherd (consecrated 1888) rises in the middle of the complex, boasting a 161-foot tower with a historic set of tubular chimes, heard every morning and evening before services, and a bronze tympanum and doors that were the first work in the United States by Scottish immigrant J. Massey Rhind (1860–1936; Rhind also created the female column-figures holding up the porch—called *caryatids*—on the West 34th Street entrance to Macy's Department Store).

Visitors enter through a modern building on Ninth Avenue (1960, O'Connor & Kilham) that replaced three Gothic-style buildings from the original plan. It contains St. Mark's Library, one of the leading religious libraries in America.

AROUND THE CORNER

➥ The Roman Catholic **Church of the Guardian Angel** (193 Tenth Ave. at 21st St. 1930, John Van Pelt. ☎ 929-5966) displays one of the most elaborate and carefully crafted Romanesque-style façades in the city. Above the marble panels set into the wall runs a hand-carved limestone frieze depicting Biblical scenes separated by angels standing guard.

➥ The Shambhala tradition of Buddhism began only in the mid-twentieth century, and the **New York Shambhala Center** (118 West 22nd St., between Sixth and Seventh Aves., 6th floor. ☎ 675-6544), founded in 1970, offers several meditation rooms, a wide variety of programs from archery to flower arranging, and a nationwide network of sister institutions. Open sessions are held on Tuesday evenings.

Edith Wharton's Wedding
SERBIAN ORTHODOX CATHEDRAL OF SAINT SAVA (LM)
15 West 25th St., between Broadway and Sixth Ave. 1855, Richard Upjohn. ☎ 242-9240

This Gothic Revival structure was built as a chapel of Trinity Church for the convenience of members who, by midcentury, were moving up around Madison Square. Social leaders included the prominent Jones family, who lived across the street and whose daughter Edith married Edward Wharton here on April 29, 1885. Edith Wharton later won recognition as one of America's greatest novelists. The Joneses were so elegant that colloquial American preserves the expression, "keeping up with the Joneses."

As the local Episcopalian community shrank, Trinity sold the property to New York's Serbian community, which rededicated the property to Sava (1169–1236), the founder of the Serbian church, nation, and culture. The church was reconsecrated as America's first Serbian Orthodox cathedral in 1944, and three years later the cathedral choir thanked Trinity Church by singing at its 250th anniversary celebrations. Early Orthodox worshipers of note here included actors Karl Malden and Brad Dexter, and Serbian King Peter II, Queen Alexandra, and Crown Prince Alexander when in exile.

The building's construction and decorating costs totaled six times the original estimate of $40,000 (the rector attributed the cost overrun to "the persuasive power of architects and the docility of building committees"). The result is the first U.S. example of the early English Gothic style, noteworthy for its lack of a tower or exterior ornamentation and for its large buttresses. Today a round mosaic of Sava above the exterior center doors adds a Byzantine note to the Gothic Revival façade, pierced by a fine rose window. The interior has a long single-aisled nave under a fully exposed truss ceiling and tall, thin stained-glass windows along the nave. Fourteen chandeliers hang from the ends of the hammerbeams, and, on the ceiling, gold stars shimmer on a field of blue. The interior walls are of stone imported from Caen in Normandy. The Serbian congregation has been adding Byzantine elements to the decor, including an oak iconostasis hand-carved at a monastery in Serbia and enriched with forty icons, and another large chandelier in the center of the nave. Today services are conducted in Old Slavonic with an a cappella choir.

Five years after the completion of the church, architect Jacob Wrey Mould designed the High Victorian Gothic parish house to the east. It's a fantasy of carved panels, little open belfries and pinnacles, polychromy, and ornamental brickwork.

A statue of Michael Pupin (1858–1935) stands in the midblock pedestrian passageway. This Serbian immigrant's inventions improved long-distance telephony, X-ray devices, and radio tuning. His 1922 autobiography *From Immigrant to Inventor* won the Pulitzer Prize and served nationwide as a school reader in citizenship.

AROUND THE CORNER
➡ General William J. Worth (1794–1849), who fought in the Mexican War, is actually buried under the **Worth Monument**, a granite obelisk on a decorated rectangular pedestal in the triangle at Broadway, Fifth Avenue, and 24th Street (1857, J. G. Batterson). The cast-iron swords that form a fence replicate the one given to General Worth by the State of New York.

➥ **Madison Square Park** just across Fifth Avenue was a potter's field from 1807 until 1814. No one knows how many people lie beneath it still today. Augustus Saint-Gaudens's 1880 monument to Admiral Farragut, America's first admiral and hero of the Civil War, stands on a base designed by Stanford White.

Spires in the Park
CHURCH OF THE HOLY APOSTLES (LM)
Episcopal. 300 Ninth Ave. at West 28th St. 1848, Minard Lafever. ☎ 807-6799

Tucked among the towers of the 1962 Penn Station South housing complex, a few church spires provide a sense of history and visual contrast. This area was rural when Holy Apostles opened for worship. Architect Minard Lafever produced a rare Manhattan example of an Italianate-style church. A square tower projects through the front of a gable-roofed body. Tiny eyebrow windows in the roof suggest clerestory windows inside. The brick tower has a fanciful unusual feature: Its cornice curves up over round windows on each side, and the cornice has exaggeratedly large brackets. On top of the tower, the belfry has the same curved and bracketed cornice, and the spire soars above the belfry.

The simple barrel-vaulted interior is typical of early Italian Renaissance churches, but it has been expanded, so Lafever's original church is now just the nave. The large round-arched windows contain work by William Jay Bolton, America's earliest stained-glass artist. Medallions depicting scenes from the life of Christ and the Acts of the Apostles are surrounded by colorful abstract and floral designs. A few of these were destroyed in a fire in 1990, but they have been reproduced.

Before the Civil War, Holy Apostles was a stronghold of abolitionism. The church was a station on the Underground Railroad, and underground passageways allowed secret hiding and escapes. Today the basement stores food for what has been since 1982 the largest emergency feeding kitchen in New York City. Each day between 900 and 3,000 people are fed.

The gay and lesbian Jewish **Congregation Beth Simchat Torah** meets at Holy Apostles.

AROUND THE CORNER
➥ Also tucked into the housing complex is the 1845 **Church of Saint Columba** (343 West 25th St., ☎ 807-8876). Its rectory dates from 1848 and its parochial school (by Thomas H. Poole) from 1911, where the most

famous students (so far) have been Caryn Johnson (Whoopi Goldberg) and Tony Orlando. Columba (521–597 C.E.) taught and preached among the Irish and the Scots, and he founded on the island of Iona a monastery that preserved Christianity during the Viking raids of later centuries. Also within the Penn South complex, the Greek Orthodox **Church of Saint Elefterios** (359 West 24th St. ☎ 924-3919), a square brick box with a dome surmounted by a gilded cross, was dedicated in 1976.

➥ Across Ninth Avenue at 28th Street is the **"doughboy" statue** created by sculptor Philip Martiny as a monument to the residents of Chelsea who fought in World War I.

The Power of Positive Thinking
MARBLE COLLEGIATE CHURCH (LM)
Reformed. 275 Fifth Ave. at 29th St. 1854, Samuel A. Warner. ☎ 686-2770

The statue of Dr. Norman Vincent Peale (1898–1993) standing in front of this church seems to address the passersby. Dr. Peale served here from 1932 until 1984, preaching an optimistic theology that drew audiences of thousands, plus radio listeners. His 1952 book, *The Power of Positive Thinking*, became a perennial best-seller, and Dr. Peale was awarded the Presidential Medal of Freedom in 1984. Peale mentored Reverend Robert Schuller, who today preaches "possibility thinking" at the Crystal Cathedral in Garden Grove, California.

Marble Collegiate (see p. 10 for its history) was consecrated as "the Fifth Avenue Church," but its building material so impressed the public imagination that the congregation formally took its current name in 1906. Its central tower contains a belfry and clock, and it is topped with a spire and weathervane. The cock on the weathervane is a reminder of Peter's having denied Christ three times before the cock crowed (Matthew 26:34 ff.). The large bronze bell in front of the church was cast in Amsterdam in 1768; it hung in an earlier Reformed church downtown through the eighteenth and nineteenth centuries.

The interior is a large auditorium with a broad open nave and galleries for maximum seating and optimal acoustics. The balconies were America's first "hanging balconies," that is, not supported by pillars. There is no altar, but a communion table. The stained-glass windows include work by Tiffany.

U.S. President Richard Nixon worshiped at Marble, and his daughter Tricia married David Finch Cox here in 1971.

Patron Saint of Ecology
SAINT FRANCIS OF ASSISI

Roman Catholic. 135 West 31st St., between Sixth and Seventh Aves. 1892, Henry Erhardt. ☎ 736-8500. Next door is a church-operated bookstore, where you can find a guidebook to the church.

Francis of Assisi (1181–1226) is probably the subject of more books, commentaries, and works of art than any other saint. He was born to wealth, but renounced it to live in poverty. He was never a priest, but he founded an order of disciples whom he humbly called the Friars Minor. With his help, Clare of Assisi soon thereafter founded the Poor Clares, and a tertiary order was founded for laymen who wished to live monastically. One day while Francis was praying, scars corresponding to the five wounds of the crucified Christ appeared on his body, a phenomenon known as stigmatization. Francis loved and respected all living things—it is said that he even preached to the birds—so he has been designated the patron saint of ecology. He was canonized only two years after his death.

When this parish was organized in a small settlement of Germans in 1844, it was way out in the country. It's still a fairly small church, yet its location (it's sometimes called "the little church among the skyscrapers") and the welcome people receive here have made it one of New York's busiest. It offers thirteen services daily in many languages. St. Francis was one of the city's first churches to offer services at "odd" hours (including the middle of the night) for the convenience of local workers and commuters. It is a Romanesque-style yellow brick church with terra-cotta trim and a copper steeple. A mosaic over the 31st Street entrance, installed 1930, shows Francis in glory over the town of Assisi. You can identify on the mosaic the basilica built in his honor shortly after his death.

Inside, sixteen columns with decorated capitals support the vaulting, and the apse is filled with a mosaic, *The Glorification of the Mother of Jesus*. This mosaic, designed in Austria, was the largest in the United States when it was installed in 1925. Mary, carrying the infant Jesus, is surrounded by Franciscan saints and other notables associated with Franciscan history. Two shrines at the back of the church (to St. Anthony and to the Sorrowful Mother) are also completely covered with mosaics.

The lower church has a crèche in a corner all year long. This display is not uncommon in Franciscan churches, because it was Francis who, in 1223, began the tradition of recreating the scene of Christ's birth at Bethlehem with small figures. The crèche at St. Francis includes what some believe is a small stone relic of the stable in which Jesus was born. Another chapel contains a twenty-four-inch-high silver cross from which is suspended an ivory body of Christ crowned with Jerusalem thorns. The cross was acquired in the Philippines in 1935, but it is in fact Spanish work of the fifteenth century, and its base contains what some believe is a relic of the true cross.

The prayer garden at St. Francis of Assisi

A tiny garden and prayer spot lighted by hundreds of candles off the corridor connecting 31st and 32nd Streets offers a peaceful retreat from the area's busyness.

In the 1950s a second entrance to the church was built on 32nd Street. Thousands of people every day touch for good luck or as a quick silent prayer the statue of St. Francis in front of that entrance.

New York's Literary Lions
THE HUMANITIES AND SOCIAL SCIENCE DIVISION OF THE NEW YORK PUBLIC LIBRARY (LM)

Fifth Ave., between 40th and 42nd Sts. 1911, Carrère & Hastings. ☎ 930-0800. Guidebooks are available in the shop.

This building of the New York Public Library exemplifies Beaux-Arts classical opulence, with virtually every detail down to the chairs and doorknobs designed by the architects and turned, carved, or hand-crafted out of the finest materials. Sculptor Edward C. Potter's two lions in front of the building, who wear holiday wreaths around their necks in December and January, are known as Patience and Fortitude. The building's collections (numbering, depending on how you count objects, at least fifteen million volumes of printed material and over twenty million other items) place it among the great research facilities of the world. It contains a large number of items of spiritual interest: sacred manuscripts of many religions in many languages in almost every form of printing or writing, illustrations and prints, medieval manuscripts, a Gutenberg Bible, and a *Bay Psalm Book* (1640), the first book printed in America in English. Tours of the building are given several times each day from the information desk in the main lobby.

AROUND THE CORNER

➡ **Bryant Park** (LM), stretching to Sixth Avenue behind the library, was a potter's field from 1823 until 1847. In the 1980s it was excavated to accommodate library stacks underground, and today, after the park's restoration in 1988–91, it feels like a bit of Paris in New York.

Home of the Fighting Chaplain
HOLY CROSS
Roman Catholic. 333 West 42nd St., between Eighth and Ninth Aves. 1870, Henry Engelbert. ☎ 246-4732

People waiting in line to buy half-price tickets to Broadway shows at the TKTS Booth (West 47th St., between Seventh Ave. and Broadway) often wonder about Father Francis Duffy (1871–1932) whose statue, by Charles Keck, stands in front of a Celtic cross at West 46th Street, facing down Broadway. He won fame as the "Fighting Chaplain" of New York's Sixty-ninth Regiment during World War I. Eyewitnesses described him scrambling from trench to trench, gas mask on his shoulder and Bible in his hand, hearing soldiers' confessions and giving last rites. He even carried some to safety, and eventually he was awarded the Distinguished Service Cross, the Croix de Guerre, and the Legion of Honor. Father Duffy returned to Holy Cross Church to work among the gangs of what was then the notorious "Hell's Kitchen" neighborhood. When Roman Catholic Al Smith won the Democratic nomination for the presidency in 1928, it was Father Duffy who wrote Smith's "Creed as an American Catholic." John F. Kennedy drew on that document to form his own philosophy of Catholicism and American democracy. When Duffy died, Alexander Woollcott wrote in *The New Yorker* that he was of "such dimensions that he made New York into a small town."

When the first Holy Cross Church was struck by lightning in 1870, the damage revealed that the church had been so poorly constructed in 1854 that it soon would have collapsed, so it had to be entirely rebuilt. This new Holy Cross is today the oldest building on 42nd Street. Behind its rather modest red brick and brownstone façade is an elegant church. The interior is a Latin cross with a high, barrel-vaulted ceiling and transepts, with a dome and lantern (the dome has been sealed and covered beneath the lantern). The chancel windows are by Mayer of Munich. Louis Comfort Tiffany designed the clerestory windows (covered today and not visible), the large circular windows of Sts. Peter and Paul in the transepts, and the window of John the Baptist, now mounted freestanding in the baptistery. In 1885 the building was extended, new marble altars installed, and a painting of the crucifixion was installed over the altar, flanked by paintings of Emperor Constantine before the Battle of the Milvian Bridge (312) and of Constantine's mother, Helena, showing the legend of her finding the true cross.

West 43rd Street to West 59th Street

The "Cathedral" of American Anglo-Catholicism
CHURCH OF SAINT MARY THE VIRGIN (LM)
Episcopal. 145 West 46th St., between Sixth and Seventh Aves. 1895, Napoleon LeBrun & Sons. Pierre LeBrun in charge. ☎ 757-5845. A guidebook is available in the office.

The dedication of this church to Mary is unusual among Protestant denominations, revealing that this is an Anglo-Catholic congregation (see p. 69). Anglo-Catholicism stresses the importance of ritual and elaborate furnishings, and St. Mary's offered ritual early on. The first high mass with incense, for example, was celebrated in 1877, and acolytes swinging smoking censers still earn the church its nickname "Smoky Mary's." The story is told that actress Talullah Bankhead once dryly warned an acolyte, "Honey, your purse is on fire." St. Mary's is affiliated with the Episcopal Diocese of New York, but it views itself as within the broadest catholic tradition, so members pray for the pope and the ecumenical patriarch of Orthodox churches, as well as for the archbishop of Canterbury.

St. Mary's congregation dedicated its first home in 1870, but the congregation soon planned a larger replacement. They specified a church in the thirteenth-century French Gothic style, with decoration restricted to the façade and the interior; an apsidal chancel at least fifty feet deep, with an ambulatory; side aisles for processions; no towers or spires (but a copper flèche over the apse); a lofty ceiling; and at least two chapels and a baptistery. St. Mary's was the world's first church constructed on a steel frame, and the architect disdained to put false buttresses on the high apsidal end, even though architects tended to put sham buttresses on Gothic-style churches. J. Massey Rhind's sculptural program on the façade exemplifies the Marian devotion typical of Anglo-Catholicism. Mary stands holding the Christ Child on the trumeau, and Mary and Child are enthroned in the tympanum.

St. Mary's interior was completely restored in 1997, and again, its elaborateness reflects Anglo-Catholic ideals. The ceiling is painted blue with golden stars. The elaborate furnishings include a marble altar, seven hanging altar lamps, cream-colored imitation marble walls, pastel stations of the cross, and murals. Woodcarver Johannes Kirchmayer contributed an extraordinary freestanding pulpit with a sounding board above, the high crown on the baptistery font, the twelve apostles under canopies on the columns along the nave, Jesus and Mary at the front of the church, and high above, a rood beam with a crucifixion scene. The Lady Chapel to the right behind the altar features figural stained glass, Gothic-style carved oak paneling, murals, and a very large and elaborate reredos.

Independence New and Renewed
SAINT LUKE'S LUTHERAN CHURCH
308 West 46th St., between Eighth and Ninth Aves. 1923, Edward L. Tilton and Alfred M. Githens. ☎ 246-3540

Each October 31, the day in 1517 on which Martin Luther is said to have posted ninety-five theses on the door to the Wittenberg castle church and thus launched the Protestant Reformation, St. Luke's displays its treasure, homilies (short sermons) hand-written by five great Reformation leaders: Luther himself, Philip Melanchthon (author of the *Augsburg Confession*, the basic document of Lutheranism), Caspar Creutziger, Justus Jonas, and Johann Bugenhagen. Luther and Melanchthon are shown in stained-glass windows on the west and east sides, respectively, of the north wall (the façade) of the church. Between them, the church's façade gable is almost filled by an arched window showing the tetramorph with two angels in fields of foliation. These three windows, as most others in the church, were made by the Zettler studios.

St. Luke's congregation was actually organized as a Reformed Church in 1850, but the congregation switched to the Lutheran denomination in 1853. Even as new Lutherans, St. Luke's continued its independent ways. In 1880 it withdrew from the New York Ministerium over synodical rulings, and only in 1987 did it join the Association of Evangelical Lutheran

Churches, which in 1988 merged with others into the Evangelical Lutheran Church.

The architect of St. Luke's, Edward Tilton, was the architect of the
Ellis Island Administration Building, and this building has a bit of the stage
set about it. The façade sprouts a variety of gables, asymmetrical towers,
and castellation that perhaps suggest medieval Germany. Some pinnacles
are simplified into plain points growing out of the wall. Inside, narrow side
aisles serve only as corridors, and the stenciling on the walls almost draws
our attention away from the windows.

Church of the Stars
SAINT MALACHY'S
Roman Catholic. 239 West 49th St., between Broadway and Eighth Ave.
1903, Joseph H. McGuire. ☎ 489-1340

Malachy (1094–1148) died in the arms of his good friend Bernard of
Clairvaux, who wrote of him, "His first and greatest miracle was himself."
What could be more appropriate to say about actors? And St. Malachy's
has always been known as Broadway's chapel for Catholic actors, where
a mass could be caught between matinees and evening performances.
The parish was founded in 1902, and this brick and limestone neo-Gothic
church dedicated the next year. An Actors' Chapel was added in the
undercroft in 1920. Thousands jammed the street outside the church at
the final tribute to Rudolph Valentino on August 30, 1926. Joan Crawford
married Douglas Fairbanks, Jr., here. George M. Cohan, Spencer Tracy,
Perry Como, Irene Dunne, Hildegarde, Florence Henderson, Lawrence
Luckinbill, Rosalind Russell, Danny Thomas, Bob and Dolores Hope, and
Ricardo Montalban worshiped here. Fred Allen, Don Ameche, Cyril
Ritchard, Pat O'Brien, and Jimmy Durante served at masses. The church
was completely renovated in the 1990s.

The Easter Parade
SAINT THOMAS CHURCH (LM)
Episcopal. Fifth Ave. at 53rd St. 1914, Cram, Goodhue & Ferguson. ☎
757-7013. Guidebooks and pamphlets are available in the office.

This is where the Easter Parade began. Over one hundred years ago, St.
Thomas's Easter services ended with a choir procession to St. Luke's Hospital, then one block north, bringing the flowers from the sanctuary and
then presenting a concert for the patients. Members of the congregation
and passersby joined.

The St. Thomas Church of that day, an 1870 building by Richard

Upjohn, was destroyed by fire in 1905, but from its ashes rose this new church, considered one of the finest in America. The architects were challenged to build a large church (it seats 1,700) on a small corner lot, and their solution was to build a tower on only one side of the entrance portal. This is rarely noticed, however, because most of the time St. Thomas is seen from up or down Fifth Avenue, and viewers admire how that one big tower anchors the corner. St. Thomas's nave (without transepts) occupies the northern part of the lot, and the architect of the building next door politely clad his tower in limestone and added vertical fins to make it look like a campanile for St. Thomas. St. Thomas's overall style is French Gothic, but it is not a copy of any specific building. Cram insisted on building St. Thomas in a true Gothic manner, without structural steel, but years later, because of an initial miscalculation and continual subway rumbling underneath, steel reinforcement had to be added.

"Doubting Thomas," who would not believe that Christ had risen until he could put his finger in the wound in Christ's side (John 20:24–28), stands on the trumeau. (Thomas is the patron of architects, and T-squares can be found in a south clerestory window and also in the narthex floor.) The tetramorph surrounds the rose window in the gable above. The four buildings on the gilded relief above the entrance doors are the buildings in which this congregation has worshiped: two on Houston Street and two on this site. The marriage feast at Cana and other figures and motifs celebrating marriage are carved over the south door, the brides' entrance.

Inside, your attention is drawn to the towering reredos. This ivory-colored stone sculpture, eighty feet high, includes more than sixty figures from the history of Christianity. This masterwork, and most of the other decoration, was designed by Bertram Goodhue and Lee Lawrie, and executed by Lawrie. Their artistic control allowed for unusual consistency. For example, every image of a particular saint throughout the church has the same face, as St. John does both in the reredos and on the lectern. Carvings throughout the church combine local and contemporary figures with historical figures, just as artists did in medieval cathedrals.

At the top of the chancel steps, a stone set in the floor was taken from the wall of Canterbury Cathedral against which Thomas à Becket fell when he was slain in 1170. Contemporary images in the carved choir furniture include an airplane, a car, and World War I generals. The oak pulpit features portraits of nineteen famous preachers, including some from New York, and the cross set into the stone column beside it is made from stones from Jerusalem's Church of the Holy Sepulchre. Samuel Yellin forged all of the ironwork. The panels on the kneeling rail show industries and historical events, including one of Christopher Columbus's ships, Theodore Roosevelt, Lee Lawrie himself (between the steamship and the telephone), a radio, J. P. Morgan's initials symbolizing finance, and medicine. St. Thomas boasts two organs, the newer of which, placed in the loft under the rose window in 1996, is one of the most authentic early Baroque-style organs in the city.

AROUND THE CORNER
➡ Across Fifth Avenue is tiny **Paley Park**, on the north side of 53rd Street between Fifth and Madison Avenues, designed by Robert Zion in 1966. Its ivy-covered walls, glade of honey locust trees, and wall of falling water make it one of the most restful spots in midtown.

Simple Decor, Surprising Behavior
FIFTH AVENUE PRESBYTERIAN
705 Fifth Ave. at 55th St. 1875, Carl Pfeiffer. Façade redesigned, plus community house and chapel, James Gamble Rogers, 1925. ☎ 247-0490

On the day after Christmas, 1965, Duke Ellington and his orchestra, accompanied by a chorus, soloists, and a tap dancer ("There is no language God does not understand," explained the Duke), gave here the New York premiere of Ellington's "A Concert of Sacred Music." "This music is the most important thing I've ever done," said Ellington, "or am ever likely to do." Some people were surprised that such an event would take place at staid Fifth Avenue Presbyterian, but this congregation has a history of surprising people.

Its founders included Scottish shipbuilder Archibald Gracie, whose Upper East Side country estate is today the mayor's official residence; Colonel Richard Varick, Revolutionary patriot and later New York City mayor; Revolutionary artillery commander General Ebenezer Stephens; and Oliver Wolcott, America's second secretary of the treasury and long-time governor of Connecticut; along with a substantial number of black New Yorkers. In 1853 Dr. Lowell Mason introduced here the use of the pipe organ in Presbyterian services. Mason was a successful composer of hymn tunes (including "Nearer, My God to Thee") and America's first holder of a doctorate in music. In 1859 the Equitable Life Assurance Society was founded in the basement of this church (then down on 19th St.). It may surprise us today that the founding of a life insurance company should have been debated in a church, but back then it was considered a theological matter. Many church leaders condemned statistical studies of human mortality as "playing God" and "gambling with human lives."

Members of this congregation, however, after lively discussion, took the position that guaranteeing the security of one's loved ones is a Christian duty. Equitable's first president was the pastor's brother. In 1937 Fifth Avenue Presbyterian launched one of America's first radio ministries, and in 1956 it introduced the nation's first "Dial-a-Prayer."

This congregation had been founded downtown on Cedar Street in 1808 and made two intermediate stops, but this building rose at the insistence of Reverend John Hall, a famous preacher called from Ulster in 1868. It is a huge oval room with few decorative details that seats over 2,000 people. Everything is focused on the pulpit, which stands on a platform above and behind a modest communion table. This congregation doesn't tolerate figures in the windows, so the windows hold only stock glass in abstract geometric and floral patterns.

The 300-foot tall tower on the south side of the façade, on the corner, was deliberately raised as the first in New York to soar higher than Trinity's steeple downtown. The shorter tower on the north side contains air intakes powered by a fan seven feet in diameter. This allowed renewal of the air inside the church every fifteen minutes, keeping it bearable in the summer.

A New Opportunity for Lutherans
THE CHURCH FOR ALL NATIONS
Lutheran Church, Missouri Synod. 417 West 57th St., between Ninth and Tenth Aves. 1886, Francis H. Kimball. ☎ 265-2867

This Romanesque Revival building was erected by the Catholic Apostolic Church, a charismatic Christian movement founded in England in 1826. Twelve new apostles were chosen, and they alone could ordain ministers, called angels. The denomination believed that Christ would return to Earth in 1835, so they did not originally provide any means of succession. A New York congregation organized in 1848 worshiped in a small Romanesque-style church (today's **French Evangelical Church** at 126 West 16th St.), before erecting this building. The denomination struggled along in New York, but when the last "angel" died in 1949 at the age of ninety-four, the church started on an irreversible decline. In 1995 the few remaining members telephoned Life's Journey Ministries, a Lutheran urban mission, and asked if they wanted the building, on the condition that it remain a house of worship.

The Lutheran Ministry completely renovated it and rededicated it in 1997. In order to guarantee light in this church's midblock site, the architect planned a truncated cross with a short transept, and he kept the aisles low and narrow, so the center was allowed to soar over the nave. Clere-story windows capture both east and west light. The façade shows a high square tower flanked by low wings, where the entrances are. The tower has an arcade of windows, a large wheel window, and then turrets and a pediment. The whole building is red—both the brick and the terra-cotta details, such as small angels' heads over the doors. Inside, the Lutherans added a symbolic Lutheran cross and rose to the center of the crossing of the barrel-vaulted ceiling.

Who Needs Artifacts?
CALVARY BAPTIST CHURCH
123 West 57th St., between Sixth and Seventh Aves. 1931, Rosario Candela. ☎ 975-0170. A church-owned bookstore is in the storefront to the west.

Calvary Baptist was organized as Hope Chapel on lower Broadway in 1847, and yet, curiously, the congregation has very few artifacts of its long history. That fact emphasizes that Calvary Baptist is a preaching church. The record of the life of this congregation, say its members, is not to be found in old Bibles or candlesticks, but in the changed lives that the work of this congregation has brought about.

Several of its pastors have won national fame. Its third, A. D. Gillette, served as chaplain to the four men convicted of President Lincoln's assassination. He spent the night before their execution in their jail cell and stood on the gallows with them the next morning. He later served as chaplain of the U.S. Senate. In the 1920s, Calvary Pastor John Roach Straton, accompanied by a cornetist, preached in the streets from a platform-pulpit extending out over the hood of a specially built car, and in 1923 Calvary opened the first church-owned-and-operated radio station in the country.

Calvary Baptist's present home is one of New York's multipurpose houses of worship. The congregation replaced its 1883 Gothic-style church structure with this sixteen-story church/apartment/hotel. A four-story portal announces the church at street level, above which we read in stone, "We Preach Christ Crucified, Risen, and Coming Again." Clusters of flattened piers rise to an elaborate Gothic-style crest at the sixteenth floor, and the water tower is disguised as a belfry. The entrance to the hotel is to the east of the church portal; income is used for worldwide missionary work. The church interior is a plain open preaching space, with a choir loft above and behind the preacher and a baptismal pool concealed to the side. The grand piano (one of the congregation's few historical artifacts) was donated by parishioner pianist Van Cliburn in 1958 in thanksgiving for winning, at age twenty three, the first International Tchaikovsky Competition in Moscow. His achievement, during the height of the Cold War, made front-page news around the world, and he was celebrated by New York City's only ticker-tape parade ever given for a classical musician. President Eisenhower kept in his desk a Bible that was a gift from Calvary

CHURCHES IN MULTIPURPOSE BUILDINGS

Soaring twentieth-century real estate values encouraged some Manhattan houses of worship to abandon their freestanding buildings and to tuck new sanctuaries into either office buildings or residential buildings. That way, rent rolls from commercial or residential tenants supplement the collection plate. In 1921, the *New York Times* moaned, "We are told that it is good business. Are we then to look forward to a landscape free from ecclesiastical architecture? Must we visualize a New York in which no spire points heavenward?"

In 1922 architect A. D. Pickering incorporated the **Fifth Church of Christ, Scientist**, into an office building and gave the church its own splendid façade at 9 East 43rd Street. **Second Presbyterian Church** tore down its building on the corner of West 96th Street and Central Park West and replaced it with a high-rise residential building with a church tucked into 9 West 96th Street in 1929. Orthodox Congregation Poel Zedek Anshe Ileya bought the 1890 Presbyterian Church at 130 Forsyth Street (designed by J. C. Cady) and converted the entire ground floor along its Delancey Street side to shops. (That building is today's **Templo Adventista Del Septimo Dia**.) **Saint Peter's Lutheran Church** (see p. 157) is one of the most recent congregations to continue this trend.

Templo Adventista Del Septimo Dia

Baptist Church, which also presented one to President Bill Clinton in 1992.

The New York School of the Bible, launched in 1971 as an interdenominational evening school on Calvary's premises, has grown to offer a catalogue of courses and certificates at an ever expanding number of sites throughout the metropolitan area.

Dynamic Preaching
UNITY CENTER OF PRACTICAL CHRISTIANITY (LM)
Nonsectarian. 213 West 58th St., between Seventh and Eighth Aves. 1903, York & Sawyer. ☎ 582-1300

The Unity Center is founded on Christian principles, spiritual values, and the healing power of prayer, but it is nonsectarian. The Unity movement began in 1889 when Charles and Myrtle Fillmore published *Modern Thought*, a metaphysical magazine. A small group began to pray together for health, prosperity and for help through life challenges, and this group grew into today's Silent Unity, a ministry of prayer that has spread around the world. New York's first Unity services were held in 1936. In 1961 the charismatic preacher Eric Butterworth was named minister of New York's Center, and by 1976 Sunday morning services moved to Avery Fisher Hall in Lincoln Center, where they are still held. The Center offers lectures and workshops through the week at its 58th Street home, a French Renaissance-style building that was originally a carriage house, built for Helen Miller Gould, daughter of financier Jay Gould.

CHAPTER SIX

---- ✿ ----

𝒯he Upper East Side: From East 59th Street to East 110th Street

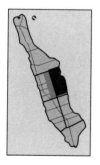

Until the end of the Civil War, today's Upper East Side was where fashionable New Yorkers escaped city summers. A series of estates followed the shore of the East River all the way to Harlem. The Boston Post Road, today's Third Avenue, and steamships on the East River provided access to the city, which still lay miles to the south. By the late 1860s, however, the summer houses were being converted to year-round use by pioneering commuters, and soon elevated railroads on Second and Third Avenues opened the area to working-class people. Industry developed along the river north of 86th Street. High Society arrived on the western edge of the Upper East Side in 1894, when Caroline Schermerhorn Astor built a mansion on Fifth Avenue at 65th Street. The ballroom of this mansion held 400 people comfortably, and thus "Society" has ever since been defined as "the 400." In their view, Central Park provided an attractive front yard and a buffer to the west, and the railroad on today's Park Avenue (before it was covered in 1907) provided a barrier against the workers to the east. Later, the best apartment houses rose on the Upper East Side, and, although (less elegant) apartment buildings continue to rise, the Upper East Side remains a generally high-income district with an aspect of gentility and privilege.

The East 60s

The Methodist "Cathedral"
CHRIST CHURCH, METHODIST
520 Park Ave. at 60th St. 1933, Ralph Adams Cram. ☎ 838-3036

In 1930 the Planning Committee for what was then the Madison Avenue Methodist Church announced, "The largest Protestant denomination in the United States should contribute an outstanding cathedral-like church to the country's greatest city, and it is counting on [us] to build such a structure. The eyes of the church at large are upon us."

"The eyes of the church at large" certainly ought to be dazzled by what they see here. This building offers one of the most resplendent interiors in New York. The congregation chose the Byzantine style (see p. 60), which uses mosaics, variegated marbles, and gilding to achieve the color effects that stained-glass windows give to Gothic churches.

A visitor steps first into a narthex with deep purple marble walls and a gilded mosaic ceiling. It strikes the note of brilliant hard-edged splendor. The nave beyond glistens with 14,000 square feet of mosaics composed of over seven million pieces (*tesserae*) in thousands of colors. The materials were made by the oldest company in Venice, and they left Italy on the last ship bound here before World War II. The gilded high barrel vault leads the eye to the semidome of the apse, where Christ sits enthroned not as judge, but as Lord and teacher. His right hand is raised in blessing, and in his left he holds the Gospel of St. John open to 8:12, "I am the light of the world." Below him the four evangelists stand on the mullions between windows. Additional mosaic patterns along the walls illustrate Moses, John the Baptist, and Christian symbols.

Aside from these walls of mosaics, the interior is covered by thirty-four different kinds of rare and precious marbles. You have to see them for yourself, because a catalogue reads like overwrought romantic poetry: monolithic columns of Italian Purple Levanto marble alternate with piers of French Rosato d'Or inset with panels of Fleur de Pêche framed by lighter Hauteville. Small green Italian Cippolino columns frame an altar of Spanish Sienna-gray, and the lectern and pulpit are of Rosato d'Or inset with Bresche Rose. The floor is a checkerboard of pink Tennessee and dark green Verde Antique. And more. The chapel adjoining and opening from the north aisle is a miniature version of the nave, and it, too, dazzles with marbles and mosaics. The diamond-shaped inset on its altar is a particularly rare African marble. The chapel ceiling is of decorated and painted wood, in the style of Spanish and Sicilian medieval buildings.

Several aspects of the interior echo those of Byzantine Orthodox churches. The reredos that closes off the apse behind the altar (as an iconostasis would conceal the altar in an Orthodox church) displays sixteenth-century icons from the collection of Czar Nicholas II and a pair of seventeenth-century royal doors from the iconostasis of an historic Russian Orthodox cathedral. More icons adorn the top of the reredos and the nearby walls, including, in the north transept, a rare image of Christ in the robes of a Byzantine emperor.

Christ Church is a preaching church. The pulpit and lectern stand forward in the chancel, and the congregation's longtime pastor, Ralph W. Sockman (served from 1917 to 1961) won renown through thirty-five years of nationally broadcast sermons.

Today's Christ Church combines the Madison Avenue Church (founded in 1881) and another Methodist church that was founded in 1863 and met in a hall over Dingeldein's Third Avenue Lager-Beer Saloon.

AROUND THE CORNER

➥ Author **Willa Cather** (1876–1947) died in her apartment at 570 Park Avenue. Her 1927 novel *Death Comes for the Archbishop* tells of nineteenth-century missionary work among Native Americans in New Mexico.

➥ Down the street to the east, the **Mount Vernon Hotel Museum and Garden** (LM, 421 East 61st St., between First and York Aves. 1799) was a carriage house built on land once owned by President John Adams's daughter Abigail and her husband, William Smith. The Colonial Dames of America restored the stone building, which sits in a landscaped and planted half-acre, and furnished it with period pieces.

➥ A cable car over the East River from Second Avenue at East 60th Street provides access to **Roosevelt Island**. In the 1970s a "new town" for over 5,000 people was built here, but before that time city institutions had long occupied the island. The Episcopal Mission Society built a small Victorian Gothic chapel, and that building, originally called the **Chapel of the Good Shepherd** (LM, 1889, Frederick Clarke Withers; restored in 1975 by Giorgio Cavaglieri) is today an Ecumenical Center hosting both Episcopal and Roman Catholic services. Other historical buildings on the island (all LM) include, from north to south, a lighthouse on the northern tip (1872, James Renwick, Jr.); the ruins of the City

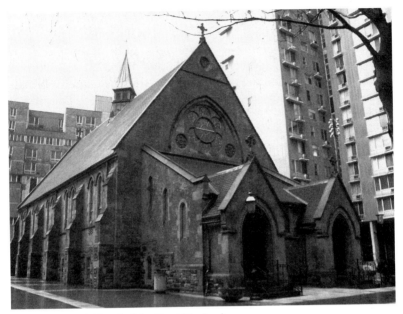

The Ecumenical Chapel of the Good Shepherd

"Lunatic Asylum" (1835, A. J. Davis); the old farmhouse of the Blackwell family (ca. 1796); and, at the southern end, the Strecker Pathology Laboratory (1892, Withers & Dickson) and the smallpox hospital (1854, James Renwick, Jr.).

The "Home" of Reform Judaism
TEMPLE EMANU-EL (LMD)
Reform. Fifth Ave. at 65th St. Robert D. Kohn, Charles Butler, and Clarence Stein, 1929. ☎ 744-1400

One of Temple Emanu-El's most treasured possessions is the Schiff Torah Shield, an elaborately worked silver, enamel, and gilded emblem to be hung on one of the Torahs in the ark to indicate which Torah is to be read on a given week or holiday. Front-and-center on the shield is an eagle whose wings hold tablets of the Ten Commandments. This is unmistakably an *American* eagle, for its breastplate displays the stars and stripes, testifying beautifully to confidence in a vibrant Judaism in America. Financier Jacob Schiff and his wife Theresa commissioned the shield in Mr. Schiff's native Frankfurt, Germany, and they presented it to Temple Emanu-El in 1890 in honor of the confirmation of their daughter, Frieda. The story of the founding of Temple Emanu-El as New York's first Reform congregation was told earlier (see p. 22), and the confirmation of young women is itself a Reform ceremony, unknown to Orthodox synagogues.

From humble beginnings, Emanu-El consolidated with several other congregations, moved through a series of homes, and finally, here on one of the most fashionable avenues in the world, built the largest synagogue in the world—registered as such in the *Guinness Book of World Records*. It replaced on this site the Astor mansion (of the famous ballroom—see p. 197) and has the same grandeur and beauty as the Roman Catholic cathedral a few blocks down Fifth Avenue and the Episcopal cathedral uptown.

Emanu-El's limestone exterior echoes that of B'nai Jeshurun (see p. 253), built a few years earlier. Both adapt and combine Byzantine and early Romanesque styles with Moorish-style decorations. The façade of Emanu-El presents a single giant recessed arch that shelters a wheel window with a Magen David in the center. All of the elaborate decorations of the façade are drawn from traditional Hebrew iconography. The twelve petals of the window represent the twelve tribes of Israel, and three sets of bronze entrance doors below it carry similar symbols. The main sanctuary occupies the corner of Fifth Avenue and 65th Street. Along 65th Street, an expanse of plain wall surface terminates in the community house, which is topped with water tanks and elevator machinery camouflaged as a bell tower.

Emanu-El's austere monochromatic exterior belies the splendor of its interior. It's an immense uninterrupted space 150 feet long, 100 feet wide, and 103 feet high. The basilica-type sanctuary needs no internal columns because the load-bearing side walls carry steel beams across the nave to support the roof. The ceiling supports are covered in stone and plaster and painted in gold and rich colors modeled on the exposed ceiling timbers of the El Transito synagogue in Toledo, Spain, dating from 1357. Red, green, and yellow marble columns support low

Temple Emanu-El

side galleries over the shallow aisles of the nave, so total seating capacity reaches 2,500.

At the east end of the sanctuary, a high marble mosaic arch echoes the arch on the façade, enclosing the organ grille and a choir gallery above the ark. The ark is represented as an open Torah scroll, and the *ner tamid* hangs before it. Tall menorahs stand on each side of the ark. Decorative motifs include the Magen David, the Lion of Judah, various fruits, and a crown, the traditional Torah ornament. A stained-glass window at the southwest corner of the sanctuary shows the immediate former homes of Temple Emanu-El and of Beth-El Congregation.

Beth-El Congregation ("House of God," organized in 1874), with which Emanu-El consolidated in 1927, is remembered in the name of a chapel opening from the nave to the north. (From the outside, it can be seen to sit behind a small garden along Fifth Avenue.) Samuel Yellin produced the ornamental ironwork throughout both the chapel and the main sanctuary.

Temple Emanu-El is historic, but thoroughly up-to-date. It was the first religious institution to broadcast a webcast of a service. When it made the Seder available on the Internet for the first thirty-nine hours of Passover in 1996, the site received over 122,000 hits from thirty-two countries around the world. By the end of the week of Passover, there had been more than 224,000 visitors to the site.

During your visit, you may see the Schiff Torah Shield, its accompanying finials (*rimmonim*) and Torah pointer (*yad*), and many other objects of interest in the Herbert and Eileen Bernard Museum in the community house at 1 East 65th Street.

God's Dogs
SAINT VINCENT FERRER (LM)
Roman Catholic. 869 Lexington Ave. at 66th St. 1918, Bertram Goodhue.
☎ 744-2080

A dog with a blazing torch in its mouth is seen everywhere in the decor of the Church of St. Vincent Ferrer, served by the Dominican Order of priests. The story goes that when Dominic's mother was carrying him, she saw the dog in a dream, symbolically setting fire to the world. The order her son founded in 1216, officially known as the Order of Preachers (O.P.), sees its duty as fiery preaching of God's word, and, after all, Dominicans note, "Dominicans" sounds like "*Domini canes*," "God's dogs." Vincent Ferrer (1350–1419) was a Spanish Dominican whose sermons attracted large crowds as he traveled throughout Spain and France. In the south aisle of this church a life-size marble statue shows him wearing a *cappa*, a black preaching cloak; his hand is raised in benediction, and the Holy Spirit flames above him. He can also be seen in an oil painting on the reredos leading a group of people (including recognizable members of the parish when this church was built) in a procession out of this church. Vincent has a special significance for Jews because on several occasions he protected them from attacks by angry Christian mobs.

St. Vincent's Church is a cruciform Gothic-style structure, and it displays some of the finest stained glass in the United States. The artist Charles Connick came close to achieving here the perfect synthesis of color, glass, and wall. The windows along the nave show Dominican saints paired with other famous figures. For example, the great naturalist and scholar Albertus Magnus is shown with Aristotle in the easternmost window on the south side. (Aristotle has what looks like a green halo, but in fact it's a laurel wreath.) The stained-glass windows in this church can be enjoyed more than those in many other houses of worship because the light fixtures in St. Vincent's direct most of their light downward.

We can list only a fraction of the art in this church. The statue of Our Lady of Fatima in the north aisle was carved by priest/sculptor Thomas McGlynn, who interviewed one of the children who had seen a vision of Mary at Fatima, Portugal, in 1917; this statue is the prototype for the ones now at the basilica in Portugal and in the pope's private apartment in the Vatican. Father McGlynn also carved the angels supporting the font in the baptistery off the narthex and the statue in the north aisle chapel of Martin de Porres (1579–1639), a Peruvian mestizo who became a Dominican lay brother, was canonized as a saint in 1962, and is today associated with work for interracial justice and harmony. Samuel Yellin wrought the ornamental ironwork throughout the church. The stations of the cross are unusual because Christ seems to have changed his robes from one station to the next. This irregularity was deliberate, in order to suggest that the paintings were given at various times and placed together as a set, although in fact they were all painted by the same artist. The oak pulpit stands under a canopy whose spire has tiers of carved saints. Tucked into the wall by the altar in the north aisle is the only Easter sepulchre in the United States. An Easter sepulchre is a special repository in which consecrated bread is placed before Good Friday, the day of the crucifixion. It is brought out again—"resurrected"—on Easter Sunday. The pelican is another traditional Christian symbol seen throughout St. Vincent's. It represents sacrifice, because tradition has it that a pelican would pluck its own breast to feed its young its own blood, as Christ in the Eucharist feeds with his blood. ("I am like a pelican of the wilderness," Psalms 102:6.). The church treasures an important collection of relics, including a piece of the true cross.

St. Vincent's façade presents one bulky tower that seems hollowed out by steps leading up to the double door. Francis of Assisi, Vincent Ferrer, and Dominic stand in the tympanum, and over thirty other saints, popes, and doctors of the church can be found. The stunning crucifixion scene above the portal, carved by Lee Lawrie, was the first ever placed on the exterior of a church in the United States. Above the crucifixion, lancet windows rise to a rose window of unusually intricate tracery. A gallery at the top of the tower connects the two massive buttresses that flank the entrance portal. The exterior is of rough-hewn granite with limestone trim, detailing, and sculpture.

Bertram Goodhue thought St. Vincent's was his best church.

Bastion of Orthodoxy in a Vibrant Building
PARK EAST SYNAGOGUE (LM)
Orthodox. 163 East 67th St., between Lexington and Third Aves. 1890, Ernest Schneider & Henry Herter. ☎ 737-6900

In the 1880s, several of the historic German Jewish congregations moved to the Upper East Side from the Lower East Side, and that geographic move was often accompanied by a theological move from Orthodoxy to Reform. Congregation Zichron Ephraim was founded in 1889 by German Jews who felt that the Reform movement was abandoning too much Jewish tradition and that Orthodox Judaism could be reconciled with American lifestyles. The founders of this synagogue had already been among the

Park East Synagogue

founders of the Orthodox-sponsored Jewish Theological Seminary in 1886, and they founded this synagogue as an Upper East Side redoubt of Orthodoxy. Zichron Ephraim means "Memorial of Ephraim," for it was dedicated to the father of a founder-benefactor. The congregation treasured traditional practices, but it also pioneered in the use of English in services and in religious instruction for the young. Magician Harry Houdini (born Ehrich Weisz) studied in the synagogue school's first class. Today Park East is one of the few synagogues in New York still owned by the congregation that built it.

It's hard to exaggerate the exuberance of this building's orange brick and ruddy terra-cotta Moorish Revival façade. Asymmetrical towers flank a central flat-topped gable pierced by a rose window in a red frame. Horseshoe arches screen a porch narthex, and the entire surface is rich with arches, small columns, and other ornaments. This exuberance contrasts sharply with the interior—a surprisingly plain space made nominally Jewish through "Middle Eastern" decorative details.

AROUND THE CORNER

➥ **The Zen Studies Society** (223 East 67th St., between Second and Third Aves., converted from a carriage house in 1968, ☎ 861-3333), founded in 1956, offers a rigorous Zen experience that makes few concessions to Western traditions. The building is decorated in traditional Japanese Zen style, complete with a stone garden.

➥ **The Urasenke Tea Ceremony Society** at the Urasenke Chanoyu Center (153 East 69th St., between Lexington and Third Aves., ☎ 988-6161) offers lessons, by appointment, in the traditional Japanese tea ceremony.

SOME UPPER EAST SIDE MUSEUMS

The Asia Society (725 Park Ave. at 70th St. 1981, Edward L. Barnes Associates. ☎ 288-6400) offers changing exhibitions, lectures, gallery tours, and a variety of other programs to expand understanding of Asian cultures. Its art collection includes sacred and secular sculptures, porcelains, prints, and manuscripts. The building also contains a bookshop.

The Frick Collection (1 East 70th St. LM, 1914, Carrère & Hastings. ☎ 288-0700), once the home and private art collection of steel magnate Henry Clay Frick, contains many important pieces of religious art, including Giovanni Bellini's painting *St. Francis in Ecstasy* and Duccio's *The Temptation of Christ*.

The Metropolitan Museum of Art (Fifth Ave. at 82nd St. LM, central Fifth Ave. façade, 1902, by Richard M. Hunt and Richard H. Hunt; many other architects have designed wings through the years. ☎ 535-7710) contains, in its encyclopedic collections, great works of art from virtually every religious tradition.

The Met even has a number of restful retreats and reconstructions of sacred spaces: a Ming dynasty Chinese courtyard, Hindu temple settings, a garden courtyard in the American Wing, a small medieval chapel, a rooftop sculpture garden with a stunning view (not open year-round), an Egyptian temple in a setting meant to suggest its original placement on the banks of the Nile River, a mosque setting, and more. The Met's uptown branch, the Cloisters (see p. 296), focuses on the art of the European Middle Ages.

The Cooper-Hewitt Museum (the Smithsonian Institution's National Museum of Design, 2 East 91st St. at Fifth Ave. LM, 1901, Babb, Cook & Willard. ☎ 849-8400) occupies what was the mansion of steel baron Andrew Carnegie. The collection was begun by members of Peter Cooper's family, and it was originally housed at the Cooper Union School downtown (see p. 126). Changing exhibitions feature selections from its extensive collections of drawings and prints, ceramics, glass, furniture, woodwork, textiles, and metal work. Many items are religious objects.

The Jewish Museum (1109 Fifth Ave. at 92nd St. LM, 1908, C. P. H. Gilbert; 1993 addition in the same style by Kevin Roche. ☎ 423-3200) offers generous samples of Judaica from its permanent collection, plus periodic exhibitions on special topics of interest. The French Renaissance-style chateau housing the museum was the home of Felix and Frieda Warburg; it was Frieda (born Frieda Schiff) whose parents gave Temple Emanu-El the Schiff Torah Shield in honor of her confirmation (see p. 200).

The Museum of the City of New York (Fifth Ave. at 103rd St. LM, 1930, J. J. Freedlander. ☎ 534-1672. To be relocated in the near future.) was founded to teach New Yorkers the history and culture of their own city. It exhibits dioramas, models, furniture, silver, paintings, prints, and other collections reflecting every aspect of the city's history.

El Museo del Barrio (1230 Fifth Ave., between 104th and 105th Sts. ☎ 831-7272), founded in 1969, is New York City's museum devoted to Puerto Rican, Caribbean, and Latin American art. It offers exhibitions, education, workshops, lectures, and festivals. Its building formerly housed the Society for the Prevention of Cruelty to Children.

The East 70s

The Church that Turned Itself Around
SAINT JAMES (LMD)
Episcopal. 863 Madison Ave. at 71st St. 1884, R. H. Robertson. Rebuilt 1924, Ralph Adams Cram. ☎ 288-4100

When St. James's doors are open to Madison Avenue, even the most casual passerby stops to admire the church's gilded reredos. Pedestrians weren't able to see into the church, however, until the building turned itself around.

When St. James's congregation first built here in 1884, the entrance was in a gable facing East 71st Street down toward Park Avenue. The body of the church ran parallel to 71st Street to the square tower on the Madison Avenue corner, and the rear (apse) of the church faced Madison Avenue. In 1922 the congregation asked architect Ralph Adams Cram to turn the building around, so that the congregation would more appropriately face an altar in the east, and to increase the seating. First, he replaced the apse with a grand new entrance on Madison Avenue. It features a beautiful rose window, and incorporates a narthex and a gallery above that. Then he built a large new chancel at the east end. He raised the side walls, put tall thin lancet windows into them, and flattened the roofs of the side aisles. He added a north transept with a chapel in it. The tower got a modest spire (since replaced by what you see today)—and thus a "new" church appeared on Madison Avenue.

St. James was founded in 1810 as the summer church for people who had estates "way out here" in the country but who wintered in town, which was then below City Hall. Far in advance of actual settlement, New York City planners had designed streets and avenues northward with occasional "squares" to break the grid for parks, schools, or religious institutions, and the first St. James was built in 1810 on one of those squares—Hamilton Square, at the southwest corner of Lexington Avenue and 69th

Street—where Hunter College stands today. St. James offered services only in the summer until 1827, and it shared a rector with St. Michael's on the West Side until 1842. St. James served not only "society"—the Stuyvesants, Beekmans, Van Rensselaers, and Gracies—but also a neighborhood of African Americans just to the north. In fact the second marriage registered in St. James was that of Peter Japan and Priscilla Hicks, a black couple, in 1817.

This congregation has a fine sense of history, for it has saved and brought along appointments from all of its earlier homes. The congregation treasures a pair of silver altar chalices given by Peter Schermerhorn, the congregation's first warden, in 1814. When the church got its new main altar and reredos (a Spanish rococo design in gilt and polychrome), the old altar and its reredos went into the chapel. It also uses a rare old organ, fixtures, pews, and lectern. The tower holds the bell saved from the congregation's first home. The baptismal font, some stained glass, and the iron fence come from Holy Trinity Church on 42nd Street, with which St. James merged in 1895. Note the Della Robbia terra-cotta plaque in the baptistery; the stained glass by Charles Connick and Tiffany Studios; and the furnishings of the mortuary chapel. Here St. James held the funeral of actor Montgomery Clift in 1966. He was a Quaker, and he's buried in Brooklyn's Quaker cemetery, but his mother wanted the funeral here.

St. James's attributes, the pilgrim's staff and cockle shell associated with the pilgrimage to Santiago in Spain (see p. 99) can be seen on the façade and above the door to the parish house next door.

Saint Nicholas in New York
THE GREEK ORTHODOX ARCHDIOCESAN CATHEDRAL OF THE HOLY TRINITY
319 East 74th St., between First and Second Aves. 1932, Kerr Rainsford, John A. Thompson, Gerald A. Holmes. ☎ 288-3215

The only relic of New Amsterdam's patron saint, Nicholas, in Manhattan is kept here in the Greek Orthodox Cathedral. Nicholas, patron of children, sailors, Greece, Sicily, and Russia, as well as New York, is traditionally identified as a fourth-century bishop of Myra in Asia Minor. His relics were stolen from Myra in the Middle Ages and taken to Bari, Italy, and a fragment was brought to New York from Bari and placed in a chapel on the north side of the nave in this cathedral in 1972.

Holy Trinity Greek Orthodox Church was founded in New York in 1892. Its first pastor, Reverend Paisios Ferentinos, was a native of Patmos, the Greek island where John the evangelist had once lived in exile, and

Reverend Ferentinos had been a monk there in St. John's Monastery. Holy Trinity occupied different locations downtown before it purchased an Episcopalian church building on East 72nd Street in 1904. The purchase was made possible by showman P. T. Barnum's daughter, who had been married at Holy Trinity downtown to a handsome young Greek into whose arms she had stumbled and fallen while climbing a pyramid in Egypt. The 72nd Street church burned down, and the cornerstone for this new church was laid in 1931 in the presence of Eleanor Roosevelt, who represented her husband, then–New York State Governor Franklin D. Roosevelt.

Greek Orthodox congregations in the Western Hemisphere were more or less subject to authorities in Greece into the early twentieth century, but political strife in Athens made that arrangement untenable. Therefore, in 1921, the Greek Orthodox Archdiocese of North and South America was incorporated under the direct jurisdiction of the ecumenical patriarch of Istanbul, who is the spiritual head of all Orthodox churches. Holy Trinity in New York has been the seat of that archdiocese since 1961.

The cathedral is one of New York's little-known treasures. It is a cruciform building in Romanesque style made of red brick with limestone trim. A chancel platform, called a *solea*, extends in front of the iconostasis, which screens the sacred space in the apse behind. High above, the half-dome of the apse is frescoed with the Virgin and Child enthroned. The Ten Commandments are carved on the wall to the left of the apse, and the Nicene Creed to the right. The building is everywhere adorned with rich marbles, mosaics, paintings, and glass.

The cathedral was long the seat of the legendary Archbishop Iakovos, who retired in 1996 after serving thirty-seven years. He marched in Selma, Alabama, with Reverend Martin Luther King, Jr., in 1965, and the two made the cover of *Life* magazine. For nine years he was copresident of the World Council of Churches, and in 1959 he was the first Greek Orthodox archbishop to visit a pope (John XXIII) in over 400 years. In 1980 President Jimmy Carter awarded him the Presidential Medal of Freedom, the nation's highest civilian honor. In 1999 Demetrios Trakatellis became archbishop. He is a former professor at Harvard Divinity School. Famous members of the congregation have included shipowner Aristotle Onassis and Spyros Skouras, the president of Twentieth Century-Fox Films from 1942 to 1962.

The headquarters of the Greek Orthodox Diocese of America is on East 79th Street, a portion of which was renamed "Patriarch Bartholomew Way" when Ecumenical Patriarch Bartholomew I visited New York in October 1997.

SANTA CLAUS

The early Dutch settlers chose Nicholas as their patron saint because the saint was the figurehead of *The New Netherlands*, the ship that brought the first colonists. "Santa Claus," however, as we know the figure today, is entirely a creation of New Yorkers. In the Netherlands, St. Nicholas's Feast Day (December 6) is a children's holiday, but New Yorkers moved his gift day to Christmas Day, which is the traditional English gift holiday. Early in the nineteenth century, New York author Washington Irving first described Santa Claus's habits; Clement Moore wrote a poem about "A Visit from St. Nicholas" (better-known by its opening line: "Twas the Night Before Christmas") in 1822; cartoonist Thomas Nast first drew the character we recognize today in *Harper's Weekly* in 1863, and in 1897 editor Francis Church of the *New York Sun* reassured a little girl named Virginia O'Hanlon that, yes, there really is a Santa Claus.

Today New York has a Greek Orthodox Cathedral of St. Nicholas, a Russian Orthodox Cathedral of St. Nicholas, and many other churches dedicated to the popular saint. The Dutch Reformed denomination, however, dissolved St. Nicholas Reformed Church in the 1940s.

The Exposition of the Blessed Sacrament
SAINT JEAN BAPTISTE (LM)
Roman Catholic. 1067 Lexington Ave. at 76th St. 1914, Nicholas Serracino. ☎ 288-5082

This impressive Italian Mannerist-inspired building was the gift of financier Thomas F. Ryan, who came to New York from Virginia an impoverished orphan and made a fortune consolidating street railways. After once having had to stand during crowded services at an earlier, smaller church, he told the priests to build a new church and send him the bill. Its façade presents a porch with four freestanding Corinthian columns on a high base. Two carved angels support a globe with a monstrance on it on a parapet between a pair of bell towers, and two more angels blast trumpets from pedestals beside the towers below the cornice.

The parish was originally language-based, established for a local community of French Canadians in 1882; thus it bears the French name for John the Baptist. Its first pastor was Father Charles De La Croix, whose modest adopted name concealed his true name, Castries, of French ducal rank. St. Jean is staffed by members of the Congregation of the Most Blessed Sacrament, founded in France by Peter Eymard (1811–68), a saint of whom the church displays a relic. This order advocates the perpetual display of consecrated hosts for worship, hence the monstrance on the façade. At St. Jean Baptiste, the consecrated host (Blessed Sacrament) is exposed in a golden monstrance forty feet high on an elaborate marble altar protected by a shimmering mosaic baldachin. That form is echoed by a mosaic in the apse. The church also remembers Peter Eymard's friend and associate in France, John-Baptist Vianney (1786–1859); his tirelessness in the service of his parishioners won him designation as the patron saint of parish clergy.

A recent restoration and additional decoration of St. Jean's interior by contemporary New York artist and restorer Felix Chavez has brought new life to it. Vivid new painting plus gold, silver, and copper leafing pick out details of carving and plaster, rosettes and angels' heads in the ceiling, walls, and woodwork. New marbleizing adds dignity to the tall columns. Arches and fluted pilasters support the barrel vaulting over the three naves.

St. Jean Baptiste

The words to the hymn "Lauda Sion" encircle the clerestory in gold leaf. Inside the dome at the crossing (175 feet above the floor and 45 feet in diameter) twelve twentieth-century stained-glass windows from Chartres, France, each fourteen by eight feet, depict the apostles.

This church also contains the National Shrine to St. Anne, the mother of the Virgin Mary. The first chapel to the right upon entering the church contains a relic of St. Anne sent to the New World by Pope Leo XIII.

"Blossom and Bear Fruit"
CONGREGATION SHAARAY TEFILA
Reform. 250 East 79th St. at Second Ave. Reconstruction of a corner movie theater (1959) and construction of the community house next door (1963), both by John J. McNamara and Horace Ginsbern & Associates.
☎ 535-8008

Congregation Shaaray Tefila ("Gates of Prayer") was organized as an Orthodox congregation in 1845, when a group of English Jews left Congregation B'nai Jeshurun (see p. 253) on the Lower East Side. The congregation first worshiped over a stable on Franklin Street, but in 1847 they dedicated their own building. Their first rabbi, Rabbi Samuel Isaacs, had served at B'nai Jeshurun, but he came with the splinter group to form the new congregation. Isaacs had been born in Holland and raised in England, and when he had come to America in 1839, he was said to be the only English-speaking rabbi in New York City, and one of only two in the entire country. Isaacs was a man of tremendous intellectual distinction. He started ed a newspaper, *The Jewish Messenger*, organized the Hebrew Free School Association, and lectured at Yale University on Judaism. Shaaray Tefila's second rabbi, Frederick de Sola Mendes, was an eleventh-generation rabbi in his family, as was his brother H. Peirera Mendes, who served at Shearith Israel (see p. 246). The two brothers were instrumental in founding what is today Montefiore Hospital in the Bronx.

In 1859 Shaaray Tefila initiated the formation of the Board of Delegates of American Israelites, the first central organization to speak and act for American Jewry as a whole. When the provision for chaplains for the Civil War specified "Christian ministers," this Board protested to Congress and raised funds to support a Jewish chaplain. In 1878 the Board merged with the Union of American Hebrew Congregations.

From its first synagogue downtown on Wooster Street, Shaaray Tefila moved uptown several times, and in 1894 settled into a synagogue on West

82nd Street designed by architect Arnold Brunner, the great-grandson of their own first president. A terrible fire there in 1937 destroyed much of the congregation's material history, including historic Torahs that had to be buried, but still today members parade historic Torahs through the aisles of the sanctuary at annual Simchat Torah celebrations. An artistic highlight of today's sanctuary is the set of six bronze bas-relief panels by sculptor Chaim Gross, installed in 1965. Each depicts a single event from the creation story.

In the 1880s the congregation evolved from Orthodox to Conservative Judaism. They simplified the service and introduced more English into it, replaced individual seats with pews, began seating women and men together, bought an organ, and launched a mixed choir. Eventually Shaaray Tefila joined the Reform movement in 1921, and it is today one of the city's largest and most distinguished Reform congregations.

The congregation still cherishes the trowel with which Rabbi Isaacs cemented the cornerstone of the congregation's first synagogue in 1846, when he said, "The seed of Judaism here sown will blossom and bear fruit in the courts of God. . . ."

The East 80s

Two American Restoration Congregations
The Christian Church (Church of Christ/Disciples of Christ) is one of the largest indigenous American denominations. One of its founders was Thomas Campbell, a Presbyterian minister who broke with that denomination because of his belief in universal communion. In 1809 he published his "Declaration and Address," which outlined his beliefs that creeds, clerical titles, and authority have no justification in Scripture; that Communion should be served every Sunday; and that baptism should be by immersion for adult believers. Thomas's son Alexander Campbell became a famous preacher of what was called the American Restoration Movement.

In New York, a group of Scottish immigrants (one a cousin of poet Robert Burns) who had been attending various Baptist churches withdrew in 1810 and organized under the name Church of Christ. In the late nineteenth century, the American Restoration Movement split into the Churches of Christ and the slightly more liberal, ecumenically minded Disciples of Christ. New York's original Church of Christ became today's Park Avenue Christian Church (Disciples of Christ). A new Manhattan Church of Christ was founded in 1920.

THE MANHATTAN CHURCH OF CHRIST

48 East 80th St., between Madison and Park Aves. 1968, Eggers & Higgins. ☎ 737-4900

This congregation is dedicated to following the teachings of the New Testament strictly: "Speak where the New Testament speaks, but remain silent when the New Testament remains silent." Singing, therefore, is entirely a cappella, because the New Testament has no references to any musical instruments. The congregation prides itself on the quality of its singing. Pat Boone was long a member of this congregation.

The sanctuary is a simple preaching space, and the baptismal pool is located in a lower chapel below the main sanctuary. The building's façade of cast concrete and thick stained glass (designed by J. Duval) reveals a colorful "shattered" cross when illuminated at night from within.

PARK AVENUE CHRISTIAN CHURCH

1010 Park Ave. at 85th St. 1911, Cram, Goodhue & Ferguson. ☎ 288-3246

This congregation differs from the Church of Christ in only a few doctrinal matters, including, for example, that it uses a pipe organ during services. Their Gothic-style building (of true Gothic construction—it has no steel frame) was built as the South Reformed Church and then served a Presbyterian congregation until it was bought by this congregation in 1945. A reminder of the Reformed congregation can be seen above the front entrance, where a Dutch coat of arms bears two mottoes: in Dutch, "Unity makes strength," and, in Latin, "Without the Lord, all is vain." The delicate high lead flèche over the crossing is lighted at night and furnished with chimes that play hymns on Sunday morning and at twilight during the Christmas season.

In the chancel is a small old table upon which, it is said, Alexander Campbell celebrated communion in 1830; the new communion table is a solid block of granite quarried near Jerusalem. Here the baptismal pool was installed at the front of the nave. The east windows depict the nativity, baptism, and resurrection of Christ. These were made by Tiffany for an earlier home of South Reformed Church, where they were so admired that they were removed for exhibition at the Chicago World's Columbian Exhibition of 1893 and eventually installed here in 1911.

In 1963 the present congregation built a new education and office building on the site of the original parish house south of the church, but the congregation insisted on saving the Park Avenue façade of the original building. The kitchens of this new facility, where meals are prepared for the homeless, were donated by Colonel and Mrs. Harland Sanders, of Kentucky Fried Chicken fame.

The Worship of God and the Service of Man
UNITARIAN CHURCH OF ALL SOULS
1157 Lexington Ave. at 80th St. 1932, Hobart Upjohn. ☎ 535-5530

This is the fourth home of what was incorporated in 1819 as the "First Congregational Church of New York." The church's first pastor, William Ware, won fame for his novels about the Roman Empire; another early minister, Charles Follen (served 1836–38), a native of Germany, introduced the custom of decorating Christmas trees to New England and New York. Many early American leaders were members. The dedicatory sermon for its first building was delivered by Edward Everett—statesman (later vice-presidential candidate), orator (he preceded Lincoln at Gettysburg),

CHRISTMAS TREES

Today's Christmas tree originated in late medieval Strasbourg, Alsace, where a popular play about Adam and Eve in the Garden of Eden hung apples on a fir tree and called it "the Paradise Tree." Some people set up such a tree in their own homes on December 24, the religious feast day of Adam and Eve, and they hung wafers on it to symbolize the Eucharist as the means of redemption from the sin of Adam and Eve. The wafers were often later replaced with cookies. Candles symbolized Christ. Christmas trees were widespread in German Lutheran homes by the eighteenth century, and in the nineteenth century they became a general northern European tradition. German settlers had also brought the tradition to North America early on, and they became more fashionable in the United States after the German Prince Albert, Queen Victoria's husband, introduced Christmas trees into England in the nineteenth century. Some New Yorkers adopted the custom in the 1840s, although the stricter Protestant denominations did not accept the tradition until the end of the century (see p. 224).

and author (*The Man Without a Country*). Early parishioners also included poet and journalist William Cullen Bryant (who wrote five hymns for its first hymnbook), author Herman Melville, Nathaniel Currier (of Currier & Ives), and inventor Peter Cooper (who founded Cooper Union).

The architect of this church, Hobart Upjohn, was the son of Richard M. Upjohn and the grandson of Richard Upjohn, both of whom had been personally committed to High Church Anglicanism and to the Gothic Revival style. Richard, Sr., had once even refused to design a Unitarian church. Hobart, however, accepted the commission for this Unitarian church, and he gave the congregation a simple geometry of red brick and sandstone boxes that might be called Georgian Revival. The entire narthex is a rectangular base from which a square lantern rises to an octagonal steeple. A slate tablet states the congregation's beliefs: "In the freedom of the truth and in the spirit of Jesus/We unite for the worship of God and the service of man."

The narthex opens into a large vaulted sanctuary with a high pulpit placed prominently in the center. White pews are framed in mahogany, and tall arched windows of clear glass provide strong light. One of sculptor Augustus Saint-Gaudens's finest works stands on the right wall: a life-sized bas-relief of Dr. Henry W. Bellows. Bellows was an extraordinary man: pastor of All Souls from 1839 to 1882; founder of the Unitarian National Conference; Overseer of Harvard University; organizer, during the Civil War, of the U.S. Sanitary Commission, the forerunner of the Red Cross; and a founder of the Metropolitan Museum of Art, although he wondered who would administer it, because "men of affairs and enterprise and executive ability are seldom interested in art or marked with taste. . . . [and] artists [are] a brooding, dreamy, meditative class." Another portrait of Dr. Bellows, a marble bust by Hiram Powers, stands in the foyer. Visitors to FDR's estate at Hyde Park, seventy-five miles up the Hudson River, may notice that the framed marriage certificate for the president's parents, Sara Delano and James Roosevelt, was signed by the presiding minister—Dr. Henry Bellows. Upstairs at All Souls is a signed photograph of William Howard Taft, the only Unitarian President of the United States; he spoke at All Souls' 100th anniversary in 1919. The church still uses its original communion set, made by New York silversmith William Thomson in 1821. In November 2000 All Souls hosted the first *goma*, sacred fire ceremony of the Japanese Agon Shu Buddhist sect, ever held in the Western Hemisphere.

 The design of the church and parish house allowed space for a small outdoor seating area, today planted with bushes, trees, and flowers.

Tragic Memories
ZION-SAINT MARK'S EVANGELICAL LUTHERAN CHURCH

339 East 84th St., between First and Second Aves. 1889, J. F. Mahoney. ☎ 650-1648

This Gothic Revival stone building houses two historic German Lutheran congregations that merged in 1946. One of them, Zion Lutheran, was founded in 1892 and bought this building from a previous German Evangelical Church of Yorkville (whose name survives over the door). The other congregation, St. Mark's, organized downtown in 1847, moved to 6th Street in 1848, and eventually spun off both today's St. John's Lutheran on Christopher Street and Grace Lutheran on West 71st Street.

The altar furnishings in Zion-St. Mark's are from old St. Mark's, and it was that congregation that suffered in 1904 one of the greatest tragedies in New York history. Each year, the church's German immigrant parishioners enjoyed a picnic excursion, and on June 15, 1904, they boarded the steamboat *General Slocum* for a cruise and picnic on Long Island Sound. Virtually all of the more than 1,300 passengers were women and children; only nine were male heads of families. Unfortunately, the vessel was a disaster waiting to happen, with rotting life jackets and an incompetent crew. It caught fire just after passing through the Hell Gate between Randalls Island and Queens, and it broke up near North Brother Island, just off the South Bronx. The crew never even tried to launch the lifeboats (there were only six), because they were wired in place and virtually glued to the chocks by many coats of paint. Forty minutes after the *General Slocum* had sailed from the East 3rd Street pier, 1,021 of the holiday makers were dead. The funeral procession had to use every hearse in the city, and Wilhelm II, the German emperor, sent a telegram of sympathy to President Roosevelt. Two memorials commemorate the disaster: one in Tompkins Square Park, and the other in Lutheran Cemetery in Queens, where almost 1,000 of the victims are buried. The tragedy broke the spirit of the German Lower East Side, and a mass migration of the families of the victims ensued, with many of them relocating up to the East 80s, which came to be known as German Yorkville. St. Mark's Church (consecrated in 1848 at 323 East 6th St., between First and Second Aves.) became a synagogue in 1940—today's **Orthodox Community Synagogue**.

Church minutes record the pain German-Americans suffered during World War I. In 1915 and 1916, before the United States entered that war, the congregation sent money to Germany for the widows and orphans of dead soldiers. By 1918, however, after the United States had been a combatant against Germany for a year, the minutes list local widows and orphans of men who died fighting against Germany.

Today Zion-St. Mark's carries on its traditions (services every Sunday in both German and English), but offers a variety of new community programs, too. The coffee socials downstairs, overseen by portraits of the church's pastors through history, provide a bit of German conviviality in Yorkville (see p. 219).

For the Greater Glory of God
SAINT IGNATIUS LOYOLA (LM)
Roman Catholic. 980 Park Ave. at 84th St. 1898, William Schickel & Isaac Ditmars. ☎ 288-3588. A guidebook is available in the office.

Ignatius Loyola was a Basque aristocrat who, during a long convalescence from a battle injury, began to write *The Spiritual Exercises*, a series of reflections and prayers leading to mystical union with God. The number of readers of this book and its influence through the centuries could scarcely be exaggerated. In 1540 Ignatius and nine companions formed the Society of Jesus (Jesuits), whose members take a special vow to be at the pope's disposal anytime anywhere. Jesuit missions almost immediately fanned out around the world to begin their work in education and battling the challenge of the Protestant Reformation.

This complex of church, schools, and residences on Park Avenue began in 1866, when New York's Archbishop Hughes asked the Jesuits to staff what was then the small country parish of St. Lawrence O'Toole, established in 1851. Lawrence was a twelfth-century bishop of Dublin. The Jesuits soon started work on a new church, the basement of which was finished in 1886. Along East 84th Street, you can still see the rough-cut stone buttresses that were intended to support a Gothic-style church. The Jesuits changed their design plans, however, and, at the same time, they petitioned Rome to rededicate the church to St. Ignatius. The Vatican approved recognition of Ignatius as titular copatron with the Irish saint, so today the upper church is dedicated to Ignatius, and the lower church serves as a parish hall.

The church's overall plan derives from that of the Gesu in Rome, where Ignatius is buried. On the limestone façade, superimposed pilasters support entablatures, and high above, the Jesuit motto proclaims: "Ad majorem Dei Gloriam," "For the greater glory of God." A planned pair of tall towers was never built. St. Ignatius's symmetrical and relatively austere exterior belies the richness of the interior, which illustrates the Jesuit belief in honoring God by beautifying the sanctuary. Three bronze doors

TEILHARD DE CHARDIN
AND THE INTERNET

The Jesuit priest and paleontologist Pierre Teilhard de Chardin (a discoverer of Peking Man) came to St. Ignatius Loyola in 1946, and he died there on Easter Sunday 1955. He tried to reconcile Christianity with evolution, seeing evolution as biological, intellectual, and spiritual. He proposed a theory of "convergence," that technology is creating a "single nervous system for humanity," a "living membrane . . . a stupendous thinking machine." Chardin's writings inspired the Canadian scholar Marshall McLuhan, who popularized the phrase "the global village." McLuhan, a convert to Roman Catholicism, wrote, "The Christian concept of the mystical body—all men as members of the body of Christ—this becomes technologically a fact under electronic conditions." It has been argued that what Chardin called "the noösphere," we now call the Internet.

lead from the marble narthex into the long, high, gilt-coffered barrel-vaulted nave that focuses on the apse. Monolithic polished pink granite columns separate the nave from flanking lower side aisles. Lavish decoration is set off by unadorned flat expanses of marbles. The coat of arms of the house of Loyola decorates the center of the pavement. Three mosaics above the main altar show Ignatius's wounding at the Battle of Pamplona; his receiving the papal bull confirming the Society of Jesus; and, in the center, his reception into heaven. The gallery at the back of the nave houses a four-manual, sixty-eight stop, 5,000-pipe direct tracker-action pipe organ dedicated in 1993. In 1994, the world watched the funeral of Jacqueline Kennedy Onassis here (broadcast from the outside only).

The Voices of Faith, Hope, and Love
IMMANUEL EVANGELICAL LUTHERAN
122 East 88th St. at Lexington Ave. 1886, Arthur Crooks. ☎ 289-8128

Every Sunday morning three large bronze bells named Faith, Hope, and Love (1 Corinthians 13:13) ring out here as they have since this church was dedicated in 1886. These bells were a personal gift of Augusta, Empress of Germany, and the tower that houses them soars 200 feet over this Gothic Revival church in Yorkville, which was then a bustling German neighborhood. Immanuel Lutheran had been founded in 1863, just a few months after riots protesting the Civil War draft had swept downtown New York City, about five miles away. In the next few years so many German immigrants would be drafted that by war's end, German was a common language of command in the Union Army. German immigration continued, and by 1890 Germans were the leading national group in New York City. Immanuel Lutheran anchored German Yorkville for 100 years.

Yorkville isn't so German anymore, but Immanuel Lutheran is still here. The interior reveals exposed wooden ceiling trusses, and galleries decorated with a motif of pointed arches surround three sides of the nave. The focus of the church is a stunning reredos in which almost-life-sized figures of Christ, Moses, and John the Baptist stand in an elaborate structure of Gothic-style canopies. This reredos was hand-carved in the Black Forest about 1900. In the early 1970s, blasting for construction of a new building next door shook and damaged the church, so the construction company had to pay for the new stained-glass windows designed by Benoit Gilsoul.

The Loire Valley in Manhattan
CHURCH OF THE HOLY TRINITY (LM)
Episcopal. 312 East 88th St., between First and Second Aves. 1897, Barney & Chapman. ☎ 289-4100. A guidebook is available in the office.

🍃 A quiet moment spent in the enclosed garden of this church is about as restful as a Manhattan experience can be. The French Gothic-style church and tower, and Renaissance Revival rectory and parish house could almost be found somewhere along the Loire Valley. The complex was designed, however, as a community facility for the poor Irish and German immigrants in what was then a slum. Just to the north were three huge breweries, a sawmill, and other factories. The church complex was a gift of Serena Rhinelander in memory of her father and grandfather. The Rhinelander family had arrived in New York in 1686, and they had owned this property since 1798. Serena had already given the neighborhood the Children's Aid Society Building, still standing just to the east of the church (1891; Vaux and Radford). She lived in a mansion on Washington Square, and she gave her own church, Ascension, its reredos and the mural by John LaFarge (see p. 171). Personally, she was shy and retiring. Contemporary accounts report only two public appearances in her 85 years: once to witness the dedication of the Washington Memorial Arch (1895), and once to see Holy Trinity Church.

Holy Trinity was designed by the same architects who designed Grace Chapel—today's Immaculate Conception—on East 14th Street three years

Holy Trinity Episcopal Church

earlier (see p. 133). The bricks and terra-cotta of Holy Trinity are a warmer yellow, and the tower that rises from the exact center of the property has three open belfry slots on each side (it contains a ten-bell carillon), turrets and pinnacles, and an octagonal spire on top. (Architect J. Stewart Barney brought his sweetheart to the top of the tower to propose to her.) The base of the tower is the entrance to the church, the nave of which extends parallel to the street behind a garden, which the *New York Evening Post* called "in effect, a park for the surrounding tenements" when it opened. The rectory (at the east end of the church) and the parish house (at the west) extend out to the sidewalk to embrace the garden, which is then closed off by an iron fence, creating the feel of a half-open cloister. An arcaded gallery connects all of the buildings. The parish house (St. Christopher's) contains meeting rooms, an auditorium, library, gymnasium, splash pool, and communal baths and showers for locals who lacked private plumbing. The parish house was actually finished and opened before the church.

Deep arches above the church's door shelter groups of sculpted figures, and the tympanum depicts the Trinity with saints. All sculpture on the exterior and interior is by Karl Bitter (1867–1915), a Viennese immigrant who designed many of the best sculptures around the city, including the fountain in front of the Plaza Hotel. This church is rich with details and furnishings. The unusual dark brown terra-cotta interior sets off the stained-glass windows by Henry Holiday, considered among the finest by this British artist. The transept windows of the crucifixion and the ascension are among the largest in America.

Holy Trinity was long administered by St. James parish on Madison Avenue, but it became independent in 1951.

God's Servant First
SAINT THOMAS MORE
Roman Catholic. 65 East 89th St., between Madison and Park Aves. 1870, Hubert & Pirsson. ☎ 876-7718

This small "rural" church, built for an Episcopal congregation but serving a Catholic congregation since 1950, coincidentally commemorates a Roman Catholic who gave his life after the Anglican church was founded by King Henry VIII. Sir Thomas More was lord chancellor of England and Henry's dear friend, but he refused to deny papal authority and to acknowledge the king's supremacy, and therefore he was executed. Sir Thomas insisted on the scaffold that he was always "the king's good servant—but God's first." More was declared the patron saint of politicians on October 31, 2000. You can see More's portrait from life by Hans Holbein at the Frick Collection (see p. 205).

St. Thomas More is in the Gothic Revival style, with an unusual tall tower with chamfered corners and an asymmetrical pinnacle. A tiny plot of lawn in front still preserves its rural charm. Some people are surprised to see a Magen David in the window tracery over the door and ask whether this church was built as a synagogue. The Magen David, however, is often found on Christian churches in remembrance of the fact that Jesus was a Jew, of the house and lineage of David. From inside, one can see that the Magen David frames the Holy Spirit descending as a dove in a glorious window showing the resurrection.

The interior displays the same olive-gray Nova Scotia sandstone used in some of the walls surrounding Central Park, a high central nave with abstract clerestory windows, and a hammerbeam ceiling. St. Thomas More held the official memorial service for John F. Kennedy, Jr., after he died in an airplane crash in 1999.

St. Thomas is the second oldest church building on the Upper East Side—after the Episcopal **Church of the Resurrection** (115 East 74th St., between Park and Lexington. 1869, Renwick & Sands. ☎ 879-4320).

A Reminder of Nazi Terror
PARK AVENUE SYNAGOGUE

Conservative. 50 East 87th St., between Park and Madison Aves. 1927, Walter Schneider. ☎ 369-2600

The Nazis planned that after they had eliminated the Jews and other peoples they considered "inferior," they would build a museum to vilify these peoples. Torah scrolls, prayer books, and ceremonial objects from destroyed synagogues—the possessions of entire congregations sent to the death camps—were gathered in Prague. After the war, British Jews discovered these sacred objects, repaired them (if possible), and sent them to congregations in need of such items. The damaged scrolls that could not be used were entrusted to synagogues around the world as memorials. At the front of the sanctuary of Park Avenue Synagogue, a case holds Torah scroll Number 375, written by a scribe at the end of the eighteenth century and treasured at the synagogue in Horazodvice, Czechoslovakia, until the synagogue was destroyed and its members killed in 1942. A tablet beneath the scroll quotes Deuteronomy 25:17, "Remember what Amalek did unto thee. . . ." Amalek harried the Jews as they left Egypt under Moses, and he represents all evil men. What the Nazis intended to display in a perverted museum has become a shrine to victims of Nazi atrocities.

Today's Park Avenue Synagogue—Agudat Yesharim ("The Association of the Righteous")—is New York's largest and one of its leading Conservative synagogues. Its membership combines several congregations that have moved and merged since a group of German-speaking Jews founded a synagogue on East 86th Street in 1882. Their present home is one of New York's Moorish-style synagogues, with a huge arched cast-stone decorated façade, Arabesque dadoes along the interior walls, and an octagonal stained-glass skylight dome. The balcony is not to separate the sexes, but to provide additional seating. Ex-President Dwight Eisenhower worshiped with this congregation on May 28, 1965, the twentieth anniversary of the liberation of concentration camps by troops under his command. Leonard Bernstein, Lukas Foss, Morton Gould, Darius Milhaud, and other leading twentieth-century composers all wrote music for services of this congregation.

A bas-relief over the door to the synagogue's school and office building on Madison Avenue at East 87th Street (1980, J. R. Jarrett, and Schuman Lichtenstein Claman & Efron) shows Dr. Janusz Korczak, the world-famous pediatrician, whose wards from an orphanage clung to him as they all went together to their deaths in the gas chambers at Treblinka concentration camp.

The East 90s to East 110th Street

A Ceiling of Bridal Lace

OUR LADY OF GOOD COUNSEL

Roman Catholic. 236 East 90th St., between Second and Third Aves. 1892, Thomas H. Poole. ☎ 289-1742

Brides-to-be telephone many months in advance and from surprising distances to reserve this church for their weddings; a more fairy-tale interior could hardly be imagined. The fan vaulting that traces lacey webs onto the ceiling is probably the church's rarest and most beautiful feature. Behind the marble high altar from Venice, five fifteen-foot-high paintings by 1887 Paris Salon Prize-winner Alexander Rossi depict the annunciation, the nativity, the crucifixion, the resurrection, and the ascension. Statues of saints and apostles decorate the columns that support the galleries on three sides of the nave. Sun streams in through handsome stained-glass windows lining the nave, and a five-light window opposite the altar shows the many roles of the Virgin. All of these windows were installed by Mayer of Munich.

The marble façade of Our Lady is a gable with a double-s curve (called an *ogee*), flanked by two towers, each of which has two pinnacles. Two sets of stairs rise from the sidewalk, then turn toward each other and unite in a narthex, which is screened from view by the front wall. The shape of the church is unusual. It is a basilica form (the main door is opposite the altar), but the church is wider than it is deep.

➡ AROUND THE CORNER

 The Ruppert Towers Apartment Complex across the street includes a couple of small but delightful park spaces.

Home of Revolutionary Ideas

BRICK PRESBYTERIAN CHURCH (LMD)

1140 Park Ave. at 91st St. 1940, York & Sawyer; Lewis Ayres, designer. Chapel of the Reformed Faith, 1952, Adams & Woodbridge. ☎ 289-4400. A guidebook is available in the office.

In 1883 the new pastor of this church, Reverend Henry van Dyke, shocked the congregation by celebrating Christmas and Easter. Brick Church was one of the more fundamentalist churches in New York that had traditionally ignored those holidays. The parishioners argued that nobody could really know when Christ was born, and "Eastre" was a pagan goddess celebrated on the vernal equinox. Therefore, many New York Presbyterians regarded the celebration of Christmas and Easter as pagan. Many older church members took offense when Reverend van Dyke read the Christmas story instead of giving a sermon on December 25, although the younger generation took to the new custom.

Brick Presbyterian is steeped in history. The congregation organized downtown in 1767, and the belfry on the congregation's present building holds the bell from their first church, opened in 1768. The spire is topped by the original weather vane. The architect of that first church, Scotland-born John McComb, was the father of the architect of New York's City Hall, John McComb, Jr. Benjamin Franklin recommended their first pastor, Dr. John Rodgers, later chaplain of the Revolutionary Army. Rodgers's 1783 sermon, "The Divine Goodness Displayed in the American Revolution," earned a thankful letter from General Washington that Brick Church treasures still. In 1826 Charles Scribner set up his first printing press in Brick's chapel in order to print the pastor's writings. Samuel Clemens (i.e. Mark Twain; 1835–1910) was buried from Brick Presbyterian when it was down at Fifth Avenue and 37th Street.

Brick moved uptown and merged a few times before settling on Park Avenue, where Mayor La Guardia helped lay the cornerstone for this church. The congregation chose a Colonial Revival style to echo that of their first home downtown. The red brick is trimmed with white stone. A grand portico with columns recessed into the façade (*distyle in antis*) shelters the entrance, and a simple tower and steeple rise behind the portico. The elegant interior, virtually one rectangular room lighted by tall arched

The Brick Presbyterian Church

clear glass windows, is comparable to St. Paul's Chapel downtown (see p. 92). Large Corinthian columns support the church and lateral arches over side aisles, and ornamental ironwork by Samuel Yellin sets off the chancel, which contains a simple communion table and the organ. Clarence Dickinson, organist and choirmaster here from 1909 to 1965, helped found the School of Sacred Music at Union Theological Seminary and the American Guild of Organists.

AROUND THE CORNER

➡ The **Church of the Heavenly Rest** (LMD; Episcopal) on Fifth Ave. at East 90th Street (1929, Hardie Philip of Mayers, Murray & Philip. ☎ 289-3400), features exterior sculpture by Ulrich Ellerhausen and Lee Lawrie and a pulpit Madonna by Malvina Hoffman. The rather stern, minimalist exterior might be called art deco Gothic. The great rose window by J. Gordon Guthrie, which is an unsymmetrical arrangement of glass without imagery, is said to have been inspired by John 1:5: "And the light shineth in darkness; and the darkness comprehended it not." Louise Carnegie, the widow of Andrew Carnegie, whose mansion is today the Cooper Hewitt Museum across the street, sold the lot to the congregation with the stipulation that their new home not rise so high as to obstruct the sun in her garden.

An Upper East Side Essential
THE 92ND STREET "Y"
1395 Lexington Ave. at East 92nd St. 1930, Necarsulmer & Lehlbach; and Gehron & Ross; 1968 extension, Gilbert Seltzer. ☎ 427-6000

This is the best known of the Young Men's and Young Women's Hebrew Associations in New York, which are nonsectarian cultural, educational, and recreational centers under Jewish auspices, but without religious affiliation. It was founded in 1874 by a group of German Jewish men, and originally housed on West 21st Street. After several moves, financier-philanthropist Jacob Schiff donated this land in 1898, and the Y moved here.

It is today one of the city's cultural landmarks, offering concerts, lectures, readings, classes, and plays, as well as recreational facilities, a camp program, a day care center, and a senior citizens' program. Although without religious affiliation, the Y has offered facilities for Yom Kippur and Rosh Hashanah services since 1900.

Manhattan's First Purpose-Built Mosque
UPPER EAST SIDE ISLAMIC CULTURAL CENTER AND MOSQUE

201 East 96th St. at Third Ave. 1991, Skidmore, Owings & Merrill; minaret by Swanke Hayden Connell. ☎ 722-5234

This building was not planned and constructed by a congregation. It was, rather, built by a nonprofit organization founded in 1963 by the Islamic states represented at the United Nations. The Board of Trustees is made up of UN ambassadors of Muslim countries, and although Saudi Arabia, Libya, and Malaysia contributed for its construction, more than half of the total cost was ultimately borne by Kuwait. It was dedicated in the presence of the Emir of Kuwait. Imams are provided by Egypt from the prestigious Al-Azhar University in Cairo.

The Islamic Cultural Center mosque was the first purpose-built mosque in Manhattan. Its designers carefully followed the traditional architectural criteria for a Muslim house of worship. Worshipers gather in an outdoor forecourt and then enter a small below-grade structure in the courtyard for ritual ablutions. The mosque is turned 29 degrees off the Manhattan street grid so that the *mihrab*, placed opposite the entrance, properly indicates the direction toward Mecca. The entrance portal to the prayer hall is created from layers of overlapping green-toned glass panels that are stepped to form an arch. Green is associated with paradise, and shades of green are supplied by the glass, celadon walls, and a green marble border on the floor. Strong steel trusses allow a vast column-free interior, and a suspended women's gallery. The entire space is covered by a copper-clad steel and concrete dome that seems to float on a band of clear glass. In addition to this skylight band, the interior is illuminated by a huge circle of suspended lights. Islam forbids figural art, so a modern adaptation of Kufic Arabic calligraphy is used as ornament over the main portal, around the *mihrab*, and

The Upper East Side Islamic Cultural Center and Mosque

in the dome. Both the mosque and the companion minaret are clad in granite. In addition to the mosque, a school, library, lecture hall, museum, and a residence for the imams are under construction.

The New Yorkers worshiping at the mosque today reflect recent Muslim immigration to the city, rather than the countries that paid for the mosque. Bangladeshis and Pakistanis, in particular, outnumber Arabs and Malaysians here.

Symbol of Historic Russian-American Friendship
SAINT NICHOLAS RUSSIAN ORTHODOX CATHEDRAL (LM)
15 East 97th St., between Fifth and Madison Aves. 1902, John Bergessen. ☎ 289-1915

In 1899 Nicholas II Romanoff, Czar of all the Russias, donated 5,000 rubles toward the construction of an Orthodox Cathedral for New York. A Russian congregation had been founded downtown in 1894 and, with the Czar's help plus additional funds from the Russian Synod of Bishops, it was able to lay the cornerstone for this church in 1901 and to dedicate it the next year.

The man chiefly responsible for this success was Reverend Alexander Hotovitzky. He would serve as Dean here until 1914, and during his service Hotovitzky would be called on to celebrate a Te Deum in Portsmouth, New Hampshire, at the signing of the peace treaty ending the Russo-Japanese War. Later he would welcome Theodore Roosevelt, who had negotiated that treaty, to St. Nicholas. Hotovitzky eventually returned to Moscow and became bishop at Christ the Savior Cathedral. Stalin soon decided to destroy that church, built to commemorate the defeat of Napoleon, as a symbol of the old regime, so Stalin sent Hotovitzky to Siberian exile and death. Today the Russian government is rebuilding Christ the Savior Cathedral.

Soon after New York's St. Nicholas was finished, the diocesan seat of North America was transferred here from San Francisco by Bishop Tikhon, the first Russian bishop to visit North America. Tikhon returned to Russia in 1908 and rose to become patriarch of Russia. The communist government imprisoned him, but he was canonized in 1995. St. Nicholas Cathedral treasures a relic of Tikhon, as well as a relic of St. Innocent, who brought Christianity to Alaska in the 1820s, when it was a Russian colony (both relics are found on the west wall). Innocent translated the Bible into Aleut. Framed on the wall next to the relic of Innocent is the letter from the bishop of Irkutsk sending Innocent to Alaska.

St. Nicholas Russian Orthodox Cathedral

The cathedral exemplifies an architectural style called Moscow Baroque, which was revived in the late nineteenth century. The main entrance is in a central two-storied gabled bay, and the entire exterior is rich with polychromatic crosses, arches, and other ornamentation of majolica tiles, colored brick, and terra-cotta. Arches shelter winged white cherubim against a ground of blue and gold. Four small onion domes surround a central dome, and each is topped with a cross.

The interior is a large cube illumined by stained-glass windows and one huge chandelier. Winged angels' heads top the pilasters around the walls. An oak iconostasis closes off the apsidal chancel. The cross on the altar came from the chapel of the Russian battleship *Retvizan*. The ship was under construction in Philadelphia in 1901, so Russian sailors from its crew made up the choir at the laying of St. Nicholas's cornerstone. Some of those very sailors may have lost their lives when the *Retvizan* was sunk in the Japanese raid on Port Arthur on November 23, 1904. Today's choir (a cappella) sings from a gallery over the rear of the nave. The bishop has a throne behind the iconostasis and another in the middle of the floor, but worshipers (except the infirm) stand during services.

A "Flower Garden" of Nationalities

Upper East Side Ethnic Churches

During the period of great immigration between the Civil War and World War I, a tremendous number and variety of "ethnic churches," representing the immigrants' native countries and traditions, organized on the Lower East Side. As many of these congregations prospered in their new country, they moved to the Upper East Side. These buildings survive, and although the pronounced ethnic elements of the congregations have been diluted, the buildings still tell their stories by revealing details of national decor.

The Swedish Baptist Church (today **Trinity Baptist**, 250 East 61st St., between Second and Third Aves. LMD, 1931, Martin Hedmark) exemplifies ethnic architecture at its best—a style from home practiced here for a specific national cultural community. In a brochure for the church's open-

Trinity Baptist Church

ing, its architect criticized the theory of America as a "melting pot," and suggested instead the metaphor of a garden, "where the different nationalities are represented as flowers, each with different qualities." The tall street-wall of this church, crowned by a stepped gable, reflects features found on buildings around the Baltic Sea, and the metal-capped bell towers imitate Swedish churches' wooden steeples. The color of the exterior brick grades from brown to orange rising to buff. Other distinctive national touches include the flat hand-hammered metalwork on the doors, the "Angel Forest" above the entrance door, and the stylized figures of

Adam, Eve, and the angel Gabriel. The interior is a large square topped by a light, circular drum and shallow dome, and everywhere there are fine details: hammered metal, molded terra-cotta, relief sculpture, and expressionist stained-glass windows. The church changed its name to Trinity Baptist and adopted English as the language of worship in 1942.

The Roman Catholic Church of **Saint John Nepomucene** (Nepomuk), (411 East 66th Street at First Ave. 1925, John Van Pelt) houses a Slovak congregation that moved up into this stunning Romanesque-style church. The iconography reveals that it was built for a Slavic congregation. A mosaic above the altar depicts scenes from the lives of Saints Cyril and Methodius, missionaries to the Slavs. Cyril is said to have invented the Cyrillic alphabet. Another mosaic shows John Nepomuk, a Bohemian priest who was bound and dumped into the Vltava River for refusing to divulge the confessions of the king's wife. John is often shown in church decorations with a finger to his lips (as in a window in the narthex at Holy Cross Church on West 42nd St.—see p. 187).

Another Roman Catholic Church, **Saint Elizabeth of Hungary** (211 East 83rd St., between Third and Second Aves.) was founded as a second Slovak parish, but this one was for Slovaks loyal to their pre-World War I Hungarian overlords. Elizabeth (1207–31) was a Hungarian princess who married a German prince; she won sainthood for her care for the poor. Today this church, no longer Slovak, occupies what was originally a Lutheran church from the 1890s. The building is a yellow brick Gothic Revival church with polished oak doors and towers and turrets topped by bright green copper. The interior has a painted ceiling and stained-glass windows.

Roman Catholic Hungarians had their **St. Stephen of Hungary** (408 East 82nd St., between First and York Aves. 1928, Emil Szendy), a yellow brick Romanesque-style church with a tile hipped roof. Stephen was a king baptized in 1001 who spent the rest of his life converting his people to Christianity.

Protestant Hungarians organized the **First Hungarian Reformed Church** (346 East 69th St., between First and Second Aves. 1916, Emery Roth). This is a picturesque adaptation of Hungarian vernacular—a stucco façade ornamented with brightly colored faience and capped by a tiled roof. A conical turret tops the eighty-foot bell tower. The **Hungarian Baptist Church** (225 East 80th St., between Second and Third Aves.), a brick and terra-cotta "Italian palazzo," was built about 1890. Today's **First Russian Baptist Church** (429 East 77th St., between First and York Aves.), a one-room brick Romanesque Revival church, opened in 1885 as a German Baptist Church, then served a Czechoslovak congregation before welcoming its present occupants.

Protestant Czechs founded in 1888 the **Jan Hus Presbyterian Church** (347 East 74th St., between First and Second Aves.), a Richardsonian Romanesque building (architect unknown) decorated with dazzling ironwork. Jan Hus was a Czech nationalist and forerunner of the Protestant Reformation who was burned at the stake as a heretic in 1415. In December 1999, Pope John Paul II apologized for his "cruel" execution. **St. John the Martyr** (252 East 72nd St., between Second and Third Aves.) is an almost fortresslike brownstone Romanesque Revival church built as the Knox Presbyterian Church in 1888, a Bohemian congregation named in honor of Protestant reformer John Knox. It became a Catholic church in 1904.

Other Eastern European congregations can be found elsewhere in Manhattan. Slovene Catholics have a small church—virtually a chapel in a brownstone—**St. Cyril**, established in 1916 at 62 St. Mark's Place. In 1913 the Catholic Croats organized a national parish, **Sts. Cyril and Methodius**, in a former Lutheran church at 552 West 50th Street. In 1974 they merged with St. Raphael's parish and moved into that Gothic-style church (fine windows) at 502 West 41st Street at Tenth Avenue, dating from 1902. The Croats' former 50th-Street church is still dedicated to Cyril and Methodius, but it became the **Bulgarian Orthodox Cathedral of New York**.

———— ✹ ————

CHAPTER SEVEN

The Upper West Side: From West 59th Street to West 110th Street

THE UPPER WEST SIDE is bisected by Broadway, originally a Native American trail and historic highway to the north. A few small villages sprang up along it in the nineteenth century, and Broadway still serves as a spine to the area, with its mix of shops and services. New means of transportation—trains then subways—brought new development. Eastern European Jews and other immigrants from the Lower East Side moved up here in the early part of the twentieth century, and the area still has a large Jewish population. The West 60s and 70s once housed a mixed lower-income black, Irish, and Puerto Rican population (*West Side Story* took place here) that was displaced by gentrification after the construction of Lincoln Center in the 1960s. Riverside Drive along the western edge saw the construction of mansions and upper-middle-class town houses, but most of these were replaced by apartment houses in the 1920s, as Central Park West, too, developed into a wall of elegant apartment buildings. The north-south avenues are generally commercial, but the cross streets mix brownstones and apartments.

Heaven-Sent

Central Park (LM)

From 59th St. (Central Park South) to 110th St., between Fifth Ave. and Eighth Ave. (Central Park West). Opened 1859; Frederick Law Olmsted and Calvert Vaux.

Central Park is not a consecrated space, but New Yorkers never doubt that this, the first large-scale landscaped public park in the United States, was "heaven-sent." Europe's leading cities had public grounds by the mid–nineteenth century, but in the United States land-scaped "rural-style" cemeteries still filled that role. Brooklyn's Green-Wood Cemetery became a leading metropolitan tourist attraction soon after it opened in 1838 (see p. 317), and poet William Cullen Bryant led the drive for a general-use public space of similar design in New York. In 1857 Olmsted and Vaux won the contest to design such a park with their entry, called "Greensward," which combined pastoral areas (such as the **Sheep Meadow**), picturesque areas (such as the **Ramble**), and formal areas (such as the **Mall** and **Bethesda Terrace**). Today the 843-acre park is enjoyed by millions of people annually, for physical recreation, for rest and relaxation, or just to commune with nature. Maps and guidebooks may be found at the **Dairy** (midpark at 65th St.). Free milk was distributed to children here in early park days, but since the 1980s the Dairy has served as the park's visitor information center. Following is a selection of spots of spiritual significance.

The **Maine Monument** (southwest entrance to the Park, 59th St. at Columbus Circle) commemorates the

Relaxing in Central Park's Sheep Meadow

258 sailors who died when the battleship *Maine* exploded in Havana Harbor on February 15, 1898. The incident triggered the Spanish-American War, but today we know it was an accident. The architect of the monument was H. van Buren Magonigle, and the sculptor was Attilio Piccirilli. It was dedicated in 1913.

The **Memorial to the 107th Infantry** of World War I (Fifth Ave. at 67th St.) was the work of Karl Illava, who had himself served in the war. It was dedicated in 1927.

Central Park contains thirteen Great Trees of New York (see p. 129). The Mall, for example, just south of

A quiet corner in Central Park

the 72nd Street transverse road, is lined by what is believed to be the largest **grove of American elms** anywhere, and to walk beneath the arching canopy of green they create when lush in foliage is one of New York's unique experiences. (The park's oldest tree is probably the London Plane growing along the Bridle Path at the northeast corner of the Reservoir near the East 96th St. entrance.)

The subject of the **Angel of the Waters at Bethesda Fountain** (mid-park at 72nd St.; angel by Emma Stubbins; fountain by Jacob Wrey Mould and Calvert Vaux, 1868) derives from John 5:2 ff., which tells of a miraculous pool at Bethesda whose waters, stirred by an angel, cured the sick. The angel is Raphael, whose name means "God healing." The fountain honors the Croton Aqueduct, which first brought pure water to New York in 1842. *Bethesda* means "the place of mercy," and it is frequently the name given to hospitals, orphanages, and other social service institutions.

The construction of Central Park involved the destruction of **Seneca Village**, a mostly African American settlement located between the north end of today's Great Lawn and Central Park West at about 85th Street. It had boasted three churches and a cemetery, bones from which were still being found as recently as 1959. Irish-American political boss George Washington Plunkitt (famous for summing up: "I seen my opportunities and I took 'em.") had been born here in 1842. If you walk into the park on the sidewalk on the north side of the road entering at West 85th Street (Mariner's Gate), you can see a small remnant of the foundations of an old church on your right at the top of the gentle hill. Continuing on that path you will find the **Arthur Ross Pinetum**, with over 600 pine trees representing seventeen species from around the world. The **Conservatory Garden** (closed off from Fifth Ave. at 105th St. by the wrought-iron gates from a former mansion) is a formal area, offering perennials and wildflowers in a setting of fountains and quiet walks.

The 1980 murder of musician John Lennon in front of the Dakota apartment building at Central Park West and West 72nd Street sparked such an outpouring of public grief that a nearby tear-shaped 2.5-acre section of Central Park was dedicated as **Strawberry Fields**, from the name of one of his songs. It was landscaped with 161 species of plants—one for each country of the world, but no strawberries (the birds ate them). A plaque set in stone dedicates the nations to work for peace. The city of Naples, Italy, contributed a star-shaped mosaic, laid in the sidewalk, inscribed "Imagine," the title of another Lennon composition.

Religious services are occasionally held in the park. **Pope John Paul II** celebrated a mass on the Great Lawn in October 1995, and the **Dalai Lama** preached in the East Meadow in August 1999.

The West 60s

An "Otherworldly Interior"
SAINT PAUL THE APOSTLE
Roman Catholic. Columbus Ave. at 60th St. 1885, Jeremiah O'Rourke and Father George Deshon; 1990s renovation by the Eggers Group. ☎ 265-3495. A guidebook is available in the bookshop.

The Missionary Society of St. Paul the Apostle was America's first indigenous society of priests, founded in 1858 by Father Isaac Hecker with four other priests, all of whom were converts to Catholicism. Their purpose was to reach out to non-Catholic America at a time when American culture was still largely anti-Catholic. Hecker founded *The Catholic World*, which writer William Cullen Bryant called "the first high-toned and first-class literary periodical devoted to the interests of the Roman Catholic

Church which has yet appeared. . . ." Later the Paulists opened one of America's first radio stations, and many still enjoy speaking in secular settings, wherever anyone wants to learn about Catholicism.

Their Gothic Revival home church was built mainly of stone from an old uptown aqueduct, and the building's deep embrasures and lack of side windows earned its nickname "Fort Deshon." Father Deshon had in fact been a military engineer at West Point, where he roomed with Ulysses S. Grant. Two flights of steps approach the main portal, flanked by life-sized statues of

St. Paul the Apostle

saints, over which a large travertine and blue-glass bas-relief shows the moment of Paul's conversion, when the heavens opened and Jesus asked, "Why persecutest thou me?" (Acts 9:4) Tall spires planned for the twin towers were never built.

Several of the finest artists of the American Renaissance movement collaborated at St. Paul's to create an interior that the *New York Tribune* described in 1885 as "the most august, otherworldly interior on the continent." Most of it was created or coordinated by Father Hecker's friend John LaFarge, together with Stanford White. The marble baptismal font LaFarge designed has recently been placed in a pool at front and center, since baptism is the entry to Christian life. Beyond, massive columns of blue limestone, alternately round and octagonal, frame a wide nave and vaulted side aisles with skylit shallow chapels. The nave vault is painted blue with the pattern of gold stars as they were at midnight on the church's dedication, January 25, 1885.

The original high altar, designed by Stanford White, is of marble, gold, alabaster, and onyx, and protected by a golden baldachin supported by eight marble columns. Frederick MacMonnies created the three gilded bronze angels kneeling on the baldachin. Today this altar serves as a reredos for the new altar, which has been moved forward into the nave. The chapel of Thérèse of Lisieux contains a painting of her by Augustus Vincent Tack, who also designed the pendant votive lights in all the chapels. The church also treasures one of only two bronze copies ever made of Michelangelo's *Madonna and Child* from the Cathedral of Bruges, Belgium. St. Paul's contains many other fine sculptures and paintings.

LaFarge designed the stained-glass program. The church has no side windows, but only the opalescent windows high in the clerestory, so being in St. Paul's seems like being in a mysterious underwater palace.

AROUND THE CORNER

➡ **The American Bible Society** (1865 Broadway at 61st St. 1966, Skidmore, Owings, & Merrill. ☎ 956-2099) is an interdenominational religious organization formed in New York City in 1816. It is dedicated "to provide the Holy Scriptures to every man, woman and child in a language and form each can readily understand, and at a price each can easily afford." The society's home building offers exhibitions of Bibles and other religious objects, as well as a large library and collection of rare and unusual Bibles.

➡ **The West Side Branch of the Young Men's Christian Association** (LMD, 5 West 63rd St., between Central Park West and Broadway. 1930, D. J. Baum. ☎ 787-1301) is the largest "Y" facility in New York. The YMCA was founded in London as a prayer group in 1844, and its first branch was opened in New York in 1852. The organization evolved from its initial focus on street-corner evangelism and Bible study to more secular activities, including educational, cultural, and recreational opportunities, and even dormitory facilities, as here on the West Side.

➡ **The New York Society for Ethical Culture** (LM in LMD, 33 Central Park West at 64th St. 1910, Robert D. Kohn. ☎ 874-5210) is a religious humanist association formed in 1876 by Felix Adler, a leading exponent of Reform Judaism who was the son of Rabbi Dr. Samuel Adler of Temple Emanu-El (see p. 200). The society belongs to the American Ethical Culture Union, which is recognized as a religion but which supports no single theology, doctrine, or creed. Carving on the building proclaims that it is "Dedicated to the ever-increasing knowledge and practice and love of the right." It holds that human life is of the utmost value and that improved social, interpersonal, and ecological relations are possible through dedication to the potential and betterment of human beings.

➠ **Makor** (35 West 67th St., between Columbus Ave. and Central Park West, ☎ 601-1000), which opened in October of 1999, offers a wide variety of contemporary arts and entertainment with possibilities of Jewish spiritual exploration and edification. Makor features a live music café and bar, a film screening room, an art gallery, lecture hall, seminar rooms, and more. Courses offered include Jewish ethics, Kabbalah, artistic expression, and Bible study. It is a branch of the 92nd Street "Y".

Promoting Gratitude to God
CHURCH OF JESUS CHRIST OF LATTER-DAY SAINTS
2 Lincoln Square, Columbus Ave., between 65th and 66th Sts. 1975, Schuman, Lichtenstein & Claman. ☎ 873-1690

The Church of Jesus Christ of Latter-Day Saints, as the Mormon Church is officially known, was organized in upstate New York in 1830. In addition to the Bible, the Mormon faith is based on revelations experienced by its founder, Joseph Smith, and transcribed by him in *The Book of Mormon*. Mormons believe that revelation from God has never ceased, but continues through living prophets, and the presidents of the Mormon Church are seen as prophets in the same way that Moses and other biblical leaders were. Another belief unique to Mormons is that of proxy baptism. A living Mormon may undergo baptism several times to win access to heaven for deceased ancestors (Mormons find scriptural justification in 1 Peter 4:6). Thus, Mormons maintain prodigious genealogical archives. The Mormons were driven to today's Utah by persecution, and there they founded Salt Lake City in 1847. Mormons remain the majority in Utah and parts of adjacent states; the eastern states are regarded as mission territory.

Joseph Smith visited New York City in 1832 and noted its grandeur, but he also noted "ingratitude to God" here. Latter-Day Saints were fully organized in New York City by 1934 and counted almost twenty congregations by 2000, including one in each borough. The number of members was growing rapidly.

Mormons differentiate churches, where worship services are conducted, from temples. Temples are closed on Sundays, but open on other days for marriages and other sacred ordinances. Only Mormons may enter a temple. There are no professional clergy and, in fact, few full-time employees in the entire worldwide church. Services are led and staffed by lay members.

This building contains a Mormon Church, not a temple; therefore, worship services are held here, but no sacraments can be performed. The facility welcomes visitors, and its Family History Center contains books, microfilms, and computers linked to the church's international family research capabilities, making it an invaluable resource for anyone interested in genealogy.

The Music of Bach in a Sacred Context
HOLY TRINITY (LMD)
Lutheran. Central Park West at 65th St. 1904, William Schickel. ☎ 877-6815

For over thirty years Holy Trinity's Bach Vespers Choir has offered the only opportunity in America to hear Bach's cantatas on their appointed day in the context of a worship service. Martin Luther was himself a composer, and music plays a special role in Lutheran church services. The musical core of early Lutheran liturgy consisted of chorale melodies composed or compiled by Luther or his immediate disciples. Each is appropriate to a certain day in the Christian calendar and to the biblical text for that day. Johann Sebastian Bach's 300 cantatas expanded this musical repertory. A cantata is a piece in several movements for a number of performers, including soloists and a chorus. Secular cantatas can be about anything (Bach even wrote one about the evil of drinking coffee), but each sacred cantata is a kind of musical meditation on both the melody and the biblical text. Bach

Holy Trinity Lutheran Church

MUSIC IN NEW YORK CHURCHES AND SYNAGOGUES

New York newspapers and magazines will accept paid advertisements for concerts, and they occasionally list special holiday concerts, but they do not announce the weekly buffet of literally hundreds of organ concerts, choir concerts, and recitals in the city's synagogues and churches. Perhaps it would be too much. Many churches and synagogues have concert series featuring choirs, organs, chamber ensembles, and soloists. Just to name a few: St. John the Divine regularly hosts the entire New York Philharmonic Orchestra; Holy Trinity offers its Bach concerts; St. Ignatius's concerts are well-known; Ascension has a distinguished series; Corpus Christi offers its respected "Music Before 1800" series; St. Bartholomew's and Temple Emanu-El feature regular organ concerts; St. Thomas has its Boys' Choir; Park Avenue Synagogue has regularly commissioned and premiered works from leading composers.

The best way to find out about the many events is simply to ask. Synagogues and churches are happy to add your name to their mailing lists so you can receive announcements of their concerts and recital series.

elaborated Martin Luther's hymn "A Mighty Fortress Is Our God," into his Cantata Number 80, for the Feast of the Reformation (October 31). The German poet Heinrich Heine called this work "the Marseillaise of the Reformation." Bach's genius made his cantatas great music, and his personal faith endowed this music with unmistakable emotional power. Holy Trinity reenforces its "Bacchanalian" reputation by offering Bach's complete organ works in January concerts through a cycle of four years, one-quarter each year.

This congregation was organized in 1868 to be an English-language Lutheran congregation. Its present structure is an ornate German Gothic-style church with a flèche over the crossing and bright red front doors facing Central Park. Its rose window and clerestory windows were made to Schickel's design, but Lamb Studios and Tiffany supplied the windows along the nave.

Cherished Remnants of Synagogues
CONGREGATION HABONIM
Conservative. 44 West 66th St., between Central Park West and Columbus Ave. 1957, Stanley Prowler and Frank Faillance. ☎ 787-5347

Adolf Hitler ordered the destruction of all synagogues in Germany, and the devastating pogrom on November 9, 1938, came to be known as *Kristallnacht*, from the sound of the shattering glass. Some of the Jews who fled Germany and found refuge in the United States founded New York's Congregation Habonim ("the builders") on November 9, 1939, the first anniversary of *Kristallnacht*.

In the lobby of the synagogue stands a *bimah* made of stones collected from the ruins of synagogues destroyed in 1938, including those of Aachen, Cologne, Essen, Hanover, Dortmund, Würzburg, Nuremberg, and Mannheim. The large Corinthian capital that forms the top of the altar was salvaged from the ruins of the magnificent synagogue on Berlin's Fasanenstrasse. Some current members of Congregation Habonim remember worshiping with their parents and grandparents in the synagogues of which these stones were once a part. The lobby also displays a scorched Torah parchment scroll, a sacred remnant recovered from the ashes of the Great Synagogue of Essen on the morning after *Kristallnacht*.

This modern building is basically a cube with stained-glass walls (by Robert Sowers) set at an angle against the sidewalk. The congregation calls itself "a Liberal Jewish synagogue, on the Conservative side of Reform."

New Jerusalem on Central Park West
SECOND CHURCH OF CHRIST, SCIENTIST (LMD)
77 Central Park West at 68th St. Finished in 1901 but dedicated in 1911. Frederick R. Comstock. ☎ 877-6100

"And I, John, saw the holy city, new Jerusalem, coming down from God out of heaven. . . . And the city lieth foursquare. . . . The length and the breadth and the height of it are equal." (Revelation 21:2, 16)

The great marble box of the Second Church of Christ, Scientist, symbolically reproduces that vision. It is almost exactly 110 feet wide, deep, and high to the top of the green copper dome.

Christian Science was founded by Mary Baker Eddy, who wrote its textbook, *Science and Health with Key to the Scriptures*, in 1875. She founded the Mother Church in Boston "to commemorate the words and works of our Master (Jesus Christ), which should reinstate primitive Christianity and its lost element of healing" (*Church Manual*). Her teaching generally emphasized the spiritual over the material, including an element of healing through faith.

Mrs. Eddy took a personal interest in the organization of New York's Second Church. This building went up before First Church, thirty blocks north, and Mrs. Eddy bequeathed the money to pay off what was left on the mortgage so it could be dedicated in 1911. The building is in the classical style, which appealed to Christian Scientists because it avoided the more traditional Christian symbolism of the Gothic tradition. This classical building is simple, but no expense was spared in the materials. It has the costliest marble, mosaic, and bronze work throughout, detailed down to the door handles.

The interior has been redesigned and redecorated several times since it opened, but it has remained a simple preaching space—a huge cube with galleries below enormous round-arched abstract stained-glass windows on three sides, with organ pipes on the fourth. The ground-floor pews converge concentrically on the speakers' platform. The skylights of the dome have been sealed, and the inner surface, a stained-glass window reading "Love," has been backlit.

Christian Scientist churches often collect Bibles. Second Church displays in the lobby a copy of the first Bible printed in New York. Subscribers to it received installments printed through the year 1792, including twenty full-page copperplate engravings by Amos Doolittle, John Dunlap, and other leading American artists of the day. The subscribers are listed in the back. Number one is George Washington.

Elizabeth Taylor attended Sunday school at Second Church. Albert Einstein used to frequent its reading room, and the story is told that one day he said to the librarian, "Mary Baker Eddy was right. There is no mass; it's all spirit."

AROUND THE CORNER

➥ About thirty blocks north, the **First Church of Christ, Scientist** (LM, 1 West 96th St. at Central Park West. 1903, Carrère & Hastings. ☎ 749-3088) was organized by Mrs. Eddy's follower Augusta Stetson in 1887. She won a large following and ruled the congregation with a heavy hand, threatening to usurp Mrs. Eddy's position. In 1909, while Miss Stetson was still the leader of First Church, she was excommunicated from the Mother Church in Boston. She then left First Church, but continued to live in her house next door until her death in 1928 (at one point suing First Church for planning an extension that would block her light).

First Church of Christ,
Scientist (detail of a pew)

This building abounds with columns and exterior architectural details recalling the works of the English architect Sir Nicholas Hawksmoor (1661–1736). The interior impresses with rich marbles, Circassian and French walnut pews (seating 2,400), and six Italian hand-crafted bronze chandeliers brilliant with 650 lights. The gracefully curving stairways and other details throughout the building are typical of Beaux-Arts architecture. This large church was one of the first in New York to combine a variety of facilities in one building: a library, meeting halls, and even a basketball court.

Today Christian Scientists have twenty-two churches in New York City, and each maintains a reading room of Christian Science publications.

Speak to the Congregation, Not for It
STEPHEN WISE FREE SYNAGOGUE (LMD)

Reform. 30 West 68th St., between Central Park West and Columbus Ave. 1950, Bloch & Hesse. ☎ 877-4050

Stephen Wise, born in Budapest in 1874, served as assistant rabbi at B'nai Jeshurun in New York (see p. 253) before going to Portland, Oregon, in 1900. There he won a national reputation as a religious leader, but he returned to New York and founded a new synagogue in 1907. It was called "Free" because it advocated freedom of the pulpit, abolition of distinctions between rich and poor members' privileges, full participation in social services, and identification with the Jewish faith and Israel. Theodore Herzl named Rabbi Wise as American secretary of the Zionist movement, and Wise headed the delegation of the American Jewish Congress to the Paris Peace Conference after World War I. The founding of Israel was not his only concern. He was an early member of the NAACP and a crusader for the rights of American labor. In 1919, when he criticized U.S. Steel for battling the unionization of its workers, so many resignations poured into the synagogue that Rabbi Wise tendered his own resignation. The chairman of the synagogue's executive council, Oscar Straus, rejected it. "The pulpit must be forever free," insisted Straus. "It must be understood that the Rabbi, speaking the truth as he sees it, speaks to the congregation, not for it."

The Free Synagogue continues to be a progressive congregation, dedicated to "worship, education, social service, and social action." Services here encourage participation of the congregation, including singing. Men and women participate equally; it was in fact the first synagogue in the world to install a female rabbi (Rabbi Sally Priesand, in 1972), as well as the first in New York City to offer a shelter for the homeless, and it sponsored the first Jewish Gay and Lesbian Conference in 1987. The pulpit has been open to an astounding list of speakers, including President Woodrow Wilson, William Jennings Bryan, Dr. Martin Luther King, Jr., Supreme Court Justices Louis Brandeis, Benjamin Cardozo, and later William O. Douglas, social reformers Jacob Riis and Jane Addams, novelist Thomas Mann, scientist Albert Einstein, Atlanta's mayor Andrew Young, astronomer Carl Sagan, and South Africa's Bishop Desmond Tutu.

The present fieldstone Gothic-style building was begun in 1940, but construction was suspended during World War II, so it was not dedicated until 1950, nine months after Rabbi Wise died. Its cornerstone comes from the Temple in Jerusalem.

The West 70s

War May Be Hell, But This Church Is Heaven
BLESSED SACRAMENT (LMD)
Roman Catholic. 152 West 71st St., between Columbus and Broadway. 1916, Gustave Steinback. ☎ 877-3111

Sherman Square, a tiny triangle on the West Side of Broadway at 70th Street, is New York's smallest parcel of park property. It memorializes the Union General William Tecumseh Sherman (1820–91), a great Civil War commander, whose own comment on war was the pithy, "War is hell." An equestrian statue of him by Augustus Saint-Gaudens stands at Fifth Avenue and 59th Street. Sherman lived on West 71st Street just off Central Park, and his funeral was conducted by his own son (a Roman Catholic priest) and the priest from Blessed Sacrament. The parish had been founded in a nearby stable in 1887—the only place available to them—but eventually it obtained this midblock location, on which this is the second building.

It's a large Gothic-style church. Its façade is set back from an open gable above the portal and virtually hollowed out by a rose window thirty feet in diameter—one of the largest in America. On either side, buttresses gradually step back to paired pinnacles. The relief over the main door is after Raphael's Vatican fresco, *The Triumph of the Eucharist*, but with two additional strips of unidentified clerics and laypersons. The façade of the rectory to the church's west pulls back from the sidewalk deferentially, so that the church can be seen from Broadway.

Visitors enter a long nave, on either side of which clusters of stone columns develop into stone ribs supporting the vaulting ninety feet above the floor. Most of the windows, including the great rose, are by Clement Heaton, an Englishman who migrated to West Nyack, New York, in 1912. The sanctuary behind the altar is unusual in having three tapestries, hand-woven here in America, on the theme of sacrifice: the high priest Melchizedek blessing Abraham; the crucifixion; and Abraham about to sacrifice Isaac. Above the tapestries, a cantilevered baldachin protects the altar, and high above that hangs a large carved and painted crucifix.

North America's Oldest Jewish Congregation
CONGREGATION SHEARITH ISRAEL (LM)
Orthodox. 99 Central Park West at 70th St. 1897, Arnold Brunner & Thomas Tryon. ☎ 873-0300. Brochures are available in the office.

This synagogue, also known as the Spanish and Portuguese Synagogue, is the fourth home of "Remnant of Israel," the nation's oldest Jewish con-

gregation, which was founded in 1654 (see p. 20). It built its first home in 1730, and in today's building a small room called the "Little Synagogue" reproduces the interior of that first synagogue, incorporating many original furnishings and ornaments: the benches, fifteenth-century Spanish brass candlesticks, the *tebah* and its railing, the *Shabbath* lamp hanging in the west window, and panels over the ark carved with the Ten Commandments. The *ner tamid* here has burned since 1818.

Congregation Shearith Israel

The building itself is probably the first of the Classical or Beaux-Arts synagogues (see p. 64). It actually mixes historic classical styles. For example, on the façade, the attic and pediment are Greek, the four giant Corinthian columns are Roman, but setting those columns on high bases on a flight of steps is typical of the Renaissance, as are the balustrades at the three tall windows over the three entrances secured by bronze gates. A Greek temple would have figures in the pediment, but since this congregation's faith does not permit figural art, the pediment displays only a pattern of vine tendrils (called *rinceaux*).

The ark contains Torahs decorated with multicolored embroidered cloaks and silver *rimmonim* made by the noted silversmith Myer Meyers (1723–95), who was president of the congregation. The *tebah* is in the middle of the room, and the pews face it, perpendicular to the ark. The floorboards under the *tebah* date back to that first synagogue of 1730. The round-arched Tiffany windows have abstract designs, so on sunny days, the interior glows with geometric patterns.

Members of this congregation have included Commodore Uriah Levy, the first Jewish flag officer of the U.S. Navy, who saved Thomas Jefferson's Monticello from neglect and decay; poet Emma Lazarus; and U.S. Supreme Court Justice Benjamin Cardozo.

The congregation receives one symbolic dollar per year in rent from the congregation of historic Touro Synagogue in Newport, Rhode Island, America's oldest synagogue. When that congregation asked for financial assistance in 1763, Shearith Israel paid for a building for them. Shearith Israel still owns the building and leases it to the Newport congregation.

The Generosity of a Revolutionary Hero
RUTGERS PRESBYTERIAN CHURCH
236 West 73rd St., between Broadway and West End Ave. 1926, Henry Otis Chapman. ☎ 877-8227

Revolutionary War hero Colonel Henry Rutgers gave his name to Rutgers Street through his lower-Manhattan property, and he gave this congregation a lot on that street for its first home in 1796. He also gave it title to a lot on Henry Street, but with the stipulation that the city could retain the property as long as a school stood on the site. New York's P.S. 2 still stands at 122 Henry Street. That wasn't the end of Rutgers's largesse. He also donated to the new Rutgers Street Presbyterian Church (they dropped "Street" in 1874) two silver tankards, six silver goblets, and five pewter plates, all of which are today on loan to the Metropolitan Museum of Art.

Colonel Rutgers also donated land for the college in New Jersey that bears his name.

The church moved uptown with the general flow of population, settling on the corner of Broadway and West 73rd Street in 1890. Their new church didn't occupy all the land they owned, so the congregation allowed the construction of a neighboring building on Broadway, originally on condition that no business be transacted there on Sundays (a condition dropped long ago). Their corner property, however, soon became so valuable that the congregation decided to tear down their church, erect a commercial building on the corner, and build new facilities back in the block along West 73rd Street. Their architect gave them three buildings in red brick trimmed with stone, but in three slightly different styles: a faintly classical bank building on the corner, an Elizabethan-style community house with a chapel, and an English Gothic-style church. The congregation called this property development "putting real estate values, which are idle, to work for the Kingdom of God." Rutgers has always maintained a tradition of generous public service.

In 1946 Rutgers Presbyterian triggered one of America's first court cases testing an artist's right to his work. The church had held a nationwide competition in 1937 for a design for a chancel mural, and the design of the winning artist, Alfred Crimi, was painted and dedicated in 1938. The 26-by-32-foot fresco, entitled *The Spreading of the Gospel*, showed Christ preaching. It was popular, but in 1946 Rutgers' pastor suddenly had it all painted over, complaining that it flouted Presbyterian tenets against the figurative representation of Christ in sanctuaries. Many members of the congregation, however, suggested that the pastor was just angry because the towering heroic figure of a well-built Christ had distracted the parishioners' attention from the pastor during services. Crimi sued. A court eventually ruled that the artist should have reserved rights in the work when it was contracted, but he hadn't, so he could claim no damages.

If These Stones Could Speak
WEST END COLLEGIATE CHURCH (LM)
Reformed. 368 West End Ave. at 77th St. 1892, Robert W. Gibson. ☎ 787-1566

A millstone sits in the narthex of West End Collegiate Church; another is embedded in the wall of the Collegiate School, and two more sit in the narthex of Shearith Israel Synagogue a few blocks away (see p. 246). This is the history of those stones.

A 1626 New Amsterdam document records: "Francis Molemaecher is busy building a horse-mill over which shall be constructed a spacious room sufficient to accommodate a large congregation, and then a tower is to be erected where the bells brought from Porto Rico will be hung." That mill stood at what is today 20 South William Street, in downtown Manhattan. Two years later the first clergyman arrived, Jonas Michaelius, and in 1628 the first Reformed services were held in the loft above the mill. When a new minister arrived in 1633, a new Reformed Church was constructed, and the mill property was eventually taken over by Shearith Israel. Now the details get vague. In 1730 Shearith Israel constructed a synagogue on that property, the first purpose-built synagogue in New York, somehow using the millstones as construction material, probably for the floor. Thus, these stones supported the first homes of both the first Protestant church and the first Jewish congregation in America. When Shearith Israel abandoned that downtown site in 1834, the stones were used to pave the back courtyard of a small building. Fifty years later, a member of Shearith Israel went downtown, dug up the stones, gave two to the Collegiate Church and kept two for Shearith Israel.

Today's West End Collegiate Reformed Church is a picturesque building modeled after the seventeenth-century public meat market of Haarlem, Holland. It's a romantic allusion to the congregation's historic Dutch roots. The orange brick body is lined with several stone string courses, and details include a stepped central gable, pinnacles, terra-cotta decorations, and ornate dormers.

Inside, wall panels suggest a Renaissance Revival style, but the dark timber A-frame beams supporting the roof are in the Flemish tradition. The large octagonal pulpit above the simple communion table and the choir stalls are elaborately carved. The choir sits to the right of the pulpit; what seems like a second choir stall to the left is actually the consistory pew. To this day it is the responsibility of the deacons and elders to sit here and listen attentively for any signs of heresy in the preacher's sermon. The Apostles' Creed is writ large on the front (north) wall. The east wall holds a window, *Then Shall Light Break Forth as the Morning*, by Clara Burd, dating from 1913, just after she quit working for Tiffany and opened her own studio. It identifies Jesus, the Light of the World, with the dawn, and it is positioned on the wall perfectly to capture the sunrise. Another window, *Little Children Come unto Me* in the baptistery, is by Tiffany. The armorial devices in the large circular window in the south gable are those of the various Dutch provinces in the 1579 Union of Utrecht, and also those of the United States and of New York City.

In the 1940s this church and the attached school were a center for

Dutch war-relief measures, when it was visited twice by then Princess Juliana. The Collegiate School is now independent of the church, but it has stayed on in the 77th Street wing.

In the late nineteenth century and into the twentieth, West End Collegiate supported a hospital and medical missionaries in Xiamen, China, whose people sent the temple bell on the 77th Street porch in thanks.

The Wonders of Earth and Space

AMERICAN MUSEUM OF NATURAL HISTORY (LM)

Central Park West, between 77th and 81st Sts. First wing and general plan, 1872–77, Calvert Vaux and Jacob Wrey Mould, but it is today an interconnected complex of twenty-two buildings. ☎ 769-5000

This museum covers virtually every aspect of natural science from anthropology to zoology. Exhibits include the world's largest and most important collection of vertebrate fossils, dioramas of animal habitat groups, and the world's largest cut gem. Halls of various "peoples" from around the world describe their cultures, environmental adaptations, and spiritual lives. The Rose Center for Earth and Space, including a new Hayden Planetarium, opened in 2000. The 15.5-ton Willamette Meteorite on display there, the largest ever discovered in the continental United States, crashed to Earth some 10,000 years ago. The museum has transferred legal title to this object to the Confederated Tribes of the Grand Ronde Community of Oregon and mounted a plaque explaining that it was of religious significance to the Clackamas Indians, who believe that the meteorite united Earth, sky, and water when it rested on the ground and collected rainwater in its many basins.

The walls of the museum subway stop on the B and C lines display mixed-media artistic installations that depict the evolution of extinct, existing, and endangered life-forms—from single-celled organisms to the great dinosaurs.

AROUND THE CORNER

➥ The New-York Historical Society (LM in LMD. Central Park West, between 76th and 77th Sts. 1908, York & Sawyer. ☎ 873-3400) was the city's first museum, founded in 1804. Highlights of its holdings today include the original watercolors for John James Audubon's *Birds of America* (see p. 293), silver, furniture, over 500,000 photographs from 1850 to the present, paintings of the nineteenth-century Hudson River School of landscape artists, and one of the finest historical libraries and archives in the country.

Due Process in Church and State
FIRST BAPTIST CHURCH
265 West 79th St. at Broadway. 1893, George Keister. ☎ 724-5600

This is the historic mother congregation of New York Baptists. The congregation was organized downtown in a rigging loft on Cart and Horse Street (today's William Street) in 1745, and the congregation emphasized its moral position on some issues from the start: Slaves were welcomed as members, but not slave owners. First Baptist's Reverend John Gano served as chaplain to the Continental Army, and he offered the prayer of thanksgiving at Newburgh, New York, on April 19, 1783, when General Washington announced the end of the hostilities. Oral tradition has it that Reverend Gano baptized George Washington himself. Gano returned to the city and reassembled the tiny Baptist congregation, one of whose early prominent members was Melancton Smith. At the convention held to determine whether New York State would ratify the proposed U.S. Constitution, Smith led the faction insisting on a written Bill of Rights to include the words "due process of law." This was the first time those words were used in constitutional discourse, and perhaps they reflect the traditionally independent spirit of Baptist congregations.

First Baptist made five successive uptown moves before settling into this Romanesque Revival church. George Keister was a celebrated designer of theaters, including Harlem's famous Apollo Theater, and he gave this congregation an eclectic, busy, restless building. He placed the church's triumphal-arch-like entrance diagonally on the busy corner, thus breaking Manhattan's relentless right-angle street grid. The large rose window above the entrance is illuminated at night from within. The church's two wings extend from that façade up Broadway and along West 79th Street.

The most striking feature of the interior is a triple-vaulted stained-glass skylight ceiling. It was covered over some years ago, but today backlighting reveals the beauty of the abstract patterns. Another abstract stained-glass skylight (still open to the sky) fills the semidome of the apse. At the rear of the apse, a colonnade screens the baptismal pool. Over 1,000 people can sit in the semicircular auditorium, and yet, every seat offers a good view of the pulpit.

AROUND THE CORNER

➡ Just a few blocks away is **Central Baptist Church** (166 West 92nd St. at Amsterdam Ave. 1916, architect unknown. ☎ 724-4004), a congregation that was organized downtown in 1843 and, after several moves and mergers, built this building in 1917. A stained-glass window virtually fills the Amsterdam Avenue gable with scenes of John the Baptist preaching, the baptism of Christ, and the Acts of the Apostles. Robert Lowry, who served as pastor of this church from 1858 to 1861, wrote many popular hymns, including "Shall We Gather at the River."

The West 80s

Protective Angels
SAINT PAUL AND SAINT ANDREW (LM)
United Methodist. 540 West End Ave. at 86th St. 1897, Robert H. Robertson. ☎ 362-3179

This church was built by St. Paul's congregation when there were no other Methodist churches in this part of Manhattan, and the local Methodist population was large and growing (the church seats over 1,000 people). St. Andrew's congregation merged here in 1937.

The building combines many architectural influences. Its wide entrance porch set in front of a high peak-roofed nave, high clerestory flanked by flat-roofed side aisles, basilican form, and prominent campanile are all features reminiscent of sixth-century Christian churches found in the region of Ravenna, Italy. Some other features are German Romanesque-style: the two unmatched (and bell-less) towers, round windows, and shallow transept. Italian Renaissance-style details include the arched entrance porch and the bays separated by Corinthian pilasters on West 86th Street, as well as the cherubs on top of the corner tower and at the front marble steps. The six elegant terra-cotta angels on the façade, clad in flowing robes and carrying scrolls and palm branches, are reminiscent of the women painted by American Renaissance artists such as Edwin Blashfield, Thomas Dewing, and Abbott Thayer. The use of pale brick and buff-colored terra-cotta reflects the fashion of the 1890s.

The interior is a simple preaching space of painted plaster and varnished oak overseen by life-sized angels with outspread wings standing high at each corner. One stained-glass window shows Paul before Agrippa, but the others are all abstract. Andrew was a Galilean fisherman, the first-called among the followers of Jesus. Very little is known about his life, and even the story that he was crucified on an X-shaped cross (today his symbol) was unknown before the late Middle Ages.

The Jewish congregation of B'nai Jeshurun (see below) is holding services in this building as well as in its own nearby synagogue. B'nai Jeshurun began renting space here when its synagogue was being restored several years ago.

"No Word of God Is the Last Word of God"
CONGREGATION B'NAI JESHURUN (LMD)
Conservative. 257 West 88th St., between Broadway and West End Ave. 1918, Henry B. Herts and Walter Schneider. ☎ 787-7600

B'nai Jeshurun (BJ to its friends) is one of New York's oldest and most historic congregations, but it is also one of today's most vibrant. The "Children of Israel," New York's first Ashkenazic synagogue, was founded in 1825 by a group of English and German Jews unaccustomed to the Sephardic ritual of Shearith Israel. They modeled their services on those of London's Great Synagogue. Their first home (this is their fifth) was down on Pearl Street, and successive buildings followed the general movement of settlement northward on Manhattan. In 1860 B'nai Jeshurun's rabbi, Dr. Morris J. Raphall, was the first ever invited to open Congress with a prayer of invocation. During the Civil War this congregation paid the salaries of many Jewish chaplains, and, at war's end, the congregation marched in a

Congregation B'nai Jeshurun

body from their Greene Street synagogue to Union Square on April 25, 1865, to participate in the public demonstration of grief over the assassination of Abraham Lincoln.

Under the influence of the development of Reform Judaism in New York, worship at B'nai Jeshurun evolved away from Orthodoxy in the 1870s. Confirmation was introduced, seats were altered into pews, a choir combined male and female voices, and an organ was purchased. B'nai Jeshurun officially affiliated with the Conservative movement in 1884, played a leading role in the founding of the Jewish Theological Seminary (1887), and published its own prayer book in 1889. Through the late nineteenth century, Russian and Polish Jews slowly replaced English and German Jews in the congregation, representing the new immigrant population.

In 1918 the congregation moved into the present building, whose architect, a well-known theater designer, adopted an exotically eclectic Middle Eastern/Byzantine Revival style. It mixes Coptic designs with Moorish and Persian motifs. The rough mottled granite façade is relieved by stunted copper turrets, an abstract cornice, and a single giant deeply-recessed, richly-ornamented portal arch, which shelters the entrance and a wheel window focused on a Magen David. The architects insisted that the design was patterned after an Egyptian temple at Aswan, and the building set a style soon adopted by other congregations.

During the 1960s and 1970s, B'nai Jeshurun's membership declined, but that changed dramatically with the coming of Rabbi Marshall T. Meyer in 1985. Rabbi Meyer was born in Brooklyn in 1930 and educated in the United States and Israel, but in 1959 he went to Argentina, where he achieved astounding success in revitalizing Judaism. In 1962 he founded, in Buenos Aires, South America's first rabbinical seminary. He also established planned parenthood and mental health clinics, and he edited and published in Spanish over seventy volumes of Jewish classic and theological literature. After the fall of the military government, he served on President Raul Alfonsín's National Commission for Disappeared Persons, and Argentina eventually awarded him its highest decoration for a noncitizen, the Order of the Liberator San Martín. His return to New York to B'nai Jeshurun was like a whirlwind, and his dedicated work of social justice, education, and inclusive approach to community and worship multiplied BJ's membership to over 2,000 by the time of his death in 1993.

B'nai Jeshurun continues to seek ways to incorporate elements of all Jewish theological movements into its spiritual expression, in keeping with the wisdom of the twentieth-century scholar Abraham Joshua Heschel that "no word of God is the last word of God." For example, it is committed to devising liturgy through which a nonpatriarchal tradition can be achieved, and BJ is not a member of United Synagogue for Conservative Judaism because of USCJ's discrimination against gay people. Today BJ continues to practice the traditional teaching that the world rests on three pillars: study of Torah, prayer, and deeds of love.

AROUND THE CORNER

➡ **The Soldiers' and Sailors' Monument** (LM, Riverside Drive at West 89th St. 1902, Stoughton & Stoughton with Paul E. M. DuBoy) is dedicated "To the Memory of the Brave Soldiers and Sailors Who Saved the Union." It is adapted from the classical Greek Choragic Monument of Lysicrates (the same model for the tower at St. Paul's Church—see p. 92), but, at ninety-six feet high, it's much bigger. An interior polished marble chamber contains five niches designed for bronze statues, but the statues were never executed.

➡ **The West Side Community Garden** (between 89th and 90th Sts., Columbus and Amsterdam Aves.) offers 17,500 square feet of beautiful plantings, subdivided into individual kitchen gardens and a sunken garden with benches and chairs.

West 90th Street to West 110th Street

For Tiffany Fans
SAINT MICHAEL'S
Episcopal. 225 West 99th St. at Amsterdam Ave. 1891, Robert Gibson.
☎ 222-2700

The ecclesiastical decorative work of Louis Comfort Tiffany and his studio has won renewed interest in America through recent years, and for those who want to see the most comprehensive surviving example of Tiffany work in the home of an historic congregation, this is the place. The work here was installed between 1893 and 1923.

In one vast scene around the apse, installed in 1895, archangel Michael marches forward in triumph while angels throng the heavens to celebrate his victory over the dragon (Revelation 12:7–9). The scene covers seven stained-glass windows, each measuring five by twenty-five feet. Much of the work was done by Tiffany's chief designer Frederick Wilson, an Englishman who arrived in the 1890s and worked for the studio for over thirty years. His signatures are the elegant Pre-Raphaelite bodies and facial types

St. Michael's Episcopal Church

with long slender noses, broad foreheads, high cheekbones, and reddish hair and beards. The vibrancy of the colors and the sweep of the figures in this tableau dominate the church interior.

Shortly thereafter, Tiffany Studios decorated the dome of the apse and installed the altar, reredos, credence, altar rail, pulpit and other apse decorations. In 1920 Tiffany completed the decorations of the Chapel of the Angels, which holds two more stained-glass windows, a large glass mosaic (that Tiffany described as "Gloria in Excelsis in Color") behind the altar, a small marble altar and altar railings, mosaic columns, and elaborate light fixtures. All in all, it's so splendid that Tiffany's publicity felt it necessary to emphasize "the legitimacy of using the fine arts in the embellishment of God's house, as aids to devotion." This suggests that there must have been some lingering distrust of the appropriateness of such elaborate decorations in what had, after all, started out as a Low Church. In the 1990s the congregation voted to restore the Tiffany stained-glass windows and decorative finishes and, further, to adorn parts of the apse and sanctuary that had not been embellished by Tiffany. Felix Chavez of New York not only restored the Tiffany finishes, but also proposed and executed an extensive decorative treatment of the architectural surround and of the nave based on the color scheme Tiffany used.

Tiffany is not the only artist represented by outstanding stained glass here. The church boasts work by J. & R. Lamb, F. L. Stoddard, D. Maitland Armstrong, and a set of nine medieval-style windows by Charles Connick.

St. Michael's is a cruciform church in the Italian Romanesque style; the congregation specifically refused Gothic Revival. The rounded apse of the church, the parish house, arcades, and a rectory are all arranged around a quiet garden and dominated by a beautiful tower.

St. Michael's is one of New York's few congregations that began as a country church and became a city church without ever moving. It was founded in 1806 by wealthy families living along the Hudson River. Alexander Hamilton's widow was one of the original pew holders. At the time, there were no other churches between St. Mark's in the Bowery and St. John's in Yonkers except a single Dutch Reformed Church in Harlem. St. Michael's also supported a chapel in Seneca Village, where Central Park is today (see p. 235). This is the parish's third church at this site.

AROUND THE CORNER

➡ Another fine tower is visible to the North at **West End Presbyterian Church** (325 Amsterdam Ave. at West 105th St. 1892, Henry Kilburn. ☎ 663-2900). West End's tall tower marks the corner, and the Romanesque-style church wraps around it to present one gable to 105th Street and another to Amsterdam Avenue. This church is a tour-de-force of decorative yellow brick, limestone, and bands of ornamental terra-cotta. West End was New York's largest Presbyterian congregation early in the twentieth century, and it introduced radio broadcasts of services in 1923.

➡ At Riverside Drive and West 93rd Street stands an equestrian **statue of Joan of Arc** (1412–31), the "Maid of France" (LMD). Obeying angelic voices, Joan led a French army to several victories over the English and persuaded Charles Valois to be crowned Charles VII at Reims Cathedral. She was later captured and burned at the stake. Anna Hyatt Huntington, the sculptor, explained, "The work looks at Joan from a spiritual rather than a warlike point of view. . . . She is holding [her sword] up to her God and praying for guidance." The statue was unveiled in 1915, five years before Joan's canonization, which was not for her military valor, but for her virtue and her faithfulness. John Van Pelt designed the pedestal that incorporates stones both from Reims Cathedral and from the dungeon where Joan was imprisoned at Rouen. The statue was a gift to the city from a private group of French and American citizens.

➡ **The Firemen's Memorial** (Riverside Dr. at West 100th St. Architect H. van Buren Magonigle; sculptor Attilio Piccirilli; 1913) commemorates the firemen who have given their lives in service. It includes an approach of stairs, a platform with balustrade, a fountain basin, and a sarcophagus-like block with a bas-relief showing three galloping horses pulling a fire engine. (A bronze tablet embedded in the plaza commemorates the horses that lost their lives, too.) To the north and south are marble allegorical figures of Sacrifice and Duty, respectively. That of Sacrifice, a woman supporting the limp body of her fireman husband, is a pietá of a quality equal to many of the Italian Renaissance.

The Lotus Garden

➥ Local activists prevailed upon the owner of a parking garage on West 97th St. to cover the entire 7,000-square-foot roof of the building with topsoil. The garden tended there today, called the **Lotus Garden** (between Broadway and West End Ave. ☎ 580-4897), includes goldfish ponds, fruit trees, and a great variety of flowers. The rooftop sanctuary is open to the general public only on Sunday afternoons, but you can become a lifetime member simply by buying a key for just a few dollars.

The Founder Keeps Watch
NEW YORK BUDDHIST CHURCH AND AMERICAN BUDDHIST STUDY CENTER (LMD)
331–32 Riverside Dr., between 105th and 106th Sts. 331 dates from 1902, Janes & Leo; 332 dates from 1963, Kelly & Gruzen. Church ☎ 678-0305; Center ☎ 864-7424.

A monumental statue of Shinran-Shonin (1173–1262 C.E.), founder of the Buddhist Jodo Shinshu sect, guards this church and study center. The statue withstood the atomic bomb blast at Hiroshima in 1945.

The New York Buddhist Church was found in 1938 to minister to New York's Japanese population, and it still offers many traditional Japanese arts and activities. Participation, however, is open to all. The church blends Eastern and Western approaches to Buddhism: Japanese liturgy and traditional arts, but two Sunday morning sermons delivered in Japanese and English. The school of Buddhism followed here tries to achieve a naturally enlightened state of mind without too much rigorous meditation or asceticism; these, they believe, backfire as egocentrism.

The Study Center (formerly called the American Buddhist Academy) has recently launched new programs, including a lecture series, discussion seminars, and even a publishing arm. The center owns a large library of Buddhist materials in many languages, plus non-Buddhist materials useful for interfaith studies.

New York Buddhist Church and American Buddhist Study Center

AROUND THE CORNER

➦ **The Nicholas Roerich Museum** (319 West 107th St., between Broadway and Riverside Dr. ☎ 864-7752) was the home of Nicholas Roerich (1874–1947), a Russian-born archaeologist, traveler, and mystic who was deeply influenced by Asian religions. The museum, a three-story brownstone, has a selection of Asian artifacts, plus about two hundred of Roerich's paintings, which feature lamas, monasteries, Buddha images, and metaphorical landscapes. It also hosts occasional concerts and poetry readings.

CHAPTER EIGHT

*H*arlem and the Heights

Central and East Harlem

Harlem is traditionally defined as the three square miles bounded by the high ridges of Morningside Heights and St. Nicholas Terrace to the west, by the East and Harlem Rivers to the east, and by Central Park to the south. The small village of New Harlem, established in 1658 about ten miles north of New Amsterdam, retained its pastoral charm and separateness for two centuries, but the coming of the railroad in the 1830s transformed it into a growing suburb. When the elevated trains reached Harlem in 1880, its blocks were subsequently developed with fine apartment houses and brownstone homes. This phase of Harlem's history peaked with the opening of Oscar Hammerstein's Opera House on West 125th Street in 1889. From then until World War I, Germans were the leading element of the local population, followed by the Irish, but with Jewish and Italian segments, too. Many churches and synagogues still standing were built at that time.

Meanwhile, New York City's black population had moved northward repeatedly through history, usually forced by racism and violent attacks. When whites had assaulted the small black settlement around Greenwich Village during the 1863 Draft Riot, African Americans moved up to Midtown on the West Side. In 1900, whites rioted again. Historic black congregations sold their properties and moved to the northernmost reaches of Harlem. Good opportunities in real estate could be found there because the arrival of the subways had triggered overbuilding and consequent deflation. African Americans first settled between 130th and 140th Streets, and by 1920, 200,000 black New Yorkers lived in Harlem.

THE DRAFT RIOT OF 1863

New York's Draft Riot of 1863 was a four-day binge of rioting, looting, burning, and killing that resulted partly from anger at the inequities of conscription during the Civil War. Laboring people generally supported the Northern war effort, but they were outraged that some men could buy their way out of service for $300. After the drawing of names began on July 11, 1863, mobs (mostly of foreign-born workers) surged onto the streets assaulting people, attacking draft headquarters, and burning buildings.

The riot was also associated with racial competition for jobs. Workers feared that the emancipation of slaves (the Emancipation Proclamation had been issued on January 1, 1863) would cause an influx of African American workers from the South; employers did in fact use blacks as strikebreakers at the time. Thus the white rioters directed some of their wrath at black-owned homes, businesses, and churches. At least eleven blacks were lynched, and the Colored Orphan Asylum on Fifth Avenue at 43rd Street was burned to the ground. Overall, more than 1,000 people were killed or injured, and property damage was estimated at $1,500,000 at the time. The riot was finally quelled by police cooperating with the Seventh N.Y. Regiment, which had been hastily recalled from Gettysburg.

During the 1920s, Harlem emerged as the cosmopolitan capital of black America, triggering an explosion of creativity known as "the Harlem Renaissance." Writers included Countee Cullen, W. E. B. Du Bois, Zora Neale Hurston, Langston Hughes, Claude McKay, Wallace Thurman, Jean Toomer, and James Weldon Johnson, but the Renaissance also encouraged the music of Eubie Blake, Bessie Smith, Louis Armstrong, Fletcher Henderson, and Duke Ellington, as well as painters, sculptors, and architects.

THE HARLEM RENAISSANCE
AND
SPIRITUAL LITERATURE

Some of the authors associated with the Harlem Renaissance were from deeply religious backgrounds, and their writings made unique contributions to American spiritual literature. James Weldon Johnson (1871–1938), for example, was a lawyer trained in music, and he and his brother, John Rosamond Johnson (1873–1954), a composer, wrote many songs. "Lift Every Voice and Sing," based on James's 1900 poem of that name, became something of an anthem to many African Americans and to the National Association for the Advancement of Colored People, in which the brothers were active. The brothers also collaborated on two pioneering anthologies: *The Book of American Negro Poetry* (1922) and two books of *American Negro Spirituals* (1925, 1926). These anthologies are milestones in the recognition of African American arts. Countee Cullen (1903–1946), the son of the pastor of Harlem's Salem Methodist Episcopal Church, won recognition as one of America's finest lyric poets. Helen Keller wrote him, "Your poetry has magic to turn my prison-house into a Garden of Delight," and Senegalese poet-president Léopold Senghor testified that Cullen's works inspired racial pride throughout colonial Africa. Zora Neale Hurston (1903–1960) combined many important themes in her powerful feminist novel of 1937, *Their Eyes Were Watching God*, which deals largely with the role and rights of women in the small Florida town in which she had grown up—Eatonville, America's first incorporated all-black city. The heiress A'Lelia Walker Robinson gave financial assistance to several of the lights of the Harlem Renaissance. Her mother, Madam C. J. Walker (1867–1919), had started a cosmetics company and risen to become the richest self-made woman in America, as well as America's first African American millionaire-entrepreneur. Her personal creed remained "Lord, help me live from day to day/ In such a self-forgetful way/ That when I ever kneel to pray/ My prayers shall be for others." The site of the Walkers' Harlem mansion is today the **Countee Cullen Branch of the New York Public Library** (104 West 136th St., between Malcolm X and Adam Clayton Powell, Jr., Blvds. 1942, L. A. Abramson. ☎ 491-2070).

Documentation for this period—and for all aspects of African American life—can be found at the **Schomburg Center for Research in Black Culture**, a branch of the New York Public Library (515 Malcolm X Blvd., between West 135th and 136th Sts. 1978, Bond Ryder Associates. ☎ 491-2200), and one of the world's leading research facilities devoted to the preservation of materials on the African and African diaspora experiences. Arthur Schomburg (1874–1938) was a Puerto Rican who, after having been told by a schoolteacher as a boy that blacks had no history, went on to gather the world's largest collection of materials documenting the history and culture of people of African descent. Today the collection includes books, photographs, posters, personal papers, recordings, and other artifacts. After World War II, Harlem's black population expanded south to 110th Street, and what had remained Italian East Harlem became largely Hispanic.

Harlem's main East–West boulevard is named in honor of the Reverend Martin Luther King, Jr. (1929–68), who led the U.S. civil rights movement from the mid-1950s until his assassination in 1968. He promoted nonviolent tactics, such as the massive 1963 March on Washington, and his leadership was fundamental in ending the segregation of blacks in the South. He was awarded the Nobel Peace Prize in 1964. Most of Dr. King's work was accomplished elsewhere, but he visited New York on several occasions, and a high school on Amsterdam Avenue at West 65th Street in Manhattan also carries his name.

Today Harlem contains a fine housing stock and a concentration of some of the most splendid houses of worship in the city. Its economy is reviving, and many of its fine properties are being renovated. New communities of faith are forming, and old houses of worship are being restored.

A Parade on Three Kings' Day
SAINT CECILIA'S (LM)
Roman Catholic. 120 East 106th St., between Park and Lexington Aves. 1887, Napoleon LeBrun & Sons. ☎ 534-1350

Virtually nothing is known of St. Cecilia, but she is thought to have been an early Roman patrician convert to Christianity and a martyr. Medieval church references have her "singing to God in her heart," so she is recognized as the patron saint of music. The red brick façade of her church incorporates a very large terra-cotta bas relief of her playing an organ, with angels at her feet. The church was landmarked with the adjoining convent, called Regina Angelorum (Neville & Bagge, 1907), which is also in the Romanesque Revival style. The priest who founded this parish saved money by serving as general contractor for the church building, commissioning various bricklayers, carpenters, and plasterers from the neighborhood. The parish today is largely Hispanic, so each January 6th, Three Kings' Day, which is especially significant to Hispanics, the neighborhood features a parade of donkeys, camels, and sheep.

A Home for Several Faith Groups in Turn
MOUNT NEBOH BAPTIST CHURCH
1883 Adam Clayton Powell, Jr., Blvd. at 114th St. 1909, Edward T. Shire.
☎ 866-7880

The Bible recounts that it was from the top of Mount Neboh that Moses saw the promised land, although he could not enter it (Deuteronomy 34:1).

In 1920, a Roman Catholic congregation took the Magen Davids off the towers of this Neoclassical-style building, built to house Temple Ansche Chesed, and moved in. In 1980 that congregation was replaced by the Mount Neboh Baptist Church, founded in 1937. The Baptist congregation has left the exquisite hand-painted Italian tiles surrounding each of the tall round-arched windows along the nave, but it has removed the marble from the apse and built there a large choir loft. Mount Neboh's gospel choir has won fame on its regular tours of Europe, and it attracts many visitors to its home.

GOSPEL MUSIC

Today so many tourists are visiting Harlem to hear fine gospel music that the large number of visitors often threatens to disrupt religious services, or at the very least, to alter the meaning of the services. Congregations do not want to exclude guests, but some fear the loss of their integrity. When a service becomes a performance for spectators, it erodes its authenticity. Furthermore, some tourists snap photographs, use camcorders, and leave before the service is over.

Harlem churches encourage visitors to call ahead to inquire about their visitor policies. Alternatively, visits can be arranged through a number of New York tour companies.

Superb gospel music can also be heard in the outer boroughs—see the entries in that chapter.

Our Lady of Mt. Carmel

Sanctuary of the Virgin
OUR LADY OF MOUNT CARMEL
Roman Catholic. 448 East 115th St., between First and Pleasant Aves. 1884, original architect unknown. ☎ 534-0681

The Archdiocese of New York has never been able to control the Madonna of Mount Carmel. Her veneration began spontaneously within the Italian immigrant community, and her cult is strengthened today by many Haitians who believe she represents the voodoo spirit Ezili Danto.

Italian immigrants began settling East Harlem in the 1870s, finding work laying new trolley tracks and in the local trolley yards. Some of these immigrants from tiny Polla, just south of Naples, formed a Mutual Aid Society and named it for the Madonna, Protectress of Polla. They received a statue from Italy, set her up in a member's house, and launched an annual July 16 *festa*. Festivities included veneration, but also a street procession, dancing, and feasting. All of this began with little cooperation from church officials, who frowned on such "street religiosity." Shortly thereafter, however, New York's Bishop Corrigan, who admired the social service work that Italian Pallotine Fathers had done in London, invited them to come to work among New York Italians. A church eventually rose on East 115th Street, and the Fathers coaxed the Society to lodge their Madonna in the church crypt. In 1903, partly in response to fears that New York Italians were converting to Protestantism, Pope Leo XIII reached out to them by elevating this shrine to a "Sanctuary of the Virgin," of which there are only three in the Americas—Guadalupe in Mexico, Our Lady of Perpetual Help in New Orleans, and Mount Carmel. Leo's successor, Pius X (who has since been canonized as a saint), provided the emeralds that are in the Virgin's and the Child's crowns. The Madonna nevertheless stayed in the basement until the church finally got an Italian pastor, who moved the statue up to the main altar on June 23, 1923. Mount Carmel became the focus of community life. Each year on July 16, thousands of people—penitents, school groups, and marching bands—joined a procession of the Virgin as it wound around East Harlem.

Since the late 1950s, many Hispanics and Haitians have moved into East Harlem, but veneration of the Virgin has not diminished. The festival

SYNCRETIC RELIGIONS

New York has hundreds of small shops called *botánicas* that sell herbal formulas for complaints ranging from the purely physical (pain) to the emotional (depression) or even social (potions to help you find a mate). These formulas are sold in an atmosphere of religiosity, usually including appeals to the Virgin Mary and other Christian saints, as well as saints, spirits, or gods traditional to a variety of other religions.

Botánicas exemplify *syncretic religions*, that is, religions that combine aspects of several different faiths or cults. Voodoo (from the god Vodun) is one example. The basic features of voodoo were brought to the Western Hemisphere by slaves from West Africa, particularly Dahomey, where the name originated. Caribbean peoples combined African religious beliefs and practices with Christian elements. African deities and spirits, for example, became identified with Christian saints, as many Haitians fuse Elizi Danto with Our Lady of Mount Carmel. Ritual often involves ecstatic trances and magical practices. A highly developed voodooistic religion known as Candomblé originated in Brazil.

and procession still occurs every July 16, but now it is preceded by masses in Italian, Spanish, French Creole, and Latin. The rest of the year, the Madonna presides from the high altar.

The interior has tall columns supporting a long central barrel vault with frescoed medallions of religious scenes; side aisles are flat-roofed. By special dispensation, this church has retained its communion rail, and it is one of the few that offers masses in Latin. Vincent Pallotti (1795–1850, canonized in 1963), founder of the Pallotines, can be seen in a window on the west wall.

AROUND THE CORNER
➡ A private nonprofit group intends to open, in 2001, the **National Museum of Catholic Art and History** next door to Our Lady of Mount Carmel Church. It will occupy what was originally the church's parochial school.

The Man Behind the Name of Both Boulevard and Mosque
MASJID MALCOLM SHABAZZ
102 West 116th St. at Malcolm X Blvd. Building converted to a mosque 1965, Sabbath Brown. ☎ 662-2200

This building was originally the Lenox Casino, and then it served as Elijah Muhammad's Temple of Islam. Malcolm X preached here before his break with Muhammad and the Nation of Islam. Malcolm Little (1925–1965), born in Omaha, Nebraska, was introduced to the Nation of Islam while serving a prison term, and he became a Nation of Islam minister upon his release in 1952. He split with Elijah Muhammad and formed his own organization, the Muslim Mosque, in 1963. The following year, after a pilgrimage to Mecca, he announced his conversion to Orthodox Islam and to the belief that there could be brotherhood between black and white. In that same year his *Autobiography* (as told to Alex Haley) was published. He was assassinated in 1965, but his murderers have never been identified.

Membership in the mosque has grown since it has turned to mainstream Islam and as substantial numbers of Muslim immigrants from West Africa have moved into this Harlem neighborhood. The aluminum onionshaped dome surmounted by a crescent is visible from far up the boulevard now named for Malcolm X.

The site of Malcolm X's 1965 assassination, the **Audubon Theater and Ballroom** (3960 Broadway at 165th St., 1912, Thomas R. Lamb. ☎ 795-3475) is today property of the City of New York. Its Broadway façade pre-

Masjid Malcolm Shabazz

serves the polychrome glazed terra-cotta decorations, and there are plans for the building to house business offices, plus the Harlem-Heights Historical Society, the Audubon Tourist and Information Center, and the Malcolm X (El Hajj Malik Shabazz) Memorial Museum. Part of the property, however, has been altered, enlarged, and renovated (1996, Davis Brody Bond) into the Mary W. Lasker Biomedical Research Building of Columbia University College of Physicians and Surgeons.

AROUND THE CORNER
➥ **The Studio Museum in Harlem** (144 West 125th St., between Malcolm X Blvd. and Adam Clayton Powell, Jr., Blvd. ☎ 864-4500) took over an old office building in 1968 in order to provide studio spaces for African American artists, and in 1979 it started a permanent collection, which is today divided into three categories: African American art from the nineteenth century to the present; twentieth- and twenty first-century Caribbean and African art; and traditional African art and artifacts. The museum also offers a sculpture garden.

St. Thomas the Apostle

A Mix of Styles
SAINT THOMAS THE APOSTLE
Roman Catholic. 260 West 118th St. at St. Nicholas Ave. 1907, Thomas H. Poole & Co. ☎ 662-2693

This is all-in-all one of the most original buildings in the city, inside and out. It has been called English Gothic, Flemish Renaissance, and Venetian fantastic, but "eclectic erratic" probably describes it best. The interior reveals a fan-vaulted ceiling and a complete set of windows by Mayer of Munich. Organ lovers know that it boasts one of the few ever built by W. W. Kimball of Chicago.

Magen Davids in a Baptist Church
MOUNT OLIVET BAPTIST CHURCH (LMD)
201 Malcolm X Blvd. at West 120th St. 1907, Arnold W. Brunner. ☎ 864-1155

The Bible records that Mount Olivet (the Mount of Olives) was the scene of David's flight from Absalom (2 Samuel 15:2), of Christ's weeping over Jerusalem (Matthew 24:3), and of his ascension (Acts 1:9–12).

This Classical Revival structure was once one of the city's most prestigious synagogues. It was built as Temple Israel for a German-Jewish congregation that had been founded in 1870. From 1920 to 1925 it served as the First Church of the Seventh-Day Adventists, and in 1925 it became the home of this Baptist congregation founded in 1878.

Despite these several changes in use and neighborhood population, the building remains largely unchanged. Magen Davids can still be seen on the exterior, carved in the capitals of the Corinthian columns and at the bases of the windows, as well as inside, in the stained-glass windows (none of which are figural). Rampant Lions of Judah protect tablets of the Ten Commandments by the organ pipes. The gilded doors that originally held the ark now surround the baptismal tank. The ground floor pews radiate concentrically from the pulpit platform, and two levels of galleries seat a substantial congregation.

Two Historic Episcopal Churches, Now Merged as One Parish

In 1942 St. Luke's and St. Martin's, two historic Episcopal congregations occupying two significant church structures (today both LM), merged.

SAINT MARTIN'S

230 Malcolm X Blvd. at West 122nd St. 1885, William A. Potter. ☎ 534-4531

You may hear St. Martin's tall tower even before you see it, for it houses one of New York's rare genuine (manually played) carillons. Its forty-two bells celebrate the restoration of the church after a terrible fire in 1939. Queen Juliana of the Netherlands, where the bells were made, came to hear them in 1952.

The tower is the punctuation mark for a Richardsonian Romanesque complex. An arched doorway at the tower's base on West 122nd Street leads into the church; the rectory is east of that on the street, and the

St. Martin's Episcopal Church

parish house fronts Malcolm X Boulevard along the western side. The rough-hewn granite walls are pierced by windows with brownstone trim, but they could be those of a fortress.

A predominantly white congregation built the church as Holy Trinity, but after a fire destroyed the interior in 1925, that congregation decided to move north to Inwood, and a new largely African American congregation rededicated the church to Martin of Tours. Martin (315–397 C.E.) was a Roman soldier in what is today France who converted to Christianity after he recognized Christ in a naked beggar to whom he had given half his cloak. Martin preached widely, founded monasticism in France, and was later one of the first holy men who was not a martyr to be publicly venerated as a saint. St. Martin's Church in Canterbury is the oldest Christian church in England, dating from Roman Empire times, and a stone from its walls is built into New York's St. Martin's. Many members here are from the West Indies, where the Anglican/Episcopal tradition is strong. One of them, Robert L. Douglas, was the owner, manager, and coach of the Renaissance Basketball Team, an all-black team that toured the country in the 1920s and 1930s, laying the foundation for the urban popularity of basketball today.

During the Depression, St. Martin's was one of the most socially active churches in Harlem. Its dynamic rector, Reverend John Johnson, led a campaign to win African Americans more jobs in Harlem's businesses, which were still largely white-owned, under the slogan "Don't buy where you can't work." In 1937 St. Martin's founded New York's first church credit union, which has since funded housing and many other local community projects. For many years the congregation has remembered loved ones by commissioning mosaic reproductions of great paintings. Today the interior walls boast reproductions of works by José Ribera (his *St. Martin of Tours*), Da Vinci, El Greco, Botticelli, Raphael, and other masters.

SAINT LUKE'S
285 Convent Ave. at West 141st St. (up in Hamilton Heights) 1892, R. H. Robertson. ☎ 926-2713

St. Luke's congregation was founded in Greenwich Village but moved uptown in 1886 (see p. 163). Their first uptown facility was **the Grange** (LM, 1802), Alexander Hamilton's one-time home. Hamilton left this house on the morning of July 11, 1804, to meet Aaron Burr for the duel in which Hamilton was killed. St. Luke's eventually sold the Grange, which since 1962 has been a National Monument owned and operated by the U.S. Department of the Interior (☎ 283-5154).

St. Luke's Episcopal Church

While worshiping in the Grange, the congregation built next door a massive Richardsonian Romanesque church in two contrasting shades of rough-textured stone, like St. Martin's. This building, however, has not been completed in its original design. A tall tower planned for the corner was never built, and the capitals of the columns on the curving front porch were never carved.

Today this congregation, too, now led by Reverend John Johnson's son, Johan, is expanding its services to the community. A visitor entering this formidable building finds its basement full of humming computers—part of a training class for local youngsters.

Christ Is Still the Cornerstone
GREATER METROPOLITAN
BAPTIST CHURCH (LM)

147 West 123rd St., between Malcolm X Blvd. and Adam Clayton Powell, Jr., Blvd. 1897, Ernest W. Schneider & Henry Herter. ☎ 678-4284

This site tells the story of Harlem's changing population. In 1865, when Harlem was a new settlement both for new immigrants and for Germans from downtown, St. Paul's German Evangelical Lutheran Congregation erected the first building here. The congregation replaced that building with this one in 1897, so the cornerstone reads: "Christus Unser

Greater Metropolitan Baptist Church

Eckstein (Christ Our Cornerstone) 1865/1897." By 1939, however, there weren't many German New Yorkers left in Harlem, so that dwindling congregation joined Grace Lutheran (now **Grace and Saint Paul's**) on West 71st Street, where the pastor was the son of St. Paul's pastor. This building became the 12th Church of Christ, Scientist, founded in 1927 as New York's first black congregation of that faith. In 1985 the Christian Scientists moved to smaller quarters on Adam Clayton Powell, Jr., Boulevard at 136th Street and sold this building to the Greater Metropolitan Baptist Church, a congregation that had recently split off from the Metropolitan Baptist Church.

Each owner of this building remodeled the interior, but the grand exterior is remarkably unchanged. The ornate Gothic-style façade boasts marble facing. A central gable with a single recessed portal and a rose window is flanked by square towers with small doors, lancet windows, and spires with finials. The church has impressive windows by Mayer of Munich.

AROUND THE CORNER

➡ **Marcus Garvey Memorial Park** (bounded by 120th and 124th Sts., Mount Morris Park West and Madison Ave.) was named for the Jamaica-born Pan-Africanist (1887–1940) who, after his arrival in Harlem in 1917, sought to instill black pride and independence. Attracting much interest, he recruited thousands into the Universal Negro Improvement Association (UNIA), which he had founded in Jamaica a few years earlier. He formed other community organizations, like the African Community League, the Order of the Nile, the Black Cross Nurses, and the Universal African Legion, as well as a newspaper. In 1925,

Garvey, a devout Catholic, was sent to prison on federal charges of mail fraud that were clearly motivated by politics. After his release in 1927 he was deported to Jamaica.

The Congregation Kept the Faith
SAINT ANDREW'S CHURCH (LM)
Episcopal. 2067 Fifth Ave. at 127th St. 1873, Henry M. Congdon; enlarged 1891. ☎ 534-0896

St. Andrew's was the first Episcopal congregation established in Harlem—in 1829, when Harlem was just a small village. The parish received an early shock when its rector, Reverend James R. Bailey, became convinced of the truth of the Anglo-Catholic movement (see p. 69), converted to Roman Catholicism, and rose to become Archbishop of Baltimore. Nevertheless, the congregation held fast, St. Andrew's flourished, and today it remains one of the few nineteenth-century Protestant churches in Harlem continuously occupied by the same congregation.

This building was originally constructed a few blocks away, but when the congregation outgrew it, the congregation hired the original architect to dismantle it stone by stone, enlarge it, and reconstruct it on this more prestigious location. It has received landmark designation as one of the city's finest Victorian Gothic churches. Its tower is a strong feature; it is not set at the corner of the intersection, but against the south transept along East 127th Street. Late Victorian Gothic buildings usually sport polychrome stonework, but this one is of solid rock-faced granite. The congregation celebrated its 170th anniversary in November 1999 by dedicating a new altar.

Unique Rose Windows in the Clerestory
ALL SAINTS CHURCH
Roman Catholic. East 129th St. at Madison Ave. 1894, Renwick, Aspinwall & Russell. ☎ 534-3535

This grand Gothic-style church of varicolored brick laid in geometric patterns was designed by W. W. Renwick, the son of James Renwick, Jr., and some critics have called it "better than St. Patrick's." The 129th Street façade presents a single portal, a large wheel window, and a central gable flanked by a pair of delicate towers. On each side, a smaller wheel window is topped by a smaller gable with a single tower, and a tall bell tower marks the church's north end. The church's side aisles do not go to the height of the nave, and the clerestory windows are extraordinary because they are not conventional arched windows, but a series of rose windows. Several windows along the nave exhibit American opalescent glass. The interior furnishings include open-work carved pews, an elaborately carved high altar, candlesticks, and, high above in the apse, a carved crucifix with angels.

The Venetian Gothic–style rectory next door at 47 East 129th Street (1889; Renwick, Aspinwall & Russell) would fit anywhere along Venice's Grand Canal.

Antecedents to 1704
SAINT PHILIP'S CHURCH (LM)
Episcopal. 210 West 134th St., between Seventh and Eighth Aves. 1911, Vertner W. Tandy and George W. Foster, Jr. ☎ 862-4940

The cornerstone of St. Philip's Church dates its founding as 1818, but the congregation may claim to date back well before that. The London-based Society for the Propagation of the Gospel established an "African Episcopal Catechetical Institution" in New York in 1704. That institution eventually fell to the responsibility of Trinity Church and moved out of

Trinity as the Free African Church of St. Philip (Philip the Evangelist, who reportedly converted the first Ethiopian to Christianity; Acts 8:26–27). It was finally confirmed as an independent Episcopal parish in 1818. Its first independent home was on Centre Street downtown.

St. Philip's has moved uptown several times, either following its parishioners or, occasionally, to escape persecution. For example, in 1834 antiabolitionist rioters damaged the church (then on Centre Street), and when rioters again targeted blacks and

St. Philip's Church

their institutions during the 1863 Anti-Draft Riots, federal troops had to occupy St. Philip's (then on Mulberry Street). The U.S. government paid the congregation $333.33 in rent, and the city added $1,100 for damages, but repairing the damage cost still more. In 1886 the church moved up to West 25th Street, which was then an African American residential area, and it was from there that the church established a mission on 134th Street in 1907, thus becoming one of the first institutions to attract African Americans to Harlem. The church accumulated tenements and row houses around its uptown mission, and in 1909 St. Philip's hired Tandy and Foster, two of America's first black registered architects, to build a new home uptown.

Its neo-Gothic home is a utilitarian structure. The main façade is a single large gable with emphasis at the roof and top, surmounted by a cross and pierced by a large arched window. This façade is of salmon-colored Roman brick and contrasting cast-stone aggregate, but the other sides, originally concealed behind neighboring buildings, are of common red brick. The interior is spare, open, and elegant, with stained-pine hammer-beam roof trusses. Some features were designed specifically to facilitate circulation of processions, which are significant in St. Philip's liturgy.

Parishioners have included Thurgood Marshall, the first black U.S. Supreme Court justice; author and civil rights advocate W. E. B. Du Bois; and poet Langston Hughes.

Mother to a Denomination
MOTHER AFRICAN METHODIST EPISCOPAL ZION CHURCH (LM)
140 West 137th St. near Malcolm X Blvd. 1925, George W. Foster, Jr. ☎ 234-1545

Mother Zion is the oldest independent black congregation in New York and the "mother" church of the A. M. E. Zion denomination (see p. 29). The story of "Mother Zion" begins with Peter Williams, a black slave who served as sexton at the John Street Methodist Church (see p. 87). When Williams's owner threatened to take him back to England after the Revolution, or to sell Williams at public auction, the church trustees bought him privately for forty pounds. Williams eventually gained his freedom, went into the tobacco business, and prospered. The John Street Church condemned slavery, but it still discriminated against its own black members, who, for example, had to take communion separately. Therefore, Williams, together with his friends James Varick and Christopher Rush, broke away from the John Street Methodist congregation. They held their first services in a rented house on Cross Street, between Orange and Mulberry Streets, downtown. In 1800 they incorporated a separate Methodist society, the Zion Church, and laid the cornerstone for their own house of worship on the southwest corner of Church and Leonard Streets, where they stayed until 1864.

Zion churches were long known as the Freedom churches because of their role in the abolitionist movement; several, including Mother Zion, were stations on the Underground Railroad. Sojourner Truth, born a slave in New York State and freed on the state's Emancipation Day in 1827, was a member of Mother Zion. Harriet Tubman was a Zion Conference member, and Frederick Douglass was pastor of A. M. E. Zion in Rochester, New York. The church's abolitionist activity triggered violent backlash. Mother Zion's downtown building was vandalized during the 1834 antiabolitionist riots, so Mother Zion, like other black churches, was forced to move uptown in several steps to Harlem.

This neo-Gothic building, the congregation's sixth home, was designed by one of America's first African American registered architects. Inside, the plan is not cruciform, as might be expected in a Gothic-style church, but auditorium-style, with seats arranged in arcs as in a meeting hall. Seating focuses on the pulpit, which stands on a raised shallow platform. From this pulpit Langston Hughes, W. E. B. Du Bois, Marian Anderson, and countless other African American personalities have spoken, including Paul Robeson, whose brother Benjamin was pastor of Mother Zion for many years. The downstairs Children's Chapel displays the wooden pulpit from an earlier church on Bleecker Street (1864–1904). Many historic plaques and mementos are on display in the church's vestibule. In a crypt beneath the sanctuary are the remains of James Varick, who served as Mother Zion's first bishop.

Spellbinding Orators
ABYSSINIAN BAPTIST CHURCH (LM)

132 West 138th St., between Malcolm X Blvd. and Seventh Ave. 1923, Charles Bolton and Son. ☎ 862-7474

The Acts of the Apostles recounts that an Abyssinian, or Ethiopian, was one of the first converts to Christianity, and Ethiopia was among the first Christian nations. In 1808 a group of Abyssinian merchants in New York protested the racially segregated seating at the First Baptist Church and, together with some African Americans, broke off to form their own church, the Abyssinian Baptist Church. The congregation's first home was

Abyssinian Baptist Church

downtown on Worth Street, but the church moved uptown with New York's African American population, especially after angry antiabolitionist mobs damaged all three black churches south of Canal Street in 1834: Abyssinian, St. Philip's Episcopal (see p. 276), and Mother Zion (see above). The *New York Post* reported that "the windows of the African [Abyssinian] Baptist Church were broken to atoms." Abyssinian made three intermediate stops before reaching Harlem in 1923.

Abyssinian Baptist chose the Bolton family architectural firm from Philadelphia to design their church, although the Boltons had not before built in New York. They had, however, built at least ten Baptist churches in Philadelphia. (The father and son eventually built over 500 churches across the United States.) The Gothic style was chosen for this building, constructed of a fine-textured bluish-gray sandstone and trimmed with white terra-cotta. The façade is a central gable almost filled by an enormous pointed-arch window. The gable is flanked by two square towers that contain the entrances. Gable and towers are crenellated. The inside is a virtually unadorned lecture hall that can hold 1,000 people arranged in arcs focused on the pulpit, both on the main floor and in balconies above. Its superb acoustics have echoed concerts by the New York Philharmonic and other orchestras, as well as the church's own outstanding choir. Its first and foremost function, however, is as a preaching space. This is a plain auditorium church wrapped inside a neo-Gothic skin.

Two spellbinding orators, the Reverend Dr. Adam Clayton Powell, Senior (1865–1953) and Junior (1908–1972), occupied the pulpit here for many years, during which this was the nation's largest Protestant congregation. Adam Jr. was elected to the U.S. House of Representatives in 1944, and there he pioneered reform legislation in education and in civil and labor rights. His flamboyant personal style offended some other legislators, and in 1967 he was censured and stripped of his office. The Supreme Court, however, reinstated him in 1969. Today a Powell Memorial Room displays artifacts of his life, and the principal north-south thoroughfare through Harlem was named Adam Clayton Powell, Jr., Boulevard, shortly after his death in 1972.

Under the leadership of Reverend Dr. Calvin O. Butts, III, the congregation has remained dedicated to social activism. Cuban leader Fidel Castro addressed the congregation in 1958 and returned in 1995, when he was excluded from festivities celebrating the fiftieth anniversary of the United Nations.

Morningside, Washington, and Hamilton Heights and Inwood

Uppermost Western Manhattan consists of a series of bluffs raised above Harlem to the east by a cliff defined by today's Morningside and St. Nicholas Parks. These heights were settled after the opening of the parks in 1887 and 1891, respectively. The high ridge is breached east to west only by Martin Luther King, Jr. Blvd. (125th St.) and Dyckman Street.

Morningside Heights (roughly 110–125th Sts.) has attracted centers of learning and faith, including Columbia University, the Union and Jewish Theological Seminaries, Barnard College, the Cathedral Church of St. John, and Riverside Church. Hamilton Heights (125–155th Sts.) was named for Alexander Hamilton, whose country estate still stands among some lovely turn of the nineteenth-century homes in the Hamilton Heights Historic District (see p. 272). Most development, however, occurred after the coming of the IRT subway in 1904. The buildings of the City College branch of the City University date from 1904 to 1907. Washington Heights (155th to Dyckman Sts.) was once an Irish neighborhood, but is today home to a population mix including blacks, Hispanic groups, and Chinese. Inwood, north of Dyckman Street, is another neighborhood of mixed population.

New York's Episcopal Cathedral
CATHEDRAL OF SAINT JOHN THE DIVINE

Amsterdam Ave. at West 112th St. 1892–1911, Heins & LaFarge. Work continued 1911–42, Cram & Ferguson. ☎ 865-3600. Guidebooks are available in the shop.

The Cathedral of St. John the Divine is, quite simply, stupendous. It is about twice the size of St. Patrick's downtown and almost as big as St. Peter's in Rome. Its cornerstone was laid on December 27 (St. John's Day), 1892, and the first service was held in the crypt in 1899. When completed, it will seat 15,000 people. That, however, is the rub. Its construction has absorbed labor and treasure for over one hundred years. It has undergone transformations in style and purpose, and it's still only two-thirds complete. Nevertheless, what's here to see is incomparable within the United States.

The cathedral offers not only worship services, a retreat for meditation and prayer, and a wide range of social services, but also arts programs, performances, training, a forum for public debate on social issues, and the site of such popular events as the annual "blessing of the beasts," at which thousands of pets ranging from gerbils to elephants assemble for a benediction on the first Sunday in October. The art and historical treasures it holds range from the beginning of Christianity to modern artist Keith Haring's triptych, *The Life of Christ.* Jazz bands perform here, as well as the New York Philharmonic, opera stars, and folk groups. The Episcopal Diocese of New York, for which this is the cathedral, covers three counties of New York City (New York, Staten Island, and the Bronx), plus seven upstate: Westchester, Putnam, Dutchess, Rockland, Orange, Sullivan, and Ulster.

Construction began on a Romanesque-style design, and by 1911 work had been completed on the apse, choir, and crossing. By then, however, Bishop Henry Potter, who initiated the work, was dead and the original architects were out of favor. The job was given over to architect Ralph Adams Cram, who recast the cathedral plan from Romanesque to Gothic. Other architects have worked on the cathedral through the years (including Thomas Nash, Henry Vaughan, and Carrère & Hastings), but the grand scheme remains Cram's.

The view of the west façade down West 112th Street from Broadway reminds one of views of medieval cathedral façades seen in cramped European cities. Two incomplete towers frame five recessed portals adorned with figures of saints and prophets, martyrs and preachers. The central portal's gold-plated bronze doors depict biblical events. The central Portal of Paradise counts thirty-two biblical matriarchs and patriarchs, and it includes contemporary references. The traditional scene of the fall of Jerusalem, for example, has been replaced with one of mushroom clouds looming over New York's World Trade Center.

When you step inside, the view down the nave into the choir is one-tenth of a mile. The nave is much wider than is usual in Gothic (Revival) buildings because Cram had to work with the crossing that had already been built—a square 100 feet on each side. He decided to lengthen the nave eighty feet more than the original plan and to create five aisles, rather than the normal three. The side aisles are as high as the central nave (124 feet), and it's all built with stone, just as in a medieval cathedral; there is no supporting structural iron or steel.

Seven chapels along each side of the nave are dedicated to subjects as diverse as sports, the arts (where tablets record major American writers), the labors of man, the medical profession, and the legal profession. Each is adorned with artistic treasures and illumined by a twenty-six-foot-high stained-glass window. A triforium runs above these chapels, and forty-four-foot-high stained-glass clerestory windows stand above that. The bays and aisles display works from the cathedral's collection of religious art. The cathedral owns two sets of precious tapestries: the Mortlake Tapestries, woven from Raphael's designs of *The Acts of the Apostles*, and the early-seventeenth-century Barbarini tapestries, woven on the papal looms, depicting scenes from the life of Christ. Everywhere you can admire ornamental ironwork by Samuel Yellin.

Special glass in the great rose window of the west façade (at forty feet in diameter, the world's largest) responds to changing light conditions. The blues prevail during most of the day, but the reds predominate by late afternoon. The smaller rose beneath it (twenty-three feet in diameter) would alone stand out in most churches. Both windows are by Charles Connick.

The area east of the crossing can be subdivided into the choir, the sanctuary (where the altar is), the ambulatory leading around behind the sanctuary, and the crown of chapels around the ambulatory. Eight mighty columns of Maine granite (each fifty-five feet high and six feet in diameter) form a semicircle around the high altar and support the apse. Many people consider these columns the most extraordinary feature of the entire building. They were quarried as monoliths, but each had to be cut in two after the first two columns cracked while being turned and polished. Each weighs 130 tons. They form a part of the original Romanesque Revival plan, and all were standing by 1904. (For connoisseurs of stone: New York's tallest polished monolithic columns stand around the altar at the Roman Catholic **Church of Our Saviour**, 59 Park Ave. at 38th St. 1959, Paul C. Reilly. ☎ 679-8166)

The cathedral is far from finished, but work stopped when the United States entered World War II, and it has been resumed only occasionally since then, as money was available and enthusiasm rebounded. Between 1979 and 1992 fifty feet were added to the south tower of the façade, to reach 200 feet. The towers were planned for 300 feet, but still the north tower reaches only 150.

Several other buildings and art works occupy the cathedral's thirteen-acre complex, called the "close," as are the medieval cathedral greens in England. The original building on this property, an orphanage built by Ithiel Town in the Greek Revival style in 1843, still stands where the cathedral's south transept might rise someday. It currently houses the sacristy, textile conservation labs, and offices of various church programs. The cathedral close also contains an open-air pulpit—an openwork Gothic-style spire forty feet high (1916, Howells & Stokes); the Peace Fountain, a 1985 bronze statue by Greg Wyatt representing the battle between good and evil; and small bronze animal sculptures by children. A biblical garden features more than seventy flowers and plants typical of the Holy Land.

The biblical garden at the Cathedral of St. John the Divine

The Grotto of Lourdes
NOTRE DAME (LM)

Roman Catholic. West 114th St. at Morningside Dr. 1910, grotto and chapel, Daus & Otto. Nave and front elevation, 1915, Cross & Cross. ☎ 866-1500

Bernadette Soubirous, a poor and sickly fourteen-year-old girl, had a series of eighteen visions of a beautiful lady in a shallow cave along the bank of the Gave River in southwest France between February and July 1858. The lady, who eventually identified herself as the Virgin Mary, pointed out a forgotten spring and enjoined Bernadette to prayer. Some of these visions took place in the presence of others, but no one else claimed to see or hear "the Lady." Bernadette's visions were reported in a book by Henri Lasserre that eventually became one of the best-selling books of the nineteenth century. Bernadette herself entered a convent to escape the rising tide of publicity, but her health declined. She died at the age of thirty-five in 1879 and was canonized in 1933 for her humble simplicity and religious trustingness.

The grotto itself soon became the site of pilgrimages, particularly of the sick, and it was girdled with masonry and capped with a basilica. Pilgrims began arriving from throughout Europe, and today about four million pilgrims go there every year. The nightly candlelight procession of tens of thousands of devotees is one of the world's great religious spectacles. Pilgrims take a ritual bath and, for many Catholics, cures attributed to visits to Lourdes have been a sign of the truth and power of their faith.

The copy of the grotto at Lourdes that is inside this New York church was paid for by a faithful New Yorker after her son was cured at Lourdes. The rough dark stone replica of the grotto behind the altar seems to be carved out of the rock of Morningside Cliff. The altar was built into the natural rock, and the stations of the cross are carved from the same stone.

Different architects carried on the construction, giving us one of New York's finest classical churches: a Greek cross plan with a four-column Corinthian portico on the front and a semicircular apse to the rear. A band of swagged garlands follows the entablature all around the perimeter. Inside, colossal marble columns at the side aisles spring into soaring arches, creating a grand space. A planned drum and skylight dome, which would have flooded the interior with natural light, were never built, so now the church must be lighted artificially.

AROUND THE CORNER

➡ Architectural historians cherish another nearby Roman Catholic church dedicated to **Our Lady of Lourdes** (LM, 467 West 142nd St., between Convent and Amsterdam Aves. 1904, Cornelius O'Reilly. ☎ 862-4380). It incorporates parts of three important earlier buildings. The main fabric of the church, including a banded gray marble and dark bluestone façade, was saved from the High Victorian Gothic National Academy of Design that had stood on East 23rd Street (1865, Peter B. Wight). The north and east walls, including stained-glass windows, were removed from the east end of St. Patrick's Cathedral in 1902 to build the Lady Chapel that is there today. And the elaborate pedestals flanking the steps are relics of department store magnate A. T. Stewart's white marble mansion, which stood on the corner of 34th Street and Fifth Avenue until 1901 (1867, John Kellum). A critic wrote in 1907, "by picking the architecture of this church off the scrap-heap, so to say, [the priest] has managed to get an edifice far better . . . than he could possibly have obtained at the same cost, or even at a considerable multiple of it, by building it 'de novo.'" Unfortunately, architect O'Reilly didn't live to see how the pieces came together. He slipped from a ladder while overseeing construction and died in the rectory across the street. The church bears a plaque to his memory.

A Renaissance Chapel
SAINT PAUL'S (LM)
Nondenominational. On the campus of Columbia University, just off Amsterdam Ave. at 116th St. 1907, Howells & Stokes. ☎ Inquire at 854-1754

Columbia University was founded as an Anglican school, and its bylaws required it to have an Episcopal president well into the 20th century. Columbia is secular today, but this Italian Renaissance-style chapel is arguably the finest building on its campus. The four large columns of the vaulted portico are topped with winged cherubs instead of capitals. The floor plan is in the form of a short Latin cross, with a semicircular apse at the east end. A dome covers the crossing. The exterior is of brick, terracotta, and limestone, and the roof is tiled.

The interior walls are in warm salmon and buff brick, and the vaulting guarantees sonorous acoustics. Light pours in from above. The stained-glass windows illustrate the theme of teaching: the three apse windows (John LaFarge) show Paul preaching to the Athenians; the large arched windows in the transepts (Young & Guthrie) show teachers of the Old Testament (north transept) and of the New Testament (south). Windows below the dome (by D. M. Armstrong) show coats of arms of twenty-four old New York families, including the Van Cortlandts, de Peysters, Beekmans, Clintons, and Rhinelanders.

Near the building outside, look for three pairs of iron gates that were originally on the grounds of the North Dutch Church, which stood at Fulton and William Streets from 1769 until 1875. Columbia held commencements there. The gates were installed at Columbia in 1938. Two pairs flank St. Paul's Chapel, and the third is at the quadrangle formed by the chapel and Avery, Schermerhorn, and Fayerweather Halls.

AROUND THE CORNER

➥ The **General Grant National Memorial** (LM, Riverside Dr. at West 122nd St. 1897, John Duncan) is the largest mausoleum in America. Ulysses S. Grant (1822–85), Union Civil War hero and later president, was so beloved when he died that thousands of people contributed to build this mausoleum high above the Hudson River. It is in the style of an Ionic temple capped by a circular colonnade topped by a conical roof. Sculptor J. Massey Rhind's recumbent figures of Victory and Peace lean against a plaque with Grant's words, "Let us have peace." President and Mrs. Grant rest in polished black sarcophagi in a crypt under a domed rotunda, all in imitation of Napoleon's final resting place at Les Invalides in Paris. Grant's *Memoirs* remains a best-seller.

At the northern edge of this property a small stone urn was "Erected to the Memory of an Amiable Child, St. Clair Pollock," who, at the age of five, fell to his death here on July 15, 1797. This small memorial has stood undisturbed for over 200 years.

A Pulpit for a Dynamic Preacher
RIVERSIDE CHURCH (LM)
490 Riverside Dr., between West 120th and West 122nd Sts. 1930, Allen & Collens and Henry C. Pelton; Burnham Hoyt, designer. South Wing, 1960. Collens, Willis & Beckonert. ☎ 870-6700. A guidebook is available in the office.

Riverside Church is the product of the thought and work of two men: Harry Emerson Fosdick (1878–1969) and John D. Rockefeller, Jr. (1874–1960).

Harry Emerson Fosdick was ordained as a Baptist minister, but he gained fame as a popular preacher at New York's First Presbyterian Church.

THREE SEMINARIES

Three seminaries are found in Upper Manhattan, all of which can be visited.

Union Theological Seminary

Union Theological Seminary (LM, West 120th to 122nd Sts., between Broadway and Claremont Aves. 1910, Allen & Collens. Altered, 1952, Collens, Willis & Beckonert. ☎ 662-7100) was founded in 1836 as a graduate school for Protestant ministers, and it has long had a reputation for liberal religious thought and social activism. The school followed Columbia University to this neighborhood in 1910 and settled into a Gothic-style quadrangle of rock-faced granite buildings (quarried on the site) with limestone trim. The building shelters a quiet garden. Its two handsome towers and James Memorial Chapel recall medieval Oxford and Cambridge. Graduates include Reinhold Niebuhr, Norman Thomas, and Henry Sloane Coffin. The German theologian **Dietrich Bonhoeffer** (1906–45) studied here in 1929–30, then returned to Germany, where he wrote important works on ecumenism and Christianity in the modern world. He was involved in a plot to overthrow Hitler and executed by the Nazis.

The Jewish Theological Seminary (3080 Broadway at 122nd St. 1930, Gehron, Ross, Alley. David Levy, associate. ☎ 222-4663), founded in 1886 to provide American-trained rabbis and scholars, is the center of the Conservative movement in American Judaism. Its library holds the most comprehensive collection of Judaica and Hebraica in the Western Hemisphere, and its **rock garden** was inspired by Exodus 16:6: "Behold, I will stand with you at the rock at Horeb, and you shall strike the rock, and water shall come out of it that the people may drink."

Yeshiva University (West 183rd to West 187th Sts. along Amsterdam Ave. Main building: 1928, Charles B. Meyers Associates. ☎ 960-5400) is the oldest and most distinguished Jewish university in America, having evolved from the first Jewish parochial school (1886) into a full school with a seminary ten years later. Today it offers both undergraduate and graduate education, while the associated Rabbi Isaac Elchanan Theological Seminary trains rabbis and cantors. This is an Orthodox Jewish institution. The main building is a flamboyant Near Eastern Romanesque-Byzantine-Moorish Revival structure.

In the 1920s theological struggles between fundamentalists and liberal modernists bitterly divided U.S. Christians. Fosdick was a noted liberal, and his 1922 sermon "Shall the Fundamentalists Win?", a plea for tolerance, became one of the most famous sermons in American history. Political leader William Jennings Bryan and other fundamentalists tried to oust him from his pulpit, and Fosdick finally resigned in 1925. (Bryan went off to help prosecute John Scopes for teaching evolution in a Tennessee public school, and he died five days after his own beliefs were there subjected to cross-examination by defense counsel Clarence Darrow. These events provided the material for the classic American play, then film, *Inherit the Wind*, by Jerome Lawrence and Robert Lee.)

John D. Rockefeller, Jr. (see also p. 297), admired Fosdick, and he subsidized the printing and distribution of Fosdick's 1922 sermon. Rockefeller was himself a member of Park Avenue Baptist Church (and a Sunday school teacher there), and he was ready to sponsor a move of that congregation or even the construction of a new interdenominational church where Fosdick's thousands of followers could hear him preach each Sunday. Fosdick accepted the pastorate of Park Avenue Baptist Church on three conditions: "First, affirmation of faith in Christ must be the only requirement for membership. Second, any Christian, regardless of denomination, seeking admission to the church, must be freely welcomed. Third, a new and larger building and a more expansive ministry should be planned in a neighborhood critical to the life of the whole city." These ideas represented a radical departure from Baptist tradition, and Fosdick's views on baptism and ecumenism nearly provoked a schism at the 1925 Baptist convention. Nevertheless, the new Riverside Church rose, and Fosdick stayed there (and taught at nearby Union Seminary) until his retirement in 1946. He organized Alcoholics Anonymous groups, birth control clinics, and other social programs. His sermons, books, and radio broadcasts made him one of the most prominent clergymen in the world. Riverside became famous as a forum for nonsectarian, interracial, and international ideals. Today it is affiliated with both the Baptist Church and the United Church of Christ.

Rockefeller purchased an ideal setting for the new church: the crest of a steep bluff with a view of the Hudson River to the west, Harlem to the north and east, and Manhattan's West Side to the south. The design of the building imposes a Gothic-style exterior upon a steel-framed multipurpose structure. Its architects had had a small-scale trial run just a few years earlier, when they had built Park Avenue Baptist Church (today's **Central Presbyterian**, Park Avenue at 64th St.), also with Rockefeller's money. From the exterior, that church seems traditional Gothic in style, but what looks like a clerestory is really offices and school spaces stacked above the

Riverside Church, detail from the west side portal

auditorium; it's all cloaked in a neo-Gothic skin. Riverside imitated that example, but expanded it to a gargantuan scale. Seen from miles away, Riverside looks like a Gothic church with a single tower over the entrance. But the "tower" is an office skyscraper (you don't even enter the church here), and the "nave" behind it is an enormous building containing not only spaces for worship, but also community facilities such as a gymnasium, bowling alleys, and a theater.

The main entrance to the church, on the west side, is based on that of the Porte Royale at Chartres. A tiny chapel off the entrance lobby con-

A GREAT VIEW
FROM THE TOWER

From the lobby of Riverside Church you may ascend to the observatory and to the Laura Spelman Rockefeller Memorial Carillon of seventy-four bells, including one of twenty tons. Both the carillon and that bell are said to be the largest in the world, and the view from the observatory is one of the finest in Manhattan.

tains the painting *Christ in Gethsemane* by Heinrich Hofmann (1824–1911), one of the most-reproduced Christian religious paintings.

Riverside was most emphatically to be a preaching church, so the nave is exceptionally wide; it seats 2,500 people. The chancel screen portrays seven aspects of the life of Christ and people who have fulfilled the divine ideal, including individuals as diverse as Dr. Louis Pasteur, Savonarola, Florence Nightingale, Johann Sebastian Bach, Booker T. Washington, Michelangelo, Dr. Walter Reed, Hippocrates, John Ruskin, Jane Addams, and John Milton. The fifty-one stained-glass windows include two rose windows above the second gallery, clerestory windows that are copies of those at the Cathedral of Chartres, in France (made by French glassmakers), and, on the aisle level, windows illustrating both modern and historical motifs.

LABYRINTHS

The marble floor of the chancel at Riverside Church displays a small copy of the labyrinth that was paved into the floor of Chartres Cathedral in France in 1220. A labyrinth—not to be confused with a maze—is a winding path inward to the center of a circle. The same path is then followed out again; the walker has only one path to follow, and is never confused. A labyrinth is a sanctuary, or a metaphor for the spiritual journey inward. The labyrinth at Chartres was available for people who were unable to make a pilgrimage to the Holy Land, and walkers of it were believed to have entered sacred space.

We do not know where or when labyrinths originated, but labyrinthine designs have been found in cultures throughout the world dating as far back as 3,500 years. In recent years, increasing numbers of Americans have been drawn to walking labyrinths as a way of encouraging meditation. Reverend Lauren Artress of Grace Cathedral in San Francisco triggered the popularity of labyrinths, and she has toured the country promoting their creation. Even hospitals have found that they offer a calming experience for patients and their visitors. In New York, a walkable labyrinth has been created at Riverside Church, and others can be found at Judson Memorial Church and at the Cathedral of St. John the Divine. The Department of Parks has allowed the creation of a labyrinth at the north end of Union Square (17th St., between Broadway and Park Ave. South.)

Explaining the Mass in English
CORPUS CHRISTI
Roman Catholic. 529 West 121st St. at Broadway. 1936, Wilfred E. Anthony. ☎ 666-9350

Corpus Christi parish was founded in 1906, and it includes Columbia University, so you may well imagine that it has a history of intellectual innovation and ferment. Here in 1935 that one priest celebrated the traditional Latin liturgy at the altar while another provided an English translation and running commentary from the pulpit. Eventually full translations of the priest's words were placed in the pews for the congregation to read along. This was thirty years before Vatican II decreed that mass should be celebrated in the language of the people.

Even the architecture of Corpus Christi is highly unusual for a Roman Catholic church. It is in the Colonial Revival style usually associated with Congregational or Presbyterian churches. The belfry, however, echoes that of architect Charles Bulfinch's original Roman Catholic Holy Cross Cathedral in Boston (since replaced), and the gilded cross surmounting the tower is in the form of a monstrance, symbolizing the mystery of the Eucharist, to which this church is dedicated. A stone from the fifth-century Basilica of Santa Maria Maggiore in Rome can be found set into the wall of the narthex, and the stained-glass windows in the apse contain

THOMAS MERTON

Thomas Merton (1915–68) was a graduate student at Columbia University when he began to work in a Catholic settlement house in Harlem. One day, while reading about the Jesuit poet Gerard Manley Hopkins, Merton heard a voice saying, "You know what you ought to do. Why don't you do it?" Merton was instructed in Catholicism at Corpus Christi, baptized, eventually ordained, and entered a Trappist monastery. He died while attending an ecumenical conference of Catholic and Buddhist monks in Thailand, but his works of religious prose and poetry remain perennial best-sellers, especially his 1948 autobiography *The Seven Storey Mountain*. In the introduction to the Japanese edition, Merton wrote, "I seek to speak to you, in some way, as your own self. Who can tell what this may mean? I myself do not know, but if you listen, things will be said that are perhaps not written in this book. And this will be due not to me but to the One who lives and speaks in both."

glass fragments recovered from Reims Cathedral in France after it was bombed in World War I.

Music is a strong tradition at Corpus Christi. The choir at the 11:15 A.M. Sunday mass, composed of professional singers, has the longest tradition of liturgical chant and polyphonic music in New York. Since 1975 Corpus Christi has also been the home of "Music Before 1800," a nonprofit group that sponsors a series of early music concerts on Sunday afternoons through the winter.

A "Rural" Church and Cemetery
CHURCH OF THE INTERCESSION (LM)
Episcopal. 550 West 155th St. at Broadway. 1915 Bertram Goodhue. ☎ 283-6200

🍃 The name of this church means that this is a congregation of intercessors, people who appeal to God in prayer for the welfare of others. The church was founded as an independent country parish and consecrated its first building here in 1846, but in 1907 the parish was financially insolvent and "demoted" to the status of a chapel of Trinity parish. Therefore, Trinity erected this 1915 building, but then in 1976 Trinity launched it again as an independent parish. The Gothic Revival complex of church, parish house, and vicarage, all of which can be entered from a cloister surrounded by a vaulted arcade, mounted high on a clear open site overlooking the Hudson River, presents a vision of medieval times.

Inside the church, columns down the long nave support a brightly colored wood hammerbeam roof. On the front of the high altar, designed by L. C. Tiffany, a pattern of stones inlaid in brass creates a "historic tree" of the growth and life of the church. The first stone is from Bethlehem; others are from Nazareth, the banks of the Jordan River, the Mount of Olives, and churches throughout England. The altar also contains a stone from the London church where explorer Henry Hudson took communion before his voyage across the Atlantic and up the river that now bears his name. The altar is protected by a high baldachin and dossal decorated with a pattern of the symbolic pelican. All of the stained-glass windows except those in one side chapel are abstract.

Architect Bertram Goodhue must have loved this church, because he chose to be buried in it. His marble wall tomb in the north transept, sculpted by Lee Lawrie, shows his buildings in a frieze above his recumbent figure. The text reads, "His great architectural creations that beautify the land and enrich civilization are his monuments." In 1929 Intercession

The Church of the Intercession

opened in the crypt below the nave the first columbarium (place for urns containing ashes after cremation) in any New York church.

Behind the church is part of its original graveyard. The plot of naturalist John James Audubon (1785–1851), who once owned this land and lived here, is marked by a tall Celtic cross donated by the New York Academy of Sciences in 1893. Birds and a relief portrait are carved on one side, and animals on the other. It stands on a base sculpted with rifles and a powder horn, a palette and paintbrushes.

AROUND THE CORNER

➡ **Trinity Cemetery** (153rd St. to 155th St., Broadway to Riverside Dr.) is just across Broadway. An annual Christmas Eve service at Intercession is followed by a candle-lit procession across Broadway to the graves of Clement C. Moore (d. 1863), the author of "A Visit from St. Nicholas," and Alfred Tennyson Dickens (d. 1912), the son of Charles Dickens, the author of *A Christmas Carol*. Alfred Dickens died in New York while on a lecture tour.

Trinity Church purchased J. J. Audubon's farm and laid out in 1843 what is still Manhattan's largest cemetery. This area had witnessed history before then, for it was the site of the fiercest fighting during the battle of

Washington Heights on November 16, 1776. The cemetery contains some fine examples of funerary art, sculpture, and private mausoleums. One mausoleum is the final resting place of Eliza Brown Jumel (1775–1865), who started her career as a prostitute in Rhode Island, married the rich Mr. Jumel, and later became Mrs. Aaron Burr. She lived in the nearby mansion that had been Washington's headquarters during September 1776. Today the **Morris-Jumel Mansion** is a public museum with a garden (LM, 65 Jumel Terrace. 1765, architect unknown. ☎ 923-8008).

Trinity Cemetery is the only cemetery in Manhattan still receiving interments. In the year 2000, it had room in new community mausoleums, as well as available columbarium niches. (Open to the public daily.)

The American Acropolis
AUDUBON TERRACE (LMD)
Opening onto Broadway between 155th and 156th Sts. 1912, Charles Pratt Huntington. Remodeled in 1925 by Lawrence G. White of McKim, Mead & White.

Audubon Terrace was intended by its founder, railroad heir Archer M. Huntington, to be an American acropolis, a concentration of cultural institutions to serve both scholars and the general public. Huntington first organized the Hispanic Society of America and commissioned his cousin Charles Pratt Huntington to design a museum and library for it. The Hispanic Society is one of the city's least-known repositories of artistic and historical treasures. Its art collection, displayed around an interior courtyard, contains masterpieces of painting (including works by Velasquez, Goya, and El Greco, and a sixteenth-century *Holy Family* by Luis de Morales that has a diagram of Christ's horoscope), sculpture, and metalwork, and its library holds almost 300,000 volumes and manuscripts, mainly about Spanish and Portuguese history, literature, and art. (☎ 926-2234)

The Hispanic Society was joined by the American Numismatic Society (which holds an extraordinary collection of coins, medals, and paper money, plus a comprehensive library; ☎ 234-3130), but in the year 2000 that organization announced plans to move and open a new museum at 140 Williams Street, in downtown Manhattan. The Museum of the American Indian left this location in the 1990s (see p. 83), but its building has been purchased by the Hispanic Society for eventual expansion. In another building, the American Geographic Society has been replaced by today's Boricua College. What is today the American Academy and Institute of Arts and Letters (☎ 368-5900) moved here in 1923.

All the buildings are Italian Renaissance–style and sit around a plaza featuring sculpture by Archer Huntington's wife, Anna Hyatt Huntington. Sculptures include a monument to El Cid Campeador, the legendary Spanish hero, and equestrian reliefs of the fictional Don Quixote and of the historical Boabdil, the last Muslim king of Granada, Spain.

The complex also includes New York's second oldest Spanish-language parish, **Our Lady of Esperanza** (Roman Catholic. 624 West 156th St. 1912, C. P. Huntington. ☎ 283-4340). Originally, stairs led up from the sidewalk to a small terrace in front of the church, but in 1925 architect Lawrence G. White (Stanford White's son) extended the church's façade forward to the lot line and added a vestibule, which brought the stairs up to the sanctuary inside. The green and gold church interior contains a marble high altar with a demilune (semicircular) relief of the Madonna and Child adored by angels, various articles given by the prominent Have-meyer and Vanderbilt families (probably because of their friendship with Huntington), and a hanging sanctuary lamp donated by King Alfonso XIII of Spain when the church opened.

The First American Citizen Saint
THE SHRINE OF MOTHER CABRINI
701 Fort Washington Ave. at 190th St. 1959, DeSina & Pellegrino. ☎ 923-3536

The closest many of us will ever get to sainthood is the experience of sitting on the favorite bench of Frances (Mother) Cabrini (1850–1918), the first American citizen to be proclaimed a saint of the Roman Catholic Church. The bench, painted red and installed in an elaborate carved-stone frame under an enormous statue of Christ, sits in front of the Shrine of Mother Cabrini in Washington Heights.

When Mother Cabrini founded the Missionary Sisters of the Sacred Heart in 1880 in her native Italy, she intended to go to China. Pope Leo XIII, however, told her to "find her China in the West," that is, to go to New York and help the struggling Italian immigrants here. Her meeting with the pope is shown in a stained-glass window at Our Lady of Pompeii (where she taught school in 1899; see p. 165). She arrived in New York in 1889 and set right to work, opening an orphan asylum in that year and a hospital in 1892. Hospital funding eventually came partly from sponsoring New York's first Columbus Day Parade in 1900. She called it Columbus Hospital, but today it's Cabrini Hospital (227 East 19th St., between Second and Third Aves. ☎ 995-6000). In 1899 she bought property in Washington Heights and opened Sacred Heart Villa, a school for girls.

The red bench was on that property. Mother Cabrini became a U.S. citizen in 1909, and she eventually founded sixty-seven hospitals, schools, and orphanages across the United States, Latin America, and Europe, one for each year of her life. When she was beatified, her remains were placed in the chapel of the new Mother Cabrini High School built here, but after she was canonized in 1946, work began on the shrine next door (designed, appropriately, by a man named Pellegrino, "pilgrim"). Her remains (encased in a wax replica) rest in a crystal coffin under the main altar. A showcase in the small gift shop displays photographs and various personal items belonging to her. The Vatican named Mother Cabrini the patroness of all immigrants in 1950.

More Than a Museum—a "Medieval Environment"
FORT TRYON PARK AND THE CLOISTERS (LM)

Early Dutch settlers referred to this heavily wooded high ground overlooking the Hudson River as the "Long Hill," and the strategic battlements of Fort Tryon were later built on that hilltop. In November, 1776, it was here that 3,000 American soldiers, including the legendary woman cannoneer Margaret Corbin, defended the hill against over 8,000 British troops, but they were forced to surrender before George Washington's order to escape arrived. Over 2,800 defenders were sent to die in British prison ships moored in the harbor (see p. 309).

In 1916, John D. Rockefeller, Jr., began to acquire the land to establish a park, but the city, fearing the cost of necessary improvements, declined the gift. Rockefeller offered the fifty-six acres again in 1927 with the funds necessary to landscape it, and the city accepted. The landscaping plan by the Olmsted brothers (the son and stepson of F. L. Olmsted) included building over nine miles of retaining walls to preserve the natural beauty of the site and open up the views.

The Cloisters (1938, Charles Collens. ☎ 923-3700), at the northern end of the park, has been called "the most perfect museum created in the twentieth century, the ideal environment for great works of art." It is a new construction that incorporates sections of a twelfth-century chapter house from Pontaut, France, parts of cloisters from five medieval European monasteries, and the apse from a twelfth-century Spanish church. Visitors insist that it is more than a museum. With its courtyard gardens, balconies, central tower, exterior landscaping, medieval music (recorded music is played regularly, but the Cloisters also offers regular live concerts), and superlative art works, it is an evocation of the

Middle Ages. The three men most instrumental in creating it were John D. Rockefeller, Jr. (see also p. 288), George Grey Barnard, and James J. Rorimer.

Rockefeller was a devout Baptist, and he appreciated medieval art for the careful way many of its artists anonymously wrought their work as an offering to God. One of the highlights of Rockefeller's collection was a set of tapestries showing *The Hunt of the Unicorn* (ca. 1500), a sophisticated allegory of Christ. They are among the most magnificent and best-preserved Gothic tapestries in existence, despite having been used during the French Revolution to wrap potatoes in a freezing cellar. Rockefeller bought them from Count Gabriel de la Rochefoucauld, who, the story goes, wanted the money to build a golf course on his estate.

As Rockefeller was accumulating medieval art, American sculptor and art dealer George Grey Barnard was touring the French countryside, buying up architectural fragments from abandoned churches and monasteries. He spirited his collection out of France just two days before a new law would have prohibited their export as national treasures, and, in 1914, he opened a "cloister museum" of medieval sculpture and architectural elements on Fort Washington Avenue. In 1925 Rockefeller gave the Metropolitan Museum the money to buy Barnard's collection as an uptown branch.

Rockefeller and the Metropolitan soon began to feel that the Fort Washington Avenue site was inadequate, and that is why in 1927 Rockefeller renewed his offer to New York City to donate the land along the Long Hill, if four acres at the northern end could be reserved for a cloisters museum. The city accepted the gift of what is today Fort Tryon Park, and the Cloisters had a new home.

Architect Charles Collens first proposed a fortresslike medieval building, but Rockefeller felt that would be inappropriate to display religious art, so Collens redesigned his model to imitate the general shape and structure of a medieval monastery, without imitating any one in particular. At that point the Metropolitan's brilliant young curator James J. Rorimer entered the picture. Rorimer and Rockefeller together configured the building, the placement of many of the architectural fragments, and even of individual art works within it. As the museum rose, they visited the construction site almost every day together. As a concluding gesture of exceptional vision and generosity, Rockefeller bought the wooded cliffs on the west side of the Hudson River and presented the land to the Palisades Interstate Park Commission in order to preserve the view from the Cloisters for all time. The Cloisters opened to the public in 1938.

A Native American Sacred Site
INWOOD HILL PARK

The Urban Ecology Center is at West 218th St. and Indian Road. ☎ 800-201-7275 or 888-697-2757

Manhattan's oldest known sacred ceremonial site is here, set among the last stand of natural forest at the very northwest corner of the island. The rock ledges and overhangs on the steep hillside just beyond the park entrance at 218th Street and Indian Road are known as the Indian Caves. The many artifacts found here (now in the Museum of the American Indian—see p. 83) testify to the ceremonies observed by the Shorakapkock, who believed that the swirling water of the Hell Gate area of the Harlem River was a portal to the underworld. Several Native American bands held councils under an ancient tulip tree that stood here until it fell in 1938, at which time it was probably the oldest living thing in Manhattan. The meeting at which Peter Minuit bought Manhattan was possibly at this spot, and that event is commemorated by a marker on historic Tablet (or "Shorakapkock") Rock just inside the Park. The city bought the land for a public park in 1916, and today Urban Park Rangers maintain a year-round schedule of free walking tours.

CHAPTER NINE

𝒯he Four
Outer Boroughs

MANHATTAN ISLAND IS THE FOCUS of New York City's
history and wealth, but each of the city's four "outer boroughs" (Brooklyn,
Queens, the Bronx, and Staten Island) contains the population of a good-
sized city, and each boasts enough architectural masterpieces, historic sites,
pleasant retreats, and lively communities of faith, worship, and service to
fill a large volume. Unfortunately, this chapter can only suggest the
extraordinary diversity of sacred spaces and peaceful places throughout
these boroughs.

Each of the outer boroughs has historic individual settlements, and
Brooklyn was an independent city for some sixty years. Furthermore, the
immigrants who are arriving in New York City from virtually every country of the globe today more frequently settle in the outer boroughs than in
Manhattan. Therefore, the outer boroughs are seeing rapid growth in the
number of houses and communities of worship that are serving many of
the world's faith traditions.

The outer boroughs' botanical gardens are of great spiritual interest.
They offer a variety of theme gardens, including classical Asian landscape
designs and plantings that reflect how some Asian religions emphasize
God in nature, or God *as* nature. In these special gardens, the contemplation of nature is interpreted as a form of worshipful meditation. The beautiful rural-style cemeteries in the outer boroughs also reflect a meditative
approach to nature.

Because of space limitations, this chapter introduces just a few places in each of the outer boroughs. These locations are often widely dispersed even within each borough. The chapter includes a few neighborhoods through which you might comfortably walk (Brooklyn Heights, Flushing, etc.), but in other cases you will have to count on transportation among the individual sites profiled. Each listing provides the nearest subway stop (and commuter train where available), and if the site is not within five blocks of a subway stop, a bus from the nearest subway stop to the site is suggested.

Brooklyn

Brooklyn is the most populous of all of the city's five boroughs, and its tradition of building houses of worship long ago earned it the nickname "The borough of churches." Fine steeples punctuate its skyline still. Mention of Brooklyn brings to mind a roll call of its tree-shaded brownstone neighborhoods, adorned by dignified houses of worship: Brooklyn Heights, Clinton, Bedford-Stuyvesant, etcetera.

When Europeans first arrived, the Native American inhabitants of western Long Island were mostly of the Canarsie band, but the Canarsies were decimated or displaced as the Dutch chartered independent villages: 's Gravensande (today's Gravesend, 1645); Breuckelen (today's Brooklyn, originally named for a small town south of Amsterdam, 1657); 't Vlacke Bos (Flatbush, 1652); Nieuw Utrecht (1662); Nieuw Amersfoort (Flatlands, 1666); and Boswijk (Bushwick, 1660). Each of these settlements provided a focal point for growth and development, and each still contains houses of worship of great age and renown. New York State chartered the city of Brooklyn in 1834, and Brooklyn expanded to cover all of Kings County before consolidating with New York City in 1898.

Brooklyn Heights, the high promontory facing Manhattan from across the East River (*Ihpetonga*, "high sandy banks," to the Canarsie), sprouted New York's first suburb after inventor Robert Fulton inaugurated steam ferry service across the river in 1814. **The Brooklyn Bridge** (LM, 1883) knit Brooklyn with New York City more tightly. This engineering marvel was built by John Augustus Roebling (who pioneered in the use of steel cable and built a factory for manufacturing it in Trenton, N.J.) and his son Washington Augustus Roebling. Both men sacrificed themselves to the bridge. The father's leg was crushed by a ferryboat during the work, and he died of tetanus. The son collapsed while working in a pneumatic caisson, and he was paralyzed by decompression sickness. He supervised the bridge's final completion through a telescope from his home in Brooklyn Heights. The Roeblings' masterwork, when dedicated, was more than twice as long as any other bridge in the world. Its masonry-clad support towers, with soaring Gothic Revival arches, are a surprisingly old-fashioned feature of what is otherwise a technologically innovative construction. When Gustave Eiffel built the Statue of Liberty in 1886 and his tower in Paris three years after that, he knew that, in terms of engineering prowess, he was competing with the Brooklyn Bridge.

Brooklyn Heights and Downtown Brooklyn

Brooklyn Heights has retained its grace and charm, and in 1965 it was the first New York City neighborhood to be designated a Landmark Historic District. The area is rich in historic houses of worship, and of the approximately 1,100 houses in the Heights today, some 600 were built before 1860. There are several guidebooks to the area available in the bookshops on Montague Street. The following are just a few of the places of spiritual interest.

Many subway lines 🚇 converge on Brooklyn Borough Hall or Jay Street (M, N, R, 2, 3, 4, 5, A, C, F) and it's just a short walk to the Heights from there.

America's Earliest Figural Stained Glass
SAINT ANN AND THE HOLY TRINITY (LMD)
Episcopal. 157 Montague St. at Clinton St. **Brooklyn Heights**. 1847, Minard Lafever. ☎ 718-858-2424

In 1844 John Bartow, a prosperous mill owner, underwrote the construction of Holy Trinity Church on the highest point in Brooklyn Heights. St. Ann's Church and the Holy Trinity Church merged in 1966. Architect Lafever commissioned twenty-six-year-old William Bolton and his brother John to design sixty

St. Ann and the Holy Trinity

stained-glass windows for this church, the first figural stained-glass windows made in America.

AROUND THE CORNER
➡ **The Brooklyn Historical Society** (LMD, corner of Pierrepont and Clinton Sts. 1878–80, George B. Post. ☎ 718-624-0890) was founded as the Long Island Historical Society in 1863, and its collections (125,000 books, plus maps, newspapers, memorabilia, and more) include materials about all of New York City and State. The Society offers tours of Brooklyn, and its permanent exhibits present the stories of the Brooklyn Dodgers, Brooklyn Bridge, Coney Island, and famous Brooklynites. The building is a handsome combination of Romanesque and Classical Revival styles in red and brown terra-cotta and pressed brick.

The Maronite Rite
OUR LADY OF LEBANON (LMD)
Maronite Rite of the Roman Catholic Church. 113 Remsen St. at Henry St. **Brooklyn Heights**. 1846, Richard Upjohn. ☎ 718-624-7228

Even the most casual passerby will notice the bronze doors on the west and south portals to this church. These works of art came from a passenger ship. In 1942 the French luxury liner *Normandie* caught fire and sank as it was being refitted for use as a troop ship at a pier in Manhattan. Sabotage was at first suspected, but now it is believed the fire was an accident. After the disaster, articles found in the wreckage were auctioned off, and among the decorative items salvaged were the pair of bronze doors originally in the ship's banquet room, now on the south portal, only a few of whose medallions are religious in inspiration. Another set of bronze doors with ten medallions, nine showing churches in Normandy and a tenth showing the *Normandie*'s sister ship, the *Ile de France* were installed on the west portal. The doors were purchased by the priest at this church.

Our Lady of Lebanon

The doors are not the only inventive feature of this building, for when it went up it was the first Romanesque Revival church in the United States. It was built as a Congregational church—the Church of the Pilgrims—by a congregation made up largely of migrants from New England who moved to Brooklyn Heights in the decades before the Civil War. A piece of Plymouth Rock was embedded in the church tower, but when the congregation merged into the Plymouth Church a few blocks away in 1934, they took the rock fragment with them (see p. 304). Lebanese Maronite Christians bought this building in 1944, and they gave the church its present name in 1977. The Maronites separated from the Church of Rome in the seventh century, but returned to communion with the pope in the twelfth century. Today their head (under the pope) is the patriarch of Antioch, who lives in Lebanon. Maronite priests are allowed to marry.

Awake!
JEHOVAH'S WITNESSES

More than thirty buildings in **Brooklyn Heights** have been purchased or built by the Watch Tower Bible and Tract Society, which is the publishing arm of the Jehovah's Witnesses (for general information ☎ 718-625-3600).

Jehovah's Witnesses grew out of a Bible-study group begun in Pennsylvania by Charles Taze Russell in 1870. The group started to print a magazine, today's *The Watch Tower*, in 1879, and, after incorporating in 1884, the group eventually took the name of the Watch Tower Bible and Tract Society. The society moved to Brooklyn in 1909 and later changed its name to Jehovah's Witnesses (Isaiah 43:10–12). Witnesses believe that the Bible is the inspired word of God and that it is historically accurate, so all religious teachings should be subjected to the test of agreement with it. The Witnesses do not have any clergy or churches in the usual sense. Their meeting places are called Kingdom Halls, and all Witnesses are considered ministers. Baptism is by total immersion. Witnesses carry on intensive proselytizing, distributing their publications internationally and even walking from house to house offering Bible literature. The society distributes books, booklets, and tracts in the hundreds of millions. *Awake!*, for example, another magazine, claims a circulation of eleven million in fifty languages.

The group has constructed some new office and dormitory buildings in Brooklyn Heights, but it also occupies some historic buildings, and it has been commended for how it has preserved and cared for these.

At 107 Columbia Heights is the Brooklyn Heights Residence of Jehovah's Witnesses (1959, Frost and Associates), where a garden and fountain provide a pleasant spot to rest.

AROUND THE CORNER

➥ At 110 Columbia Heights originally stood the home of Brooklyn Bridge builder **Washington Roebling** (when the bridge was opened, the celebratory parade made a detour here to pay tribute to the invalid engineer, see p. 300), and later of **Hart Crane**. In 1930 Crane published *The Bridge*, a book of poems in which he attempted to create an epic myth about American history, using the Brooklyn Bridge as a symbol of the evolution of civilization ("O harp and altar of the fury fused,/ [How could mere toil align thy choiring strings!]"). This same house was later occupied by **John Dos Passos**, who wrote here part of his trilogy of novels together called *U.S.A.* The fifty-foot tree at 151 Willow Street is an exotic Dawn Redwood, a Chinese conifer that drops its needles every fall.

➥ **The Brooklyn Heights Esplanade** offers unforgettable views of Manhattan and of New York harbor. The Esplanade, with benches, is cantilevered over the Brooklyn-Queens Expressway, which was completed in 1950.

➥ Number 31 Grace Court was owned by playwright **Arthur Miller** from 1947 to 1951, and by civil rights leader **W. E. B. Du Bois** from 1951 to 1961.

Abolitionist Stronghold
PLYMOUTH CHURCH OF THE PILGRIMS (LMD)
Congregational. Orange St., between Hicks and Henry Sts. **Brooklyn Heights**. 1849, Joseph C. Wells. The Tuscan porch was added early in the twentieth century, and a garden and church house by Woodruff Leeming were added in 1913. ☎ 718-403-9546

Henry Ward Beecher, preacher here from 1847 until 1887, won national fame as one of America's most dedicated—and flamboyant—abolitionists. His sister Harriet Beecher Stowe had already written *Uncle Tom's Cabin* in 1851, when Henry, in the spring of 1856, started raising money to send guns to abolitionists in Kansas. Fighting had broken out there between abolitionists and slaveholders in a prelude to the Civil War, earning Kansas the nickname "Bleeding Kansas." The rifles Beecher sent, packed in boxes labeled "Bibles," came to be known as "Beecher's Bibles." Beecher later brought the horror of the slave trade right into this church by holding two mock slave auctions here. On June 1, 1856, Beecher auctioned off a twenty-two-year-old woman, the slave daughter of a Virginia slave owner. "Come Sarah," said Beecher to the sobbing girl, "come up upon the platform." Turning to the congregation, Beecher went on, "This is a marketable commodity. . . . What will you do now? May she read her liberty in your eyes?" The *New York Times* reported "the most stoical and the most refined shed tears like rain." The cash and jewelry that went into the collection plate bought Sarah her freedom on the spot.

On February 5, 1860, Beecher "sold" a nine-year-old girl named Pinky. Beecher saved a small ring from the collection plate and gave it to the girl, renaming her Rose Ward, after Rose Terry, who had given the ring, and for Ward Beecher, Henry's brother, also a clergyman. (Rose later moved to Washington, but she returned to this church in 1927, sat in the same chair she had used sixty-seven years earlier, and donated the ring Beecher had given her to the congregation.) Three weeks after that auction, Abraham Lincoln attended services here. Plymouth Church had earlier invited him to speak, but he had spoken instead at Cooper Union in Manhattan (see p. 126). Lincoln's pew (no. 89) is marked by a silver plaque, and a bas-relief of Lincoln by sculptor Gutzon Borglum can be seen on the wall outside. Lincoln later asked Beecher to deliver an oration at Fort Sumter on April 14, 1865, acknowledging the end of the Civil War (which he did). That evening Lincoln was assassinated.

Many other famous abolitionists spoke from this pulpit, including Wendell Phillips, William Lloyd Garrison, Charles Sumner, and John Greenleaf Whittier. English author Charles Dickens spoke here on his second visit to America, and journalist Horace Greeley, author Mark Twain, and civil rights leader Booker T. Washington worshiped here. Hungarian freedom fighter Louis Kossuth spoke here in 1851 and raised $10,000 for the cause of Hungarian liberty.

Total church membership was only 343 when the first service was held in this building in 1850, but within a few months the auditorium began to fill on Sundays, and by 1857 the congregation sometimes reached 3,000. The church is a barnlike structure virtually without exterior ornamentation, and its interior, probably designed by Beecher himself, reveals that it is dedicated to preaching. Instead of a rectangle with straight rows of pews, this building is square, with pews focusing on the platform, around which Beecher strode freely as he preached. It may be the first such auditorium-type plan for a church. The acoustics are so good that an ordinary voice in a conversational tone can be heard throughout the building, and no pillars obstruct anyone's view of the speaker. The pulpit furniture (dating from 1868) was constructed from an olive tree brought from Jerusalem's Mount of Olives by members of an excursion to the Holy Land, made famous by Mark Twain in his book *Innocents Abroad*.

Today an arcade connects the church to a new parish house, and the two buildings enclose a garden with a bronze statue of Henry Ward Beecher by Gutzon Borglum (1914). Beecher stands on a granite base on which are seated two slave children, one of whom is Rose Ward. The passageway inside the arcade displays a collection of historical memorabilia, including the ring Beecher gave Rose. A special niche holds the fragment of Plymouth Rock that was brought when the Church of the Pilgrims merged here in 1934 (see p. 303).

AROUND THE CORNER

➥ North of Brooklyn Borough Hall in **Cadman Plaza** (a civic center redevelopment of the 1950s—eight acres of open space named for Reverend S. Parkes Cadman, the nation's first radio preacher) is another sculpture of **Henry Ward Beecher** by John Quincy Adams Ward (1891), with a pedestal by Richard Morris Hunt. The day Beecher died, Ward received an urgent telegram commissioning him to make a death mask, and he later made this eight-foot-high statue.

Historic Roots
THE CATHEDRAL-BASILICA OF SAINT JAMES
Roman Catholic. 250 Cathedral Pl., at Jay and Tillary Sts., just east of Cadman Plaza. **Downtown Brooklyn**. 1903, George H. Streeton. ☎ 718-852-4002

When the Diocese of Brooklyn separated from the Archdiocese of New York in 1853, Brooklyn's new Bishop John Loughlin chose the original church on this site (built in 1822) as his cathedral. Successive bishops have chosen to keep their *cathedra* (throne) here, despite the construction of grander Roman Catholic churches in the diocese, undoubtedly in recognition of this church's rich history. St. James was the first Roman Catholic church on Long Island. From 1853 until 1957, the Diocese of Brooklyn included all of Long Island, but in that year Nassau and Suffolk counties were designated as the new Diocese of Rockville Centre, leaving just Brooklyn and Queens in the Diocese of Brooklyn. With 1.6 million parishioners, the Diocese of Brooklyn has today the largest Catholic population of any of the 164 dioceses in the United States, and yet the diocese's territory comprises the smallest of all dioceses in the United States.

Pope John Paul II visited St. James on October 3, 1979, and in 1982, the Vatican designated St. James as a *basilica* (see p. 50). Today you see the symbols of that distinction—a *tintinnabulum* (a small bell) and an *ombrellino* (a small multicolored round umbrella)—at the front of the sanctuary. The interior of this red brick Georgian-style structure has recently been restored in a neo-classical style, so gilded capitals gleam at the tops of the Corinthian pilasters. Light streams in all four sides through windows by Mayer of Munich.

 A high brick wall surrounding the cathedral property protects a small churchyard cemetery, the first Roman Catholic cemetery on Long Island. Some 7,000 people were buried here between 1823 and 1849. The cemetery may be visited for prayer and meditation.

A Home of Long Island's First Jewish Congregation
BNOS YAKOV OF PUPA
274 Keap St., between Marcy and Division Aves. **Williamsburg, Brooklyn.** 1876, William B. Ditmars. 🚇 *Marcy Ave. stop on the M, J or Z subways, or the Hewes St. stop on the M or J.*

The first Jewish congregation on Long Island organized in 1850 as the Kahal Kodesh Beth Elohim, following the Orthodox tradition. When the congregation moved into this building, it changed its name to Temple Beth Elohim and its ritual to Reform. The congregation merged with Temple Israel in 1921 to form Union Temple, today at 17 Eastern Parkway, and this building is today a Hassidic girls' school, "The Daughters of Jacob of Pupa," a town in Hungary. The building exemplifies High Victorian Gothic, with its multicolored brick and painted brownstone, terra-cotta, stained glass, fine tiles, and iron gates.

"The Chance to Live Decently"
WARREN PLACE WORKINGMEN'S COTTAGES AND THE TOWER AND HOME APARTMENTS (LMD)
Warren Place (between Warren and Baltic Sts. just east of Hicks St.) and Tower Apartments and Home Apartments (Hicks St., between Baltic and Congress Sts.) **Cobble Hill, Brooklyn.** 1876–79, William Field & Son. 🚇 *four blocks west of the Bergen St. stop on the F or G subways.*

The Warren Place housing complex could be part of an idyllic village in the countryside, but instead it was part of a pioneering effort to provide affordable housing for the urban working class. Businessman Alfred T. White wanted to give workingmen "the chance to live decently, and to bring up their children to be decent men and women." Twenty-six attached red brick cottages face a central garden; each is twenty-four feet high (just the width of the garden) and only eleven and a half feet wide. At the ends of the Place, four-story cottages enclose the garden and lower row houses. Although each cottage rented for only $18 per month, the overall project achieved White's goal of practicing philanthropy while achieving a profit: "Philanthropy plus 5 percent." (The garden is not open to the public.)

White's Tower Building and Home Building around the corner not only provided sanitary plumbing (community facilities were in the basement), but they also offered separate entrances, sunshine, and air. The design featured outside recessed balconies and open stairtowers. Each building even has a central courtyard recreation area. A four-room apartment here rented for $7 per month. The "progressive" design of these buildings inspired the design of housing in Europe and the U.S. in the 1920s.

The first *publicly sponsored* low-income housing project in the United States was not to be built for over fifty years: First Houses in Manhattan (29–41 Ave. A and 112–138 East 3rd St. LM, 1935–36, Frederick L. Ackerman.)

AROUND THE CORNER

➥ Two blocks north at 197 Amity Street (near the corner of Court St.) is where **Jennie Jerome**, daughter of wealthy financier Leonard Jerome, was born on January 9, 1854. She moved to England and married Lord Randolph Churchill in 1874, and in that same year gave birth to their son Winston, who frequently returned to New York with his mother during his childhood. Winston Churchill went on to become one of the great public figures of the twentieth century, serving as prime minister of Great Britain from 1940 to 1945 and again from 1951 to 1955. During World War II, he frequently reminded Americans that he was himself half American.

An Old Congregation in a Historic Home
CONGREGATION BETH ISRAEL
ANSHEI EMES (LMD)

Conservative. 236 Kane St. at Tompkins Pl. **Cobble Hill, Brooklyn**. 1855, original architect unknown. ☎ 718-875-1550. 🚆 *Bergen St. stop on the F or G subways.*

This congregation originally occupied Brooklyn's first synagogue building, which was built in 1862 on State Street at Boerum Place. In 1905, however, the congregation purchased this building from Trinity German

Lutheran Church. The building had been built as the Middle Dutch Reformed Church. It is in the Romanesque Revival style, of brick and brownstone, but today it is covered with stucco.

Fort Greene and Clinton Hill

"Rebels, Turn Out Your Dead."
FORT GREENE PARK (LM)

🚊 *Lafayette Ave. stop on the A or C subways; Fulton St. stop on the G; Nevins St. stop on the 2, 3, 4, 5; DeKalb Ave. stop on the D, M, N, Q, R.* Offering a commanding view of downtown Brooklyn and the Manhattan skyline, Fort Greene Park was Brooklyn's first public park (1850), and it contains one of the most important monuments to American Revolutionary War heroes anywhere in the country, **The Prison Ship Martyrs' Monument.**

During the American War of Independence, the British Navy anchored a flotilla of twelve decrepit ships in a nearby bay (since filled-in) and converted the ships to floating prisons for captured American seamen. Some of the prisoners were black slaves fulfilling their masters' military obligations. The ships were allowed to deteriorate into filthy, crowded, disease-ridden hulks, in the hope that conditions on the ships would induce the men to volunteer to serve in the British Navy. Few men did, and, ultimately, death claimed an estimated 11,500 to 12,500 prisoners. Each morning, at the cry of "Rebels, turn out your dead," the bodies of those who had died during the night were hauled on deck, rowed ashore, and buried in shallow graves. In 1808 as many remains as could be recovered were unearthed and reburied nearby, and in 1844 a monument to the martyrs was erected. Walt Whitman, then editor of *The Brooklyn Eagle* newspaper, campaigned for the creation of the 1850 park, which was enlarged and landscaped by Calvert Vaux and Frederick Law Olmsted in 1867. They combined the memorial with the site of an old fort from the Revolutionary period, Fort Putnam, that had been refortified and renamed Fort Greene (for Revolutionary General Nathaniel Greene) during the War of 1812. The new thirty-acre park received its crown in 1908, when President William Howard Taft dedicated the monument as we see it today: A grand stairway leads up to a 220-foot square plaza, and in the center of the plaza stands a 148-foot-high granite Doric column (the world's tallest), topped by a large bronze lantern. The monument was designed by Stanford White. In 1976, during America's bicentennial, Spain's King

Juan Carlos II dedicated a plaque memorializing the Spanish volunteers who also died in the prison ships.

Today the monument is in a state of disrepair. The crypt is closed, and visitors are no longer allowed to climb to the top of the column (a planned elevator was never constructed). A perpetual flame at the top of the column was never lit.

Richard Wright (1908–60; who lived at 175 Carlton Ave.) walked up to the top of this hill almost every day and wrote most of his novel *Native Son* (1940) sitting here. It sold over 215,000 copies in three weeks and launched Wright as the first black writer in America whose books would be immediate best-sellers.

AROUND THE CORNER

➡ The Romanesque Revival **Lafayette Avenue Presbyterian Church** (LMD, Lafayette Ave. at South Oxford St. 1860, Joseph C. Wells. ☎ 718-625-7515. 🚇 *Lafayette Ave. stop on the A or C subways; Fulton St. stop on the G*) was the church of poet **Marianne Moore** (1887–1972), who lived in the Cumberland Apartments at 260 Cumberland Street. Its Tiffany windows date from 1890. The large one in the Underwood Chapel (1920) was the last window made before the firm went out of business.

The Roman Catholic **Queen of All Saints Church and School**, on the northwest corner of Lafayette and Vanderbilt Streets (LMD, 1911, Gustave Steinback. ☎ 718-638-7625. 🚇 *Clinton-Washington Aves. stop on the G subway*) combines a French Gothic-style church with a school building. The building's extraordinary walls of windows (by Locke Decorative Company) transform the interior into a jewel-box of color and light. The building was commissioned by parish priest George Mundelein, who went on to become bishop of Chicago.

A Beautiful Interior
EMMANUEL BAPTIST CHURCH (LM in LMD)

279 Lafayette Ave. at St. James Pl. **Clinton Hill, Brooklyn**. 1887, Francis H. Kimball. ☎ 718-622-1107. 🚇 *Clinton-Washington Aves. stop on the G subway.*

This church was known as "The Standard Oil Church" because it was financed largely by Charles Pratt, a founder of Standard Oil and Brooklyn's wealthiest man. Pratt withdrew from Washington Avenue Baptist Church and founded (and funded) this one when the pastor at the Washington

Emmanuel Baptist Church

Avenue Church wrote a satire of monopolies. The yellow stone Gothic Revival complex consists of a towered chapel (designed by E. L. Roberts and opened before the church itself), the sanctuary, and a school building.

The Gothic-style exterior conceals an interior called by the Landmarks Preservation Commission "perhaps the finest surviving nineteenth-century church interior in New York City." The congregation has taken wonderful care of it. A fanlike seating plan spreading out from the pulpit emphasizes that this is a preaching church. The interior is an expanse of dark woodwork brightened up by light streaming in through stained-glass windows on three sides and by four big brass chandeliers. Two huge brownstone columns support the gallery. Since the 1940s, the congregation has come to be made up mostly of African Americans, who have recently had an Ethiopian Coptic cross, signifying African origins, added to the stenciling around the lower walls.

Charles Pratt also funded the nearby **Pratt Institute** (Willoughby Ave. to Decal Ave., Clawson Ave. to Hall St. 1887), now a professional school of art and design, architecture, engineering, and computer sciences. The institute's library (LM, 224–228 Ryerson St. 1896, W. B. Tubby) was Brooklyn's first free public library, but it was removed from the Brooklyn Public Library system in 1940.

AROUND THE CORNER

➡ The **Apostolic Faith Mission**, next door to Emmanuel Baptist, (LMD, 265 Lafayette Ave. on the NE corner of Washington St. 1868, S. C. Earle. ☎ 718-622-2295) was built in the Lombard Romanesque Revival style for a congregation of Orthodox Quakers. Today the brick building is painted white with red trim.

➡ **Underwood Park** (LMD, along Lafayette Ave. from Waverley to Washington Sts.) was built on the site of the home of wealthy typewriter manufacturer John T. Underwood. His will specified that his house be demolished to provide a public park.

➡ Four blocks further east on Lafayette Avenue stands New York's first Landmark Tree, a *Magnolia Grandiflora* planted about 1885 at the northern edge of this species' range. This great tree towers before three houses (677, 678, and 679 Lafayette Ave. between Marcy Ave. and Tompkins Ave., ca. 1883) which have been converted into **The Magnolia Tree Earth Center**, an environmental studies facility (☎ 718-387-2116).

A Grand Urban Space
GRAND ARMY PLAZA (LM)

The oval Grand Army Plaza (🚋 *Grand Army Plaza stop on the 2 or 3 subways*) was designed in 1862 by Frederick Law Olmsted and Calvert Vaux as an approach to Prospect Park. The arch, groups of sculpture, and dedication to the Union Army came later. At the time of the original plan, the city of Brooklyn still lay a mile to the north. Entering the plaza from the north, a visitor passes through a formal circle of sycamores, then mounts a terrace to see New York City's only official **monument to John F. Kennedy**: a dark green bronze bust by sculptor Neil Estern (monument by Morris Ketchum, Jr. and Associates, 1965). Behind that, **Bailey Fountain** (1932; architect Edgerton Swarthout; central sculpture group by Eugene Savage) shows male and female figures representing wisdom and felicity standing on the prow of a ship in front of Neptune and his tritons together with a young boy holding a cornucopia.

On the south side of the plaza is a great triumphal arch: **The Soldiers' and Sailors' Memorial Arch** (1892, John H. Duncan), dedicated to the Union forces of the Civil War. General William Tecumseh Sherman laid its cornerstone in 1889. The granite arch measures eighty feet high by eighty feet wide, with an aperture thirty-five feet by fifty feet. The arch is adorned by several sculptures, including, on top, a *quadriga* (four-horse chariot) with a female figure carrying a banner and sword flanked by two winged figures of Victory, all in bronze by Frederick MacMonnies (1898). Pedestals on the south side of the arch display military groupings by MacMonnies (1901) representing the Army (on the left; MacMonnies included himself as the figure with a raised sword in the foreground) and the Navy (on the right). The inside of the aperture has bronze equestrian bas-reliefs (1895) of President Lincoln (the only known equestrian portrait of him) and of General Ulysses S. Grant (both figures by William O'Donovan; both horses by Thomas Eakins). Visitors are occasionally allowed to climb to the top of the arch to enjoy the view. (For information ☎ 718-788-0055).

The main branch of the **Brooklyn Public Library** (LM, Flatbush Ave. at Eastern Prkwy. 1941, Githens & Keally. ☎ 718-780-7722) also faces Grand Army Plaza.

A Grammy Award-Winning Choir
BROOKLYN TABERNACLE
Nondenominational. 290 Flatbush Ave. at Seventh Ave. **Park Slope, Brooklyn.** ☎ 718-783-0942. 🚇 *Seventh Ave. stop on the D or Q subways.*

The fame of the Brooklyn Tabernacle has spread far beyond its home, for its 240-voice choir has performed around the world and (as of the year 2000) sold almost two million copies of its eighteen albums of gospel music. Three albums have won Grammy Awards. The choir is directed by Carol Cymbala, who started it in 1973 with eight other people. Carol has had no formal training in music, and she does not read sheet music, but the choir rehearses up to five hours every Friday night, and it demonstrates, Carol and the members proudly point out, what is possible with God's help.

The Tabernacle's pastor, Jim Cymbala, Carol's husband, never received formal seminary training, yet he has authored several best-selling inspirational books, and he has nurtured Brooklyn Tabernacle from under 100 members when he took over in 1971 to its present congregation of over 10,000. Today the Tabernacle holds four two-hour services each Sunday.

The Tabernacle currently meets in a converted movie theater, but in 1998 it purchased Loews Metropolitan Theater, built in downtown Brooklyn in the early 1920s as a vaudeville and movie house. This theater is being restored to its original architectural grandeur, and, when reopened as the Tabernacle, 4,000 people will be able to attend each service, and there will be room for over 700 children in Sunday school.

AROUND THE CORNER

➡ CONGREGATION BETH ELOHIM (LMD)
Reform. Eighth Ave. at Garfield Pl. **Park Slope, Brooklyn**. 1909, Eisendrath & Horowitz. ☎ 718-768-3814. 🚇 *Grand Army Plaza stop on the 2 or 3 subways.*

This imposing Classical Revival synagogue, characterized by a high dome and a chamfered corner entrance flanked by tall columns, is pentagonal. Its five sides represent the Five Books of Moses. The congregation was organized in Brooklyn Heights in 1861 as Brooklyn's first Reform congregation, and it had several homes before settling in Park Slope. Its pulpit is the oldest in any Brooklyn synagogue in continuous use.

The Green Soul of Brooklyn

PROSPECT PARK AND BROOKLYN
BOTANIC GARDEN (LM)
🚇 *Grand Army Plaza or Eastern Parkway/Brooklyn Museum stops on the 2 or 3 subways, or Prospect Park stops on the F, D, Q, S subways.*

Prospect Park rivals Central Park (see p. 234). Its 562 acres include scenic woodland (six Great Trees—see p. 129), broad meadows, picturesque bluffs, plantings, ponds, playing fields, recreational facilities, a zoo, and a Dutch colonial farmhouse. A preexisting Quaker burying ground remains inside the park. The city of Brooklyn began acquiring land for the park in 1859 and accepted Olmsted and Vaux's design in 1866. A visitor walking into the park from the formal entrance on Grand Army Plaza climbs a small hill before Long Meadow comes into view—a broad vista of undulating green with clusters of trees. It might well be one of the finest views in North America (and the design "father" of every par-five golf hole).

Contiguous to the park to the east is the fifty-acre **Brooklyn Botanic Garden** (1910, landscaping by Harold Caparn. ☎ 718-623-7200). This facility combines a scientific research center and a library, as well as specialized gardens, including the first Japanese Garden to open in the United States (1915; completely restored in 2000). It represents the traditional Shinto religion of Japan, according to which the gods, or *kami*, reside in nature—in a tree, a rock, or a piece of moss. A *torii* gate, modeled after a famous Japanese example, symbolizes that you are entering a sacred place. Other highlights include Fragrance Hill, the first garden in the world to be designed for the blind; a garden of plants mentioned in Shakespeare's works; an herb garden; a cherry esplanade with more than forty

Brooklyn Botanic Garden

varieties of blooming cherries; an Italian-style formal garden; a garden of wildflowers native to New York City; ten of New York's Great Trees (see p. 129); and a collection where plants are displayed in the order in which they evolved on Earth.

AROUND THE CORNER

➡ **The Brooklyn Museum** next door (LM, 200 Eastern Prkwy. 1897– 1924, McKim, Mead & White with later additions. ☎ 718-638-5000. ▯ *Eastern Parkway/Brooklyn Museum stop on the 2 or 3 subways*) is one of America's largest and finest art museums. Its encyclopedic collections include one of the world's best Egyptology collections, plus American art, and representative collections from each world region and tradition. Its grand Beaux-Arts building features sculptures on the façade by D. C. French and others. A statue of Muhammad (by Charles Keck) still stands here among great lawgivers, although in 1955 Muslim nations successfully petitioned the State of New York to remove a statue of the prophet (perceived by them as an idol) from the Appellate Courthouse at Madison Square Park in Manhattan.

Flatbush Reformed Dutch Church

Earliest Dutch Roots
FLATBUSH REFORMED DUTCH CHURCH (LM)

890 Flatbush Ave. at Church Ave. **Flatbush, Brooklyn.** 1798, Thomas Fardon. ☎ 718-284-5140. 🚇 *Church Ave. stop on the D or Q subways.*

Dutch Governor Peter Stuyvesant ordered the first church to rise here at 't Vlacke Bos ("the wooded plain") in 1654, so this site vies with that of Stuyvesant's own chapel (today's St. Mark's in Manhattan, p. 127) as being in longest continuous use for European religious purposes in New York City. The present church, the third to be erected here, is a stone and brick building in the Federal style with an elegant clock tower and steeple. The steeple still has the original bell imported from Holland and donated by a parishioner in 1796. It tolled the death of George Washington in 1799 and of every president since. Today immigrants from the Dutch Caribbean island of Aruba are living in this neighborhood and reviving the use of Dutch in this historic church.

The church graveyard, dating back to the seventeenth century, contains famous local families (Vanderbilts, Lefferts, Cortelyous, and Bergens), as well as many of the dead from the 1776 Battle of Brooklyn during the American War of Independence.

AROUND THE CORNER
➥ A few miles away is the **Flatlands Dutch Reformed Church** (3931 Kings Highway at East 40th St. **Flatlands, Brooklyn.** 1848, Henry Eldert.

☎ 718-252-5540. 🚊 *From the Flatbush Ave./Brooklyn College stop on the 2 or 5 subways, take the Flatbush Ave. B41 bus to Kings Highway, then walk two blocks.*) This church was also chartered by Peter Stuyvesant in 1654, but it was not until 1663 that the congregation built its first church here. Today's Greek Revival building is the third church on the site.

🍃 In the graveyard, which dates back to the seventeenth century, rests Dominie Ulpianus Van Sinderen, who, during the War of Independence, preached in favor of American victory to British soldiers; they didn't know what he was saying, because he preached in Dutch. Early settler Pieter Claesen Wyckoff and his wife, Margaret, rest under the church's pulpit. Their 1641 **Wyckoff farmhouse** (LM) stands nearby at 5902 Clarendon Road—in part the oldest surviving man-made structure in New York State (open to the public ☎ 718-629-5400).

An Early African American Community
HISTORIC WEEKSVILLE (LM)

The Society for the Preservation of Weeksville and Bedford Stuyvesant History can be reached at 1698 Bergen St. **Weeksville, Brooklyn.** ☎ 718-756-5250. 🚊 *Crown Heights/Utica Ave. stop on the 3 or 4 subways, or the Fulton St. stop on the A or C subways.*

Hunterfly Road was an important highway to eastern Long Island during Dutch days, and remains of the highway now survive in the middle of a block surrounded by Bergen Street and St. Mark's, Rochester, and Buffalo Avenues. This was the eastern boundary of Weeksville, one of the earliest free African American communities in New York. Little is known about the history of Weeksville, but it was established around 1827 (the year of emancipation in New York) and named for James Weeks, an early landowner. The population was black until after the Civil War, and African Americans fleeing the 1863 Draft Riot (see p. 262) found refuge here when whites attacked and murdered blacks in Manhattan. Archaeological evidence reveals that Weeksville supported a school and several churches. The four surviving houses date from about 1830.

The Solace to Be Found in Nature
GREEN-WOOD CEMETERY

🍃 Main entrance just east of the intersection of 25th St. and Fifth Ave. Landscape design of the 478-acre cemetery by David Bates Douglass, 1838; gates, gatehouse, chapel, office, and shelters by Richard Upjohn and Son, 1861–63. ☎ 718-768-7300. A map and guide are available at the office. 🚊 *25th St. stop on the M, N, R subways.*

Green-Wood Cemetery's design illustrates the "rural-type cemetery," inviting contemplation of nature. The committee planning the cemetery selected a commanding site with a view of the harbor, intending to please the living who were expected to visit. Typical names for landscape features include Halcyon Lake, Vista Hill, Camelia Path, and Sylvan Cliff. Romantic theory recommended that people enjoy sheets of water reflecting moonlight, so Green-Wood includes streams and artificial lakes. Scattered wooden shelters exemplify various picturesque styles: Gothic Revival, Italian villa, and Swiss chalet. Soon after Green-Wood opened, it was the

RURAL-STYLE CEMETERIES

The ancient world buried its dead along roads leading out of the cities. Athens had its Dipylon Gate for this purpose, and Rome its Via Appia. Medieval Christianity brought burial into the city, in the churchyard or right in the church itself. But as cities expanded, community graveyards ran out of space, and soon most urbanites wanted new burial grounds established outside the city walls.

The design of burial grounds reflects the beliefs and philosophies of the people who build them. One type, called a *necropolis* ("city of the dead") is predominantly architectural. Monuments crowd upon one another and overwhelm nature. The contrasting model is the rural-style *cemetery* ("place of sleep"). In the late eighteenth century, at the time of our national birth, European romantics were just discovering the sublimity of nature, but Americans have long felt a special affinity with nature. Cemeteries are designed not only as resting places for the dead, but also as places for the living to find solace and consolation in the contemplation of nature. Beautifully designed rural-style cemeteries serve as arboretums, wildlife sanctuaries, sculpture gardens, and tours-de-force of architecture and landscape design, as well as repositories of history. Rural-style cemeteries were in fact America's first open public places, precursors of our public parks.

Père Lachaise Cemetery, built outside the city limits of Paris in 1804, was the first rural-style cemetery designed as a retreat from a city. Mount Auburn in Cambridge, Massachusetts (1831), was America's first, nonsectarian and detached from any church, and Green-Wood soon followed (1838). Woodlawn in the Bronx (see p. 334) is another example.

metropolitan region's leading tourist attraction. By 1850, some 500,000 people visited each year (even for strolls by moonlight). The cemetery inspired Manhattan's Central Park. Here lie politician De Witt Clinton, abolitionist preacher Henry Ward Beecher, inventor-philanthropist Peter Cooper, newspaperman Horace Greeley, the piano-manufacturing Steinways, the Brooks Brothers clothiers, musicians Louis Moreau Gottschalk and Leonard Bernstein, and other famous Americans.

A Bright Star of David
YOUNG ISRAEL-BETH EL OF BOROUGH PARK
Orthodox. 4802 15th Avenue. **Borough Park, Brooklyn.** 1920, Shampan & Shampan. ☎ 718-435-9020. 🚇 *50th St. stop on the B or M subways.*

Just to the south of Green-Wood cemetery lies the neighborhood of Borough Park. Its Jewish population of about 250,000 makes it the country's largest Jewish American neighborhood. Borough Park's identity had already evolved before World War I, when Orthodox Jews from Lithuania began to settle here. Through the twentieth century, the Lithuanians were followed by other Orthodox and ultra-Orthodox groups, including the Hasidim (see p. 23).

Borough Park contains about sixty *yeshivas* (schools) and 250 synagogues, and Young Israel-Beth El was its first Jewish congregation, organized in 1906 at 4002 12th Avenue (a building presently inhabited by Congregation Anshe Lubawitz). The congregation's current home is in the Moorish Revival style, with a massive dome, the interior of which is coffered and designed as a Star of David composed of 120 lightbulbs. The main sanctuary is noted for its near-perfect acoustics.

Hand-Painted Tiles from Turkey
FATIH MOSQUE
59–11 Eighth Ave. at 60th St. **Sunset Park, Brooklyn.** ☎ 718-438-6919. 🚇 *Eighth Ave. stop on the N subway.*

Fatih mosque was founded by Turkish Muslims; Fatih, "the conqueror," was the sultan who conquered Constantinople in 1453. The building was a movie theater before it was converted into a mosque in 1980. The marquee is gone, and the mosque façade presents now a low, broad arcade. A small room off the former lobby contains a fountain for the ritual ablutions. The fountain is covered with hand-painted tiles, a specialty of the Turkish city of Isnik since the fifteenth century. The main sanctuary was formerly the theater's auditorium, a large space beneath a shallow dome, lit by a large crystal chandelier. To convert the theater into a mosque, with the *qibla* toward Mecca, the design of the theater had to be reversed. Today's *qibla* was the theater's back wall, and today's women's gallery replaced the screen. A private passageway allows the women access to that gallery, separated from the men's area by lace curtains. The *qibla* in Fatih mosque is extraordinary. To a height of fifteen feet, it is covered with exquisite Isnik tiles. Islam forbids figural art, so the tiles are of intricate, traditional floral patterns, with bold inscriptions from the Qur'an in Turkish and Arabic. The *minbar*, too, from which *hutbas* are given in Turkish, Arabic, and in English, is covered with tiles.

The United American Muslim Association, which operates the mosque, offers a weekend school for children, a dormitory for students visiting from Turkey, rooms for ceremonies, receptions, and meetings, and a night school. American Muslims of all national backgrounds worship at Fatih mosque.

Queens

When the Dutch arrived, most of today's Queens was inhabited by Native Americans of a band called the Rockaways, and their name survives in the name of the peninsula stretching across Jamaica Bay on the borough's south side. The Dutch took possession of the land in 1639 and shortly thereafter chartered the first towns: Mespat (today's Maspeth, 1642), Middleburgh (Newtown, 1652), and Vlissingen (Flushing, 1654). In 1683 these towns were organized as Queens County, taking its name in honor of Queen Catherine of Braganza, the Portuguese-born wife of King Charles II. In 1898, when Queens County voted to join the newly consolidated New York City, the easternmost half of the county broke off to form a new Nassau County, but much of the remaining Queens County was still rural and agricultural as late as 1900. Mass transit and highways spread residential development across the borough in the twentieth century.

Flushing

It has been argued that the historic Remonstrance of Flushing (see p. 30) was the forerunner of the First Amendment to the U.S. Constitution, guarantor of religious freedom in America. Flushing preserves several sites intimately connected with the very foundations of American freedom of worship. In addition,

*new immigrants are bringing their faiths to Flushing, so a short tour of the his-
toric village presents an astonishing array of sacred sites.*

*A walking tour may begin at the corner of Main Street and 41st Avenue
(🚆 take the Long Island Railroad/Port Washington Branch to the Flushing Main
St. station) or one block to the north at Main Street and Roosevelt Avenue (🚆
Flushing Main St. stop on the 7 subway).*

No More Prayers for the King
SAINT GEORGE'S CHURCH (LM)
Episcopal. Main St., between 38th and 39th Aves. **Flushing, Queens**.
1854, Frank Wills and Henry Dudley. ☎ 718-359-1171

This congregation was organized as a mission of the Society for the
Propagation of the Gospel in Foreign Parts as early as 1702, erected its first
church building here in 1746, and received a charter directly from King
George III in 1761. Today's Gothic Revival building is the third on the site.
The bell in the tower, still rung every Sunday, was recast in 1854 using the
metal from the original bell, dating to 1760. The stained-glass windows
exemplify fine late-nineteenth-century English work.

Francis Lewis, a signer of the Declaration of Independence, served as
warden and vestryman here from 1769 to 1790 (he's buried in Manhattan's
Trinity churchyard). It may have been at his instigation that the prayer for
the royal family was so conspicuously crossed out in the 1754 copy of the
Book of Common Prayer that the church today displays in the parish house.
The Reverend Samuel Seabury served here as rector from 1757 to 1765
and later became the first bishop of the Episcopal Church in America.
When the United Nations first met in Flushing in 1947, this church was
designated for the use of the delegates. Today it houses three growing
congregations: one English-speaking, one Chinese-speaking, and a third
Spanish-speaking.

 St. George's churchyard contains graves dating back to the early
eighteenth century, but, unfortunately, all records have been lost.

New York's Oldest Religious Structure
FRIENDS MEETING HOUSE (LM)
137–16 Northern Boulevard, between Main and Union Sts. **Flushing,
Queens**. 1694; additions 1716–19. ☎ 718-358-9636

This is New York City's oldest surviving structure in continuous use for
religious purposes, except for the period between 1776 and 1783, when the
British used it as a prison and hospital. The plain rectangular wooden
building with its hipped roof (that is, it slopes upward from all four

Friends Meeting House

corners) illustrates virtually-medieval building techniques that were still common in the early American colonies. Hand-hewn forty-foot oak beams cut from a single tree are still in place in the second story. Two doorways on the open front porch (the building faces to the south, with its back to the cold north winds) offer separate entrances for men and women, who then sat on benches on opposite sides of a large central room. There are no altar, pulpit, sacristy, or other liturgical features; the simple room reflects the Quaker spirit of undistracted devotion. One of two cast-iron stoves dates from 1760. The hand-wrought iron door hinges, latches, and locks are over 300 years old. The first public antislavery meeting in New York was held here in 1716, when this part of Long Island was largely worked by slaves. John Bowne (see p. 31) rests in the little burying ground in front of the building, as does John Murray, the founder of both the New York Society for the Manumission of Slaves and the New York Public School Society.

F. Scott Fitzgerald placed the climactic scene of his novel *The Great Gatsby*, the killing of Myrtle Wilson in front of her husband's gas station, just a couple of blocks to the west on Northern Boulevard. The characters' actions had taken place underneath a giant billboard of one eye that stood here. Fitzgerald insisted that the image of the eye, symbolizing God, illustrate the book's jacket cover. The area west of here, then a dump, was later landscaped into today's 1,316-acre **Flushing Meadows–Corona Park**, site of the 1939 World's Fair.

It All Started Here in the Kitchen
BOWNE HOUSE (LM)
Bowne St. at 37th Ave. **Flushing, Queens**. 1661, original architect unknown. ☎ 718-359-0528

This is the house in which English settler John Bowne first allowed the
Quakers to worship, for which he was punished (see p. 31). He later converted to Quakerism himself. Bowne's descendants lived here until 1946.
The house is today a museum preserving many of its original furnishings.
The focal point is the kitchen, where Bowne entertained George Fox, the
founder of the Friends, when he visited Flushing in 1672. Fox preached
under the oak trees (long gone) at Fox Oaks Rock on Bowne St. between
Northern Boulevard and 37th Avenue. William Penn visited the Bownes
at home in the 1670s, and gave the dining room highboy as a wedding gift
to John Bowne's daughter, Mary. The yard contains a monument to the
Flushing Remonstrance (see p. 30).

AROUND THE CORNER
➥ Just across 37th Avenue is two-acre **Weeping Beech Park** (LM), which
honors one of America's most extraordinary trees. A beech tree with
hanging branches was uprooted in Belgium in 1847 by American
horticulturist Samuel Bowne Parsons (1819–1907) and, after being
replanted here in Queens, saplings were sold from it, so it became the
source of all weeping beeches in America. As its branches touched the
ground and rerooted, it produced eight offspring in a circle with a diameter
of eighty feet. Unfortunately, the parent tree had to be cut down in 1999,
but the offspring still stand. Parsons and his son Samuel Jr. (1844–1923)
established a nursery in this neighborhood and introduced rhododendrons,
flowering dogwoods, Japanese maples, and many other species of trees to
America. The first nursery in Flushing had been established as early as
1738 by William Prince, and local street names (Geranium, Juniper,
Poplar, Quince, etc.) reflect the historic importance of the neighborhood's
nurseries. The house next to the park, the **Kingsland Homestead** (LM,
1785, architect unknown. ☎ 718-939-0647), today houses the Queens
Historical Society.
➥ Just around the corner stands the **Sikh Center of Flushing** (38-17 Parsons Blvd. 1989, Paul Moc. ☎ 718-460-3581). This purpose-built temple
replaced an earlier building that was converted into a Sikh temple in 1975.
The Sikh sacred scriptures, the *Adigranth*, are taken to an upper floor each
evening and brought down to the main sanctuary each morning, just as a
living teacher would retire for the night.

➧ The **Bowne Street Community Church** (143-11 Roosevelt Ave. 1892, G. E. Potter. ☎ 718-359-0758). This massive red brick Romanesque Revival structure with a high bell tower was built as a Protestant Reformed church. Today it is affiliated with the United Church of Christ as well as the Reformed Church, and services are in English and Chinese. Its windows were designed by Agnes Fairchild Northrup, an artist and congregation member who worked with Tiffany.

➧ Continuing south on Bowne Street, you will pass by (or within a block) churches of several Christian denominations (many of them Asian American congregations), including an historic A. M. E. Zion Church, several synagogues (one of which rents its space on Sundays to a Korean Presbyterian congregation), a couple of mosques, and several small Hindu and Buddhist temples.

America's First Hindu Temple Built According to Ancient Texts
HINDU TEMPLE OF NORTH AMERICA
45–47 Bowne St., between 45th and Holly Aves. **Flushing, Queens.** 1977, Barun Basu. ☎ 718-460-8484

This Temple Society was founded in 1970, and here in 1977 they dedicated the first Hindu temple in the United States built according to ancient texts. Over 200 traditional craftsmen in India took two years to complete the carvings, which were then shipped to Flushing. The temple has an east-west axis, with the sanctum situated in the west, from which the main deity, Ganesha, gazes on the rising sun and the approaching devotee. Its three pavilions are covered with intricate carvings of deities and religious symbols, surmounted by pyramidal roofs with gilt finials, and a main spire marking the entrance. Shrines to major deities mark the corners of the sanctuary, carved friezes along the walls illustrate Indian religious tradition, and the black shrine of Lord Ganesha dominates the center. With his elephant head and human form, he represents the universality of creation. Ganesh Chathurthi is an annual nine-day festival in August or September (depending on the lunar calendar) honoring him. Special prayers are recited, and decorations are made with flowers and fruit. At the end of the festival, Ganesha is carried around Flushing in a procession.

AROUND THE CORNER
➧ Six blocks west of the Hindu Temple along 45th Avenue, the **Kissena Arboretum** and the thirty-three acre **Queens Botanical Garden** compose a park corridor that connects Flushing Meadows–Corona

Park to Kissena Park. (The park contains several rare species of trees; ask at the Ranger Center for a free map.)

Under Royal Patronage
THAI BUDDHIST TEMPLE
76–16 46th Ave. **Elmhurst, Queens.** 1999, P. Uthong, V. Prangpituk, and M. Pao. ☎ 718-803-9881. 🚇 *Walk south on 74th St. from the 74th St.–Broadway stop on the 7 subway or the Jackson Heights/Roosevelt Ave. stop on the E, F, G, R subways.*

An elaborate blue-and-yellow glazed ceramic tile portico protects the door to an otherwise-plain rectangular yellow brick building. The ground floor holds a main sanctuary with carved and gilded images of Buddha, and the second floor provides housing for resident monks. Perched on the flat roof of the building, however, like a penthouse, is an exquisite small temple with a blue-tiled steeply sloping roof decorated with elaborate birds' beaks, flame symbols, and hanging bells. Its gables bear a ceramic emblem of King Bhumibol of Thailand, marking that this temple enjoys royal auspices. This rooftop "inner sanctum," a symbolic mountaintop, houses the principal Buddha image, a nineteen-inch replica of a jade image preserved in Thailand.

AROUND THE CORNER
➥ **Masjid Al-Falah,** New York City's first purpose-built mosque, is just to the east (42–12 National St., between 42nd and 43rd Aves. **Corona, Queens.** 1982. ☎ 718-476-7968. 🚇 *103rd St.–Corona Plaza stop on the number 7 subway*)

➥ Six blocks to the north, the home where jazz musician **Louis Armstrong** ("Satchmo") lived from 1943 until his death in 1971 has been converted into a museum of Armstrong's career and the history of jazz (34–55 107th St. at 37th Ave. ☎ 718-478-8274).

➥ **Forest Hills Gardens** is a private residential development reaching roughly from 71st Avenue to Union Turnpike, from the Long Island Railroad line to Greenway South (**Forest Hills, Queens.** 1913, architect Grosvenor Atterbury and landscape architect F. L. Olmsted, Jr. 🚇 *Forest Hills/71st Ave. stop on the E, F, G, R subways, or take the Long Island Railroad to the Forest Hills station*). Alfred T. White, who pioneered in the construction of worker housing in Brooklyn (see p. 307), was also instrumental in promoting this residential development for middle-income workers. Its layout of winding streets, large lots, generous plantings, and romantic picturesque architecture, conveys the feeling of an

English village. The idyllic **Church in the Gardens** (50 Ascan Ave. 1915. ☎ 718-268-6704) is a multicultural, ecumenical, Community Congregational Christian Church.

The Needs of the Total Person
ALLEN AFRICAN METHODIST EPISCOPAL CATHEDRAL

110-31 Merrick Blvd. at 110th Ave. **Jamaica, Queens**. 1997, Harry Simmons, Jr. ☎ 718-206-4600. Books are available in the shop. *Jamaica/ Sutphin Blvd. stop on the E, J or Z subways; from there take the number 85, Q4, or Q5 bus to Merrick Blvd.*

Ever since the Allen A.M.E. Church was founded in 1834, it has been central to the life of the community. It founded the first school for blacks in Jamaica, and it was in Allen's sanctuary that the Jamaica branch of the NAACP was founded. The list of social services provided by the church is staggering: housing programs, home care, a school, transportation services for the elderly and handicapped, a federal credit union, a multipurpose center that offers health care, a Head Start Program, psychiatric services, and a Women, Infants and Children Program, among others. Its mission statement insists: "We are called to address the needs of the total person, as our Savior did . . . through our commitment to praise, worship, stewardship, evangelism, and economic development." Allen A.M.E. and its subsidiaries employ over 800 people.

Today the congregation numbers over 9,000 members. The pastor since 1976 has been Reverend Floyd H. Flake, who also represented the community in the U.S. House of Representatives from 1986 to 1998. Among the many pieces of legislation Reverend Flake sponsored in Congress, The 1994 Bank Enterprise Act has increased bank lending in distressed neighborhoods.

The church's new home was dedicated in 1997, the largest church built in the city in the second half of the twentieth century. It offers a sanctuary seating 2,500, classrooms for community programs, a fellowship hall for 1,000, a book and gift shop, print shop, and administrative offices.

A Blend of Eastern and Western Artistic Traditions
ISAMU NOGUCHI GARDEN MUSEUM

32–37 Vernon Blvd. at 33rd Rd. **Long Island City, Queens**. 1985, Shogi Sazao. ☎ 718-721-1932. *From the Broadway stop on the N subway, walk west on Broadway. Turn left on Vernon Blvd. and go 2 blocks.*

This museum and outdoor sculpture garden features the work of Isamu Noguchi (1904–88), who was born in Los Angeles and started his career as a sculptor in New York City. His works include the gardens for the headquarters of UNESCO in Paris; a sculpture garden at the Israel Museum in Jerusalem; a piazza in Bologna, Italy; and works of landscape design and sculpture throughout Japan, Mexico, and across the United States. Noguchi moved his home and studio into this former photo-engraving factory in 1961, and he opened the Garden Museum in 1985. The tranquil garden demonstrates Asian attitudes toward nature, with stone sculptures, a trickling fountain, and careful plantings.

AROUND THE CORNER

➡ **Socrates Sculpture Park** (31–29 Vernon Blvd., **Long Island City, Queens.** ☎ 718-956-1819). This wind swept field near the Noguchi Museum along the East River is one of the few places in New York to see large-scale sculptures by emerging artists. The site was formerly a marine terminal, then a garbage-strewn lot, but it was leased and developed in 1986 by sculptors Mark di Suvero and Isamu Noguchi.

The Bronx

The Bronx is the only borough of New York City that is part of the American mainland. The Dutch took possession of the land in 1639, and in 1641 a Dane named Jonas Bronck settled along what is today the Bronx River. The parallel Hutchinson River was named for Anne Hutchinson (see p. 24), and Throg's Neck for John Throgmorton, an Anabaptist who settled here in 1644. Conflicts between the Dutch and the Native Americans plagued the area during the seventeenth century, but after the transition to English rule and the arrival of English landowners (notably the Pell and Morris families), settlement began in earnest. Villages sprang up along the roads to Albany and Boston, and these later developed as commercial centers of neighborhoods: Mott Haven, Kingsbridge, Morrisania, and others.

As means of transportation to and from the City of New York improved, Irish immigrants came to settle, then Germans, and eventually eastern European Jews. Independent towns in the western part of the area joined New York City in 1874, and towns in the eastern area merged in

1894. Consolidation in 1898 created the borough of the Bronx. Today the borough has some of New York's wealthiest neighborhoods and some of its poorest. Substantial Hispanic and Asian immigration has diversified the population mix and, as a result, its sacred spaces as well.

A Prominent Early Family
SAINT ANN'S CHURCH (LM)
Episcopal. 295 St. Ann's Ave. at 140th St. **Mott Haven, the Bronx**. 1841, original architect unknown. ☎ 718-585-5632. 🚇 *Brook Ave. stop on the 6 subway.*

This, the oldest surviving church in the Bronx, was erected on the country estate of Gouverneur Morris, Jr., as the centerpiece of the burial ground at the family estate, Morrisania. The cemetery is much older than the building, and it contains the graves of many members of this prominent early-American family. These include Judge Lewis Morris (d. 1746), the first Lord of the Manor of Morrisania and the first governor of the Province of New Jersey; General Lewis Morris (1726–98), a member of the Continental Congress and signer of the Declaration of Independence (he tried to get the U.S. capital established here on the family estate); Gouverneur Morris, Sr. (1752–1816), who had a key role in drafting the U.S. Constitution, served as U.S. ambassador to France during the Reign of Terror (the only foreign representative who stayed at his post through

St. Ann's Church

that period) and U.S. senator from New York 1799–1803; and Gouverneur Morris, Jr., himself (1813–88), a pioneer railroad builder. Ann Cary Randolph Morris (?–1837) of Roanoke, Virginia, wife of Gouverneur Morris, Sr., a lineal descendant of the Native American Princess Pocahontas, is interred in a large vault beneath the chancel. The family retained perpetual burial rights in the church (the recent Governor Kean of New Jersey is a descendant), as well as the right to veto any new minister.

The church building is a simple fieldstone church articulated by Gothic-style windows and door openings trimmed in red brick. It is capped by a Greek Revival steeple. It faces south from a small rise, and it originally looked out over isolated manor houses and farms. The local neighborhood first attracted German and Irish settlers, who were followed in turn by African Americans by the 1940s, then Puerto Ricans. Today services in the church are held in both English and Spanish.

AROUND THE CORNER

➥ Just north of the church, along Westchester Avenue between St. Ann's and Brook Avenues, the firm of **Janes, Kirtland & Co.** produced architectural ironwork. Its most notable production was the 8.9 million-pound dome of the U.S. Capitol in Washington D.C., in 1863. Nothing remains of the firm.

➥ **The Missionaries of Charity,** an order of nuns founded by Mother Teresa in India in 1950, operate a soup kitchen and shelter at 335 East 145th Street (between Third and College Aves. ☎ 718-292-0019. 🚇 *Third Ave./138 St. stop on the 6 subway).* Mother Teresa was born in Albania in 1910, but she went to India to work among the poor in 1928 and became an Indian citizen in 1949. She was awarded the Nobel Peace Prize in 1979, and when she died, consideration of her canonization began virtually immediately.

Mother Teresa visited this mission several times. Her last visit was on June 21, 1997, with Lady Diana, the Princess of Wales. Lady Diana died seven weeks later in a car accident, and Mother Teresa six days after Lady Diana.

An Early School and Seminary
FORDHAM UNIVERSITY CHAPEL (LM)

The campus is between Fordham Rd. and Kazimiroff Blvd., Webster and Crotona Aves. ☎ 718-817-1000. 🚇 *Fordham Rd. stops on the 4 or D subways, or take Metro-North's Harlem or New Haven Lines to the Fordham station.*

What is today the campus of Fordham University was settled by Europeans late in the seventeenth century, but the oldest building now on campus (the administration building) was built in 1838 as part of a private estate called Rose Hill. New York's Bishop Hughes bought the estate in 1839 and opened St. John's College and St. Joseph's Seminary on the property in 1841. (The college became a Jesuit institution in 1846 and took its present name in 1907, after St. Joseph's had moved away to Westchester.)

Bishop Hughes sent his brother-in-law, architect William Rodrigue, out to the Bronx to beautify the campus, and Rodrigue built several buildings while living here and also serving as a professor—of penmanship. One of his designs was the stone Gothic Revival St. John's Church (1845). The bell in the tall tower over the entrance may have inspired the poem, "The Bells," by Edgar Allan Poe, who lived nearby. The church nave boasts six tall stained-glass windows that France's King Louis Philippe sent as a gift for St. Patrick's Old Cathedral downtown (see p. 116). They didn't fit there, so they were sent up here. The four evangelists plus Peter and Paul are each identified in French. The altar served at the new St. Patrick's Cathedral on Fifth Avenue from 1879 until 1941, when the cathedral received new furnishings and Cardinal Spellman gave the old altar to Fordham. The painted reredos behind it from the 1930s, by Hildredth Meière, is unusual. The Virgin Mary presides over a company of Jesuit saints, but Christ is nowhere to be seen. Architect Emile Perrot enlarged the church in 1929, adding transepts and an elaborate decorated copper lantern over the crossing, based on that of Ely Cathedral, in England.

AROUND THE CORNER

➥ **The Hall of Fame of Great Americans** at nearby Bronx Community College (originally New York University, University Ave. at W. 180th St. **University Heights, the Bronx**; constructed 1894–1912, McKim, Mead & White. ☎ 718-289-5100. 🚇 *Walk up the hill to the west from the Burnside Ave. stop of the 4 subway*) is a colonnade exhibiting busts of noted American scientists, statesmen, writers, and educators. The colonnade curves behind Gould Memorial Library, one of architect Stanford White's masterpieces and the centerpiece of the campus's complex of classical-style buildings.

➥ **Poe Park** (LM, 2640 Grand Concourse at Kingsbridge Rd. **Bedford Park, the Bronx**. ☎ 718-881-8900. 🚇 *Kingsbridge Rd. stops on the 4 or D subways*). In 1846 Edgar Allan Poe brought his wife Virginia to the humble white frame farmhouse (ca. 1812) that now stands in this small park, hoping that the country air would cure her tuberculosis. Virginia died during the winter, but Poe stayed on until 1849, and here he wrote "Ulalume," "The Bells," and parts of "Annabel Lee," a eulogy to his wife, whom he had married when she was just thirteen years old. The simple museum/home (moved here from a block away in 1913) contains period furnishings.

Modeled after Hagia Sofia
SAINT ANSELM'S CHURCH
Roman Catholic. 673 Tinton Ave., between E. 152nd St. and Westchester Ave. **Melrose, the Bronx**. 1917, Anton Kloster. ☎ 718-585-8666. 🚆 *Jackson Ave. stop on the 2 or 5 subways.*

This area was described as "wooded swampland" in 1892, when Benedictine fathers from St. John's Abbey in Minnesota arrived hoping to build a new monastery here in the Bronx. They celebrated the first mass in a chapel below the current church in 1893, and although they never built the monastery, they did dedicate this astonishing building on Christmas night, 1917. St. Anselm's relatively modest exterior of brick trimmed with glazed decorative tiles conceals what is arguably the finest Byzantine-style church in America, a miniature of the Hagia Sofia in Istanbul. A huge shallow central dome, the interior of which is a gold mosaic of the Benedictine medal, rests on four massive pillars (called *pendentives*), and six polished granite columns with elaborate carved capitals support galleries

St. Anselm's Church

on each side. The church seats about 800, but it seems even larger. Decorations include marble facings, bronze lamps and candelabra, terra-cotta stations of the cross, and two-toned green tilework.

The paintings throughout the interior constitute an outstanding example of a style of art known as Beuronese, from its development in the ancient Benedictine Abbey of Beuron (Germany) at the end of the nineteenth century. Dom Adelbert Gesnicht, O.S.B., the foremost exponent of Beuronese art of the time, worked at St. Anselm's with two assistants for five years to complete the decorations. Illustrations include *Christ as the Good Shepherd*, *The Agony in the Garden*, *The Crucifixion*, and *The Last Judgment*. These were restored in 1991.

The main work above the altar shows several saints, including Anselm of Canterbury, observing the crucifixion. Anselm (1033–1109) was the son of a northern Italian nobleman, and he matured from a restless youth to become one of the great figures of the history of Christianity. His philosophical and theological works had already won him fame before he became archbishop of Canterbury in 1093. In that office he preached against slavery and for freedom of the church from royal/political interference. Dante, in his *Paradiso* (canto xii) placed Bishop Anselm (not yet then a saint) among the spirits of light and power in the Sphere of the Sun. When Anselm was canonized in 1720, he was included among the prestigious "doctors of the Church."

Benedictines from St. John's served the parish until 1976 (today it's diocesan), as its population has changed from German, Irish, and Italian to Hispanic and African American.

AROUND THE CORNER

➥ Just a few blocks northeast at number 968 along curving Kelly Street (known as "Banana Kelly"), was the last home of **Sholem Aleichem**, the Jewish humorist born Solomon Rabinowitch (his pseudonym means "Peace be upon you!"). He emigrated from his native Ukraine at age fifty-five in 1914. On a previous visit, Mark Twain had greeted him, "I wanted to meet you, for I am told that I am the American Sholem Aleichem." His collected works, written in Yiddish, run to thirty volumes of short stories, novels, and plays. The musical *The Fiddler on the Roof* is based on his writings, and today Manhattan's East 33rd Street between Madison and Park Avenues is called Sholem Aleichem Way. **Leon Trotsky** lived just north at 1522 Vyse Avenue for three months in 1917 before the Revolution called him back to Russia. In October the local newspaper headlined,

"Bronx Man Leads Russian Revolution." **Clifford Odets**, generally regarded as the best of America's social-protest dramatists, grew up around the
corner on Longwood Avenue near Beck Street; his play *Awake and Sing*
(1935) is set in an apartment here.

Dense Forest and a Waterfall
NEW YORK BOTANICAL GARDEN
200th Street and Kazimiroff Blvd. Incorp. 1891, designed 1895 by Calvert
Vaux and Samuel Parsons, Jr. ☎ 718-220-8700. 🚇 *Bedford Park Blvd. stop
on the D subway, or take Metro-North's Harlem Line to the Botanical Garden
station.*

This 250-acre facility is not only a visitors' haven, but a major educational and research institution, sponsoring biological and environmental research, expeditions, classes in everything from flower arranging to botany and botanical illustration, and scientific publications. The
grounds encompass forty-seven gardens and plant collections, thousands of
shrubs and trees (including four of the city's Great Trees—see p. 129), and
the Enid A. Haupt Conservatory (LM), one of America's most beautiful
Victorian greenhouses. The conservatory features an ecotour from misty
tropical rain forests to arid deserts, plus aquatic plants, hanging baskets,
two outdoor pools, and seasonal flower shows. A fragment of the hemlock
forest that once covered much of New York survived here until it was
destroyed in the 1990s by an insect, the woolly adelgid. Black birch and
black cherry replaced the hemlocks.

Part of the garden's grounds preserves the gorge of the Bronx River.
The brothers Peter and George Lorillard first exploited waterpower here to
grind tobacco with millstones instead of rubbing it over a grater, as other
firms did. This innovation established their fortune. The original 1792
mill was replaced by the present building in 1840. The Lorillard estate was
purchased by the city at the end of the nineteenth century, and the snuff
mill is today a cafeteria.

In 1987 a petroglyph (carved rock image) of a turtle was found on a
boulder here along the banks of the Bronx River. It had been carved by
local Native Americans between 400 and 1,000 years ago, most probably
to illustrate some aspect of a creation story. Thus, it is assumed to mark the
spot as one sacred to Native Americans. Garden authorities, working
together with representatives of the American Indian Community House,
moved the entire boulder into the Watson Building, where it can be seen
today.

AROUND THE CORNER

➡ The Bronx Zoo/Wildlife Conservation Park (LM, 2300 Southern Blvd. 1899, original architects Heins & LaFarge. ☎ 718-367-1010. 🚇 *Several stops on the 2 or 5 subways.*

Today's Wildlife Conservation Society was chartered as the New York Zoological Society in 1895, and four years later it opened what is still the country's largest urban zoo (265 acres), home to more than 4,000 animals of over 600 species, several of them endangered in their native habitats. It claims to have been the world's first zoological research center, and today zoo staff carry out conservation breeding programs and research in animal health and wildlife science. The society also sponsors research on animal life and habitats around the world.

Soldiers of the Revolution Lie Here
SAINT PETER'S (LM)
Episcopal. 2500 Westchester Ave. at **Westchester Sq., the Bronx.** The church (1855), school, and chapel (both 1868) are by Leopold Eidlitz; clerestory added and all restored after a fire in 1879 by his son Cyrus Eidlitz. ☎ 718-822-8284. 🚇 *Westchester Square/East Tremont Ave. stop on the 6 subway.*

St. Peter's congregation was established in the village of Westchester in 1693. The first church was built here in 1700, and in 1706 Queen Anne sent it a communion service consisting of a chalice and paten, a communion table, a Bible, a book of homilies, and a pulpit cloth. During the American War of Independence, Reverend Samuel Seabury infuriated the local population by preaching loyalty to the king from this pulpit, although he later became the first Protestant Episcopal bishop of the United States. Some soldiers killed in the war lie buried near the chapel. The Victorian Gothic stone building that stands here now is the third church structure on the site. The oldest stone in the cemetery is dated 1702.

Visit the Famous in a Rural Setting
WOODLAWN CEMETERY
Woodlawn Cemetery has two main entrances, one at Jerome Ave. and Bainbridge Ave. (🚇 *Woodlawn stop on the 4 subway*), the other at 233rd St. and Webster Ave. (🚇 *Woodlawn station on Metro-North's Harlem Line*). Landscape design of the 313 acres by James C. Sidney, 1863. ☎ 718-920-0500. Map and guidebook available at the office.

 By the 1860s, congestion on New York and Brooklyn city streets, as well as on the East River ferries, sabotaged the dignity of funeral

Woodlawn
Cemetery

processions from Manhattan out to Green-Wood Cemetery (see p. 317), so a group of New Yorkers looked around for a more accessible site for a new rural-style cemetery (see p. 318) Following the railroad to the north, they discovered the beautifully wooded Bronx River Valley, and here they bought 313 acres and founded Woodlawn. A wide avenue through the Bronx was soon constructed to bring New Yorkers up to a nearby race track owned by financier Leonard Jerome (Winston Churchill's grandfather), and Jerome Avenue continued on to Woodlawn's western gate. Three months after Woodlawn's first interment in 1865, the Civil War ended, and the "re-United" States launched into a spectacular era of growth and wealth which we now call "the gilded age." New York grew to dominate a burgeoning national economy, and the ambitious came here from all over the country. The interment of Civil War hero Admiral David Farragut at Woodlawn in 1870 cinched the cemetery's social prestige, and eventually Civil War heroes from both sides came to be buried at Woodlawn. So did leading industrialists and financiers (in grand mausoleums, especially after the theft of the body of A.T. Stewart from St. Mark's downtown in 1878, see p. 128), as well as creators of American culture. Woodlawn's roster today includes a remarkable variety of interesting and historically important people: musicians Duke Ellington, Irving Berlin, George M. Cohan, and Miles Davis; philanthropist Madame C. J. Walker; jurist Charles Evans Hughes; financier Jay Gould; authors Herman Melville and Nellie Bly; journalist Joseph Pulitzer; inventor Gail Borden; Dodge City Sheriff Bat Masterson; and many more. Space remains available for more interments.

Woodlawn contains six of the Great Trees of New York City (see p. 129), a weeping beech, a European cutleaf beech, a pendent silver linden, a white pine, an umbrella pine, and an American elm.

AROUND THE CORNER

➥ Since 1869, New York's potter's field has been forty-five-acre **Hart Island**, just off the Bronx in Long Island Sound. Almost 800,000 people have been interred here, and each year roughly 1,500 more join them; about one-tenth of those are nameless. Bodies are numbered, and each year 100 are claimed by friends or relatives. The only marker here is a single granite cross that reads "He calleth His children by name." Burials are performed by volunteer prisoners from Rikers Island, who cross to Hart Island by ferry, but there is no public access to the island.

An Old Family Estate
BARTOW-PELL MANSION (LM)
895 Shore Rd. in Pelham Bay Park. ☎ 718-885-1461. 🚇 *Take the 6 subway to the last stop—Pelham Bay Park—and the number 45 Westchester Bee-Line bus from there.*

Englishman Thomas Pell "bought" this land from the Native Americans in 1654. A piece of wood from the tree under which the purchase was made is exhibited in the house. The present mansion, the third on the site, dates from 1836. New York City bought the house and grounds in 1888, but in 1914 the International Garden Club took over the property, restored it, and has beautified it. Behind the house, a walkway leads to the Pell family burial plot, dating from the seventeenth century. Mayor Fiorello La Guardia used the mansion as his official summer residence.

"Your" Country Estate
WAVE HILL CENTER FOR ENVIRONMENTAL STUDIES (LM)
Independence Ave. at 249th St., **Riverdale, the Bronx.** ☎ 718-549-2055. 🚇 *231st St. stop on the 1 or 9 subways; take the BX 7 or BX10 bus from there. Alternatively, take Metro-North's Hudson Line to the Riverdale station and walk up the hill.*

Riverdale is the "Gold Coast" of the Bronx, a neighborhood of mansions dating back into the nineteenth century and overlooking the Hudson River. Wave Hill is one of these. The main mansion on this twenty-eight-acre estate was built in 1844 by a member of the Morris family (see p. 328), but it was enlarged and the grounds beautified by banker George Perkins, whose daughter gave the property to the city in 1960. When it was a home, residents or visitors included Theodore Roosevelt, William Makepeace Thackery, Thomas Huxley, Arturo Toscanini, and Mark Twain.

Today Wave Hill is an independent nonprofit cultural organization dedicated to environmental studies. It maintains gardens and greenhouses (a flower garden, wild garden, herb garden, dry garden, aquatic garden, and more), manages a woodland, provides environmental education, conducts projects in landscape history and design, and presents exhibitions, readings, concerts, lectures, and workshops. The beautiful grounds hold five of the Great Trees of the City (see p. 129) and offer a spectacular view of the Hudson River Valley and across to the New Jersey Palisades.

Staten Island

Staten Island is the least populous of the city's boroughs. Before the opening of the Verrazano Narrows Bridge to Brooklyn in 1964, much of it was still farmland. A spine of rocky hills runs down the center of the island, the highest point of which (Todt Hill, 409 feet above sea level) is the highest point on the eastern seaboard south of Maine. Settlement developed along the coastal plains to the east of the ridge, while the lands fronting Arthur Kill to the west developed commercial and industrial uses. Wealthy New Yorkers had summer homes on the spine or along the eastern shores, but older communities predated those settlements. The southern end of the island harbored fishing villages.

One section of Staten Island is named Emerson Estates, for William Emerson, a Staten Island judge and the brother of poet Ralph Waldo Emerson. In 1843 Ralph recommended **Henry David Thoreau**, later the author of *Walden Pond* (1854), as a tutor for William's son. Thoreau came to live at the Emerson home on Douglas Road near Richmond Road. The house burned down in 1855, but its stone gate survives. Thoreau wrote his sister, "The whole island is like a garden, and affords very fine scenery." Thoreau did not, however, like Manhattan, until a three-hour talk with Henry James, Sr., "naturalized and humanized New York for me."

🚌 *Public transportation to these locations is given as bus numbers from the Staten Island ferry terminal.*

SAILORS' SNUG HARBOR (LM)

Richmond Terrace, between Tysen St. and Snug Harbor Rd. **Livingston, Staten Island.** ☎ 718-448-2500. *Number S40 bus.*

Robert R. Randall, whose father had made a fortune privateering, died in 1801 and left the income from that fortune to found a home for "aged, decrepit, and worn-out sailors." After much litigation, trustees of the will bought a farm on Staten Island in 1831 and erected a row of Greek Revival temples facing the busy Kill Van Kull waterway, between Staten Island and New Jersey. Author Herman Melville often visited here when his brother Thomas was governor of the institution between 1867 and 1884. Many destitute sailors passed their final days here in dignity and tranquility, although several of them, noted visiting novelist Theodore Dreiser in 1899, relied too much on grog, while others had settled into a spirit of "pure cussedness." The central building was designed by Minard Lafever, but construction went on until the 1880s.

After over 100 years, Sailors' Snug Harbor decided to sell the buildings and move the few remaining sailors to new facilities in North Carolina. New York City bought the land and buildings, and today the eighty-three-acre park is home to the Newhouse Center of Contemporary Art, Staten Island Children's Museum, John A. Noble Collection, the Art Lab and artists' studios. Performances are regularly scheduled throughout the site, in the Veterans Memorial Hall, on the rolling South Meadow, and in the 1892 Music Hall. Sailors' Snug Harbor has two of New York's Great Trees: a grove of English yew and a royal paulownia (see p. 129).

The **Staten Island Botanical Garden** (☎ 718-273-8200), also part of the property, contains the only Chinese Scholar's Garden in the United States. It was paid for largely by the government of China, which sent forty artisans to Staten Island in 1999 to design the grounds and

The Chinese Scholar's Garden at the Staten Island Botanical Garden

assemble the Delight of the Moon Portal, the Wandering-in-Bamboo Courtyard, the Court of Uncommon Reeds, and the Court of Pure Mind and Spirit. Throughout the garden, calligraphic plaques carry couplets written by contemporary Chinese artists that link the structure to literary and artistic traditions. One near the waterfall, for example, records that "The sound of the stream is the cry of precipitous rocks."

Our Largest Community Mosque
ALBANIAN ISLAMIC CULTURAL CENTER
307 Victory Blvd. at Cebra Ave. **Stapleton, Staten Island**. 1994, Brent Porter. ☎ 718-816-9865. *Number S48 bus.*

This is considerably the largest New York City mosque built entirely with the funds (and volunteer labor) of the local congregation. No foreign government supported the work. Indeed, as war raged in Kosovo province of Serbia through the late 1990s and its local Albanian population suffered, the members of this mosque contributed generously to rebuild mosques and support orphaned children there.

The first Islamic center on Staten Island opened in 1973, and the first prayer service was held in this new mosque in 1994. Its three floors total over 50,000 square feet of space, and its minaret towers over 100 feet high. The main sanctuary is surprisingly bare. Neither the *qibla* nor even the *mihrab* are decorat-

The Albanian Islamic Cultural Center

ed, but are plain white spaces. The intention of this deliberate sparseness is to keep the congregation's thought focused on God. One banner embroidered in gilded thread framed on a side wall reads "Cling one and all to faith in God, and let nothing divide you." (Qur'an 3:103). The mosque offers regular services, plus Islamic-studies classes for children and adults, computer courses for career advancement for the mosque's members, and an Islamic academy for prekindergarten through first grade. As is true of most mosques in New York City, this mosque was inaugurated by Muslims of one national background (Albanian), but today it welcomes Muslims (and visitors) from all national backgrounds.

"Something of a Tibetan Atmosphere"
JACQUES MARCHAIS MUSEUM
OF TIBETAN ART

338 Lighthouse Ave. **Richmondtown, Staten Island.** ☎ 718-987-3500.
Number S74 bus to the intersection of Richmond Rd. and Wilder Ave., from where you will have to walk up Lighthouse Hill.

This extraordinary museum occupies two stone buildings designed to resemble a Tibetan monastery; they are set in a terraced sculpture garden affording a fine view of Lower New York Bay. The museum holds one of the largest collections of Tibetan art outside Tibet, and also exhibits sculpture, paintings, ritual objects, and musical instruments from all Asian countries. Most of the art was gathered by Jacques Marchais, which was the professional name of Jacqueline Klauber, a dealer in Asian art. Mrs. Klauber's interest in Asian art had been sparked when as a girl she discovered a trunk left by her great-grandfather, a sea captain, containing small bronze statuettes of deities. She opened this museum in 1947, and in 1991 the Dalai Lama came to visit, thanking the museum for preserving "a place where you can feel something of a Tibetan atmosphere." The main exhibition space is a large stone room with a tiered altar set up against one wall, but in it the museum can at any time exhibit only a fraction of its holdings of over 1,200 objects. Prayer flags flutter over the terraces, sending their message of peace and compassion out to the world.

An Old Island Community and School
HISTORIC RICHMOND TOWN (LM)

441 Clark Ave. ☎ 718-351-1611. *Number S74 bus.*

This 100-acre village, founded in 1690 as "Cocclestown," from the abundance of local oysters and clams, is today an historic restoration featuring buildings representing 300 years of Staten Island life. Twenty-seven historic buildings are on the site, many of which are open to the public to illustrate the evolution of village life from the seventeenth through the nineteenth centuries. In season, costumed interpreters and craftspeople reenact daily life in this rural hamlet, depicting chores, gardening, crafts, and trade. Other activities include special tours, programs, and lectures. The little frame Voorlezer's House (c. 1695) was built by the Dutch Reformed congregation for its *voorlezer* (lay reader), who lived and taught school there, making it the oldest elementary school still standing in the United States. This building also served as the community chapel from 1695 until a church was built at Port Richmond in 1701.

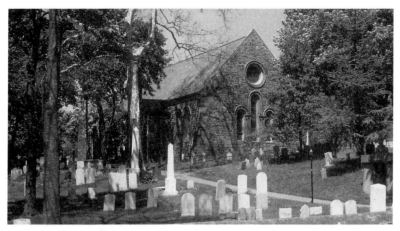

St. Andrew's Episcopal Church

AROUND THE CORNER

➡ Nearby **Saint Andrew's Episcopal Church** (LM, 40 Old Mill Rd. at Arthur Kill Rd. 1872, attributed to William H. Mersereau. ☎ 718-351-0900) is Staten Island's oldest Episcopal congregation. The original church building, dating from 1708, burned in 1867 and again in 1872. This new one, with rounded windows and carefully delineated nave, tower, and entrance porch, resembles the Norman parish churches of twelfth-century England. The church still treasures its original parish charter, plus prayer books, a silver communion service, and a bell sent by Queen Anne. Several members of the family of Saint Elizabeth Ann Seton (see p. 81) are buried in the churchyard, which provides a few inviting benches.

A Moravian Community

NEW DORP MORAVIAN CHURCH

2205 Richmond Rd. **Todt Hill, Staten Island**. 1844, original architect unknown. ☎ 718-351-0090. *Number S74 or S76 bus.*

This is one of four Moravian churches on Staten Island. The United Brethren, commonly known as Moravians, is a Protestant denomination that was born in Bohemia and Moravia in 1415, when John Hus was convicted of heresy for arguing that religious practice should be based in the Bible, not the rule of church officials. It is, therefore, the oldest Protestant denomination. Several Moravian settlements were established in America in the eighteenth century, including Nazareth and Bethlehem, in Pennsylvania, and Salem, in North Carolina. A Moravian Church was organized in New York in 1748, and in 1763 a Moravian Church rose in the Staten Island community of New Dorp.

The church sits inside the **Moravian Cemetery** (the entrance is on Richmond Rd. opposite Otis Ave.). In the section of the cemetery set aside for the exclusive use of Moravians, the dead were originally segregated by sex, although that separation is no longer practiced. One of the earliest Moravians was a Dutch settler named Jacob Van der Bilt, and, at the rear of the cemetery, on private property not open to the public, stands the Romanesque-style mausoleum of his shipping-and-railroad-tycoon descendants, the Vanderbilts (1886, Richard Morris Hunt).

A Free Community
HISTORIC SANDY GROUND

The cemetery of the Rossville A. M. E. Zion Church (LM, on Crabtree Ave., just west of Bloomingdale Rd. **Rossville, Staten Island**. Ca. 1852) is the major surviving element of Sandy Ground, a nineteenth-century settlement of newly freed black slaves from Staten Island, Manhattan, and New Jersey, plus free black oystermen and their families who moved up from Virginia and Maryland before the Civil War. Sandy Ground has been recognized as the oldest continuously inhabited free black settlement in the nation, and some descendants of early settlers still live in the area.

The Rossville Church itself is no longer standing, but the museum and library operated by the **Sandy Ground Historical Society** (1538 Woodrow Road. ☎ 718-317-5796. *Number S74 bus.*) offers a look at the history and cultural life of Sandy Ground. The society sponsors lectures, films, exhibits, and seasonal activities relating to present-day African American cultural life.

GLOSSARY

.... ✲ ....

Altar (or **communion table**): Article of furnishing from which the sacrament of the Eucharist, or the Lord's Supper, is shared.

Ambulatory: In churches, a place to walk around behind the altar.

American Renaissance: A late-nineteenth-century American art and architecture style characterized by collaboration among several artists.

Anglo-Catholicism: A nineteenth-century movement within the Anglican (Episcopal) Church drawing it more toward ceremony and emphasis on the sacraments.

Apse: A semicircular area terminating a space.

Arch: A curved structure for spanning an opening. Semicircular **round arches**, also called **Roman arches**, usually characterize Romanesque (and Romanesque Revival) architecture. **Pointed arches** generally characterize Gothic (and Gothic Revival) architecture. **Moorish arches**, also called **horseshoe arches**, widen up from their bases, then narrow toward their tops.

Ark: In a synagogue, a receptacle containing the Torah scrolls.

Attributes (or **emblems**): Symbolic objects used to identify individual saints.

Baldachin: In churches an ornamental construction covering and protecting the altar.

Balustrade: A railing with its supporting balusters (also called banisters).

Baptistery: Corner, room, or separate building for the baptismal font.

Basilica: As a style, a basilica is a rectangular building with the entrance on one of the short sides (at one end), and, in churches, the altar and pulpit at the other end. *Basilica* is also a special designation awarded by the pope to Roman Catholic churches of special historical or religious merit.

Beaux-Arts: When used as a descriptive term, usually reserved for late-nineteenth-century buildings of a particularly lush classicism, almost

Baroque in character. These buildings, including, typically, museums and court houses, boast large stone bases, grand stairways, paired columns on bases, monumental attics, grand arched openings, medallions, and sculptural figures.

Belt course (string course): A horizontal line of brick or stone often marking a division in a wall.

Bimah: In a synagogue, a platform with a lectern from which the Torah is read.

Buttress: Structure built against a wall for support.

Byzantine Revival style: A particularly ornate form of Romanesque Revival architecture characterized by complex vaulting, large open spaces, and lavish decoration with precious marbles, mosaics, and gilding.

Cantor: The synagogue official who sings liturgical solos.

Cast iron: a hard, brittle, and nonmalleable alloy of iron that is shaped by being poured into molds. It was used in building from the late eighteenth century until superseded by steel in the mid-nineteenth century.

Cathedral: The church in which a bishop keeps his *cathedra* (throne).

Chancel: In churches, the area in which the clergy performing a service move or sit.

Chantry: a small endowed chapel.

Choir chancel: The area where the choir sits, but separate from the sanctuary, where the altar is.

Classical: Any style that revives the art of the classical periods of history (the Greek, Roman, or Renaissance), especially as taught at Paris's École des Beaux-Arts.

Clerestory (clear story): A portion of an interior—usually the center aisle—that rises above the adjacent roof—usually over lower side aisles—and has windows allowing light into the interior.

Colonial Revival style: Name given to the Wren-Gibbs and Georgian classical styles when they were revived in the United States in the late nineteenth and twentieth centuries.

Corbeling: An arrangement of overlapping bricks or stones stepping upward and outward from a wall.

Crossing: The area where the transept intersects the body of a cruciform church.

Crucifix: A cross with an image of the crucified Christ on it.

Cruciform: In the form of a cross. A **Latin cross** has a long staff and two short crossing arms; a **Greek cross** has four arms of equal length.

Diocese: The territory of jurisdiction of a bishop.

Dossal: In churches, a rich fabric or tapestry that hangs behind and over the altar.

Feng-shui: The placement and design of temples, gravesites, homes, and even whole cities (in China) to guarantee propitious alignment with natural forces.

Flèche: A small roof spire, usually over the crossing, and usually containing a small bell.

Flying buttress: A freestanding pier that extends an arm against a wall to support it.

Font: The source of water for the sacrament of baptism.

Garbhagriha: The womb-chamber of a Hindu temple, where the principal deity resides.

Georgian style: A style popular during the reigns of England's first three Georges (1714–1820). It is classical, imitating northern Italian late-Renaissance architecture, particularly that of Andrea Palladio. Characteristics include a formal dignity and symmetry, solid proportions, ornate frames around doorways, stone quoins, and Palladian windows.

Gothic Revival style: A style characterized by pointed arches, buttresses, stained-glass windows, tracery, large rose windows, and sculpture with medieval inspiration. The original Gothic style predominated in Europe from about the twelfth century until the sixteenth century. **Carpenter's Gothic**, which exhibits Gothic decoration, but is not actually built according to medieval Gothic stone construction principles, is often differentiated from **Stonemason's Gothic**, which is built according to these historic Gothic construction principles. A type of late-nineteenth-century Gothic Revival style called **High Victorian Gothic** is usually characterized by the use of stones in contrasting colors.

Greek Revival style: A style imitating the buildings of ancient Greece. It is usually characterized by a portico across the front, and a roof ridge running from front to back. Doors and windows are built with posts and beams and are, therefore, rectangular, and glass windows are clear. The five classical styles of columns are: Doric, Ionic, Corinthian, Tuscan, and Composite.

High Church: A church that favors ceremony, formality, and elements of mystery, ornate vestments, candles and incense, artistic and symbolic decorations, including crosses and crucifixes.

Iconography: The study of symbols and symbolic decorations.

Iconostasis: A screen covered with icons (sacred images) dividing the nave from the chancel in an Orthodox or Armenian church.

Italianate: Italian in character, in architecture usually referring to classical Roman- or Renaissance-style designs.

Khutba: The sermon in a mosque.

Kursi: A small pulpit (or large lectern) in a mosque.

Lantern: A structure on top of a roof or dome having windows to let in light.

Lectern: In churches, a Bible-stand.

Low Church: A church that forgoes decoration and ceremony but expresses piety in plain and simple furnishings and ceremonies.

Magen David: A six-pointed star symbolizing Judaism.

Meetinghouse style: A design for a rectangular church building that places the entrance in the middle of one of the long walls, and the pulpit in the middle of the other long side.

Menorah: A candelabrum.

Mihrab: A shallow apse in a mosque that identifies the direction of Mecca.

Minaret: A tall slender tower at a mosque used to call the people to prayer.

Minbar: The tall pulpit in a mosque, usually incorporating a steep staircase.

Minyan: The minimum number of men necessarily present (10) to have a Jewish religious service.

Monstrance: An object in which the Blessed Sacrament is exposed for worship.

Moorish Revival style: A style of synagogue characterized by horseshoe- or keyhole-shaped arches and other features meant to recall the period when Judaism flourished in Muslim Iberia.

Narthex: An enclosed porch or vestibule at the entrance to the building.

Natmandir: The main sanctuary in a Hindu temple.

Nave: The part of a house of worship where the congregation stands or sits.

Ner Tamid: A continuously burning lamp in front of the ark in a synagogue.

Nonritual or nonliturgical church: A church in which the most important part of the service consists of listening to the Word, so church design usually focuses on the pulpit.

Palladian window: A large round-arched central window flanked by lower rectangular windows.

Pediment: A wide low-pitched gable on top of a colonnade or division of a façade.

Pilasters: Flat columns against walls.

Portico: A porch with a roof supported by columns, usually in front of a doorway.

Pulpit: The speaking platform from which the pastor delivers the sermon.

Qibla: In a mosque, the wall in the direction of Mecca.

Quoins: Blocks used to reinforce or decorate at a building's corners.

Rajagopuram: A steeple marking the main entrance to a Hindu temple.

Reliquary: An object displaying a relic of a saint.

Renaissance Revival style: Architecture based on the styles of the Italian Renaissance.

Reredos (or **retable** or **altar screen**): A large decorative screen behind the altar drawing attention to it.

Richardsonian Romanesque style: Architecture following the style of American architect Henry Hobson Richardson (1838–86), characterized by stone construction, round arches framing deeply recessed windows and doors, rough textures, and a horizontal heaviness.

Rimmonim: Tiny caps on the tops of Torah scrolls, often of precious metal.

Ritual or liturgical church: A church that focuses worship on the altar as the site of the ritual sacrifice of the Eucharist. Ritual churches also usually need space for processions and for the clergy.

Romanesque Revival style: Architecture usually characterized by round arches, apsidal chancels, a dome, clear glass, a bell tower, and, often, wheel windows. The original Romanesque style predominated in Europe roughly from the sixth century until the twelfth century.

Rose window: A circular window with tracery. Characteristic of Gothic and Gothic Revival architecture.

Sacristy: A room near the chancel where the robes and altar vessels are stored and where the clergy vest themselves for services.

Shrine: In churches, a special chapel dedicated to the worship of a particular saint.

Stations of the Cross: Fourteen specific scenes from Jesus' trial and crucifixion.

Tabernacle: In churches, an object containing portions of Reserved Sacrament between services.

Tebah: Sephardic for *bimah*.

Terra-Cotta: "baked earth" in Italian; a hard-fired clay, reddish brown in color, used for architectural ornaments, tiles, pottery, and for covering steel to fireproof it.

Tetramorph: An angel, a lion, an ox, and an eagle when used to symbolize the four evangelists, respectively Matthew, Mark, Luke, and John.

Torah: A scroll of parchment containing the first five books of the Hebrew scriptures (Genesis, Exodus, Leviticus, Numbers, Deuteronomy).

Trabeated: Built with posts and beams; all openings are, therefore, rectangular.

Tracery: Curvilinear openwork shapes creating a pattern within openings.

Transept: The arms of the cross in a cruciform church, crossing the nave.

Transubstantiation: The belief that in the act of consecration of the host, an ordained priest is the instrument for transforming bread and wine into the actual human flesh and human blood of Christ.

Triforium: an arcaded passageway along the nave high in the wall but below any clerestory windows.

Trumeau: The column in the center of the main door of a building. Often used for medieval church portals.

Truss: A structural frame stiffened by triangular forms.

Tympanum: The carved and decorated space above the main door of a building. Often used for medieval church portals.

Vault: An arched structure forming a ceiling or roof.

Vigil light (or **sanctuary lamp**): A light hanging beside the tabernacle and burning if the tabernacle contains Reserved Sacrament.

Wheel window: A large round window having distinctly radiating spokes. Characteristic of Romanesque and Romanesque Revival architecture.

Wren-Gibbs style: A style usually characterized by the combination of a classical portico or porch with a tower and steeple. The tower is often centered on the façade with the principal entrance at its base.

*Eldridge
Street
Synagogue*

ADDITIONAL READING

.... ✸ ....

Religion in America
Ahlstrom, Sydney. *A Religious History of the American People*. New Haven: Yale University Press, 1974.
Carroll, Bret E. *The Routledge Historical Atlas of Religion in America*. N.Y.: Routledge, 2000.
Corbett, Julia Mitchell. *Religion in America*. Upper Saddle River, N.J.: Prentice Hall, 1999.
Gaustad, Edwin S. *A Religious History of America*. San Francisco: Harper San Francisco, 1990.
Gaustad, Edwin S., and Philip L. Barlow. *New Historical Atlas of Religion in America*. N.Y.: Oxford University Press, 2000.
Gillis, Chester. *Roman Catholicism in America*. Columbia Contemporary American Religion Series. N.Y.: Columbia University Press, 1999.
Hall, David D. *Lived Religion in America*. Princeton: Princeton University Press, 1997.
LeBeau, Bryan. *Religion in America to 1865*. N.Y.: New York University Press, 2000.
Marty, Martin E. *Modern American Religion*. 3 vols. Chicago: University of Chicago Press, 1997–99 (vol. 1: *The Irony of It All: 1893–1919*; vol. 2: *The Noise of Conflict: 1919–1941*; vol. 3: *Under God, Indivisible: 1941–1960*).
———. *Pilgrims in Their Own Land: 500 Years of Religion in America*. N.Y.: Penguin, 1984.
Matlins, Stuart M., and Arthur J. Magida, eds. *How to Be a Perfect Stranger: A Guide to Etiquette in Other People's Religious Ceremonies*. 2 vols. Woodstock, Vt.: Skylight Paths Publishing, 1999.
Mead, Frank S., and Samuel S. Hill. *The Handbook of Denominations in the United States*. Nashville: Abingdon Press, 1995.
Neusner, Jacob. *World Religions in America: An Introduction*. Louisville: Westminster John Knox Press, 1994.
Porterfield, Amanda. *American Religious History*. Maldan, MA: Blackwell, 2001.
Ruether, Rosemary Radford, and Rosemary Skinner Keller. *In Our Own Voices: Four Centuries of American Women's Religious Writings*. Louisville: Westminster John Knox Press, 2000.
Seager, Richard Hughes. *Buddhism in America*. Columbia Contemporary American Religion Series. N.Y.: Columbia University Press, 2000.

Smith, Jane I. *Islam in America*. Columbia Contemporary American Religion Series. N.Y.: Columbia University Press, 1999.

Swift, Donald Charles. *Religion and the American Experience: A Social and Cultural History, 1756–1996*. M. E. Sharpe, 1998.

Tickle, Phyllis A. *God-Talk in America*. N.Y.: Crossroad Publishing, 1997.

Williams, Peter W. *America's Religions: Traditions and Cultures*. Urbana and Chicago: University of Illinois Press, 1998.

Williamson, William B. *An Encyclopedia of Religions in the United States: 100 Religious Groups Speak for Themselves*. N.Y.: Crossroad Publishing, 1992.

Wuthnow, Robert. *After Heaven: Spirituality in America Since the 1950s*. Berkeley: University of California Press, 2000.

Saints and Religious Iconography

Attwater, David. *The Penguin Dictionary of Saints*. N.Y.: Penguin, 1996.

Duchet-Suchaux, Gaston, and Michel Pastoureau. *The Bible and the Saints: Flammarion Iconographic Guides*. N.Y.: Flammarion, 1994.

Ellsberg, Robert. *All Saints: Daily Reflections on Saints, Prophets, and Witnesses for Our Time*. N.Y.: Crossroad Publishing, 1997.

Jöckle, Clemens. *Encyclopedia of Saints*. London: Parkgate Books, 1997.

Religious Architecture

Chiat, Marilyn J. *America's Religious Architecture: Sacred Places for Every Community*. N.Y.: John Wiley & Sons, 1997.

Davies, J. G. *Temples, Churches and Mosques: A Guide to the Appreciation of Religious Architecture*. N.Y.: Pilgrim Press, 1982.

Gruber, Samuel D. *Synagogues*. N.Y.: Metro Books, 1999.

Kaufman, David. *Shul with a Pool: The "Synagogue-Center" in American Jewish History*. Waltham, MA: Brandeis University Press, 1998.

Sturn, James. *Stained Glass from Medieval Times to the Present: Treasures to Be Seen in New York*. N.Y.: E. P. Dutton, 1982.

Kennedy, Roger G. *American Churches*. N.Y.: Stewart, Tabori & Chang, 1982.

Williams, Peter W. *Houses of God: Region, Religion, and Architecture in the United States*. Urbana and Chicago: University of Illinois Press, 1997.

New York City and Its History

Allen, Oliver E. *New York, New York*. N.Y.: Atheneum, 1990.

Bindser, Frederick M., and David M. Reimers. *All the Nations Under Heaven: An Ethnic and Racial History of New York City*. N.Y.: Columbia University Press, 1995.

Burrows, Edwin, and Mike Wallace. *Gotham: A History of New York City to 1898*. N.Y.: Oxford University Press, 1999.

Jackson, Kenneth T., ed. *The Encyclopedia of New York City*. New Haven and New York: Yale University Press and the New-York Historical Society, 1995.

The
Lotus
Garden

Religion, Architecture, and Religious Architecture in New York City
Cohalan, Rev. Msgr. Florence D. *A Popular History of the Archdiocese of New York.*
Yonkers, N.Y.: United States Catholic Historical Society, 1983.
Dolan, Jay P. *The Immigrant Church: New York's Irish and German Catholics,*
1815–1865. Baltimore: Johns Hopkins University Press, 1975.
Dolkart, Andrew. *Guide to New York City Landmarks.* N.Y.: John Wiley & Sons,
2nd ed., 1998.
Dunlap, David W., and Vecchione, Joseph J. *Glory in Gotham: Manhattan's Houses*
of Worship: A Guide to Their History, Architecture and Legacy. N.Y.: City and
Company, 2001.
Israelowitz, Oscar. *Synagogues of New York City.* N.Y.: Dover Publications, 1982.
Livezey, Lowell W., ed. *Public Religion and Urban Transformation: Faith in the City.*
N.Y.: New York University Press, 2000.
Morrone, Francis. *The Architectural Guidebook to New York City.* Salt Lake City:
Gibbs-Smith, 1998.
Reynolds, Donald Martin. *The Architecture of New York City.* N.Y.: John Wiley &
Sons, 3rd ed., 1994.
Stern, Robert A.M. *New York 1880* (with Thomas Mellins and David Fishman).
N.Y.: Monacelli Press, 1999.
———. *New York 1900* (with Gregory Gilmartin and John Massengale). N.Y.:
Rizzoli, 1983.
———. *New York 1930* (with Gregory Gilmartin and Thomas Mellins). N.Y.:
Rizzoli, 1987.
———. *New York 1960* (with Thomas Mellins and David Fishman). N.Y.: Mona-
celli Press, 1995.

White, Norval, and Willensky, Elliot. *The AIA Guide to New York City.* N.Y.: Crown, 4th ed., 2000.

Wilson, Jeff. *The Buddhist Guide to New York.* N.Y.: St. Martin's Griffin, 2000.

Wolfe, Gerard R. *New York: A Guide to the Metropolis.* N.Y.: McGraw-Hill, 2nd ed., 1994.

WEB SITES

················ ❁ ················

Many of New York City's sacred spaces and peaceful places have their own homepages on the World Wide Web. As existing sites change frequently and new sites are launched almost daily, it would be impossible to list them all. Here is a selection:

Abyssinian Baptist Church	http://www.adcorp.org/abyssinianchurch.html
Albanian Islamic Cultural Center	http://www.aicc-ny.org
All Souls Church	http://www.allsoulsnyc.org/
Allen African Methodist Episcopal Cathedral	http://www.allencathedral.org/
Angel Orensanz Foundation	http://www.orensanz.org/
Ansche Chesed	http://www.anschechesed.org/
Asia Society	http://www.asiasociety.org/
Asian Classics Institute	http://www.world-view.org/aci.html
Brick Presbyterian Church	http://www.brickchurch.org
Brooklyn Botanic Garden	http://www.bbg.org/
Brooklyn Museum of Art	http://www.brooklynart.org/
Brooklyn Tabernacle	http://www.brooklyntabernacle.org/
Brotherhood Synagogue	http://www.brotherhoodsynagogue.org
Cathedral Church of St. John the Divine	http://www.stjohndivine.org
Catholic Worker Movement	http://www.catholicworker.org/
Center for Jewish History	http://www.centerforjewishhistory.org/
Central Synagogue	http://www.centralsynagogue.org/
Christ and St. Stephen's Church	http://www.csschurch.org/
Christ Church (Methodist)	http://www.christchurchnyc.org
Church for All Nations (Lutheran)	http://www.cfan.net/html/
Church of Jesus Christ of Latter Day Saints	http://www.lds.org
Church of St. Mary the Virgin	http://www.stmvirgin.com/

Church of St. Paul and St. Andrew (Methodist)	http://www.gbgm-umc.org/spsaumc
Church of St. Paul the Apostle	http://www.stpaultheapostle.org
Church of St. Vincent Ferrer	http://www.fordham.edu/halsall/medny/ mchale.html
Church of the Holy Apostles	http://www.holyapostlesnyc.org/
Church of the Holy Trinity (Episcopal)	http://www.holytrinity-nyc.org
Church of the Incarnation (Episcopal)	http://churchoftheincarnation.org/
Church of the Resurrection (Episcopal)	http://www.resurrectionnyc.org/
Church of the Transfiguration (Episcopal)	http://littlechurch.org
Congregation B'nai Jeshurun	http://www.bj.org/
Congregation Beth Simchat Torah	http://www.cbst.org/
Congregation Emanu-El	http://www.emanuelnyc.org/home.html
Congregation Shearith Israel	http://www.shearith-israel.org
Eldridge Street Synagogue	http://www.eldridgestreet.org/
Fifth Avenue Presbyterian Church	http://www.fapc.org
First Chinese Presbyterian Church	http://www.fcpc.org
First Church of Christ, Scientist	http://www.csnyc.com/manhattan.html
First Presbyterian Church	http://www.firstpresnyc.org/
Fordham University	http://www.fordham.edu
Frick Collection	http://www.frick.org/html/collmnf.htm
Friends Meetinghouse	http://www.metroquakers.org
General Theological Seminary	http://www.gts.edu/
Grace Church	http://www.gracenyc.org/grace_home.html
Greek Orthodox Cathedral of the Holy Trinity	http://www.thecathedral.goarch.org
Green-Wood Cemetery	http://www.green-wood.com/
Hebrew Union College-Jewish Institute of Religion	http://www.huc.edu/
Hindu Temple Society of North America	http://www.indianet.com/ganesh/index.htm
Historic Richmond Town	http://www.historicrichmondtown.org/
Historic Weeksville	http://www.weeksvillesociety.org/ introduction.html
Holy Trinity Church (R. C.)	http://www.fordham.edu/halsall/medny/ taylor1.html
Holy Trinity Lutheran Church	http://holytrinitynyc.org

Islamic Cultural Center of New York	http://www.muslimsonline.com/~iccny
Jacques Marchais Museum of Tibetan Art	http://www.tibetanmuseum.com/
Jehovah's Witnesses	http://www.watchtower.org/
Jewish Theological Seminary	http://www.jtsa.edu/
Judson Memorial Church	http://www.judson.org
Manhattan Won Buddhism Center	http://www.wonbuddhism-un.org
Marble Collegiate Church	http://www.marblechurch.org/
Metropolitan Museum of Art and the Cloisters	http://www.metmuseum.org
Middle Collegiate Church	http://www.middlechurch.org/
Moravian Church	http://www.moraviansi.com/main.htm
Mother A.M.E. Zion Church	http://www.motherafricanmethodistezchurch.com
Museum for African Art	http://www.fieldtrip.com/ny/29661313.htm
Museum of Jewish Heritage	http://www.mjhnyc.org/home.htm
National Museum of the American Indian	http://www.nmai.si.edu/
New York Botanical Garden	http://www.nybg.org/
New York Public Library	http://www.nypl.org
Our Lady of the Scapular and St. Stephen (R.C.)	http://www.ststephenscapular.org/
Partners for Sacred Places	http://www.sacredplaces.org
Pierpont Morgan Library	http://www.morganlibrary.org/
Plymouth Church of the Pilgrims	http://www.plymouthchurch.org/
Riverside Church	http://www.theriversidechurchny.org/
Rutgers Presbyterian Church	http://www.rutgerschurch.org
Shrine of St. Elizabeth Ann Seton	http://ourladyoftherosary.catholic.org/shrineof.htm
Shrine of St. Frances Mother Cabrini	http://www.cabrinishrineny.org
Soka Gakkai International	http://www.sgi.org
St. Andrew's (Episcopal; Staten Island)	http://www.mindspring.com/~standrew/
St. Bartholomew's Church	http://www.stbarts.org
St. Francis of Assisi (R.C.)	http://www.francis.org/
St. Francis Xavier	http://www.rc.net/newyork/stfrancisxavier/
St. George Ukrainian Catholic Church	http://www.brama.com/stgeorge
St. Ignatius Loyola	http://www.saintignatiusloyola.org

St. Jean Baptiste R.C. Church	http://www.sjbrcc.org
St. Joseph's R.C. Church	http://st.joseph.greenwich-village-nyc.org/
St. Luke in the Fields	http://www.stlukeinthefields.org
St. Luke's Lutheran Church	http://www.thelutheran.org/9709/page26.html
St. Mark's in the Bowery	http://www.saintmarkschurch.org
St. Nicholas Russian Orthodox Cathedral	http://www.stnicholasronyc.com
St. Patrick's Cathedral	http://www.ny-archdiocese.org/pastoral/ cathedral_about.html
St. Patrick's Old Cathedral	http://www.oldsaintpatricks.org
St. Peter's Lutheran Church	http://www.stpeters.org
St. Sava Serbian Orthodox Cathedral	http://members.aol.com/saintsava/
St. Thomas Church (Episcopal)	http://www.saintthomaschurch.org
St. Vartan Armenian Cathedral	http://www.fordham.edu/halsall/medny/ stvartan1.html
Staten Island Botanical Garden	http://www.bbg.org/
Stephen Wise Free Synagogue	http://www.swfs.org/
Studio Museum in Harlem	http://www.studiomuseuminharlem.org/
The Bronx Zoo	http://www.bronxzoo.com
The Cooper Union for the Advancement of Science and Art	http://www.cooper.edu/
The Interfaith Center of New York	http://www.interfaithcenter.org
The New York Theosophical Society	http://www.theosophy-ny.org/
The Open Center	http://www.opencenter.org
Tibet House	http://tibethouse.org
Trinity Baptist Church	http://www.tbcny.org
Trinity Church and St. Paul's	http://www.trinitywallstreet.org/
Union Theological Seminary	http://www.uts.columbia.edu/
Unity Churches Association	http://www.unity.org/
Upper East Side Islamic Cultural Center and Mosque	http://www.columbia.edu/cu/msa/nycmsa/ resources/masajid/ICCNY.html
West End Collegiate Church	http://www.westendchurch.org/
Yeshiva University	http://www.yu.edu/
Zen Center of New York City	http://www.mro.org/zcnyc/firelotus.shtml
Zen Studies Society	http://www.zenstudies.org/

ACKNOWLEDGMENTS

A list of people who helped with this book would be another book. Many pastors, priests, rabbis, and imams guided me through their houses of worship and even checked my text to certify matters of religious teachings. Congregations' secretaries were always willing to check "just one more thing" for me. Archivists, librarians, and enthusiastic members of congregations provided research materials and manuscripts. Architects, restorers, and designers drew my eye to decorative details of great beauty and spiritual significance.

Any errors in the text are entirely the fault of the author, but I would like to thank the following people for their special help:

Betty Meyer, editor of *Faith & Form* magazine, for her encouragement and for publishing an early version of the chapter on "What to Look For";

Architect Edgar Tafel, a member of the Interfaith Commission for the Study of Landmarking of Religious Buildings;

Christopher Gray of the Office for Metropolitan History, who always has an encouraging word for writers about New York;

Professor Kenneth Jackson of Columbia University, editor of *The Encyclopedia of New York City*;

Marilyn Chiat and Marjorie Pearson, two experts on architecture;

Professor John Renard of Saint Louis University;

Ken Lustbader, director of the Sacred Sites Program of the New York Landmarks Conservancy;

Kim Lovejoy, Brooklyn, NY;

And, of course, Jan-Erik Guerth, editorial director of HiddenSpring and editor of this book.

GENERAL INDEX

Numbers in **bold** indicate illustrations.

INDEX OF PERSONS

PICTURE CREDITS

Permission to use copyright material is gratefully acknowledged to the following. While every effort has been made to trace all copyright holders, the publisher apologizes to any holders possibly not acknowledged.

Albanian Islamic Cultural Center: 339

Edward F. Bergman: 39, 97, 106, 108, 195, 201

Brooklyn Botanic Garden: 315

Christian Charisius: 3, 9, 62, 72, 75, 86, 89, 99, 104, 107, 143, 147, 150, 156, 163, 175, 186, 221, 225, 227, 229, 234, 235, 258, 283, 289, 348, 351

Felix Chavez: 176, 211, 256

New York Landmarks Conservancy: 27 (courtesty of St. Peter's Episcopal Church), 93 (courtesy of Trinity Chuch), 102, 113, 114, 115, 118, 127, 138, 141, 155, 159, 169, 172, 174, 200, 204, 230, 237, 240, 244, 246, 253, 259, 266, 269, 270, 271, 273, 274, 276, 279, 287, 293, 301, 302, 311, 316, 322, 328, 331, 341

Staten Island Botanical Garden: 338

Woodlawn Cemetery: 335

Four-color insert
Brooklyn Botanic Garden: page B, top left
Christian Charisius: page B, top right, bottom right; page C, top and bottom; page D, top right and bottom
Felix Chavez: page B, bottom left
M. and P. Guerth: page A, top right
New York Landmarks Conservancy: page A, top left, bottom left, bottom right (courtesy of Mary McGee); page D, top left

ABOUT THE NEW YORK LANDMARKS CONSERVANCY

The New York Landmarks Conservancy, founded in 1973, is a non-profit organization that preserves architecturally significant buildings by providing grants, low-interest loans, and hands-on technical services. It is the only preservation organization in New York City, and one of the few in the country, to back up advocacy with financial and technical assistance. Hundreds of homes, businesses, cultural institutions, places of worship, and social service centers have benefited from its programs. The Conservancy advocates for preservation in Washington, D.C., Albany, and at City Hall. It also sponsors workshops, publications, lectures, tours, award programs, and exhibitions.

The Conservancy's Sacred Sites Program is the only statewide initiative of its kind to offer congregations of all faiths financial and technical assistance to maintain and restore their buildings. Each year, hundreds of thousands of dollars in matching grants are awarded to support planning and restoration projects. In addition, the Conservancy provides hands-on technical guidance, organizes workshops for building caretakers, and publishes *Common Bond*, an easy-to-understand journal on the preservation of religious structures.

For additional information, contact the New York Landmarks Conservancy, 141 Fifth Avenue, New York, N.Y. 10010; phone: 212-995-5260; fax: 212-995-5268; web: *www.nylandmarks.org*.